# The Nature of Endangerment in India

# The Nature of Endangerment in India

*Tigers, 'Tribes', Extermination & Conservation, 1818–2020*

EZRA RASHKOW

Great Clarendon Street, Oxford, OX2 6DP,
United Kingdom

Oxford University Press is a department of the University of Oxford.
It furthers the University's objective of excellence in research, scholarship,
and education by publishing worldwide. Oxford is a registered trade mark of
Oxford University Press in the UK and in certain other countries

© Ezra Rashkow 2022

The moral rights of the author have been asserted

First Edition published in 2022

All rights reserved. No part of this publication may be reproduced, stored in
a retrieval system, or transmitted, in any form or by any means, without the
prior permission in writing of Oxford University Press, or as expressly permitted
by law, by licence or under terms agreed with the appropriate reprographics
rights organization. Enquiries concerning reproduction outside the scope of the
above should be sent to the Rights Department, Oxford University Press, at the
address above

You must not circulate this work in any other form
and you must impose this same condition on any acquirer

Published in the United States of America by Oxford University Press
198 Madison Avenue, New York, NY 10016, United States of America

British Library Cataloguing in Publication Data

Data available

Library of Congress Control Number: 2022938823

ISBN 978–0–19–286852–7

DOI: 10.1093/oso/9780192868527.001.0001

Links to third party websites are provided by Oxford in good faith and
for information only. Oxford disclaims any responsibility for the materials
contained in any third party website referenced in this work.

The Orient was almost a European invention, and had been since antiquity a place of romance, exotic beings, haunting memories and landscapes, remarkable experiences. Now it was disappearing; in a sense it had happened, its time was over.

E. Said, *Orientalism*, 1

The future can only be anticipated in the form of an absolute danger. It is that which breaks absolutely with constituted normality and can only be proclaimed, *presented*, as a sort of monstrosity.

J. Derrida, *On Grammatology*, 5

# Contents

*List of Illustrations* ix
*List of Tables* xi
*Preface—Beyond 'Tigers versus Tribals'* xiii
*Acknowledgements* xxi

Introduction: The Nature of Endangerment 1

1. Human Endangerment Discourse: A Global Genealogy 19

2. Endangered Species & Societies in India 70

3. From Extermination to Conservation of India's 'Wild Life' 104

4. 'The Tribal Problem' 166

5. *Narmada Bachao, Manav Bachao* 205

6. A National Park for the Gond & Baiga 261

*Bibliography* 317
*Index* 355

# Illustrations

I.1. *Vanishing Tribes* by the author of *Vanishing Wildlife*. Roy Pinney, *Vanishing Tribes* (London: Arthur Baker, 1968). Fair use. — 12

1.1. Edward S. Curtis, 'The Vanishing Race—Navaho' (c. 1904), Photogravure. Public Domain. Repository: Library of Congress Rare Book & Special Collections Division Washington, D.C. LCCN Permalink: https://lccn.loc.gov/2004672872 — 27

1.2. Jimmy Nelson, *Before They Pass Away* (Kempen, Germany: TeNeues, 2013). Fair use. — 28

1.3. 'No Place for "Wild" People: Save the Nature People' & 'No Place for Wild Animals'. Peter Baumann and Helmut Uhlig, *Rettet die Naturvölker: Kein Platz für 'wilde' Menschen* (Berlin: Safari-Verlag, 1980). Movie Poster for Bernhard Grzimek and Michael Grzimek, dir. *Kein Platz für wilde Tiere* (West Germany: Okapia, 1956). Photo by author. Fair use. — 43

1.4. Advertisement for Formosan Aboriginal Cultural Village Amusement Park. Fair use. Source: *http://www.s-bus.com/tour-17-1.htm* — 54

2.1. John Edward Saché & Murray, 'Jubbulpore, Madan Mahal from the North'. Public domain. Albumen Print, Photographer's ref. 371, 1869, 228 × 279 mm. ACP: 96.20.0553. Courtesy of the Alkazi Collection of Photography. — 74

2.2. 'Tigers, "Tribes" and Forests'. Map by Sharon Lindenfeld illustrating the *approximate* distribution and location of forests, tiger reserves, and Bhil and Gond communities in India, as well as the two main field sites covered in this book: the Sardar Sarovar Dam and Kanha National Park. — 83

3.1. John Tenniel, 'The British Lion's Vengeance on the Bengal Tiger' (watercolor and gouache on paper, 1870). Public domain. Repository: Library of Congress Prints & Photographs Division Washington, D.C. http://hdl.loc.gov/loc.pnp/ppmsca.19308 — 151

3.2. Typical Odds. Public domain. Source: Bernard C. Ellison, *H R H the Prince of Wales's Sport in India* (London: William Heinemann, 1925), 29. — 126

3.3. 'The Game Laws—or the Sacrifice of the Peasant to the Hare', *Punch* 7 (1844): 197. Public domain. — 135

5.1. The Narmada Bachao Andolan Logo. *Narmada Bachao, Manav Bachao* Translation: 'Save the Narmada, Save the Humans'. Fair use. — 211

x ILLUSTRATIONS

5.2. 'Damned! Doomed! Drowned!' Photo owned by International Rivers, 'Narmada River Dams Protest: Arundhati Roy, Medha Patkar protest against dams on India's Narmada River'. Creative Commons Licence CC BY-NC-SA 2.0. https://www.flickr.com/photos/internationalrivers/3439550054/in/album-72157630547218220/ — 215

5.3. Medha Patkar, Domkhedi Satyagraha, Maharashtra, 21 Sep 1999. Photo owned by International Rivers. Creative Commons Licence CC BY-NC-SA 2.0. https://www.flickr.com/photos/internationalrivers/7646765266/in/album-72157630547218220/ — 219

5.4. 'Parley with the Bheels in the Beechwara Pass'. Robert Brown, *The Peoples of the World: Being A Popular Description of the Characteristics, Condition, and Customs of the Human Family*, vol. 4 (London: Cassell, 1892), frontispiece. — 225

5.5. Interior of a home in a resettlement colony in Nandurbar District, Maharashtra, during a wedding. Photo by author. — 251

5.6. In the searing heat, the jeep engine needed to be cooled down several times along the way. Photo by author. — 255

5.7. A home above the Narmada submergence zone, and an NBA *Jivanshala*. Photo by author. — 257

6.1. Endangered: 'The Baiga'. Fair use. *Conservation Threatens India's Baiga Tribe*. Fusion Media Company. Screenshot from: https://youtu.be/NQbcW1B4cis — 263

6.2. Mowgli's been kicked out. His jungle is now a tiger reserve. Fair use. Survival International. Source: https://www.survivalinternational.org/articles/india-evictions-jungle-book — 267

6.3. Palace of the Gond Kings of Garha Mandla at Ramnagar. Public domain. Source: Russell, R.V. and Hira Lal, *The Tribes and Castes of the Central Provinces of India* (London: Macmillan, 1916), 47. — 271

6.4. A home resettled outside of Kanha National Park. Photo by author. — 295

6.5. Save the Real Avatar Tribe. Fair use. Survival International. Source: https://www.survivalinternational.org/news/9478 — 297

6.6. Leadership of the Birsa Munda Brigade, Adivasi Mulniwasi Adhikar Parishad (Indigenous Rights Council), Self-Respect Movement, Gond Mahasabha (Gond Assembly), and the Adivasi Bachao Andolan (Save the Adivasis Movement), and others, march into the tent. Photo by author. — 300

6.7. Birsa Munda Jayanti celebration and rally. Photo by author. — 301

6.8. A Baiga farmer displaying traditional *bewar* millets. Photo by author. — 305

6.9. Baiga Dussehra: Gathering around the fire after midnight. Photo by author. — 307

# Tables

| | |
|---|---|
| 3.1. Number of 'Dangerous Wild Beasts' Killed Annually, 1875–1927 | 129 |
| 3.2. Amount Paid Annually for the Extermination of 'Wild Beasts' | 129 |
| Appendix 3.1. Tigers Killed 'Hall of Fame' | 151 |

# Preface—Beyond 'Tigers versus Tribals'

It could result in what is being called 'the biggest mass eviction in the name of conservation, ever'.[1] In February 2019, India's Supreme Court ordered the removal of millions of people from the nation's forests, such as national parks, tiger reserves, and other wildlife conservation areas—anyone who already had their land claims rejected at the state level would now be dispossessed. The Supreme Court subsequently stayed its decision, but not before it sent shockwaves through indigenous rights networks around the world. If the order stands, the Government of India now has the potential to evict anywhere from two to nine million people from forest lands in the name of tigers, wildlife, and environmental conservation, according to various estimates.[2]

Meanwhile, around the same time as India's Supreme Court decision, a major international campaign seeking to protect 30% of the earth's land and water by 2030 was quickly coalescing. Bringing together powerful players at the United Nations, over fifty national governments, environmentalist groups such as the World Wildlife Fund, organizations like National Geographic Society, and backed by the billionaire Hansjörg Wyss' Campaign for Nature, this cause has gained widespread popular support on the global stage. As in the Indian case, the aim is to save the planet's biodiversity—especially its wildlife—from extinction. But one fear is that this might happen at the expense of impoverished rural communities—especially indigenous peoples. Thus, a recent open

---

[1] Amrit Dhillon, 'Millions of Forest-Dwelling Indigenous People in India to be Evicted', *Guardian*, 22 Feb 2019. https://www.theguardian.com/world/2019/feb/22/millions-of-forest-dwelling-indigenous-people-in-india-to-be-evicted

[2] Office of the High Commissioner for Human Rights (OHCHR), 'India Must Prevent the Eviction of Millions of Forest Dwellers, Say UN Experts', 4 Jul 2019. https://www.ohchr.org/EN/NewsEvents/Pages/DisplayNews.aspx?NewsID=24786. While the OHCHR, *India Spend,* and the *Nature Conservancy Foundation* state that up to 9 million face eviction, various other predictions ranging from 2 to 8 million evictees have also been put forward. *Reuters*, the *Telegraph*, and *Survival International* claim 8 million; the International Work Group for Indigenous Affairs says 7.5 million; the *Guardian* says 5–7 million. *Quint*, the *Economic Times, Times of India,* and *Down to Earth* all report that 2 million forest dwellers face eviction.

letter signed by many scholars and activists renowned for their work with communities living in and around protected areas has raised the alarm. Scholars like Arun Agrawal, Dan Brockington, Peter Brosius, Michael Dove, Asmita Kabra, Ashish Kothari, Tania Li, Paige West, and many more, are concerned that this 30x30 approach, as it's been called, 'continues the marginalisation of rural people who will be most affected by its measures... ignores decades of research and experience on the social impacts of conservation... [and] fails to appreciate the political contexts in which protected area conservation are embedded'.[3] 'Tribal rights' groups like Survival International have gone so far as to call the 30x30 campaign 'the big green lie', again warning that 'it would constitute "the biggest land grab in history." Three hundred million people stand to lose their land and livelihood, many of them tribal and indigenous peoples'.[4]

In both of these sensational news items, what is feared endangered is not just tigers and other wildlife, and not just forests, but also forest-dwelling human communities living in proximity with that wildlife—peoples usually called tribal or indigenous, or Adivasi in the Indian context. Both stories also offer dire, catastrophic, predictions of things that have not yet (and *inshallah* may never) come to pass.

In this book, I want to show how this heightened rhetoric of tribal endangerment has long historical antecedents. The book demonstrates that so-called tribes have been projected as endangered with extinction, and have been subjected to a wide variety of conservation efforts, significantly longer than tigers and other 'wildlife' species have been. Today, some people feel that the only way to save India's forests and wildlife is to save tribal ways of life. Others really don't care about tigers and only want to protect people, or vice versa. All in all, no matter which side you are on, the discourses of saving tribes, saving forests, and saving wildlife, remain irrevocably entangled.

The view that sees both biological and cultural diversity as under threat has in recent years been called the biocultural perspective, and advocates of biocultural diversity conservation argue that it is imperative that forests, wildlife, and indigenous ways of life all be preserved together. The topic of this book—the history of these interlinking discourses of biological and

---

[3] Arun Agrawal, et al., 'An Open Letter to the Lead Authors of "Protecting 30% of the Planet for Nature: Costs, Benefits and Implications"'. https://openlettertowaldronetal.wordpress.com/
[4] 'Survival International Launches Campaign to Stop "30x30"—"The Biggest Land Grab in History"', 22 Apr 2021. https://www.survivalinternational.org/news/12570

cultural diversity endangerment and extinction in India—speaks to this foremost debate over conservation around the world today: the debate over the fate of the many millions of people living in and around national parks and other protected areas. In its most popular, but least accurate form, in India, it is known as the 'tigers vs. tribals' debate (the term 'tribals' is unfortunately often used as a noun in the Indian context).

In India's public sphere, this debate is currently centred around the Scheduled Tribes and Other Forest Dwellers (Recognition of Forest Rights) Act, also known as the Forest Rights Act or FRA. It was this act that the Indian Supreme Court's 2019 eviction order was based on. To briefly explain the history of the act: in India, in 2003, 'a new wildlife management paradigm' was launched under the auspices of Project Tiger.[5] Rather than excluding local peoples from protected areas, as in dominant models of 'fortress conservation,'[6] proponents of this populist conservation regime argue that the best way to save India's wildlife is to incentivize and involve local forest communities.[7] In this spirit, a new bill was brought before the Indian Parliament, the *Lok Sabha*. The bill, which became law in 2006 under a Congress government, promised forest dwellers, among other things, the right to remain in any forest, including wildlife sanctuaries, if they could show they had historically occupied that land.

Immediately, the Forest Rights Act was met with vociferous objections from traditional conservationists. Even within the Tiger Taskforce, which had produced the 2003 plan, there was no unanimity. Valmik Thapar, one of India's most vocal wildlife conservationists, in a strongly worded note of dissent, worried:

> The premise that there are vast areas of India where tigers and people must be forced to co-exist through some innovative scheme of increased

---

[5] Sunita Narain et al., *The Report of the Tiger Task Force: Joining the Dots* (Delhi: Union Ministry of Environment and Forests, 2005), 3. http://projecttiger.nic.in/TTF2005/pdf/full_report.pdf

[6] The term fortress conservation dates back to at least the early 1990s, despite often being credited to Dan Brockington, *Fortress Conservation: The Preservation of the Mkomazi Game Reserve, Tanzania* (Bloomington: Indiana University Press, 2002). As Brockington has communicated to me, the term was in wide use in conservationist circles at the time he published his book.

[7] Often called community-based conservation or Joint Forest Management (JFM), there is a huge literature on this. For a good annotated bibliography on the subject through 1999 see: 'Community Conservation in South Asia'. http://www.umich.edu/~infosrn/CICB/CICB_SA1.doc

use of underutilized forest resources by involving local people does not make any sense to tiger conservation especially when the human and cattle populations are constantly rising. The fact is each tiger must eat 50 cow-sized animals a year to survive, and if you put it amidst cows and people, the conflict will be eternal and perennial... The premise of continued co-existence over vast landscapes where tigers thrive ecologically, as well [as] people thrive economically, is an impractical dream, with which I totally disagree.[8]

In this view, so-called tribals truly are pitted 'versus' tigers.

The *tigerwallahs*, or tiger lovers, claim that millions of people are encroaching on parks and other protected areas in a massive land grab, and must be evicted. Conservationists like Thapar insist that 'tigers have to be saved in undisturbed, inviolate landscapes... You can either create landscapes that are undisturbed, or you don't save tigers... tigers and human beings—forest dwellers or tribal peoples—cannot co-exist'.[9] Thapar also calls the FRA a 'Forest Destruction Act'. One group of such *tigerwallahs*, which 'believes in the ideology of strictly protected wildlife reserves', is literally called Wildlife First.[10] In February 2019, Wildlife First and other petitioners succeeded in convincing the Supreme Court to order the eviction of millions of families from forests based on the logic that most claims made under the FRA were 'ineligible and bogus'.[11] Legislation that was intended to protect the rights of India's Adivasis and other forest dwellers was now being used to evict them.

On the other side are many forest rights advocates—activists, academics, administrators, and others standing up for indigenous or tribal peoples, as well as some Adivasis themselves. Groups like Survival International claim that Adivasis 'have always lived harmoniously with the tigers', 'rely on these ecosystems to survive', and that removing

---

[8] Narain et al., *Joining the Dots*, 175.
[9] Valmik Thapar quoted in Ramachandra Guha, 'Ecology for the People', *Telegraph of Calcutta*, 14 Nov 2005. http://www.indiatogether.org/2005/nov/rgh-ecology.htm
[10] Wildlife First, 'About Us'. http://www.wildlifefirst.info/about.html
[11] Shekar Dattatri, 'How a Social Justice Tool Became a Means to Grab Land in India's Forests', *Hindustan Times*, 2 Jul 2019. https://www.hindustantimes.com/analysis/how-a-social-justice-tool-became-a-means-to-grab-land-in-india-s-forests/story-TPm9hWnFzRJavD1bKN2grM.html

indigenous peoples from forests will destroy their forest-based cultures.[12] They believe that removing the forest dwellers from the forests will result in 'an unprecedented disaster'. These social activists are calling this judgement 'a death sentence for millions of tribal people in India'.[13]

Significantly, the 2006 Forest Rights Act was written by tribal advocates with the premise of addressing the 'historical injustice to the forest dwelling Scheduled Tribes and other traditional forest dwellers who are integral to the very survival and sustainability of the forest ecosystem'. The act asserts that the 'Scheduled Tribes' have traditional forest rights, defined as including 'responsibilities and authority for sustainable use, conservation of biodiversity and maintenance of ecological balance... thereby strengthening the conservation regime of the forests while ensuring livelihood and food security'. It also contains blanket statements such as, 'conservation is embedded in the ethos of tribal life'.[14]

Despite being somewhat sceptical of some of these overarching claims about tribal harmony with nature used to frame the Forest Rights Act, as well as some of the alarmist rhetoric used to defend the act, along with most forest rights advocates, I am certainly disturbed by the prospect of arbitrarily evicting millions of people from forests in the name of fortress conservation. And I am especially troubled by the 2019 eviction orders because I know from experience over the last sixteen or more years of working with Adivasi communities in western and central India, that the implementation of the FRA has been fraught at best. The FRA has been totally resisted by the conservation establishment all along. Not only have the vast majority of land claims under the FRA been rejected more or less offhand, many villagers I spoke with had never even heard of the FRA (or *van adhikar adhiniyam*) let alone been educated about their rights under it.

However, I also know that a certain amount of gaming the system happens. I have personally seen people hiking down to forest villages from the nearest town, pretending to live in a park when the forest officers come

---

[12] Jonathan Mazower, 'Modi's Escalating War Against India's Forests and Tribal People', *CounterPunch*, 31 May 2019. https://www.counterpunch.org/2019/05/31/modis-escalating-war-against-indias-forests-and-tribal-people/

[13] Survival International, '"Disaster" as Indian Supreme Court Orders Eviction of "8 million" Tribespeople', 21 Feb 2019. https://www.survivalinternational.org/news/12083

[14] Government of India, The Scheduled Tribes and Other Traditional Forest Dwellers (Recognition of Forest Rights) Act of 2006, 1, 8.

around, in order to get a resettlement package. I have also personally met people who first accepted land for resettlement, then passed these lands to their relatives to farm while continuing to live in the hills themselves.

And regardless of what some activists claim, not everyone who lives in an isolated village in a forest wants to stay there, which is probably a good thing, at least for the environment, since forest areas are small and population densities are high. I've personally met many people, especially young people, who want to get out of the hills, to live near a town, to have access to electricity, indoor plumbing, schools, hospitals, roads, motorcycles, shops, etc. They say they are sick of living without these basic amenities. Yet years later, when I interviewed *a few* of these people again in their resettlement colonies, they were deeply unhappy about their new situations and the deals they got, and *some* even wanted to go back to their old homes in the forest. They told me stories of people buying alcohol and motorcycles and unhappy endings. Still, so many others have adjusted well to life in the plains and see their resettlement as a victory.

This situation is far more complicated than the way it is typically depicted to the general public, whether in urban India or abroad. When I first started interviewing people living in and around national parks and dams in central India in 2005, asking primarily Bhil and Gond Adivasi villagers their feelings about conservation and development-induced displacement, I am willing to admit now that I was in for a bit of a shock back then. Years of exposure to activist accounts of 'tribal' people and their environmental struggles, going back to at least since I was a teenager, had prepared me only to believe that these poor, benighted, communities would be willing to do anything and everything in their power to remain in their beloved hills and forests and maintain their timeless connection with the natural world. I had been led to believe that Adivasis living in national parks and other forest areas universally wanted to continue their lives in these natural areas, and would unequivocally resist the encroachments of wildlife conservationists, the state, and industry to remove them from their forest homes. In part, this book was born as a response to my own youthful naiveté. Before ever setting foot in central India, I came to the field with the belief that Adivasis, like tribal cultures around the world, were endangered and in need of protection. It has taken me years of engagement with Adivasi communities, oral history fieldwork, archival research, and collaboration with scholars and scholarship as well as activists and administrators, to develop the more nuanced positions I now present here.

Many of the arguments in the popular sphere are so polemical, and the level of rhetoric so exaggerated, because the goal is less to educate the public, and more to spur support for particular perspectives, organizations, and agendas. The headline 'tigers vs. tribals', so prevalent in the Indian news media following the passage of the Forest Rights Act, is just one example of the kind of galvanizing rhetoric that thrives in public discourse. While eye-catching, it does grave injustice to the questions of how to best conserve Indian wildlife and how to ensure the basic human rights of peoples living in forest areas. Such phrasing presumes that it is the so-called tribals who are against, and are the main problem facing, tigers and other wildlife. Yet framing this conservation issue in terms of tigers vs. tribes also serves to grip the English-language reading public's imagination. It generates a debate in which they are encouraged to intervene. The public must either protect endangered species or endangered tribes, or increasingly in recent years, both tigers and tribes. Both require the activism of the global middle classes in order to be saved.

Thankfully, in contrast to this type of media and activist hype, the work of many scholars on the subject of tigers, communities, and conservation has been significantly more nuanced—studying the complexities of specific situations, introducing important first-hand research and fieldwork into the discussion, and providing historical background that can be used to inform public opinion and policy.[15] Weighing in on either side of this debate is not like making some abstract argument in analytical philosophy. These are not William James' theoretical 'Tigers in India', which distant foreigners do not experience in reality but know 'representatively or symbolically'.[16] A misguided conservation policy could alternatively mean the extinction of the tiger and many other species, and/or the deprivation of fundamental human rights for millions of people. This may be the kind of situation long known in policy circles as a 'wicked

---

[15] This scholarship is discussed throughout this book, and it would be impossible for me to name every researcher here. A few of the many scholars doing important work on these subjects, but not cited or acknowledged elsewhere in these pages, include: Bahar Dutt, K.U. and K.K. Karanth, Vasant Saberwal, Ghazala Shahabuddin, etc.

[16] James writes: 'Altho such things as the white paper before our eyes can be known intuitively, most of the things we know, the tigers now in India, for example, or the scholastic system of philosophy, are known only representatively or symbolically. Suppose, to fix our ideas, that we take first a case of conceptual knowledge; and let it be our knowledge of the tigers in India, as we sit here. Exactly what do we MEAN by saying that we here know the tigers?' William James, *The Meaning of Truth, a Sequel To 'Pragmatism'* (New York: Longmans, 1909), chapter 2, 'The Tigers in India'.

problem'—one where there is no clear solution that makes everybody happy and where everyone can be a winner.[17]

My work presented in this book is meant to stand in concert with existing scholarship but also hopes to contribute a new perspective. It has been suggested that conservationists rarely have a good sense of history. 'Often they have little understanding of the ways in which problems have come about, or how their predecessors understood similar problems and tried to tackle them'.[18] And so, there is a strong case to be made that environmental history has an important role to play in informing debate on social and environmental policy.[19] Thus, rather than presenting yet another elegy to endangered species and disappearing 'tribal' ways of life,[20] or an uncomplicated call for biocultural diversity conservation that overlooks the major hurdles facing this approach, this book offers reflections on the long history of discourses that have linked these two forms of endangerment—one biological, the other cultural. Exposing this history will hopefully provide useful information and critical perspectives for activists, administrators, journalists, students, general readers, and fellow scholars alike, not to mention Adivasi themselves. This stands to benefit both Adivasis communities and the environment by helping to move beyond the old fortress conservation versus coexistence debate.

Ezra Rashkow
31 May 2021
Abu Dhabi

---

[17] For the article that coined the concept of a 'wicked problem', see Horst Rittel and Melvin Webber, 'Dilemmas in a General Theory of Planning', *Policy Sciences* 4 (1973): 155–169.

[18] William Adams, *Against Extinction: The Story of Conservation* (London: Earthscan, 2004), xii.

[19] Stephen R. Dovers, 'On the Contribution of Environmental History to Current Debate and Policy', *Environment and History* 6 (2000): 131–150.

[20] Plenty of such funeral dirges exist, along with reflections on such loss. See for instance (in no particular order): Deborah Bird Rose, *Wild Dog Dreaming: Love and Extinction* (Charlottesville: University of Virginia Press, 2011); Jules Pretty, *The Edge of Extinction: Travels with Enduring People in Vanishing Lands* (Ithaca, NY: Cornell University Press, 2014); Gerardo Ceballos, Anne H. Ehrlich, and Paul R. Ehrlich, *The Annihilation of Nature: Human Extinction of Birds and Mammals* (Baltimore: John Hopkins University Press, 2015); Terry Glavin, *The Sixth Extinction: Journeys Among the Lost and Left Behind* (New York: Macmillan, 2007); David Farrier, *Anthropocene Poetics: Deep Time, Sacrifice Zones, and Extinction* (Minneapolis: University of Minnesota Press, 2019); Ursula K. Heise, *Imagining Extinction: The Cultural Meanings of Endangered Species* (Chicago: University of Chicago Press, 2016); Elizabeth Kolbert, *The Sixth Extinction: An Unnatural History* (New York: Henry Holt, 2014); Lawrence Buell, *Writing for an Endangered World* (Cambridge: Harvard University Press, 2009).

# Acknowledgements

Finalizing a book about the concept of endangerment in the middle of a global pandemic—when literally everyone everywhere is in some sense endangered, and while being isolated from most human contact—has made me really appreciate all of the wonderful connections I have had over the years. And it has made me want to offer thanks to all the people who have helped me along the way.

First, I want to thank my family for instilling a deep abiding love for nature in me from an early age, as well as a taste for environmental activism.

At the University of London's School of Oriental and African Studies, where I went to graduate school, I would like to acknowledge the intellectual influence of the following current and former faculty members: Daud Ali, Rakesh Nautiyal, Avril Powell, Peter Robb (who generously commented on a draft of the entire manuscript of this book), and Shabnum Tejani; as well the following members of my former PhD cohort: Abhishek Amar, Emma Flatt, Projit Mukharjee, Sebastian Prange, Shweta Sachdeva Jha, and Nitin Sinha. Other old SOAS friends including Yashaswini Chandra, Kevin Davis, Devon Knudsen, Sindhu Manjesh, Andrew Nelson, Subin Nijhawan, Tamar Oskanian, and Shubhangi Swarup, also warrant mention here.

My PhD dissertation began under the supervision of David Arnold as a study of previously unexplored histories of 'tribal' hunting experiences in colonial India. Much of this research on the history of hunting and conservation from below, unearthing 'subaltern consciousness' in colonial archives, was eventually published as a series of individual articles. But while in the research process, it also became clear to me that nineteenth-century colonial sources were describing Bhil and Gond so-called tribal hunting cultures as endangered as least as often as they discussed the problem of vanishing wildlife. And so, the foundations for this book about overlapping discourses of biological and cultural diversity in central India were laid at that time. This book has its origins in my PhD research, but many years of oral history fieldwork, archival research, intellectual collaborations, and developments in the fields of South Asian environmental history and anthropology since then has transformed it into a completely different animal.

In Delhi, two preeminent environmental historians, Divyabhanusinh Chavda and Mahesh Rangarajan, were extremely welcoming to me, first as a young graduate student, and subsequently on several return visits as well; engaging with them both, and being included in the intellectual life of the capital over the years, has always been a great pleasure. Also, unending thanks go to the Mangla family, especially Bhupesh, Gaurav, and Vivek, for so generously hosting me in their ancestral home in Gol Market many years ago. And, *shukriya* to Sabial and Sushila for introducing me to the Oraon community in Delhi.

Elsewhere in India, I would like to thank Deepti Ameta and Naru Mina of Seva Mandir, the Maharaja of Rewa and the directors of the Bandhavgarh Foundation, Marco Fattori, whom I originally met at a Rajasthani studies conference in Jaipur, Robin Tribhuwan of the Tribal Research Institute in Pune, Ranjan Chakrabarti of Jadavpur University, Gita Saberwal of the Madhya Pradesh State Archives, Vikram and Ranjana Kanhere of Janarth Adivasi Vikas Sanstha, Surajit Sarkar at Ambedkar University, Mohan Yadav of CGnet Swara, members of Jatan Trust in Piparia, Rakesh Bhai and family, the Subdivision Magistrate of Baihar (Balaghat District), Sunil Bhai of Kesla (RIP), members of the Birsa Munda Brigade, and Ashish Kothari and Meenal Tatpati of Ekta Parishad. For their valuable email exchanges over the years relating to the history of hunting in India, I would also like to tip my hat to Vijaya Mandala and Julie Hughes.

I benefited immensely from my time visiting as a graduate student under the tutelage of K. Sivaramakrishnan (or Shivi, as he is affectionately known) at Yale University, in 2007–2008. The ideas discussed on Friday mornings in James Scott's Agrarian Studies Seminar, and also among Shivi's first cohort of Yale graduate students—Devika Bordia, Uday Chandra, Radhika Govindarajan, Shafqat Hussain, Leah Koskimaki, Hande Özkan, and Vikramaditya Thakur—have made a lasting impact particularly when it comes to taking a rigorous analytical approach to social and environmental activist discourses in India. Uday Chandra, now at Georgetown Qatar, has recently commented on a draft of this manuscript. And Vikram Thakur, who has become one of my closest interlocutors, has supported my research and writing process in innumerable ways. Special thanks also go to one of my oldest friends and Yale librarian, Christopher Zollo, for all of the various contributions he's made over the years.

Speaking of librarians, I would also like to express gratitude to all the librarians and archivists who facilitated my research over the years at the following institutions: the American Museum of Natural History, the British Library (particularly the Asia and Africa Studies Reading Room), Bombay Natural History Society, Cambridge Centre for South Asian Studies, Columbia University, the Dehradun Forest Research Institute, Maharana of Mewar Special Library, Madhya Pradesh State Archives, Mandla District Record Room, Montclair State University, Nagpur-Berar Archives, National Archives of India in Delhi, Nehru Memorial Museum and Library, Rajasthan State Archives, Royal Anthropological Institute, Royal Asiatic Society, Senate House, Seva Mandir, SOAS, Staatsbibliothek zu Berlin, Tring Natural History Museum, University of Virginia, and Yale.

Following the completion of my PhD, I moved directly into teaching at the University of Virginia. Thanks go to Rich Barnett, Richard Cohen, Mehr Farooqi, Claudrena Harold, Walter Hauser (RIP), Thomas Klubock, Federico Marcon, Neeti Nair, and the entire History Department and South Asia Center for making me feel incredibly welcome there with such generous hospitality. Many thanks also to Philip McEldowney, for engaging me on topics and providing rare sources related to central India's history.

At Montclair State University, I am especially thankful to the following colleagues for their intellectual engagement over the years: Fawzia Afzal-Khan, Esperanza Brizuela-Garcia, Emily Cheng, Mark Clatterbuck, Richard Conway, Elspeth Martini, Ken Olenik, Sangeeta Pareshar and her husband Giri, Vikash Singh, Jeff Strickland, Neeraj Vedwan, and Leslie Wilson. I am particularly grateful to MSU for allowing me the time and space necessary to actualize this work. If I had been forced to publish earlier, it may have been a very different book.

I am grateful to Janaki Bakhle—former director of the Columbia University South Asia Institute, where I held the title of Research Associate for many years—for opening many avenues of scholarly exploration for me, particularly at the institute's weekly seminar series. Also at

Columbia, cheers to Manan Ahmed, Bill Carrick, and Divya Cherian, for the interactions over the years, and later also Sohini Chattopadhyay. And thanks to Rajbir Singh Judge for inviting me to participate in an intellectually productive panel on the 'nonhuman' along with Parama Roy and Naisargi Dave in 2019.

I started making real progress on writing this book during my 2015–2016 sabbatical year while living in Florence, Italy. I would like to thank Laelle Busch and Rebecca Olsen for making this possible with a Visiting Guest Lecturer position at the Santa Reparata International School of Art, and also thank Lorenzo Pubblici, in particular, for taking time to read and discuss some of my early drafts. I would also like to say *grazie* the humble *caffè macchiato* for sustaining my writing at this time.

Others who have graciously read and commented on drafts of select portions of this book at various points who I have not yet mentioned above include Sarah Besky, Annu Jalais, Miles Powell, and Sunil Purushotham.

Now in Abu Dhabi since 2019, I would also like to thank Mark Swislocki for including me in the pre-pandemic life of the NYUAD in 2019–2020.

And I couldn't have made it through lockdown, let alone have finished a book manuscript during a global pandemic while beached in the Middle East, without the incredible support of my wife, Sharon Lindenfeld.

But most of all, I am eager to thank all of the people who helped me on the ground in rural India with fieldwork in Madhya Pradesh, Maharashtra, and Rajasthan over the years—feeding me, housing me, teaching me about their communities, involving me in their struggles, and sharing their life stories with me. But unfortunately, for privacy reasons, they must remain unnamed here. It has always been my policy to keep the individuals and communities with whom I work from any possible negative repercussions by redacting all names and identifying information, unless they already have well-established public positions (as in the case of well-known activists or politicians). I hope that my many friends throughout the Satpuras and neighbouring regions—especially in and around the Narmada Valley and Kanha National Park, the two areas I have written about most extensively here—know how grateful I am for everything. And I hope they will find that I am doing justice to their stories and their cause.

# Introduction

## The Nature of Endangerment

> We characterize this complex as an endangerment sensibility
> Fernando Vidal and Nélia Dias,
> 'The Endangerment Sensibility'[1]

> [N]o one who wholeheartedly shares in a given sensibility can analyze it; he can only, whatever his intention, exhibit it. To name a sensibility, to draw its contours and to recount its history, requires deep sympathy modified by revulsion
> Susan Sontag, 'Notes on "Camp"'[2]

Fear of endangerment can be a powerful motivator. As many a successful politician knows, one of the more effective ways to mobilize the masses to action is to tell them that something they hold dear is under threat and therefore needs protecting. The endangered object can be anything from a way of life to life on earth itself. Everything from 'our attention spans' to 'redheads' to 'India's Hindu majority' has been called endangered by someone at some point in recent years.[3] Grammatically speaking, as an

---

[1] Fernando Vidal and Nélia Dias, 'The Endangerment Sensibility', in *Endangerment, Biodiversity and Culture*, eds Fernando Vidal and Nélia Dias (New York: Routledge, 2016), 62. In October 2011, I proposed a nascent version of the critique outlined in this book at the Max Planck Institute for the History of Science in Berlin's 'Endangerment and its Consequences Conference'. Given that much of the work on the concept of endangerment to date had stemmed from Germany, including an earlier volume by Graham Huggan and Stephan Klasen, eds, *Perspectives on Endangerment* (Hildesheim: Georg Olms Verlag, 2005), and most recently Lidia Guzy and James Kapaló, eds, *Marginalised and Endangered Worldviews: Comparative Studies on Contemporary Eurasia, India and South America* (Münster: LIT Verlag, 2017), at that conference I proposed calling this phenomenon 'the endangerment *weltanschauung*' or worldview.

[2] Susan Sontag, 'Notes on "Camp"', in *Against Interpretation and Other Essays* (New York: Farrar, Straus & Giroux 1966), 276.

[3] Ruth Walker, 'Is the Paragraph an Endangered Species?' *Christian Science Monitor*, 11 Jun 2015. https://www.csmonitor.com/The-Culture/Verbal-Energy/2015/0611/Is-the-paragr

2 THE NATURE OF ENDANGERMENT IN INDIA

adjective or past participle, the word 'endangered' can be applied to literally almost anything. And yet all it takes to bring about action is the belief that the object at hand is threatened—because endangerment discourse is often based on the *perception* of endangerment, rather than some quantifiable measurement of the degree of threat. And even such quantification is susceptible to error, manipulation, interpretation. This inability to pin down what exactly is threatened, how much it is endangered, or whether it is even truly threatened at all, is often precisely what makes this generalizable anxiety of endangerment such an effective mobilizing tool, and also such a fascinating object of study.

> endangered, adj.
> Etymology: < ENDANGER v. + -ED suffix
> a. That is or has been exposed to danger....
> b. *spec.* (of an animal or plant) in danger of extinction;
> esp. in *endangered species* (also transf. and fig.).
> 1964 Congress. Rec. 8 July 16099/1 A partial list of extinct and endangered species of the United States and Puerto Rico is attached.[4]

The *Oxford English Dictionary* reports (above) that the term 'endangered', meaning 'in danger of extinction', (a) refers specifically to animals or plants and (b) first appeared in print in 1964. Both points are in error. Originally, the term 'endangered' as in 'in danger of extinction' never referred to animals or plants.[5] Instead, it typically referred to humans, and

---

aph-an-endangered-species; Tom Phillips, 'No, Redheads Are Not in Danger of Going Extinct', *BuzzFeed*, 9 Jul 2014. https://www.buzzfeed.com/tomphillips/gingergeddon-is-cancelled. D. Anand, *Hindu Nationalism in India and the Politics of Fear* (New York: Palgrave, 2011); Francois Gautier, 'The Hindu Future of the World', *Times of India Blog*, 27 Jan 2017. https://timesofindia.indiatimes.com/blogs/francois-gautiers-blog-for-toi/the-hindu-future-of-the-world; Madhav Godbole, 'Is India a Secular Nation?' *Economic & Political Weekly* 51, no. 15 (9 Apr 2016); M.R., 'The Erosion of Secular India', *The Economist*, 4 Feb 2020. https://www.economist.com/the-economist-explains/2020/02/04/the-erosion-of-secular-india

[4] 'endangered, adj.', *OED Online* (Oxford: Oxford University Press, 2017). http://www.oed.com/view/Entry/61876?redirectedFrom=endangered

[5] Probably the earliest usage of the terms 'endangered plants' and 'endangered animals' with the specific meaning of 'threatened with extinction' dates back to 1871. Henry Walker, *Saturday Afternoon Rambles Round London: Rural and Geological* (London: Hodder And Stoughton, 1871), 111 writes: 'Here, in Kew Gardens, are instances in which the extirpation of the weaker individuals and tribes of plants is prevented by attentions which is as necessary to preserve the endangered plants as are iron bars for endangered animals'. Note the description of plant and animal species as 'tribes'.

today it refers to objects besides plants and animals at least as often as it refers to them. The usage of 'endangered' as the term-of-art to mean 'threatened with extinction' also certainly appeared in print well before 1964. Even with specific reference to the extinction of plants and animals, numerous uses appear several decades before the US Endangered Species Act. For instance, by 1939 an article entitled 'Fauna of the Empire' in the British daily *The Times* discussed 'endangered species'.[6] Surveying articles from the mid-twentieth century, one finds titles ranging from 'Endangered Elms' (1933) as Dutch elm disease ravaged the American elm tree population, to 'Existence of Jews held Endangered' (1945) in the wake of World War II.[7] Quite quickly, the phrase 'endangered species' was also being twisted in wordplay, as in this title—*Endangered Species: Our Children*.[8] In contrast to meaning 'threatened with extinction', using the term endangered to mean 'in danger' goes back far further in general usage, with Milton, for example, in 1645 CE, writing of 'the endangerment of our souls'.[9]

While the *Oxford English Dictionary* etymology conforms to the commonly held assumption that the concept of endangerment meaning 'in danger of extinction' derives from a particular moment in the history of environmental sciences (i.e. within conservationist circles of the 1960s), this book shows that fears and threats of extinction were first historically associated with groups now referred to as indigenous peoples well *before* they were ever applied to non-human species.[10] In fact, long before there

---

[6] The article reads: 'Among the numerous societies which are interested in the study and preservation of wild life the Society for the Preservation of the Fauna of the Empire takes a high place. Its declared object is to ensure that no more species of wild creatures shall be exterminated within the British Empire, and its members are confident that all the now endangered species can be preserved without any impediment to the economic development and civilization of British territories'—'Fauna of the Empire', *The Times*, 28 Dec 1939, 7. As early as 1909, one article in *The Times* reported 'that the very existence of species was endangered'—'Dr. A.R. Wallace On Darwinism', *The Times*, 23 Jan 1909, 9. See also: the 1959 foreword to Lee Merriam Talbot, *A Look at Threatened Species: A Report on Some Animals of the Middle East and Southern Asia which are Threatened with Extermination* (London: Fauna Preservation Society, 1960), which used the term 'endangered species'.
[7] 'Endangered Elms', *New York Times*, 9 Sep 1933; 'Existence of Jews held Endangered', *New York Times*, 24 Dec 1945.
[8] Gospel Tract Society, *Endangered Species: Our Children* (Independence, MO: Gospel Tract Society, nd [1970?]). Thanks to Esther Park, Archives & Special Collections Assistant at the Fuller Theological Seminary Library, for helping me locate this peculiar item.
[9] Milton cited in 'en'dangered, adj.', *OED Online* (Oxford University Press, 2017). http://www.oed.com/view/Entry/61876?redirectedFrom=endangered
[10] A few early English language examples might be useful here to support the point that people and what they valued were literally being called 'endangered' with extinction long before plants or animals ever were: 'Miraculous appearances and operations of providence, for the deliverance

was even scientific awareness that other animal species could become extinct, there was a common belief that cultures coming into contact with Europeans in the age of empire were vanishing. Although there was some limited cognizance of environmental degradation among early modern scientists before the nineteenth century, human endangerment attracted far wider attention than the problem of extinction of plants and animals even in the age of Darwin. As a modern environmental consciousness emerged in the late nineteenth and early twentieth century, the two forms of endangerment and extinction discourse intersected in remarkable ways.

## The Sixth Extinction?

Today, there is widespread acknowledgement—and attendant horror—that we are living in the sixth period of mass extinction in the history of the earth. Whereas most previous periods of mass extinction were attributable to natural disasters such as volcanoes or meteors, this Sixth Extinction wave is unique in that we humans are causing it, i.e. it is anthropogenic.[11] Extinction may be a naturally occurring phenomenon that is part of the evolutionary struggle, but human impact is now causing extinctions at an alarming, perhaps even catastrophic, rate. Some, therefore, say that it is less an extinction event and more an 'extermination event'.[12] One commonly cited figure is E.O. Wilson's: since the mid-twentieth century, more than 27,000 species have been going extinct each

---

of God's oppreffed, endangered people, may not now be expected; yet God has very strange and unthought of ways', in Samuel Dunbar, *The Presence of God with His People* (Boston: S. Kneeland, 1760); 'The conftitution is in danger, religion is in danger, the very exiftence of the nation itfelf is endangered; all perfonal and party confiderations ought to vanifh', in *The Parliamentary Register: Or, History of the Proceedings and Debates of the House of Commons*, vol. 37 (London: J. Debrett, 1794), 137; 'That barbarous people, who felt that their very existence as a separate tribe was endangered, becoming desperate, vanquished their enemies in two great battles', in David Brewster, *Edinburgh Encyclopaedia* (London: John Murray, 1830), 728; 'Morning and night some warning voice will be raised to us—some other enslaved or endangered population will cry out', in *The Portfolio: A Collection of State Papers* (London: F. Shoberl, 1836), 202; '... to labor for securing justice to suffering or endangered tribes', in 'The Indian Association', *The Indian's Friend* 16, no. 2 (Oct 1903), 2; 'It Is the Function of Art to Meet Impending Disaster to Insure the Survival of the Endangered Race', in Percy Leo Crosby, *Patriotism: A Dialogue* (New York: Percy Crosby, 1932), 15.
 [11] Richard Leakey and Roger Levin, *The Sixth Extinction* (New York: Double Day, 1995).
 [12] Justin McBrien, 'This Is Not the Sixth Extinction. It's the First Extermination Event', *Truthout*, 14 Sep 2019. https://truthout.org/articles/this-is-not-the-sixth-extinction-its-the-first-extermination-event/

year. Some estimate that the current number of extinctions may be as high as 50,000 or even 100,000 species per year.[13] Counting only birds and mammals, for which the data are reasonably reliable, on average, one species or subspecies became extinct every four years in the period 1600–1900, and one each year thereafter.[14]

There are several key problems with the rhetoric of extinction just outlined, however. Firstly, though numerous authors have now latched onto the designation of 'the Sixth Extinction', in fact the number of extinctions in the earth's history could be significantly higher (or lower) depending on how you count them.[15] For example, if one considers Anthropocene extinctions starting in the modern era to be a separate extinction wave from the late Pleistocene megafauna extinctions occurring some 11,000 years before the present, then this would be 'the Seventh Extinction', not the sixth.[16] Additionally, many scientists have argued that Pleistocene extinctions were also human-induced, some going as far as alleging that hunter-gatherers led a *blitzkrieg* of extinction against ancient megafauna.[17] If some version of this position were correct, that it was our early ancestors who caused the extinctions of sabre-tooth tigers

---

[13] Edward O. Wilson, *The Diversity of Life* (Cambridge, MA: Belknap Press, 1992), 280; Paul G. Irwin, *Losing Paradise: The Growing Threat to Our Animals, Our Environment, and Ourselves* (Square One Publishers, 1999), 104–105; Walter V. Reid and Kenton R. Miller, *Keeping Options Alive: The Scientific Basis for the Conservation of Biodiversity* (Washington: World Resources Institute, 1989).

[14] William Adams, *Against Extinction* (London: Earthscan, 2004), 26–27.

[15] There really is no scientific consensus on how many mass extinctions there have been, or even on what constitutes a mass extinction. Pincelli Hull, 'Life in the Aftermath of Mass Extinctions', *Current Biology* 25, no. 19 (2015): R943, discusses several different ways of counting mass extinctions: 'One recent authoritative estimate placed the total number of mass extinction events in the last half billion years at 18, with earlier estimates ranging from nearly thirty to more than sixty events', and also argues for the downgrading of the Late Devonian extinction, writing: it 'is probably not a mass extinction at all, but rather a mass depletion of biodiversity driven by low speciation rates'. Other studies have advocated for adding various mass extinction events to the list of the superlative extinctions. See, e.g. Michael R. Rampino and Shu-Zhong Shen, 'The End-Guadalupian (259.8 Ma) Biodiversity Crisis: The Sixth Major Mass Extinction?' *Historical Biology* 33, no. 5 (2021): 716–722; and Eric Hand, 'Sixth Extinction, Rivaling That of the Dinosaurs, Should Join the Big Five, Scientists Say', *Science Magazine*, 16 Apr 2015 http://www.sciencemag.org/news/2015/04/sixth-extinction-rivaling-dinosaurs-should-join-big-five-scientists-say

[16] Similar critiques have been levelled at another term intended to grab headlines and the public imagination—the Anthropocene. Donna Haraway, 'Anthropocene, Capitalocene, Plantationocene, Chthulucene: Making Kin', *Environmental Humanities* 6, no. 1 (2015): 159–165; Donna Haraway, Noboru Ishikawa, Scott F. Gilbert, Kenneth Olwig, Anna L. Tsing, and Nils Bubandt, 'Anthropologists Are Talking–About the Anthropocene', *Ethnos* 81, no. 3 (2016): 535–564.

[17] P.S. Martin, 'Catastrophic Extinctions and Late Pleistocene Blitzkrieg: Two Radiocarbon Tests', in *Extinctions*, ed. M.H. Nitecki (Chicago: University of Chicago Press, 1984), 153–189.

and the like, then the current one is not the first anthropogenic extinction episode in world history, and the rhetoric of 'the Sixth Extinction' loses some of its dramatic punch, if not significance. As Ursula K. Heise puts it: 'Many of the numerous books about the presumed sixth mass extinction are textbook examples of the rhetoric of decline'.[18]

Furthermore, though precise extinction rates are notoriously difficult to ascertain, E.O. Wilson's self-described 'conservative estimate' that 27,000 species every year are facing extinction has captured the public imagination and is commonly cited by environmentalists and the popular press as a scientific certainty.[19] The problem here is that this extinction estimate is just one among many, one 'based on the rate of tropical deforestation'. Such extinction estimates also rely on estimates of the total number of species as-yet described by science, numbering 'anywhere between 1 and 100 million species', and so 'choosing a higher number gives a higher number of total extinctions and thus a higher rate', raising questions about hyperbole. Thus, Ladel and Jepson point out that such 'shockingly high numbers ... were guaranteed to attract the attention of the world's polities and strongly supported the narrative of environmental crisis', and they argue that 'there is nothing fundamentally wrong with such extrapolations, but without an appreciation of the underlying assumptions, such crude statements may give a false impression of certainty to non-scientists'.[20] Such alarming statistics, so often shared without an understanding of the wider scientific literature or the methods by which they were generated, are effectively reduced to rhetoric.

This gap between science, the media, and popular understanding is a well-established problem.[21] The point here is not to undermine claims to the gravity of the current environmental crisis that we face as a planet, but

---

[18] See Ursula K. Heise, 'Lost Dogs, Last Birds, and Listed Species: Cultures of Extinction', *Configurations* 18, no. 1–2 (2010): 60. Ironically, Heise's own article begins exactly by opening with a dramatic exhortation that we are now living through 'the Sixth Extinction', and she does not herself question the underlying validity of this rhetorical construct. Further, though Heise's article is called 'cultures of extinction' and points to a wider 'rhetoric of decline' around the Sixth Extinction concept, her article does not discuss the link between rhetorics of cultural and biological endangerment and extinction.

[19] Edward Wilson, *The Diversity of Life* (Cambridge: Belknap Press, 1992), 280.

[20] Richard J. Ladle and Paul Jepson, 'Origins, Uses, and Transformation of Extinction Rhetoric', *Environment and Society: Advances in Research* 1 (2010): 102–103.

[21] Hans Peter Peters, 'Gap between Science and Media Revisited: Scientists as Public Communicators', *Proceedings of the National Academy of Science USA* 110, Suppl. 3 (2013): 14102–14109.

rather to demonstrate how this sense of gravity is rhetorically produced, and to argue that, quite often, simplistic headline-grabbing sound bites simply fail to do justice to complex underlying realities. After all, people have been predicting the end of the world at least since the beginning of recorded history, and so in order to be taken seriously, scholarship must do more than just generate apocalyptic rhetoric.

## Biocultural Diversity Endangerment

There is little doubt that the general scientific consensus that we are now living through one of the greatest extinction events in the history of the earth is correct,[22] but a key question now being asked by a multitude of voices around the world is: in this sixth (or seventh? or eighteenth?[23]) extinction, are more than just species being lost? By the late 1980s, several widely reputed studies had established that links exist between biological, linguistic, and cultural diversity.[24] And since the start of the twenty-first century, there has been growing concern that links also exist between biological, linguistic, and cultural endangerment and extinction.[25] Comparisons between threats to cultural and biological diversity

---

[22] One doubter is Doug Erwin, a Smithsonian paleontologist who entirely denies claims that we are living through a mass extinction event. He puts it this way: 'People who claim we're in the sixth mass extinction don't understand enough about mass extinctions to understand the logical flaw in their argument ... To a certain extent they're claiming it as a way of frightening people into action, when in fact, if it's actually true we're in a sixth mass extinction, then there's no point in conservation biology', because at that point it would be too late to save anything. Peter Brannen, 'Earth Is Not in the Midst of a Sixth Mass Extinction', *Atlantic*, 13 Jun 2017. https://www.theatlantic.com/science/archive/2017/06/the-ends-of-the-world/529545/

[23] Richard K. Bambach, 'Phanerozoic Biodiversity Mass Extinctions', *Annual Review of Earth and Planetary Sciences* 34 (2006): 127, states that '18 intervals during the Phanerozoic have peaks of both magnitude and rate of extinction that ... all fit Sepkoski's definition of mass extinction'.

[24] Madhav Gadgil, 'Diversity: Cultural and Biological', *Trends in Evolution and Ecology* 2, no. 12 (1987): 369–373; R.F. Dasmann, 'The Importance of Cultural and Biological Diversity', in *Biodiversity: Culture, Conservation, and Ecodevelopment*, eds M.L. Oldfield and J.B. Alcorn (Boulder: Westview, 1991), 7–15; B.Q. Nietschmann, 'The Interdependence of Biological and Cultural Diversity', *Center for World Indigenous Studies Occasional Paper* 21 (1992), 1–8; P. Mühlhäusler, 'The Interdependence of Linguistic and Biological Diversity', in *The Politics of Multiculturalism in the Asia/Pacific*, ed. D. Myers (Darwin: Northern Territory University Press, 1995), 154–161; D. Harmon and L. Maffi, 'Are Linguistic and Biological Diversity Linked?' *Conservation Biology in Practice* 3, no. 1 (2002): 26–27; J.L. Moore et al. 'The Distribution of Cultural and Biological Diversity in Africa', *Proceedings of the Royal Society of London* 269 (2002): 1645–1653. Luisa Maffi, 'Linguistic, Cultural, and Biological Diversity', *Annual Review of Anthropology* 34 (2005): 599–617.

[25] K. Anim Suckling, 'A House on Fire: Linking the Biological and Linguistic Diversity Crises', *Animal Law Review* 6 (2000): 93–202; M. Lizarralde, 'Biodiversity and Loss of Indigenous

have long been commonplace, and some anthropologists such as Wade Davis have argued that the worldwide threat to cultural diversity is even greater than that to biological diversity:

> And just as the biosphere has been severely eroded, so too has the ethnosphere—and, if anything, at a far greater rate. No biologists, for example, would dare suggest that 50 percent of all species or more have been or are on the brink of extinction because it simply is not true, and yet that—the most apocalyptic scenario in the realm of biological diversity—scarcely approaches what we know to be the most optimistic scenario in the realm of cultural diversity.[26]

In confronting this existential crisis, Davis draws on Margaret Mead who once put it: we need 'to reassess our conceptions of progress, [and] see the world as a fragile, endangered whole'.[27] One article propelling this mode of thinking to the forefront of popular scientific consciousness was William Sutherland's 2003 piece in the journal *Nature* showing a correlation between endangered languages and endangered species, finding that languages are disappearing in the same regions that species are, but at faster rates.[28] Fear of co-endangered biological and cultural diversity has been called 'biocultural diversity endangerment'. And these concerns have given rise to policy plans to conserve biological and cultural diversity together—in biocultural diversity conservation.[29]

It is certainly understandable why many would want to point out that some of the same forces threatening endangered species are also

---

Languages and Knowledge in South America', in *On Biocultural Diversity: Linking Language, Knowledge, and the Environment*, ed. Luisa Maffi (Washington, DC: Smithsonian Institution Press, 2001); Rosemarie Ostler, 'Disappearing Languages', *Futurist* 33, no. 7 (1999): 16–22; Jared Diamond, *Collapse: How Societies Choose to Fail or Succeed* (New York: Viking, 2005).

[26] Wade Davis, 'Dreams from Endangered Cultures', *TED Talks*, 2003.https://www.ted.com/talks/wade_davis_on_endangered_cultures/

[27] Margaret Mead and Ken Heyman, *World Enough: Rethinking the Future* (Boston: Little Brown, 1975); quoted in Nancy Lutkehaus, *Margaret Mead: The Making of an American Icon* (Princeton: Princeton University Press, 2008), 220.

[28] William J. Sutherland, 'Parallel Extinction Risk and Global Distribution of Languages and Species', *Nature* 423 (15 May 2003): 276–279.

[29] G. Oviedo, L. Maffi, and P.B. Larsen, *Indigenous and Traditional Peoples of the World and Ecoregion Conservation: An Integrated Approach to Conserving the World's Biological and Cultural Diversity* (Gland, Switzerland: WWF International, 2000); Luisa Maffi, *Biocultural Diversity Conservation* (London: Earthscan, 2012).

threatening marginalized cultures and that the two problems sometimes intersect. It is hard to fault advocates of biocultural diversity for believing in the importance of diversity, or for believing that many kinds of diversity are today in peril. Indeed, there is a reason that biocultural diversity conservation has become enshrined in international law and is a major source of activist attention under the patronage of numerous governmental and non-government groups. This book is emphatically not intended to deny these claims. Rather, it is an exercise in pointing out several key problems with the way biocultural diversity has been conceived and rhetorically framed since the colonial era and with the ways indigenous peoples are still talked about to this day.

Tracing the complex history of entangled biological and cultural diversity endangerment discourses, with specific reference to indigenous peoples and the environment, clear connections between contemporary agendas and long-repudiated colonial positions emerge, particularly in the burgeoning field of biocultural diversity conservation. Contemporary biocultural diversity discourse, both in its scholarly and activist forms, rests on *two key ideas*: namely that biological and cultural diversity have become similarly endangered, and that they ought to be conserved together. But from such calls to conserve co-endangered species and societies, numerous problems arise. Firstly, it may be argued that biological metaphors that equate human populations to endangered and extinct wildlife populations should not be applied to marginalized peoples who have historically suffered the brunt of racist and dehumanizing animal analogies. Secondly, discourses and policies of cultural conservation have often taken paternalistic and even culturally imperialistic turns, with international organizations frequently approaching indigenous communities as in need of top-down preservation or conservation. Thirdly, when a marginalized community struggling for rights and recognition is told by outsiders that it simply does not exist, or that it will inevitably cease to exist, perhaps nothing else could be as offensive, or as disenfranchising.

One major problem with contemporary biocultural diversity conservation, which this book addresses in detail, is the disconcerting lack of awareness of the long and problematic history of human endangerment, extinction, and vanishment discourses. Luisa Maffi, one of the main voices in the field, states that 'The idea of an "inextricable link" between biological and cultural diversity was perhaps first expressed in those terms in the 1988 Declaration of Belem of the International Society for Ethnobiology'.[30] In contrast, this book contends that though the term 'biocultural diversity' may be of recent origin, awareness of these inextricable linkages is by no means new. And it offers an intellectual history of ideas linking together biological and cultural diversity endangerment. There has been precious little reflection on the fraught historical pedigree of ideas linking biological and cultural diversity. Many assume that because a term is a neologism, the underlying concept is new too.

The portmanteau phrase 'biocultural diversity' is the culmination of a variety of terms that have developed over decades. As Timothy J. Farnham noted in 2007, 'Biological diversity is considered one of today's most urgent environmental concerns, yet the term was first coined only twenty-five years ago'.[31] By 1986, the term 'biodiversity' had been used by E.O. Wilson in a report for a forum of the National Research Council to the US government.[32] Then in 1989, 'biocultural diversity' made its debut.[33] But it was not until 2001 that the term appears to have gained widespread recognition with the publication of the book *On Biocultural Diversity*, edited by Luisa Maffi.[34]

One reason why I pause to chronicle the emergence of this neologism is that though talk of biocultural diversity endangerment may appear to be of recent origin, awareness of these intricate linkages is far older. Even as far back as the Hebrew Bible or *Tanakh*, c.250 BCE, there are expressions of this correlation: 'For that which befalleth the sons of men befalleth beasts; even one thing befalleth them: as the one dieth, so dieth the other; yea, they have all one breath; so that a man hath no preeminence above a

---

[30] Luisa Maffi, 'Biocultural Diversity and Sustainability', in *The SAGE Handbook of Environment and Society*, eds Jules Pretty et al. (Los Angeles: SAGE, 2008), 268.

[31] Timothy J. Farnham, *Saving Nature's Legacy: Origins of the Idea of Biological Diversity* (New Haven: Yale University Press, 2007), from the jacket.

[32] Edward O. Wilson, ed., *Biodiversity* (Washington: National Academy Press, 1988). It is not clear whether Wilson himself coined 'biodiversity'. Some attribute the term to W.G. Rosen in 1985.

[33] Adela Baer, 'Maintaining Biocultural Diversity', *Conservation Biology* 3, no. 1 (March 1989): 97–98.

[34] Luisa Maffi, ed., *On Biocultural Diversity: Linking Language, Knowledge, and the Environment* (Washington: Smithsonian Institution Press, 2001).

beast: for all is vanity. All go unto one place; all are of the dust, and all turn to dust again.'[35]

## Endangered Species & Societies?

Today it is at least as popular as it was at the height of the colonial era to declare that indigenous peoples, their cultures, religions, languages, etc., are endangered or are even becoming extinct. Endangerment and extinction, along with the related concepts of survival and conservation, are cornerstones of activist discourse in the campaigns for the rights of indigenous peoples. According to David Maybury-Lewis, founder of Cultural Survival, globally, roughly 80% of all indigenous people (30–50 million) perished since the time of first contact with Europeans. And according to UK-based Survival International, 90% of 'Amerindian Tribes' have become extinct since Columbus, with the extinction of approximately one tribe per year occurring over the course of the twentieth century.[36]

So, let me be clear: there is certainly no denying the historical reality of indigenous genocide, a position that has convincingly been compared to holocaust denial.[37] Still, my intention as an academic taking a critical approach to problematic discourses is to first prefer complex narratives to simple ones. It is to point out that endangerment is a complicated problem that needs more sophisticated attention than the usual oversized coffee table book or activist brochure gloss, and also to point out that there are numerous problems with the way endangerment and extinction discourse has been mobilized with regards to biocultural diversity.

---

[35] *Kohelet/Ecclesiastes* KJV, 3:19–20.

[36] David Maybury-Lewis, 'Genocide of Indigenous Peoples', in Hinton, Alexander Laban, ed. *Annihilating Difference: The Anthropology of Genocide* (Berkeley: University of California Press, 2002), 43; Survival International, 'Progress Can Kill: How Imposed Development Destroys the Health of Tribal Peoples' (*Survival International, 2007*). http://assets.survivalinternational.org/static/lib/downloads/source/progresscankill/full_report.pdf

[37] Ward Churchill, for instance, warns against the 'exclusivist position' that maintains 'that there has been one, and only one, "true" genocide in all of human history'. Ward Churchill, 'An American Holocaust? The Structure of Denial', *Socialism and Democracy* 17, no. 1 (2003): 28. Yet it is also worth noting the irony that some of the most strident voices condemning indigenous genocide, such as Churchill and Andrea Smith, have themselves been accused of being non-natives who are 'playing Indian'. See Sarah Viren, 'The Native Scholar Who Wasn't', *New York Times*, 25 May 2021. https://www.nytimes.com/2021/05/25/magazine/cherokee-native-american-andrea-smith.html

One thing that spurred this critique was the overwhelming abundance of popular texts that repeatedly compare endangered species to endangered societies. While some authors naively or carelessly invoke the analogy of vanishing species, many others have done so intentionally, and shall we say, undiplomatically (see Figure I.1).

In her article, 'A Question of Semantics? On *Not* Calling People "Endangered"', Pumla Gqola argues, 'It makes little sense to embrace the scientific language of biodiversity in relation to people. This is all the more dangerous when concepts like endangerment are applied'. Gqola rightly points out 'endangerment' is a loaded word. In our day and age, the immediate association is with endangered species, and so applying

**Figure I.1.** *Vanishing Tribes* by the author of *Vanishing Wildlife*.
Fair use. Roy Pinney, *Vanishing Tribes* (London: Arthur Baker, 1968).

the concept to 'the same people who historically have had to bear the heavy yoke of racial classification, species classification and their ensuing violence' is clearly problematic.[38] These are all important considerations. Yet what Gqola fails to address is the fact that many indigenous populations had regularly been labelled as endangered for hundreds of years. In her article, Gqola does not trace the genealogy of the concept of endangerment. If she had done so, she would have had to contend with the fact that widespread concern for vanishing human societies occurred *long before* any equivalent environmentalist engagement to protect endangered species, and that in fact the environmental discourse of endangered species and wildlife conservation emerged from the language of this earlier concern.[39]

Similarly, in an article titled 'Extinction, Diversity, and Endangerment', David Sepkoski argues: 'Both the endangerment sensibility and the broader discourse of diversity share a fairly recent historical emergence that can be located, quite precisely, in the late 1970s to mid-1980s.... But why did these discourses appear at this precise historical moment?'[40] Yet, frankly, the *weltanschauung* that views everything as endangered is by no means as new as this. Sepkoski's error is that when looking for the origins of what he calls the 'new catastrophism' and 'science of diversity' of the 'later 20th century', he focuses on nineteenth or early twentieth century writings about non-human species, framing this history in terms of the rise of evolutionary biology. Had he delved further into the history of fears of human—especially tribal—endangerment and extinction, he would have found that alarm bells began to ring far earlier. Sepkoski, like Gqola, overlooks the gamut of historical voices, dating back many hundreds of years, which called for conservation or preservation of endangered tribal societies. Along with many other thinkers, both Sepkoski

---

[38] Pumla Dineo Gqola, 'A Question of Semantics? On *Not* Calling People "Endangered"', in *Perspectives on Endangerment,* eds Graham Huggan and Stephan Klasen (Hildesheim: Georg Olms Verlag, 2005), 51, 53.

[39] In another article in the same volume, Markus Schleiter does attempt to trace the history of endangerment discourse in the case of the Birhor community of Jharkhand. However, the article fails to go back far enough, suggesting the concern for endangerment started only in 1925. Markus Schleiter, 'Enduring Endangerments: Constructing the Birhor "Tribe", Development Officers and Anthropologists from Early Twentieth-Century Colonial India to the Present', in *Perspectives on Endangerment,* 79.

[40] David Sepkoski, 'Extinction, Diversity, and Endangerment', in *Endangerment, Biodiversity and Culture,* eds Fernando Vidal and Nélia Dias (New York: Routledge, 2016), 62.

and Gqola mistakenly trace the contemporary 'endangerment sensibility' to a late-twentieth-century environmental consciousness centred around the emergence of the concept of 'endangered species', thus failing to back-date this *weltanschauung*.

But before we further explore the many centuries-long history of human endangerment and extinction discourses with specific reference to indigenous communities in the next chapter, I would like to take this opportunity to explain the overall outline of the book.

## Outline of the Book

This book is written as a series of explorations, each framed around the concept or nature of endangerment and its historical parameters. I begin at the global level, and then turn increasingly towards the local, with the hills and forests of western and central India eventually becoming my main area of focus. As a historian of South Asia, who has been living and working in rural parts of Rajasthan, Madhya Pradesh, and Maharashtra over the course of the last decade and a half, it is remarkable to me how an essentially Euro-American intellectual history of ideas about tribal or indigenous peoples in global perspective has completely dominated the popular understanding of India's Adivasi ('tribal') communities since at least the 1980s. And so, in order to provincialize Europe, and in order to understand the significant differences between indigenous communities in other contexts around the world and communities such as the Bhils and Gonds with whom I work, it is important to begin with a discussion of global proportions in order to contrast it with the nature of endangerment in India.

Following this brief introduction, Chapter 1, 'Human Endangerment Discourse: A Global Genealogy', presents a broad, global, overview of the emergence of the concepts of endangerment and extinction with reference to indigenous peoples and the environment. It argues that scientific awareness that non-human species could become extinct came well after widespread focus on the problem of 'tribal' extinction. Since the very outset of the colonial encounter in the 1500s, Europeans had not only been causing but also documenting and sometimes bemoaning and fighting against the extinction of communities today referred to as indigenous. No equivalent awareness of the fate of non-human species existed for centuries. By the early nineteenth century, the phenomenon of species extinction was still disputed, and it was only by the mid-nineteenth century that the concept of extinction, long understood as impacting human 'races' and 'tribes', also came to be applied to what we now call wildlife. This newfound equivalency only further cemented and amplified the long-time practice of dehumanizing comparisons between so-called wild tribes and wild animals, now giving them a pseudoscientific basis. Studying the history of this racist, imperialist analogy reveals that postcolonial era conservation efforts have roots in—and are often guilty of repeating—the colonial past. Tracing the interwoven tropes of human and wildlife endangerment from their colonial manifestations through to their postcolonial reverberations, this chapter highlights how contemporary biocultural diversity conservation discourse is often quite indistinguishable from earlier forms of human endangerment and extinction discourse.

Chapter 2, 'Endangered Species & Societies in India', begins to document how the Indian situation departs from, and complicates, the global narrative of interlinking biological and cultural endangerment. It addresses the problems of interwoven discourses of indigenous and environmental endangerment by focusing on two major Adivasi populations in India, the Bhils and the Gonds. It explicitly challenges the common perception of these people as forest communities who are disappearing along with their forests, as hunting societies that are becoming extinct along with hunted species, or as wild tribes that are disappearing along with the wilderness. It is often said that traditional ecological lifestyles and livelihoods are becoming endangered or even extinct, and the comparison is frequently made with disappearing wildlife. Yet the parallel between endangered wildlife and human ways of life is as problematic as it is explanative. Both the Bhils and Gonds, with their massive combined populations totalling some 30 million, are not so much 'tribes' as large-scale umbrella identities, each with a wide variety of cultural ecologies and livelihood strategies. To generalize that they were all historically forest-dwelling communities that lost their forests would simply be inaccurate. Despite the complicated nature of Adivasi identity, global indigenous stereotypes of 'the ecological Indian' and 'the vanishing Indian' are still often mapped onto the Adivasi situation. Why it is assumed that the end of forest dwelling must also mean the end of Adivasi culture is the central consideration here.

Chapter 3, 'From Hunting to Conservation of India's "Wild Life"', brings the main argument of this book around full circle—showing that concern for endangered tribes and even 'tribal wildness' came long before any attempt to protect endangered species of western and central India. Carnivore conservation, in particular, came much later than the idea of tribal protection or preservation. When tribal protectionism was at a peak in the 1930s–1940s, the first official efforts at carnivore conservation were just beginning around the world. Tracing the society-wide paradigm shift from the colonial obsession with sports hunting and vermin eradication through to the zeal for wildlife conservation that dominates public discourse today, we can see that until the very end of the colonial era in India, tigers and other carnivores were rarely seen as endangered. Instead, they were seen as endangering the lives of others. Yet biocultural perspectives arguably existed already at this time. In many sources from colonial India, the language used to describe tigers and tribes overlapped and blurred. Tigers were not only referred to as a species but also as the tiger 'tribe' or 'race'. Human tribes were referred to as 'species of man', or sometimes directly, as 'savage beasts'. Whereas 'wild tribes' were often described as being 'hunted' out of their forest strongholds, there was a 'war' on 'dangerous wild beasts'. Both tigers and tribes were sometimes described as 'vermin' to be 'exterminated'. Both were eventually defended against such campaigns of eradication.

In Chapter 4, on 'The Tribal Problem', I examine how in mid-twentieth century India, politicians, administrators, anthropologists, activists, and others spent tremendous time and energy in discussing the question of the very 'existence' or 'survival' of the 'tribes'. Solutions to this so-called problem usually came down to three competing ideological approaches to these communities: isolation, assimilation, and integration. Whereas isolationists were accused of being 'no-changers' who wanted to preserve the aboriginals in a museum or a zoo as specimens, the assimilationists were lambasted as attempting to eradicate tribal culture and religion, and as seeing the tribes merely as 'backward Hindus' who ought to be incorporated into 'the mainstream'. Integrationists emerged in the 1950s as the consensus camp. While claiming they would protect tribal culture, integrationists were often more concerned with economic development, as they sought to politically integrate the tribes into the nation in the name of national unity. Although the contours of the mid-twentieth tribal problem debate are widely known amongst those interested in historical anthropology in India, this chapter provides new insight by contextualizing this debate within the wider intellectual history of tribal endangerment and conservation.

The title of Chapter 5, '*Narmada Bachao, Manav Bachao*', is taken from one of the main slogans of the Save the Narmada movement, and literally means 'Save the Narmada, Save the Humans'. Drawing on my oral history fieldwork conducted while living in a *punarvasan* or resettlement colony with Bhils displaced by the Sardar Sarovar Dam on the Narmada River, as well as fieldwork conducted in displaced villages in the hills directly above the reservoir created by the dam, I ask whether people who lived through one of the most famous environmental battles in modern Indian history, and who suffered the loss of their ancestral homes in the river valley, see themselves as 'endangered'. While *Narmada Bachao Andolan* activists often argue that Adivasi culture itself is being drowned out along with Adivasi lands and villages, displaced villagers themselves have much more complex assessments. Many of the people living in the *punarvasan* where I resided had fought long and hard for adequate resettlement packages and consider that they were victorious in their struggle.

Looking back at the history of the Bhils, this chapter then reflects on how the same general paradigm which sees the Bhils as threatened with extermination has been applied to these communities at least since the outset of the colonial encounter in the early nineteenth century. In the first half of the nineteenth century, the colonial state claimed it had saved the Bhils from extinction at the hands of the Marathas, who had treated them as vermin to be eradicated. Then, in the second half of the nineteenth century, when the British began to realize that the Bhils were now subdued, colonial administrators focused on paternalistic preservation efforts. What's fascinating in the case of the Bhils is how quickly they were transformed in the colonial imagination from a predatory and dangerous wild presence in the hills into a childlike and beleaguered minority, endangered and in need of protection, all in the course of about fifty years between the 1830s and 1880s.

Chapter 6, 'A National Park for the Baigas & Gonds?' draws on my fieldwork experiences in and around Kanha National Park in Madhya

Pradesh. Whereas most histories of national parks and indigenous peoples have largely focused on the dispossession of resident populations in the making of uninhabited wilderness areas, this chapter studies the similarly problematic history of the idea of preserving human communities today referred to as indigenous in parks. The chapter presents a case study of comparisons between human and wildlife endangerment in central India by focusing specifically on the history of Gond and Baiga Adivasis and their relationship to Kanha National Park. In 1939, anthropologist Verrier Elwin proposed a plan to establish 'a sort of National Park, in which not only the Baiga, but the thousands of simple Gond in their neighbourhood might take refuge'. This park was to be established in a '"wild and largely inaccessible" part of the country', exactly where Kanha National Park now stands. Today, still, many activists claim that what is 'endangered' in Kanha is 'not just tigers', but also 'indigenous communities'. In the very first-ever call for a national park, as well as in frequent proposals for national parks throughout the nineteenth, twentieth, and now the twenty-first century, protected areas have been envisioned as places of conservation, study, and display not only of endangered species but also of human groups perceived to be endangered. Again, the problem is not only that Adivasi groups have long been perceived as in danger of becoming extinct, and therefore paternalistically projected as in need of protection. It is also that these peoples, who have long suffered dehumanizing animal analogies, are envisioned as endangered like wildlife, and in need of protection in parks.

# 1
# Human Endangerment Discourse
## A Global Genealogy

The disappearance of wild races before the civilised is, for the greater part, as explicable as the destruction of wild animals before civilised sportsmen

Robert Brown, *The Races of Mankind*, 1873[1]

Does not almost every precise history of an origination impress our feelings as paradoxical and outrageous? Does the good historian not have grounds to constantly contradict?

Friedrich Nietzsche, *Daybreak*, 1881[2]

The concept of endangered tribes emerged well before that of endangered species. Before the mid-nineteenth century, the phenomenon of non-human species extinction was disputed, even roundly denied, and anyway was hardly considered a pressing issue by European intellectuals. Although fossils had been discovered as early as the 1670s, it was Georges Cuvier in 1796 who first presented scientific evidence to his contemporaries that the extinction of non-human species was a fact—stating with certainty that what he later called the 'mastodon' was an extinct species, distinct from the modern elephant. Still, Cuvier's position did not achieve consensus for many years to come. Just to show how little scientific understanding there was of extinction at the turn of the nineteenth century, it may be noted that in 1803, the US President Thomas Jefferson is purported to have given instructions to the Lewis and Clark expedition

---

[1] Robert Brown, *Races of Mankind*, vol. 3 (London: Cassell, Petter, & Galpin, 1873), 199.
[2] Friedrich Nietzsche, *Morgenröthe: Gedanken über die moralischen Vorurteile*, 2nd ed. (Leipzig: Verlag von E.W. Fritzsch, 1887), 5. My translation of 'Erstes Buch, Teil 1': 'Klingt nicht fast jede genaue Geschichte einer Entstehung für das Gefühl paradox und frevelhaft? Widerspricht der gute Historiker im Grunde nicht fortwährend?'

to be on the lookout for any herds of mammoths they should see wandering the Great Plains.[3] Jean Baptiste de Lamarck, for example, whom Charles Darwin later credited as being the forbearer of evolutionary theory, studied the fossil record, and in 1801 published his view that species did not go extinct, and species that seem to have done so had actually evolved into new organisms. Similarly, the man considered the founder of modern geology, James Hutton, also denied the existence of extinction, as did most deists and theologians. Along with the biblical interpretation of the universe, it had long been believed that species could neither be created nor destroyed (after Genesis and before Revelations, that is). Thus, perhaps ironically, it was a clergyman, the Reverend William Buckland, who first established the extinction of dinosaurs only in 1824.[4]

Anthropocentric as high modern Europeans tended to be, human societies were surely going to be observed to disappear first, before there was general awareness of the plight of other species.[5] Famous cases of extinction such as the dodo and Stellar's sea cow were well known to the public by the middle of the nineteenth century, and this led Lamarck to concede that in a few rare cases of catastrophe or extreme human impact, species could be wiped out entirely. Hutton, however, would reject such catastrophism, thus denying the possibility that mass extinction could even be caused by an asteroid crashing into the planet. As Henry Cowles argues, the 'modern concept of extinction' as a problem affecting non-human

---

[3] Robert L. Kelly and Mary M. Prasciunas, 'Did the Ancestors of Native Americans Cause Animal Extinctions in Late-Pleistocene North America? And Does It Matter If They Did?' in *Native Americans and the Environment: Perspectives on the Ecological Indian*, eds Michael Harkin and David Lewis (Lincoln: University of Nebraska Press, 2007), 96. In his 1781 *Notes on the State of Virginia*, Jefferson included the mammoth in the list of the local fauna, saying, 'It may be asked, why I insert the Mammoth as if it still existed? It may be asked in return, why I should omit it, as if it did not exist? Such is the œconomy of nature, that no instance can be produced of her having permitted any one race of her animals to become extinct'. Cited in Mark Barrow, *Nature's Ghosts* (Chicago: University of Chicago Press, 2009), 18.

[4] Michael Ruse, *The Darwinian Revolution: Science Read in Tooth and Claw* (Chicago: University of Chicago Press, 1979), 6–8. Dennis R. Dean, *James Hutton and the History of Geology* (Ithaca: Cornell University Press, 1992), 19–22. Anthony J. Martin, *Introduction to the Study of Dinosaurs* (London: Blackwell Publishing, 2005), 58.

[5] The history of animal protection is quite distinct from that of conserving species perceived as endangered with extinction. There had been prohibitions against hunting in ancient India dating back to at least the time of Ashoka, and there had been early prohibitions against cruelty to animals in the form of bear-baiting, bull-baiting, cock-fighting, etc., in European law dating back at least to the 1200s. However, this long history of animal protection is not the topic of this book, as at no point before the late nineteenth century was animal protection ever framed around the threat of extinction.

animal species emerged in 1860s–1870s Britain, after Darwin's *Origins*, in 'the context of mid-Victorian anxieties about the natural world and human impacts on it'.[6] And by the mid-nineteenth century, the comparison between species and societies seen as threatened with extinction and in need of protection became pervasive.

## Human Endangerment & Extinction Discourse

Whereas there was little or no awareness within the western scientific establishment of the extinction of non-human animal species until the early to mid-nineteenth century, in contrast, both human endangerment and extinction discourses with reference to indigenous peoples are as old as the colonial encounter itself. Arguably, one could trace the worldwide chorus of voices calling to protect indigenous peoples from degradation, unrecognizable transformation, and vanishment to at least 1511. In that year, a Dominican friar, Antonio de Montesinos, delivered a sermon in Hispaniola to Christopher Columbus' men condemning the scandalous behaviour of the colonizers in waging 'detestable wars' reducing the natives to 'cruel and horrible servitude', asking 'Are Not the Indians Men?'

> On what authority have you waged such detestable wars against these people who dealt quietly and peacefully on their own lands? Wars in which you have destroyed such an infinite number of them by homicides and slaughters never heard of before. Why do you keep them so oppressed and exhausted, without giving them enough to eat or curing them of the sicknesses they incur from the excessive labor you give them, and they die, or rather you kill them, in order to extract and acquire gold every day?[7]

---

[6] Henry Cowles, 'A Victorian Extinction: Alfred Newton and the Evolution of Animal Protection', *British Journal for the History of Science* 46, no. 4 (Dec 2013): 695–714.

[7] Bartolomé de las Casas, *Witness: Writing of Bartolomé de las Casas*, ed. and trans. George Sanderlin (Maryknoll: Orbis books, 1993), 66–67. Worth noting here is that both dehumanizing animal analogies as well as a critique of this dehumanization are implicit in the question 'Are Not the Indians Men?' already by 1511.

Not long after, in 1516, Bartolomé de las Casas would be appointed 'Protector of Indians' ('*Protector universal de todos los indios de las Indias*') by Cardinal Cisneros. And by 1552, a full-fledged critique of the devastation laid on indigenous societies through the colonial encounter was published by las Casas in his seminal tract, *A Short Account of the Destruction of the Indies* ('*Brevísima relación de la destrucción de las Indias*').[8]

This genealogy begins with a distinction between what I call human extinction and human endangerment discourses. As I use these terms, whereas human extinction (or eradication) discourse merely reports or sometimes even celebrates a population's extermination, endangerment discourse laments it and usually seeks to stem the tide. As far as backdating the origins of these phenomena, there is a long historiographical tradition of recognizing that las Casas was fighting to prevent the extinction of Hispanola's Taino Indian population.[9] He could therefore be considered a preacher of what I call tribal endangerment discourse. As ethnohistorian Lynne Guitar shows, while many Spanish sources declared the Taino people extinct as early as the mid-1500s, individuals continued to appear in colonial legal records long after that, and many Taino community members are still struggling to assert their existence to this day.[10] Voltaire in 1756, reflecting on the work of las Casas, wrote '*On est encore surpris que cette extinction totale d'une race d'hommes dans Hispaniola*' ('We are still surprised by this total extinction of a race of men in Hispaniola').[11] Similarly, in the 1770s, the Scottish historian and reverend William Robertson reflected back on the Spanish Empire's efforts in the 1500s to protect its new subjects from 'extinction':

> The Emperor and his ministers were so sensible of this [destruction], and so *solicitous to prevent the extinction of the Indian race*, which

---

[8] Though *Brevísima Relación de la Destrucción de las Indias* was only published in 1552 it had been written ten years earlier, in 1542.

[9] However, some Taino scholars and activists today actually blame las Casas for inventing and perpetuating the myth of Taino extinction, by exaggerating his claims about their precarity in a 'paper genocide', i.e. a genocide existing only on paper.

[10] Lynne Guitar, 'Criollos: The Birth of a Dynamic New Indo-Afro-European People and Culture on Hispaniola', *Kacike: Journal of Caribbean Amerindian History & Anthropology* 1 (2000): 1–17; Lynne Guitar, 'Documenting the Myth of Taíno Extinction', *Kacike: The Journal of Caribbean Amerindian History & Anthropology* (Online Special Issue 2002). http://web.archive.org/web/20060110160446/http://www.kacike.org/GuitarEnglish.html

[11] Francois Marie Arouet (Voltaire), *Essais sur les Moeurs et L'esprit des Nations*, vol. 6 (Neuchâtel, 1773), 19.

threatened to render their acquisitions of no value, that from time to time various laws, which I have mentioned, had been made for securing to that unhappy people more gentle and equitable treatment. But the distance of America from the seat of empire, the feebleness of government in the new colonies, the avarice and audacity of soldiers unaccustomed to restraint, prevented these salutary regulations from operating with any considerable influence. The evil continued to grow... [12]

And in the 1840s, John Sutherland also read the history of Hispaniola this way, writing: 'Las Casas received instructions to... do every thing in his power to alleviate the sufferings of the natives, *and prevent the extinction of the race*'.[13]

The attempt to identify human endangerment discourse already at the very onset of the age of exploration might be compared to various attempts which have been made to antedate the origins of present-day environmentalism to ideas circulating in the seventeenth, eighteenth, and nineteenth centuries. The most convincing of these arguments for proto-environmentalism, by historians such as Richard Grove, leave the impression that early environmentalist ideas were the precocious reckonings of a tiny European scientific community working at the margins of empire in the eighteenth century, primarily on tropical islands such as St Helena and Mauritius. But no one can claim that there were widespread environmental worries so early on, nor widespread fear of non-human endangered species threatened with extinction.[14] In contrast, both human endangerment and extinction discourse were omnipresent at this time.[15]

---

[12] William Robertson, *The History of America, Book VI, 1542* (originally published in 1777) in *The Works of William Robertson, D.D.*, vol. 10 (London: Cadell and Davies, 1817), 215. My emphasis in italics.

[13] John Sutherland, *Original Matter Contained in Lieut.-Colonel Sutherland's Memoir on the Kaffers, Hottentot, and Bosjemans of Southern Africa* (Cape Town: Pike & Philip, 1847), 117. My emphasis.

[14] Richard Grove, 'The Origins of Environmentalism', *Nature* 345 (May 1990): 11–14. 'Concerns about species extinctions in Europe developed much later than the preoccupation with rural landscape'—Richard Grove, *Green Imperialism: Colonial Expansion, Tropical Island Edens, and the Origins of Environmentalism, 1600–1860* (Cambridge: Cambridge University Press, 1995), 464.

[15] European intellectuals had also been long-obsessed with the problem of what they called 'the extinction of noble families'. Albertsen observes that 'The idea that families die out originated in antiquity', and argues that 'the interest was always in the extinction of the highest social classes'. 'Already in 1762 the Danish country vicar Westenholtz realized that "many farm families die out. But since they live in the dark without being known, yes, without having a family name, this is not noted or felt"'. Well before population calculations for vanishing species in conservation

Much as Richard Grove asks us to look back to see environmentalism in an earlier period than it is typically assumed to have existed, the postcolonial critic Robert Young argues that the origins of postcolonialism can be seen in anti-colonial critiques that can be traced as far back as las Casas.[16] But while Grove and Young have been accused of looking at the past through presentist lenses,[17] it is neither historicist nor presentist to assert that the Columbian encounter was the seminal moment in European intellectual history for discourses inspired by fear of extinction, and calling for the protection of, indigenous peoples.[18] Montesinos and Casas may have been among the first, but European voices identifying the plight and championing the rights of communities around the world today identified as indigenous certainly became widespread early in the age of exploration and empire. One need only turn to the most famous of thinkers of these ages such as Michel de Montaigne in *Des Cannibales* (c. 1580) or Jean-Jacques Rousseau's *Discours sur l'origine de l'inégalité* (1755) to see elements of the idealization of indigenous peoples, as well as arguments for their protection. In contrast to the lack of awareness of the extinction of non-human species, popular acknowledgement of the endangerment and extinction of human 'races' had already been a cornerstone of colonial discourse for centuries before the time that Cuvier announced his discovery of the extinct mastodon.[19] Pointing to a 1685 book titled *Dying*

---

biology, a long line of statisticians starting at the beginning of the nineteenth century had worked on the problem of the disappearing noble families and family names. K. Albertsen, 'The Extinction of Families', *International Statistical Review* 63, no. 2 (Aug 1995): 234–239.

[16] Robert Young, *Postcolonialism: An Historical Introduction* (Oxford: Blackwell, 2001), 75.

[17] Hal Rothman, 'Review of Green Imperialism: Colonial Expansion, Tropical Island Edens and the Origins of Environmentalism, 1600–1860, by R. H. Grove', *Environmental History* 1, no. 1 (1996): 112–113, writes: 'the effort smacks of a prescient kind of presentism'.

[18] For a discussion of the problem of presentism, or the historian's tendency to use and abuse history for present purposes, see: Friedrich Nietzsche, 'On the Uses and Disadvantages of History for Life', in *Untimely Meditations*, trans. R.J. Hollingdale (Cambridge: Cambridge University Press, 1983), 57–123; George Stocking, 'On the Limits of 'Presentism' and 'Historicism' in the Historiography of the Behavioral Sciences', *Journal of the History of the Behavioral Sciences* 1, no. 3 (1965): 211–218; and Ira Bashkow, 'On History for the Present: Revisiting George Stocking's Influential Rejection of "Presentism"', *American Anthropologist* 121, no. 3 (2019): 709–720. For a discussion of the problem of historicism, or 'the idea that to understand anything it has to be seen both as a unity and in its historical development', see Dipesh Chakrabarty, *Provincializing Europe: Postcolonial Thought and Historical Difference* (Delhi: Oxford University Press, 2001), 6–16.

[19] The problem of the extinction of human 'races' and 'tribes' was one widely discussed in the literature of the seventeenth and eighteenth centuries. A few quotations to establish this point: 'They should do nothing contrary to the will of God, if they might fave a tribe which was in danger utterly to be extinct', Thomas Lodge, trans. *The Famous and Memorable Works*

*Speeches of Several Indians*, Arnold Krupat remarks that in colonial texts, 'Indian orators have been saying good-bye for more than three hundred years'.[20] And even language extinction was an established fact long before that of non-human species.[21]

The trope of human extinction in the form of the 'vanishing American' has been well documented. As Brian Dippie observes, 'Even in 1787 the Indian seemed a spectral presence. His eastern hunting grounds were graveyards now, and from the perspective of seacoast society... he could be viewed with detachment as a legitimate American ghost.... [A] fully rounded version of the Vanishing American won public acceptance after 1814. By its logic, Indians were doomed to "utter extinction" '.[22] There are so many early instances of this human extinction discourse in North America that enumerating them all would not be practical. A few choice words of US political and military leaders, however, should help to illustrate the position of the state. George Washington in 1783 spoke to the 'analogy' between Indians and 'the wild beasts of the forest', recommending that 'the gradual extension of our settlements will as certainly cause the savage, as the wolf, to retire; both being animals of prey, though they differ in shape'.[23] Benjamin Franklin, in the autobiography he began writing in 1771, blamed foreign imports, especially alcohol, for their extinction: 'If it be the design of Providence to extirpate these savages in

---

*of Josephus: A Man of Much Honor and Learning Among the Jews* (London: F.L., 1655), 112; 'In the Thirteenth Century the Race of the Dukes of Zeringhen became extinct, which made way for the Counts of Habfpurg to inlarge their Authority', Abraham Stanyan, *Account of Switzerland: Written in the Year 1714* (London: Jacob Tonson, 1714), 19–20; 'As for the tribes of Amtem, Hashem, Abil, and Bar, all that the Orientals know of them is, that by some means or other they became extinct, most of them being cut off, and the rest incorporating with the other tribes', George Sale et al., 'The History of the Arabs', in *An Universal History, from the Earliest Account of Time*, vol. 18 (London: T. Osborne, 1748), 374.

[20] Arnold Krupat, 'Chief Seattle's Speech Revisited', *American Indian Quarterly* 35, no. 2 (2011): 192–214.

[21] George Sale et al., 'General History of the Turks', in *The Modern Part of an Universal History*, vol. 4 (London: S. Richardson, etc., 1759), 66 observed: 'the conquered people generally speak the language of the conquerors, as well as their own, which, by degrees, becomes extinct, as that of the Kopts almost already is in Egypt, where the Arabic prevails; the Celtic in Gaul, where the French takes place; and in England the British, which has been superseded by the English'.

[22] Brian W. Dippie, *The Vanishing American: White Attitudes and U.S. Indian Policy* (Lawrence, KS: University Press of Kansas, 1991), 11.

[23] Jared Sparks, ed., *The Writings of George Washington: Being His Correspondence, Addresses, Messages and Other Papers, Official and Private, Selected and Published from the Original Manuscripts*, vol. 8 (Boston: Ferdinand Andrews, 1839), 484.

order to make room for cultivators of the earth, it seems not improbable that rum may be the appointed means. It has already annihilated all the tribes who formerly inhabited the sea-coast'.[24] Thomas Jefferson put it very strongly at the age of 81 in 1824 while reflecting back on the history of his young nation: 'And where this progress will stop no one can say. Barbarism has, in the meantime, been receding before the steady step of amelioration, and will in time, I trust, disappear from the earth'.[25] Following standard nineteenth-century unilineal notions of sociocultural evolution, many men in positions of power positively felt that it was a civilizational imperative to wipe out the primitive so progress could advance. Said Navy Commander W.L. Herndon to Congress in 1854: 'Civilization must advance, though it tread on the neck of the savage, or even trample him out of existence'. And Andrew Johnson to Congress, 1867: 'If the savage resists, civilization, with the ten commandments in one hand and the sword in the other, demand his immediate extermination'.[26] As Dippie powerfully argues, the entire gamut of North American society was in concurrence:

> A popular convention, premised on a moralistic judgment, had become natural law. Romantic poets, novelists, orators and artists found the theme of a dying native race congenial, and added those sentimental touches to the concept that gave it wide appeal. Serious students of the Indian problem provided corroboration for the artistic construct as they analyzed the major causes hurrying the Indians to their graves. Opinion was virtually unanimous: 'that they should become extinct is inevitable'.[27]

The Indian as apparition was the subject of countless early American artworks including the famous Edward Curtis photograph, 'The Vanishing Race' (see Figure 1.1). And this motif is still being repeated

---

[24] Benjamin Franklin, *Mémoires de la Vie Privée de Benjamin Franklin* (Paris: Buisson, 1791); cited Dippie, *The Vanishing American*, 359 and Patrick Brantlinger, *Dark Vanishings: Discourse on the Extinction of Primitive Races, 1800–1930* (Ithaca, NY: Cornell University Press, 2003), 47.
[25] Robert Nisbet, 'Idea of Progress: A Bibliographical Essay', *Literature of Liberty: A Review of Contemporary Liberal Thought* 2, no. 1 (Jan 1979).
[26] Herndon and Johnson are both quoted in Jay Griffiths, *Wild: An Elemental Journey* (London: Hamish Hamilton, 2007), 36.
[27] Dippie, *The Vanishing American*, 10–11.

**Figure 1.1.** Edward S. Curtis, 'The Vanishing Race—Navaho' (c. 1904), Photogravure.

Public Domain. Repository: Library of Congress Rare Book & Special Collections Division Washington, D.C. LCCN Permalink: https://lccn.loc.gov/2004672872

today in numerous quasi-anthropological works. For instance, like Edward Curtis' erasing an alarm clock from a 1900 photo of an Indian chief in order to preserve an image of savage authenticity, Jimmy Nelson's dramatic photos of disappearing tribes in full regalia have been staged for full dramatic effect. In the vein of Curtis's famous photo 'The Vanishing Race', Nelson's project titled *Before They Pass Away*, first published in Germany in 2013, follows a well-trod path in art history of romantic photography of vanishing tribes, uncritically replicating a colonial theme that dominated tribal photography since the very advent of the genre (see Figure 1.2).[28]

---

[28] Jimmy Nelson, *Before They Pass Away* (Kempen, Germany: TeNeues, 2013). Tim McLaughlin, 'Review of Jimmy Nelson, Before They Pass Away', *Image on Paper*, 2 Jan 2014. http://imageonpaper.com/2014/01/02/before-they-pass-away/

28    THE NATURE OF ENDANGERMENT IN INDIA

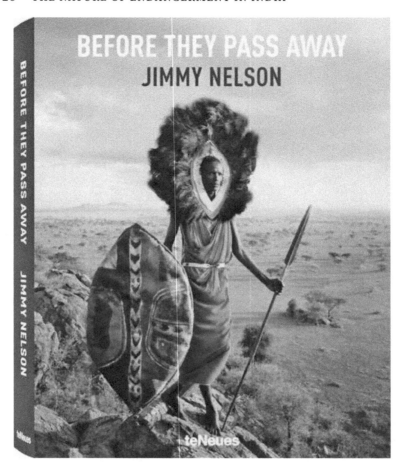

**Figure 1.2.** Jimmy Nelson, *Before They Pass Away* (Kempen, Germany: TeNeues, 2013). Fair use.

While North America was clearly a key location for the rise of endangerment and extinction discourse, it was early on a spreading global phenomenon. Patrick Brantlinger traces this discourse beyond the borders of the Americas, arguing in *Dark Vanishings* that across ideological lines in nineteenth-century European and colonial writings, there was an almost universal consensus that 'primitive races' around the world were destined for extinction, and that there was probably nothing that could be done about it. Government officials, missionaries, reformers, scientists, settlers, and soldiers were all of one mind, believing that 'primitive races' would inevitably disappear. Brantlinger and Dippie both intend to criticize the blindness of this assumption, but in doing so, both overstate the case that there was 'virtually unanimous' consensus that extinction was inevitable. For example, Brantlinger argues that even the Aborigines' Protection Society (APS), a group founded to save 'the aborigines' (and largely focusing on Asia and Africa), believed that their extinction was inevitable and unpreventable. Yet while the APS did adopt a pessimistic tone, resolving in their second annual report in 1839 that 'deep degradation and ultimate ruin… threaten barbarous tribes' due to the 'fatal results of the present system of intercourse with them', I would argue that they did so to underscore the necessity for 'protection'. As the APS itself stated: 'The object of this association is sufficiently indicated by its name. It is established as the protector of those, who have no power to protect themselves'.[29] Thus, APS literature represented a case of endangerment discourse, in contrast to those who adopted the more genocidal tone of extinction.[30]

In 1839, *The Monthly Chronicle*, a national journal in the United Kingdom, called the view that 'aboriginal populations' were 'inevitably' 'doomed to perish' an 'unworthy sentiment', writing: 'This idea, which may be traced to the worst enemies of the red race, has been readily and credulously adopted by some whose minds might have cherished juster sentiments, and whom we would forbear to suspect of hypocrisy, when they profess to be the friends of humanity'.[31] As John Bodley acknowledges: 'The problem of tribal destruction was debated by politicians, religious leaders, and scientists for 150 years'. Though I have already demonstrated that this debate existed for significantly more than 150 years, Bodley's point is well taken that there long were two vying 'philosophical camps', which he describes as 'the "realists", who felt that ethnocide was inevitable, and the "idealists", who argued that tribal survival was possible'.[32]

---

[29] *Report of the Parliamentary Select Committee on Aboriginal Tribes*, 1837.
[30] Aborigines Protection Society, *The Second Annual Report of the Aborigines Protection Society, Presented at the Meeting in Exeter Hall, May 21st, 1839* (London, 1839), 1.
[31] Anon, 'On the Practicability of Civilising Aboriginal Populations', *Monthly Chronicle* 4 (Jul–Dec 1839): 309.
[32] John Bodley, *Victims of Progress*, 6th ed. (London: Rowan & Littlefield, 2015), 285.

Official positions of 'Protector of Indians' following the model of las Casas, started to appear throughout the British Empire from the beginning of the nineteenth century. In British Guiana, the post was established at least as early as 1803. As Mary Menezes puts it, this was 'an unsalaried post of high prestige', designed with the goal of 'ensuring friendly relations with the Indians' and 'preserving the status quo of inter-ethnic colonial relations'.[33] Following an 1837 report to the House of Commons by leading members of the Aborigines Protection Society, official positions titled 'Protector of Aborigines' also began to be established throughout the British Empire in location such as the Port Phillip Protectorate (now Victoria, Australia), New Zealand, and Tasmania.[34] This is not to say that such protection was effective or uncontroversial (an issue to be addressed in later chapters). For George Augustus Robinson, the first Chief Protector of Aborigines from 1839 to 1849, 'protection' meant the removal of Truganini and the last band of aboriginals from Tasmania to Flinders Island, where, by 1876 with Truganini's death, it was said that the Tasmanians became an extinct race.

Similarly, already in the 1820s, during the build-up to Andrew Jackson's Trail of Tears in the southern United States, Indian removal was often justified in the name of 'protecting' the tribes. While President Jackson himself was said to have 'touted' a 'hollow pro-removal rhetoric ... of benevolence towards the Indians', others such as 'Quaker-born Methodist' Thomas McKenney earnestly 'saw removal as the only way for the US government to discharge its moral duty to protect Native Americans from harm at the hands of non-Native people'. As Elspeth Martini puts it, 'McKenney seems genuinely to have believed that the Jacksonian Democrats' proposed bill represented the only way to save the eastern peoples from their apparently inevitable decline and extinction'.[35]

What both *The Vanishing American* and *Dark Vanishings* do well is to draw critical attention to the consensus that emerged well before the nineteenth century that indigenous communities around the world were disappearing. Yet both books are primarily focused on documenting the

---

[33] Mary Menezes, *British Policy Towards the Amerindians in British Guiana, 1803–1873* (Oxford: Clarendon Press, 1977), 4, 117.
[34] *Report of the Parliamentary Select Committee on Aboriginal Tribes*, 1837.
[35] Elspeth Martini, 'The Tides of Morality: Anglo-American Colonial Authority and Indigenous Removal, 1820–1848' (PhD Diss., University of Michigan, 2013), 6, 189.

perception of this phenomenon, rather than addressing the empirical reality of these vanishings, or discussing the widespread endangerment discourse that mourned this loss and sought ways to prevent it (though sometimes, ironically, contributing towards decline). Furthermore, they both largely gloss over the fact that discourses of vanishing of biological and cultural diversity and their conservation were so often linked. These were not just predictions of inevitable doom; they were expressions of endangerment, with attendant calls for conservation and preservation (however misguided at times).

Even Charles Darwin publicly addressed the problem of tribal endangerment and extinction before ever dealing with the issue of species extinction. Already in 1836, Darwin recorded in his journal while on the Beagle, 'Wherever the European has trod, death seems to pursue the aboriginal. We may look to the wide extent of the Americas, Polynesia, the Cape of Good Hope, and Australia, and we find the same result... The varieties of man seem to act on each other in the same way as different species of animals—the stronger always extirpating the weaker.'[36] For many, this meant that something must be done. James Cowles Prichard, an ethnologist and a colleague of Darwin's, argued in 1839 that human endangerment was an urgent problem requiring action:

> Wherever Europeans have settled, their arrival has been the harbinger of extermination to the native tribes... [I]t may happen that, in the course of another century, the aboriginal nations of most parts of the world will have ceased entirely to exist. In the mean-time, if Christian nations think it not their duty to interpose and save the numerous tribes of their own species from utter extermination, it is of the greatest importance, in a philosophical point of view, to obtain much more extensive information than we now possess of their physical and moral characters.... How can this be obtained when so many tribes shall have become extinct, and their thoughts shall have perished with them? I cannot conclude this paper without making an appeal to the members of the British Association... to do something more than merely to record the history of the perishing tribes of the human family, and to take

---

[36] Charles Darwin, *Journal and Remarks, 1832–1836* (a.k.a. *Voyage of the Beagle*), vol. 1 (London: Colburn, 1839), 520 (New South Wales, Jan 1836).

up seriously the consideration whether any thing can be done effectually to prevent the extermination of the aboriginal tribes.[37]

The following year, Darwin and Pritchard together formed a committee of the British Association for the Advancement of Science (BAAS), where they attempted to determine what was necessary to be done in light of the fact that 'the races in question are not only changing character, but rapidly disappearing'.[38] As Jacob Gruber has shown, theirs was one of the early projects in the shaping of salvage anthropology. And as Tony Barta notes, 'Before Darwin understood species, he understood genocide'.[39]

Much of Darwin's theory of natural selection was drawn from his knowledge of human communities, and his observations of colonial impact on 'primitive tribes' around the world deeply informed his understanding of what Spencer would later call 'the survival of the fittest'.[40] In this sense, Darwin himself was a social Darwinist, even though the phrase 'social Darwinism' only started gaining traction around the time of his death. In another important sense, though, Darwin himself was not a social Darwinist. The social Darwinist position that stemmed from Thomas Malthus's population principle held that nothing could be done to save 'primitive societies'. This was because 'the struggle for existence is automatically eliminating those that are not fit to survive'. Social Darwinists thus urged a *laissez-faire* or *laissez aller* approach of allowing these communities to slip into extinction, arguing they should 'not to be tampered with because they would in course of time evolve despite all human efforts'.[41] This type of 'social Darwinism' also seems to have been

---

[37] James C. Prichard, 'On the Extinction of Human Races', *Monthly Chronicle* (1839): 497.
[38] British Association for the Advancement of Science, *Report of the Eleventh Meeting of the British Association for the Advancement of Science: Held at Plymouth in 1841* (London: John Murray, 1842), 332–339; cited in Jacob W. Gruber, 'Ethnographic Salvage and the Shaping of Anthropology', *American Anthropologist* 72, no. 6 (1970): 1294.
[39] Tony Barta, 'Mr Darwin's Shooters: on Natural Selection and the Naturalizing of Genocide', *Patterns of Prejudice* 39, no. 2 (2005): 117, 126 n28. Barta points to Sven Linquest's work to argue that even Thomas Malthus identified colonial genocide and rejected it in the 1830s.
[40] Herbert Spencer, *Social Statics* (London: John Chapman, 1851), 417, infamously argued that European imperialists will, 'exterminate such sections of mankind as stand in their way, with the same sternness that they exterminate beasts of prey and herds of useless ruminants. Be he human being, or be he brute, the hindrance must be got rid of. Just as the savage has taken the place of the lower creatures, so must he, if he have remained too long a savage, give place to his superior.'
[41] T.S. Wilkinson, 'Isolation, Assimilation and Integration in Historical Perspective', *Bulletin of the Tribal Research Institute, Chhindwara, M.P.* 2, no. 1 (Jun 1962).

closer to the view of the co-founder of evolutionary theory, Alfred Russell Wallace.[42] In contrast, Darwin appeared to hope it was possible to save vanishing tribes, at least in some cases.

## The Problem with Tribal Extinction

While the fact that many wildlife populations have dwindled and disappeared is clear enough, understanding the transformations that have taken place in indigenous societies around the world is a far more complicated issue. On the one hand, it seems to be common sense, a tautology even, to say that extinction equals extinction, whether it is human or non-human. Charles Darwin thought so. In 1871, Darwin published *The Descent of Man* in which he reflected, 'although the gradual decrease and final extinction of the races of man is an obscure problem… It is the same difficult problem as presented by the extinction of one of the higher animals'.[43] On the other hand, Darwin, in other editions of the same text, changed the language slightly to say that the spectre of human extinction was not an 'obscure problem' but rather 'a highly complex problem'.[44] And as Deborah Rose Bird et al. have recently argued, extinction 'is never a generic event'. 'There is no singular phenomenon of extinction; rather, extinction is experienced, resisted, measured, enunciated, performed, and narrated in a variety of ways to which we must attend'.[45]

---

[42] Wallace once predicted that 'the better and higher specimens of our race would therefore increase and spread, the lower and more brutal would give way and successively die out'. He also argued in favour of 'great law of "the preservation of favoured races in the struggle for life," which leads to the inevitable extinction of all those low and mentally undeveloped populations with which Europeans come in contact'. Alfred Russell Wallace, 'The Origin of Human Races and the Antiquity of Man Deduced from the Theory of Natural Selection', *Journal of the Anthropological Society of London* 2 (1864): 162–164; also cited by David Sepkoski, *Catastrophic Thinking: Extinction and the Value of Diversity from Darwin to the Anthropocene* (Chicago: University of Chicago Press, 2020), 68–69 (which was published just shortly before this book went to press).

[43] Charles Darwin, *The Descent of Man, and Selection in Relation to Sex* (London: Murray, 1871), 230.

[44] Later versions read: 'Finally, although the gradual decrease and ultimate extinction of the races of man is a highly complex problem… it is the same problem as that presented by the extinction of one of the higher animals'. Darwin, *The Descent of Man, and Selection in Relation to Sex* (London: Penguin Classics, 2004), 221–222.

[45] Cary Wolf, 'Foreword', in *Extinction Studies: Stories of Time, Death, and Generations*, eds Deborah Bird Rose, Thom van Dooren, and Matthew Chrulew (New York: Columbia University Press, 2017), viii.

When it comes to the numerous human populations already declared extinct since the colonial period, blurred boundaries and lack of clarity greet us at every turn. One of the biggest problems is resolving the question of just what precisely is a human 'population'.[46] On the one hand, we all belong to the same human race or species, therefore short of all of humanity's demise, a specific human population's extinction is not the same as a species' extinction.[47] On the other hand, it seems obvious to many that human populations can be categorized along multiple lines: ethnic, national, regional, religious, cultural, linguistic, etc., and thus that any of these population categories can become endangered or extinct. Determining the exact boundaries of a human population is therefore subject to the same lumping and splitting debates to which all systems of classification are prone. Numerous examples of the arbitrariness of the population concept complicating the phantom of human extinction abound.

For example, the Powhatans of Virginia are said to have disappeared by the mid-nineteenth century, yet were they one tribe or many? Often called a confederacy, it may be that political alliances simply dissipated and that various communities reconstituted themselves in the confederacy's wake. The Lenni Lenape or Delaware people are another example of a tribe often declared to be extinct, but they simply are not. There are some 11,000 Lenape people in Oklahoma, and the Delaware Tribe of Indians—the Lenni Lenape—are now officially registered in Bartlesville, Oklahoma. Sent there in the nineteenth century by the US government (which only recently stopped incorrectly classifying them as Cherokees), there are also thousands of Lenape descendants in New Jersey and Pennsylvania.[48]

Then there was Ishi, popularly represented as the 'last wild Indian' after he emerged starving and bedraggled from the California wilderness in 1911. For most of the twentieth century, Ishi was considered the last Yahi

---

[46] For an anthropological attempt to define extinction in human populations, see Charles Laughlin and Ivan A. Brady, eds, *Extinction and Survival in Human Populations* (New York: Columbia University Press, 1978).

[47] Of course, in the nineteenth century, the unity of the human species was not as widely accepted as today, and debate raged between those who believed in mono- and poly-genesis of human races/species.

[48] Clinton Alfred Weslager, *The Delaware Indians: A History* (New Brunswick: Rutgers University Press, 1989), 99. One variation on this existential denial has recently occurred when some officially recognized Native American tribal nations vociferously denied the existence of other unrecognized tribes, calling them 'fake tribes' or 'tribes called wannabe'.

Indian, the last member of an extinct tribe, yet research in recent decades has pointed to the fact that he was possibly multi-ethnic. Archaeologists suggest that his arrowheads more closely resemble those of tribes other than Yahi, and physical anthropologists have pointed to evidence suggesting a mixed background.[49] Still, like Shawahdunit and Truganini before him, Ishi represented the figure of the 'last' of his kind. In his evocative article 'Do Androids Pulverize Tiger Bones to Use as Aphrodisiacs?' Simon Cole puts it well: 'In those last years in the wild, Ishi personifies the tragedy of extinction'.[50]

The Tasmanians are often upheld as the most famous example of an extinct tribe. Their community has been profiled and mourned repeatedly since the colonial period.[51] In 1803 it was said there were between 5,000 and 8,000 Tasmanians alive, but their population was reduced to around 300 by 1833, when the remnant population was removed to Flinders Island and continued to decline. It was long believed that the last surviving Tasmanian died in 1876. Yet today, there is in fact a vibrant indigenous resurgence in Tasmania. Though most indigenous Tasmanians today are perceived to look indistinguishable from the wider (whiter) Tasmanian population, there are individuals of Tasmanian descent who trace their family histories back to intermarriage with other pacific islanders and colonists. The Tasmanian Palawa Aboriginal community is trying to reintroduce the Tasmanian language, called Palawa Kani, but through the twentieth century, the absence of 'full blooded' Palawa (nearly the entire community seems to have mixed with either European settlers or other South Pacific populations) meant many continued to label this population 'extinct'. Thus, the Tasmanian situation raises one of the most commonly cited debates on 'purity' and how to delineate a population.[52] And many commentators continue to maintain that all

---

[49] Russell Thornton, *American Indian Holocaust and Survival: A Population History Since 1492* (University of Oklahoma Press, 1987), *passim.*, especially 12, 109–114; Donald H. Holly Jr., 'The Beothuk on the Eve of their Extinction', *Arctic Anthropology* 37, no. 1 (2000): 79–95.

[50] Simon A. Cole, 'Do Androids Pulverize Tiger Bones to Use as Aphrodisiacs?' *Social Text* 42 (1995): 174.

[51] See for example James Bonwick, *The Last of the Tasmanians; Or, the Black War of Van Diemen's Land* (London: Sampson Low, 1870); Clive Turnbull, *Black War: The Extermination of the Tasmanian Aborigines* (Melbourne: Cheshire-Lansdowne, 1948); Robert Travers, *The Tasmanians; The Story of a Doomed Race* (Melbourne: Cassell Australia, 1968); and David M. Davies, *The Last of the Tasmanians* (Sydney: Shakespeare Head Press, 1973).

[52] Henry Reynolds, *Fate of a Free People* (Camberwell: Penguin, 2004).

indigenous Tasmanians have vanished.[53] Again, while there is no denying the historical tragedy of indigenous holocausts around the world in the age of European expansion, all of this also helps to raise awareness of the fact that the human extinction concept is more complex than is usually realized.

Declaring a marginalized population to be extinct when it is struggling for rights and recognition is not only insensitive or offensive, it is also an act of epistemic extermination. When a people's very existence is denied, states and corporations are free to appropriate resources and property without even troubling over touchy issues like compensation.[54] The impact of this type of supposed ignorance can be seen in the case of *Hoodia gordinii*, a cactus-like succulent plant of southern Africa long used by the San peoples of the region as an appetite suppressant. In 1996, the active ingredient in hoodia was patented by the South African Council for Scientific and Industrial Research and licensed to the British corporation Phytopharm under the name P57. An intellectual property rights lawsuit soon ensued, with a watchdog group for the San alleging biopiracy. The case of hoodia is well documented and need not be elaborated in detail here, except to point out that Phytopharm's 'excuse' for why it did not try to compensate the San for their traditional environmental knowledge as outlined in the Convention of Biological Diversity 'appears to be that it believed the tribes which used the Hoodia cactus were extinct'. Confronted with a San protest, the chief executive of Phytopharm 'reacted with genuine astonishment', claiming 'I honestly believed that these bushmen had died out and am sorry to hear they feel hard done by. I am delighted that they are still around and have a recognisable community'.[55]

Each one of the cases mentioned above raises various issues about the historicity, parameters, and dangers of employing the human extinction concept. Surely at some level, the extinction of a human population must

---

[53] Jim Allen et al. *The Last Tasmanian Extinction: A Search by Dr. Rhys Jones to Discover and Comprehend the Life and Death of the Tasmanian Aborigines* (California: CRM Films, 1998), video recording (61 min).

[54] Another form of cultural appropriation that can be similarly exploitative is when non-native 'plastic shamans' 'play Indian' and peddle native religions and cultures for profit. Arguably, here, peoples' existences are being denied as well.

[55] Antony Barnett, 'In Africa the Hoodia Cactus Keeps Men Alive. Now Its Secret Is "Stolen" to Make Us Thin', *Observer*, 21 Jun 2001. http://www.guardian.co.uk/world/2001/jun/17/internationaleducationnews.businessofresearch

be a possible worst-case scenario, but what about less extreme cases? If one can talk about a culture or a society as being endangered or extinct, what about a livelihood or way of life, a mode of production or ecology?[56] Can all these things, less tangible or measurable than even a population or a language, be endangered? Is this just a weakening or co-optation of the endangerment concept? Perhaps so, in some cases.

Almost anything can be threatened, thus almost anything can be called 'endangered'. Likewise, since almost anything can disappear or vanish forever, almost anything can be said to become 'extinct'. One of the problems with these declarations, then, is that they can be made even when there is patently nothing actually under threat. The rallying cry that a culture, ethnicity, etc., is disappearing is often fuelled by the rhetoric of endangerment and can be employed regardless of the underlying reality. Thus, just as the Nazis rose to power on the trope that the *deutsche Volk* was under threat from the Jews, white supremacists in the United States still today rely on the argument that the white race is endangered. But, by almost any measure, if there is any population in the world that has thrived until present, it is 'white people' in America.[57] Endangerment discourse has thus been just as powerful a tool for majoritarian forces as for those interested in protecting beleaguered minorities.

In contrast to the eagerness with which white cultural conservatives employ the language of endangerment, many indigenous activists have been far warier of this discourse. The vanishing Indian trope, for example, is an anathema to many indigenous communities, and dehumanizing animal discourse doubly so. Still, some marginalized communities have also successfully employed endangerment discourse to empower themselves and represent their interests. In the end, it is extremely important that indigenous peoples choose for themselves how to represent themselves and their interests. My hope is that raising awareness of this

---

[56] Roy Pinney, *Vanishing Tribes* (London: Arthur Baker, 1968), v, put it thus: 'The mammoth, the sabre-tooth tiger, the passenger pigeon, and the whooping crane all share the fate of losers in the contest of evolution... Man represents what he likes to think is the ultimate in evolution... However, culture, the special creation of man, has subjected him to another danger: the loss of the contest of cultural evolution, the loss of group identity. Few groups of men have ever actually become physically extinct. The loss of culture, then, whether voluntary or involuntary, is the central problem of the vanishing tribes of the world'.

[57] Richard Manson, 'Little White Lies of Endangerment: The Scary World of Supremacists and Separatists in the United State', in *Perspectives on Endangerment*, eds Graham Huggan and Stephan Klasen (Hildesheim: Georg Olms Verlag, 2005), 87–96.

long and deeply problematic genealogy will help individuals and communities make informed decisions about how to best deploy such endangerment and extinction discourse, if at all.

## From Hunting to Conserving Humans

All over the world, since ancient times, there have been dehumanizing calls for the extermination of so-called wild men alongside wild beasts. In ancient Greece, for example, one can locate the metaphor of hunting humans in Aristotle's *Politics,* where he defined hunting as 'an art which we ought to practice against wild beasts, and against men who, though intended by nature to be governed, will not submit'. In ancient India, trophic metaphors of eaters and eaten abound in Sanskrit ideas about social hierarchy. And in ancient China, the Han establishment frequently made 'unabashed' calls for 'the extermination of the [animalized] barbarians', often using the language of hunting.[58] Yet at some point in the modern colonial encounter, around the same time that large carnivores came to be identified as vermin species to be eradicated and imperialism was at its heyday, the metaphor (if it was ever *just* a metaphor) of human hunting became an all-too-common trope throughout empire. This is what Norbert Finzsch would describe as 'exterminalist discourse'[59]—a deeply disturbing rhetoric that can be seen in the following July 1763 correspondence between Colonel Henry Bouquet and Lord Jeffery Amherst, Commander-in-Chief of the British Army in North America, during the Siege of Fort Pitt, in what is now Pittsburgh, Pennsylvania:

> P.S. I will try to inoculate the Indians by means of Blankets that may fall in their hands taking care however not to get the disease myself. As it is a pity to pose good men against them, I wish we could make use of

---

[58] Aristotle, *Politics,* trans. Benjamin Jowett (Stillwell: Digireads.com, 2005), 10; Brian Smith, 'Eaters, Food, and Hierarchy in Ancient India: A Dietary Guide to a Revolution of Values', *Journal of the American Academy of Religion* 58, no. 2 (1990): 177–205; Frank Dikötter, *The Discourse of Race in Modern China* (London: Hurst, 1992), 19; Magnus Fiskesjö, 'The Animal Other: China's Barbarians and Their Renaming in the Twentieth Century', *Social Text* 29, no. 4 (Winter 2012): 57–79, esp. 62.
[59] Norbert Finzsch, ' "[…] Extirpate or Remove that Vermine" ': Genocide, Biological Warfare, and Settler Imperialism in the Eighteenth and Early Nineteenth Century', *Journal of Genocide Research* 10, no. 2 (2008): 215–232.

the Spaniard's method, and hunt them with English Dogs. Supported by Rangers and some Light Horse, who would I think effectively extirpate or remove that Vermine.

P.S. You will do well to try to Inoculate the Indians by means of Blanketts, as well as to try Every other Method that can serve to Extirpate this Execrable Race. I should be very glad your Scheme for Hunting them Down by Dogs could take Effect, but England is at too great a Distance to think of that at present.[60]

Exterminalist or extinction discourse, specifically using the threat of hunting humans, was prevalent around the world in the age of empire.[61] For example, in a Tasmanian newspaper from 1826, 'complete with bold-face capital letters':

We make no pompous display of Philanthropy—we say unequivocally—SELF DEFENCE IS THE FIRST LAW OF NATURE. THE GOVERNMENT MUST REMOVE THE NATIVES—IF NOT, THEY WILL BE HUNTED DOWN LIKE WILD BEASTS AND DESTROYED![62]

Such quotations necessarily raise the question: to what extent were colonized peoples, like wildlife, 'the hunted?' As Francis Parkman described in his 1847 book *The Oregon Trail*:

For the most part, a civilized white man can discover but very few points of sympathy between his own nature and that of an Indian… Nay, so

---

[60] Henry Bouquet to Jeffery Amherst, 13 Jul 1763, and Jeffery Amherst to Henry Bouquet, 16 Jul 1763, cited in Finzsch, '"Extirpate or Remove that Vermine"', 223.

[61] Already in 1882, at least one US commentator, George Ellis, was considering the stakes in whether to name this process 'extinction' or 'extermination', writing: 'Not unfrequently, in place of the milder word extinction the sterner word extermination is boldly used to define the alternative fate of the Indians. The difference between the words hardly needs to be morally defined here. One may speak of the extinction of the Indians as a result which might follow from natural agencies, irresistible and not requiring any external force to insure it. Extermination implies the use of violent measures to effect it'. George E. Ellis, *The Red Man and the White Man in North America* (Boston: Little, Brown, 1882), 588; Quoted in Karl Jakoby, '"The Broad Platform of Extermination": Nature and Violence in the Nineteenth Century North American Borderlands', *Journal of Genocide Research* 10, no. 2 (Jun 2008): 251.

[62] Cited in Ashley Riley Sousa, '"They Will be Hunted Down Like Wild Beasts and Destroyed!": A Comparative Study of Genocide in California and Tasmania', *Journal of Genocide Research* 6, no. 2 (Jun 2004): 202.

alien to himself do they appear that… he begins to look upon them as a troublesome and dangerous species of wild beast, and, if expedient, he could shoot them with as little compunction.[63]

In California, following the gold rush, both Indian extinction and protection discourse mounted. Around the same time that California Governor Peter H. Burnett predicted, 'that a war of extermination will continue to be waged between the races until the Indian race becomes extinct', the state also moved forward on 'An Act for the Government and Protection of the Indians'. To many white voices editorializing in California at the time, the choice was the same as with 'wild beasts': either domestication or destruction. A January 1851 letter to *The Alta California* put it thus: 'the people of California appear to have left but one alternative to these remnants of once numerous and powerful tribes, viz: extermination or domestication'.[64]

By the mid-nineteenth century, a worldwide consensus was emerging not only that many human groups coming into contact with modern Europeans were vanishing, but that non-human species were too, and that these processes were inextricably linked. In some sense, both observations reflected what Rosaldo identifies as 'imperial nostalgia'—that peculiar yearning where 'agents of colonialism long for the very forms of life they intentionally altered or destroyed'.[65] The fates of 'Wild Men and Wild Beasts', to quote the title of a popular nonfiction account of central India from the 1870s, were frequently and explicitly paired.[66] James Froud, in his colonial classic *Oceana: Or, England and Her Colonies* (1886), divided the conquered peoples of the world into two categories of animal life: domesticable and wild.

> It is with the wild races of human beings as with wild animals, and birds and trees, and plants. Those only will survive who can domesticate

---

[63] Francis Parkman, *The Oregon Trail: Sketches of Prairie and Rocky-Mountain Life* (New York: G.P. Putnam, 1849), 19.
[64] Cited in Sousa, 'They Will be Hunted Down', 193, 202.
[65] Renato Rosaldo, 'Imperialist Nostalgia', *Representations* 26 (Spring 1989): 107–122.
[66] W.G. Cumming, *Wild Men and Wild Beasts: Scenes in Camp and Jungle* (London: Hamilton Adams, 1871).

themselves into servants of the modern forms of social development. The lion and the leopard, the eagle and the haw, every creature of earth or air, which is wildly free dies off or disappears; the sheep, the ox, the horse, the ass accept his bondage and thrives and multiplies. So it is with man. The negro submits to the conditions, becomes useful, and rises to a higher level. The Red Indian and the Maori pine away as in a cage, sink first into apathy and moral degradation, and then vanish.[67]

Similarly, taxidermist and conservationist William Hornaday, on a trip to Asia, wrote in 1885:

Savage tribes deteriorate morally, physically, and numerically, according to the degree in which they are influenced by civilization.... To improve a savage race is to weaken it; to wholly civilize and convert it is to exterminate it altogether. Like the wild beasts of the forest, the children of nature disappear before the grinding progress of civilization.[68]

This back-and-forth between hunting and conserving humans and animals was not limited to English sources, and can be found across the spectrum of European language publications. Innumerable German language sources since the 1860s, for example, have addressed the concept of the *Ausrottung* or *Aussterbung* of *Naturvölker* ('nature folk').[69] *Ausrottung* and *Aussterbung* translate to English as 'extermination' and 'extinction', respectively, and today are terms more frequently applied in environmentalist discourse to *wilde Tiere* (wild animals) than to *wilde Menschen* (wild humans). The German term *Naturvölker* has a long history of problematic usage, being paired against *Zivilisationsmenschen*

---

[67] James Anthony Froude, *Oceana: Or, England and Her Colonies* (New York: C. Scribner's Sons, 1886), 300.
[68] William T. Hornaday, *Two Years in the Jungle: The Experiences of a Hunter and Naturalist in India, Ceylon, the Malay Peninsula and Borneo* (London: K. Paul, 1885), 443.
[69] E.g. Georg Gerland, *Über Das Aussterben Der Naturvölker* (Leipzig: Verlag Friedrich Fleischer, 1868); Peter Baumann and Helmut Uhlig, *Rettet die Naturvölker: Kein Platz für wilde Menschen* (Berlin: Safari Verlag, 1979). Baumann and Uhlig's title was a blatant twist on Bernhard Grzimek's famous wildlife documentary, *Kein Platz für wilde Tiere* (West Germany: Okapia, 1956).

('civilized people') and *Kulturvölker* ('culture folk') in a binary relationship. This is increasingly perceived as biased, essentializing nomenclature grounded in the assumptions of uniformity of indigenous peoples and the superiority of western civilization. Yet it might be successfully argued that the German reflects the widespread view that there was, and still remains, a category of people living in nature, and that their ecological situation is the noteworthy, defining, and endangered feature of their communities.[70] As Peter Baumann and Helmut Uhlig's 1979 book *Rettet die Naturvölker: Kein Platz für wilde Menschen* dramatically opens, 'Our thinking is so contrary, that we civilized people muster more care and understanding for wild animals and nature reserves than for the last *Naturvölker*'.[71] Overlooking this long history of human endangerment discourse, the Germany-based NGO Friends of People Close to Nature (*Freunde der Naturvölker*) says on its homepage: 'The insight that the last *Naturvölker / Indigenen Völker* around the world must be protected, came late. For some perhaps too late'[72] (see Figure 1.3).

While this comparison between 'wild peoples' and 'wild beasts' was often used to simply describe the genocidal reality that markedly resembled hunting, many nineteenth-century leftist and humanitarian observers would also resort to this type of rhetoric. They would do so not as a form of dehumanizing discourse, but with the note of urgency and even alarm that is the keystone of endangerment discourse where the subject is seen as 'in danger' and is projected as in need of protection. As Marx in *Das Kapital* tells us: 'the extirpation, enslavement and entombment in mines of the aboriginal population, the beginning of the conquest and looting of the East Indies, the turning of Africa into a warren for the commercial hunting of black-skins, signalised the rosy dawn of the era of capitalist production'.[73] Thus the hunting metaphor was occasionally

---

[70] It is also somewhat reminiscent of a move in some conservationist literature in English since the 1970s which divides humanity into opposing camps of 'ecosystem people' (tribes and peasants) and 'ecological refugees' (the dispossessed) versus 'global omnivores' (affluent, urban consumers), a taxonomy that has maintained some popularity in activist circles ever since. See Raymond Dasmann, 'Future Primitive: Ecosystem People versus Biosphere People', *CoEvolution Quarterly* 11 (1976): 26–31; M. Gadgil and R. Guha, *Ecology and Equity* (London: Routledge, 1995).

[71] Baumann and Uhlig, *Rettet die Naturvölker*, 7. (My translation)

[72] http://*www.naturvoelker.de* 'About Us'. (My translation)

[73] Karl Marx, *Das Kapital* v. 1 (Moscow: Progress Publishers, 2010), 527.

HUMAN ENDANGERMENT DISCOURSE 43

**Figure 1.3.** 'No Place for "Wild" People: Save the Nature People' & 'No Place for Wild Animals'.
Peter Baumann and Helmut Uhlig. *Rettet die Naturvölker: Kein Platz für 'wilde' Menschen* (Berlin: Safari-Verlag, 1980). Movie Poster for Bernhard Grzimek and Michael Grzimek, dir. *Kein Platz für wilde Tiere* (West Germany: Okapia, 1956).
Photo by author. Fair use.

adopted as a condemnation of capitalism by its opponents, as well as a celebration of colonialism by its advocates.

Moving beyond the realm of mere metaphor, time and again since the nineteenth century, there were individual and institutional linkages in agendas related to various forms of cultural and biological conservation, as well as linkages between early humanitarian organizations and later environmentalist ones. Perhaps, the most obvious manifestation of the direct lineage between both individuals and pressure groups founded to protect peoples and later ones founded to protect wildlife can be seen in Thomas F. Buxton, first president of the Aborigines' Protection Society established in 1839, and his grandson Edward N. Buxton, who led the creation of the Society for Preservation of Wild Fauna of Empire in 1903. In their multiple campaigns over several generations, the Buxtons, an elite family of English Quakers, show manifestations of the same romanticist and liberal desires to protect the vulnerable and those that cannot defend themselves that is the lifeblood of the top-down conservationist, or even 'white saviour', mentality.

Another fascinating and disturbing example of an individual who linked ideas of environmental and racial conservation was the infamous eugenicist, Madison Grant. The subject of an excellent biography by historian Jonathan Spiro, the book documents how Grant drafted the Adirondack Deer Bill of 1897, the Alaska Game Law of 1902, and the Migratory Bird Law of 1913, founded the Bronx Zoo, and transformed the Boone and Crockett Club from a club for wealthy sportsmen into one of the most important wildlife conservation organizations of the early twentieth century. For years, while it was the official position of the US government and the National Parks Service to eradicate predatory species seen as vermin—such as wolves, coyotes, cougars, bobcats, and even prairie dogs, fishers, martens, otters, pelicans, and eagles—Madison Grant was one of the very few voices putting forth the view that 'predators are crucial to the health of the ecological community'. Yet Grant was also one of the most hateful eugenicists of the early twentieth century, deeply concerned about white 'race suicide' and *The Vanishing of the Great Race* (as the title to his magnum opus put it). Spiro summarizes Grant's position using Grant's own words: 'conservation and eugenics were two sides of the same coin, as both were "attempts to save as much as possible of the old America"'.[74]

## People Parks

One particularly clear place where discourses of endangered tribes and wildlife have overlapped was in the construction of the national park idea.[75] In the very first-ever call for a national park, as well as in frequent proposals for national parks throughout the nineteenth, twentieth, and now the twenty-first century, national parks and other protected areas have been envisioned as places of conservation, study, and display not

---

[74] Jonathan Spiro, *Defending the Master Race: Conservation, Eugenics, and the Legacy of Madison Grant* (Burlington: University of Vermont Press, 2009), xiii. For more on links between eugenics and conservation in the US intellectual history, see: Miles A. Powell, *Vanishing America: Species Extinction, Racial Peril, and the Origins of Conservation* (Cambridge: Harvard University Press, 2016).

[75] A few paragraphs from this section appear in somewhat different form in my previously published article: Ezra Rashkow, 'Idealizing Inhabited Wilderness: A Revision to the History of Indigenous Peoples in National Parks', *History Compass* 12, no. 10 (2014): 818–832.

only of endangered species but also of human groups perceived to be vanishing or endangered. Since the nineteenth century, the vision that national parks should be inhabited by indigenous peoples has competed with the dominant conservation ideology that wilderness must be uninhabited.

The idea that national parks should be spaces for indigenous peoples has been pervasive and perennial. From antebellum calls in the United States to preserve 'Indian wilderness' to contemporary international campaigns for biocultural diversity conservation steeped in the language of the environmental sciences, the argument that national parks should be spaces for indigenous peoples has been present since the idea's inception in the early nineteenth century. While sometimes this agenda was based solely on romanticist or aesthetic visions of ecologically noble savages, other times it was based on the supposedly rational scientific grounds of cultural conservation or even specimen preservation. Similarly, while there have often been altruistic motives expressed in the examples this book will consider, this protectionist discourse has clearly leant itself to taking a patronizing and paternalistic tone. As we will see, not only must we confront a wide variety of controversial motives here, but also the idea that a primitive, authentic or traditional way of life should be preserved through parks conservation is deeply problematic.

The man considered to have written the first-ever appeal for a national park was also the first to call for preserving indigenous peoples and wildlife side-by-side in such a setting. After travelling up the Missouri River in 1832, George Catlin, the man regarded as 'the patriarch of preservation' in the United States, described his vision. Here the buffalo and the Indian:

> [M]ight in future be seen, (by some great protecting policy of government) preserved in their pristine beauty and wildness, in a *magnificent park,* where the world could see for ages to come, the native Indian in his classic attire, galloping his wild horse, with sinewy bow, and shield and lance, amid the fleeting herds of elks and buffaloes. What a beautiful and thrilling specimen for America to preserve and hold up to the view of her refined citizens and the world, in future ages! A *nation's Park,* containing man and beast, in all the wild and freshness of their nature's beauty!

I would ask no other monument to my memory, nor any other enrolment of my name amongst the famous dead, than the reputation of having been the founder of such an institution.[76]

Buffalo and Indian are paired together as both in need of protection by the steady hand of government. Both need to be 'preserved in their pristine beauty and wildness' for they are 'fleeting', endangered. In invoking the scene, not only does Catlin repeatedly refer to aesthetic considerations, repetitively using the words 'beauty' and 'beautiful' and specifically emphasizing visuals such as the 'classic attire' that the 'native Indian' would be seen wearing, but moreover the whole park is reduced to a kind of romantic image. Here the natives of the plains in all of their 'wildness' along with their primitive material culture (sinewy bow, shield, lance) are to be preserved and put on display together with domesticated and wild animals as 'thrilling specimen for America'. The park at once seems to act as a kind of museumized space filled with specimens, a place for entertainment and spectacle for 'refined citizens' of the world, and even a kind of tombstone or 'monument to my memory' where 'in future ages' civilization can have a small glimpse of the primitive and wild past, frozen in time, a kind of anthropological anachronism akin to that described by Fabian.[77] The passage thus combines so many of the elements that can be found repeatedly in calls to create 'people parks' ever since.

Since wilderness, wildness, and fear for their loss were frequently associated with indigenous people in the western imagination, it is unsurprising that the first-ever appeal for a national park included a reference to preserving wild people, wildlife, and wilderness side-by-side. As Catlin elaborates:

---

[76] George Catlin, *Letters and Notes on the Manners, Customs, and Condition of the North American Indians* (London: Self-published, 1842), 261–262. Italics in the original. Fragments of this passage are oft quoted in environmental histories of national parks. Often these sources will cursorily point out, almost as a novelty, that 'surprisingly' there are parallels between Catlin's vision and the direction that park policy in their specific case study has pursued. Interestingly, although many have hailed Catlin as giving birth to the national park idea, work tracing the history of 'people parks' back to Catlin is still rare. See, for example, Mark David Spence, *Dispossessing the Wilderness: Indian Removal, National Parks, and the Preservationist Ideal* (New York: Oxford University Press, 1999), 10; Roderick Frazier Nash, *Wilderness and the American Mind* (New Haven: Yale University Press, 1967), 728; William Adams, *Against Extinction: The Story of Conservation* (London: Earthscan, 2004), 77; Alfred Runte, *National Parks: The American Experience* (Lincoln: University of Nebraska Press, 1979), 22.

[77] Johannes Fabian, *Time and the Other: How Anthropology Makes Its Object* (New York: Columbia University Press, 1983).

> Many are the rudenesses and wilds in Nature's works, which are destined to fall before the deadly axe and desolating hands of cultivating man... Such of Nature's works are always worthy of our preservation and protection.
>
> Of such 'rudenesses and wilds', Nature has no where presented more beautiful and lovely scenes, than those of the vast prairies of the West; and of *man* and *beast,* no nobler specimens than those who inhabit them—the *Indian* and the *buffalo*—joint and original tenants of the soil, and fugitives together from the approach of civilized man; they have fled to the great plains of the West, and there, under an equal doom, they have taken up their *last abode,* where their race will expire, and their bones will bleach together.[78]

This romantic vision for the preservation of 'Indian wilderness' held popular currency in the United States up to the 1860s and beyond. Indicative of this *zeitgeist*, Ralph Emerson, Washington Irving, and James Audobon each explicitly evoked the idea of inhabited parks as a potential solution for the preservation of 'Indian wilderness'.[79] As Runte has argued, the 'original motivation for the creation of national parks had little to do with environmental preservation as we think of it today'.[80] National Parks were the US answer to artistic and architectural monuments of Europe. They were a part of the development of a national identity that emphasized the grandeur and beauty of North America. Partially, this could be achieved by preserving and showcasing Indians inside this landscape. In 1858, Henry David Thoreau also expressed much the same idea that Catlin did over a generation earlier:

> The Kings of England formerly had their forests 'to hold the King's game,' for sport or food, sometimes destroying villages to create or extend them; and I think that they were impelled by a true instinct. Why should not we, who have renounced the King's authority, have our

---

[78] Catlin, *Letters and Notes,* 260. Italics in the original.

[79] See Spence, *Dispossessing the Wilderness,* 32–35. Spence, for example, cites how Irving, through the voice of Captain Bonneville, proposed that a vast expanse of the Rocky Mountains 'must ever remain an irreclaimable wilderness, intervening between the abodes of civilization, and affording a last refuge to the Indian'.

[80] Daniel B. Botkin, *No Man's Garden: Thoreau and a New Vision for Civilization and Nature* (Island Press, 2001), 145.

national preserves, where no villages need be destroyed, in which the bear and panther, and some of the hunter race, may still exist, and not be 'civilized off the face of the earth,'—our forests, not to hold the king's game merely, but to hold and preserve the king himself also, the lord of creation,—not for idle sport or food, but for inspiration and our own true recreation? or shall we, like villains grub them all up, poaching on our own national domains?[81]

Thoreau's conclusion to his book *The Maine Woods* bears an uncanny resemblance to the concluding pages of Catlin's *Letters and Notes*.[82] Both, in their final pages, end with calls for the creation of a 'nation's park' or 'national preserves' along essentially the same lines. Whereas Catlin hoped such an area would preserve 'the buffalo and the Indian', Thoreau believed such a space would keep 'the bear and panther, and some of the hunter race', i.e. Native Americans, from being 'destroyed'. Upon his travels from Bangor to Mt Katahdin, Thoreau was depressed to pass through villages of 'Indians' he saw as having a 'shabby, forlorn, and cheerless look', and reflected on 'the Indian's history, that is, the history of his extinction'.[83] Given Thoreau's nostalgic view of authentic American Indian wildness, it is completely unsurprising that he would advocate for its preservation. After all, to Thoreau, 'in wildness is the preservation of the world'. This meant that not only land but also people—Indians in their native wild, keepers of true wildness—needed to be preserved.[84]

Such a vision was not actualized in the United States, at least not immediately or in full measure. Some fifty years after Thoreau's death, Theodore Roosevelt would justify westward expansion in the United States by arguing the land should not remain 'a game preserve for squalid savages'.[85] Instead, Native Americans were pushed into an ever-shrinking

---

[81] Henry David Thoreau, *The Maine Woods* (Cambridge: Harvard, 1884), 160.
[82] There is no incontrovertible proof that Thoreau ever read Catlin, but given the fact that Catlin was the closest thing America had to a celebrity-champion of wildness before Thoreau, as well as the fact that the end of Thoreau's *Maine Woods* parallels Catlin's *Letters and Notes* to an uncanny extent, I feel it is highly likely that Thoreau did borrow from Catlin here.
[83] Thoreau, *The Maine Woods*, 5.
[84] Dennis Martinez, 'Protected Areas, Indigenous Peoples, and the Western Idea of Nature', *Ecological Restoration* 21, no. 4 (2003): 247–250.
[85] Alexander Laban Hinton, 'The Dark Side of Modernity: Towards an Anthropology of Genocide', in *Annihilating Difference: The Anthropology of Genocide*, ed. Alexander Laban Hinton (Berkeley: University of California, 2002), 10.

reservation system, often on marginal lands surrounding national parks. The establishment of the National Parks Service in 1916 defined, created, and preserved a system of uninhabited wilderness parks that dispossessed Native Americans of their ancestral homelands. In Maine, where Thoreau had his epiphany about American wildness, Baxter Park was established 1931. Percival P. Baxter, who donated 6,000 acres including most of Mt Katahdin for the creation of the park, stipulated that the land 'shall be forever left in the natural wild state, shall forever be kept as a sanctuary for wild beasts and birds' and clearly stated in the terms of his donation that no human habitation should be allowed in the park.[86]

By the early twentieth century, around the same time that the National Park Service was becoming a bedrock institution in the American west, parks conservation was also becoming an international crusade led by Europeans. The early twentieth-century Swiss conservationist Paul Sarasin was a firm believer in the establishment of national park-like 'reserves for native tribes'.[87] Known as the founder of Switzerland's national parks, he was the first to propose a global programme for the protection of nature (*Weltnaturschutz* as he called it), as well a programme for anthropological nature conservation (*anthropologischer naturschutz*), at the League of Nations in 1920.[88] As Sarasin expressed:

> I am not yet finished with the tasks that *Weltnaturschutz* has to take on. To the contrary, I have yet to address the most important of all, and the most worthy which lies before us, namely to save the last remains of the primitive tribal peoples, the so-called *Naturvölker* (nature folk), from extinction, and to preserve them for posterity, uninfluenced to the largest degree possible.
>
> That saving these tribal groups from extinction is just as important in the list of tasks of the global nature conservation commission as

---

[86] Botkin, *No Man's Garden*, 145.
[87] Anna-Katharina Wöbse, '"The World After All was One": The International Environmental Network of UNESCO and IUPN, 1945–1950', *Contemporary European History* 20, no. 3 (2011): 331–348.
[88] Anna-Katharina Wöbse, 'Paul Sarasins "anthropologischer Naturschutz": Zur "Größe" Mensch im frühen internationalen Naturschutz: Ein Werkstattbericht', in *Naturschutz und Demokratie!?*, eds Gert Gröning and Joachim Wolschke-Bulmahn (München: Martin Meidenbauer, 2006), 207–214.

saving the other higher life forms, however, nobody can doubt... These branches of humankind urgently deserve protection.[89]

Around the world, similar ideas were proposed and acted upon in the early twentieth century. Fenneke Sysling, for example, documents how in the 1920s–1930s, the Netherlands Committee for International Nature Conservation, which was founded by P.G. van Tienhoven, worked to conserve 'natural people', publishing 'a report advocating the establishment of a reserve for mountain Papuans in the highlands of western New Guinea'.[90] Similarly, in Dutch Indonesia, the Lorentz Nature Monument (which would eventually become Lorentz National Park) was established in 1923 and was 'designed to protect indigenous tribes people from sudden contact with western civilisations'.[91] The plan for Lorentz was also 'initiated by P.G. van Tienhoven during a visit to the Dutch Indies as part of a world tour where he had visited conservation leaders in New York'. Those van Tienhoven consulted included 'leading thinkers in the social Darwinism/ eugenics discourse', and one reason put forward for the creation of Lorentz was that 'indigenous people needed "protecting" from colonial business entrepreneurs'.[92] Van Tienhoven's vision for Lorentz also makes sense, because, after Paul Sarasin's death, it was van Tienhoven who 'assumed leadership of the crusade to institutionalize international nature protection', and so the two conservationists clearly influenced each other's work.[93]

The fact that van Tienhoven was engaging with 'leading thinkers in the social Darwinism/ eugenics discourse' who were also interested in nature

---

[89] Paul Sarasin, *Über die Aufgaben des Weltnaturschutzes* (Basel: Helbing & Lichtenhahn, 1914). My translation of: 'Ich bin mit den Aufgaben, welche der Weltnaturschutz über sich zu nehmen hat, noch nicht zu Ende; im Gegenteil, die wichtigste von allen und zugleich die würdigste, welche ihm obliegt, habe ich noch namhaft zu machen, nämlich diese, die letzten der uns aufbewahrten Reste der primitiven Völkerstämme, der sogenannten Naturvölker, vor Ausrottung zu bewahren und der Nachwelt moeglicht unbeeinflusst zu erhalten ... / Dass aber die Rettung dieser Menschenstamme vor Ausrottung ebensogut in das Pflichtenheft der Weltnaturschutz-kommission gehört, wie die der andern hoheren Naturlebewesen, wird niemand bezweifeln... Diese Menschenformen beduerfen dringend des Schutzes...'
[90] Fenneke Sysling, '"Protecting the Primitive Natives": Indigenous People as Endangered Species in the Early Nature Protection Movement, 1900-1940', *Environment and History* 21, no. 3 (2015): 383.
[91] Paul Jepson and Robert Whittaker, 'Histories of Protected Areas: Internationalisation of Conservationist Values and Their Adoption in the Netherlands Indies (Indonesia)', *Environment and History* 8 (2002): 129–172.
[92] Personal communication with Paul Jepson, 9 Nov 2013.
[93] Nash, *Wilderness and the American Mind*, 358–359.

conservation, presumably points to his involvement with figures at the American Museum of Natural History in New York.[94] This is particularly relevant because Carl Akeley, the taxidermist who established the famous African Hall there, was also involved in founding the first national park in Africa, *Parc National Albert* in the Belgian Congo (formed in 1925). The Akeleys envisioned the park as an area of 'exceptional variety of flora and fauna', and if kept inviolate, believed it to be 'an almost unique opportunity to save some of the primitive African pygmies, a race now threatened with extinction'.[95] As Carl Akeley's wife Mary Jobe wrote:

> A tribe of three hundred of these little people dwell in grass huts in the Kivu forest, far removed from the ordinary Kivu natives. Since the pygmy is one of the most interesting of all primitive peoples, it is earnestly hoped that he may never come under the civilizing influence of either the white man or a higher class of blacks. He affords a unique opportunity for scientific investigation. Just as the gorilla should be observed without domesticating him, so should the pygmy be studied without instilling in him a desire for white men's goods and chattels. He should be allowed to remain in his ancestral way of living. Fortunately, under the law of the Parc National Albert, he will be free from molestation and will have with all the other wild life of the park an absolute sanctuary.[96]

Again, in this description and numerous others that the Akeleys left behind, indigenous people were paired with 'all the other wild life' as romanticized 'primitive' objects to be protected from 'civilizing influence', depicted as objects suitable for 'scientific investigation'.

As Roderick Neumann has shown, the evolution of Serengeti National Park in Tanganyika (modern-day Tanzania) followed closely in the approach laid down in Albert National Park. Various local realities and colonial ideologies prevented Serengeti National Park from becoming a human-free wilderness along the lines of the Yellowstone model

---

[94] Donna Haraway, 'Teddy Bear Patriarchy: Taxidermy in the Garden of Eden, New York City, 1908–1936', *Social Text* 11 (Winter 1984–1985): 56.
[95] Mary L. Jobe Akeley, 'Summary of Talk Given for Society for Preservation of the Fauna of the Empire by Mary L. Jobe Akeley', *Journal of the Society for the Preservation of the Fauna of the Empire* 9 (1929): 15–21; also cited in Adams, *Against Extinction*, 5.
[96] Mary Jobe Akeley, *Carl Akeley's Africa* (New York: Dodd Mead, 1929), 220.

in the United States or the Kruger model in South Africa. On the one hand, many members of the Society for the Preservation of Fauna of Empire, who were influential in the creation of the park, subscribed to the 'popular racial stereotype of "primitive" Africans as part of the natural landscape'. On the other hand, there was deep concern among some Tanganyikan officials that interfering with local customary rights might prove disastrous, especially in 1951 in light of the Mau Mau Uprising occurring in nearby Kenya, the same year that Serengeti's boundaries were set. As Neumann summarizes, these parks implemented, 'a mythical vision of Africa as an unspoiled wilderness, where nature existed undisturbed by destructive human intervention... "Primitive" Africans were often simply regarded as fauna.... The possibility of protecting them along with the wildlife could therefore be given serious consideration'.[97]

A national park explicitly founded for the protection of indigenous peoples was also created as recently as 1961 in Brazil: Xingu National Park. As in the case of all the examples of the other parks for indigenous peoples—from Sarasin's call for *anthropologischer Naturschutz*, to Akeley's call for a park to preserve the pygmies of the Congo, to Verrier Elwin's call for a national park for the tribes of Central India (discussed in Chapter 6), and numerous other such cases, the push to create Xingu was the inspired idea of prominent white activist/anthropologist administrators. While the Vice President of Brazil had proposed such a park as early as 1952, it is usually the Villas-Bôas brothers who receive full credit for founding the park. As a representative from Survival International (then transitioning from being previously named the Primitive People's Fund) put it in 1971: 'The Indians in the Xingu National Park were the healthiest in mind and body of those we saw in Brazil.... Xingu is the only closed park in Brazil, which means that it is the only area in which Indians are safe from deliberate or accidental contact with undesirable representatives of Western civilization. This is due entirely to the Villas-Bôas brothers and the total dedication of their lives to this work over the last 25 years'. Survival International then went on to urge the establishment 'before it is too late' of more such

---

[97] Roderick P. Neumann, *Imposing Wilderness: Struggles Over Livelihood and Nature Preservation in Africa* (Berkeley: University of California Press, 1998), 122–139.

'National Park[s] in which some of the remaining virgin areas of Brazil may be preserved and the Indians given a chance of survival'.[98] Much as Survival International changed its name away from 'the Primitive Peoples Fund' to escape negative stigma, Xingu replaced the title 'Parque Nacional' with the perhaps more appropriate 'Parque Indígena' in 1967, but by the time Survival International/the Primitive Peoples Fund was publishing this report in 1971, in both cases, the older terminology was still in use.[99]

Similarly, in the United States under the Carter administration in 1980, the Alaska National Interest Lands Conservation Act (ANILCA), 'designated more than 100 million acres, or 28 percent of the state', as national parks and other conservation lands. In so doing, this Act of Congress 'provided for the continuation of "customary and traditional" subsistence use in the new national park areas'. As Catton argues, 'Superficially, at least, this innovative concept for Alaska's new national parks harkened back to one of the earliest antecedents of the national park idea.... [T]he romantic appeal of Catlin's vision did not lie far beneath the surface of the legal language set forth in ANILCA's subsistence provisions'.[100]

And of course, national parks are not the only form of park that has been created to preserve and display indigenous cultures. In Taiwan, for example, Formosan Aboriginal Culture Village (see Figure 1.4) is an amusement park complete with a gondola, a steam locomotive, several water rides, roller coasters, and the tallest free-fall ride in the country.[101]

---

[98] Robin Hanbury-Tenison, *Report of a Visit to the Indians of Brazil on Behalf of the Primitive Peoples Fund/Survival International, January-March, 1971* (London: Survival International, 1971), 9–10.

[99] 'Foi apenas com a criação da Funai (em 1967, substituindo o SPI—Serviço de Proteção aos Índios) que o "Parque Nacional" passou a ser designado "Parque Indígena", voltando-se então primordialmente para a proteção da sociodiversidade nativa'. Povos Indígenas no Brasil, 'Xingu: O Parque'. https://pib.socioambiental.org/pt/povo/xingu/1539

[100] All quotations in this paragraph from Theodore Catton, *Inhabited Wilderness: Indians, Eskimos, and National Parks in Alaska* (Albuquerque: University of New Mexico Press, 1997), 1–10.

[101] As the park previously described on its own website: 'The Formosan Aboriginal Culture Village was founded in 1986 by its current president, Jung-i Chang. Mr. Chang's vision was to establish a place to both preserve and teach about Taiwanese aboriginal heritage while, at the same time, provide a spacious venue for people to spend and enjoy their leisure time. The history of his family has long been intertwined with those of Taiwanese native aborigine cultures. It was his own ancestor, Da-ching Chang, who negotiated with local tribal representatives to open to cultivation the area around modern Feng-Yuan for Chinese settlers'. The Formosan Aboriginal Culture Village>About Us>Our Roots. http://web.archive.org/web/20140316160645/www.nine.com.tw/webe/html/introduction/index.aspx

54   THE NATURE OF ENDANGERMENT IN INDIA

Figure 1.4. Advertisement for Formosan Aboriginal Cultural Village Amusement Park. Fair use.
Source: *http://www.s-bus.com/tour-17-1.htm*.

Between rides, tourists can also entertain themselves with tribal dances and other colourful performances. Reminiscent of Buffalo Bill Cody's Wild West Shows or the 'Glacier Park Indians', press reports explain that the park 'provides a window on aboriginal life with its arts and crafts demonstrations by native aborigines' and also 'offers an enjoyable insight into the aboriginal way of life in a commercial setting'.[102]

## Anthropological Museums & Human Zoos

As in the case of national parks, another manifestation of the desire to preserve and save for posterity the vanishing 'other', prevalent from the

---

[102] For Wild West Shows, see: Louis S. Warren, *Buffalo Bill's America* (New York: Knopf Doubleday, 2007). For the way that the Blackfeet of Glacier National Park were made to perform for tourists, see Spence, *Dispossessing*, 83–86. Dipal Khatri, 'Aboriginal Culture Village Shows Tribal Lifestyles', *China Post*, 19 Apr 2007.

early nineteenth century onward, were 'human zoos'.[103] Between 1800 and 1950, it is estimated that some 35,000 people from around the world were 'paraded before white Europeans and Americans' in these exhibitions.[104] Sometimes, people such as Ota Benga were literally put in cages in the company of chimpanzees and orangutans, at institutions such as the Bronx Zoo.[105] In the apparition of human zoos, all of the imperialist and racist attitudes of the era were embodied; but most importantly with regards to endangerment discourse, many of these exhibitions claimed to capture and preserve endangered specimens of humanity simultaneously for spectacle and for 'anthropo-zoological science'. Thus, an 1840s exhibit in London of Khoisan peoples from Southern Africa referred to these people as 'Bushmen' who were 'sunk in the scale of humanity to the level almost of the beasts of the forest'. J.S. Tyler, the white exhibiter of these people claimed it was 'inevitable that the Bushmen would soon be "exterminated". "Even now, London and Paris, in their museums, have stuffed skins of these people", he declared'.[106]

Though the human zoo was clearly a product of colonial modernity, unfortunately colonized populations who themselves were being subjected to European-invented racial hierarchies also sometimes embraced the logic of these exhibits. For example, between 1858 and 1863, Andaman Islanders from the Bay of Bengal were repeatedly captured and sent to Calcutta by steamship. There in the capital of British India, they were housed in the Alipore Zoo, where the Bengali public was encouraged to come to view them. It was reported that some *bhadralok* and middle-class Indian urbanites regarded them as descendants of Hanuman, the monkey god. They were also 'treated as "specimens"—when a woman and her child died of pneumonia in 1862, their bodies

---

[103] Pascal Blanchard et al., eds, *Human Zoos: Science and Spectacle in the Age of Colonial Empires* (Liverpool: Liverpool University Press, 2008).
[104] Frank Browning, 'The Human Zoo: Invention of the Savage', *Huffington Post*, 3 Feb 2012. For more on human zoos, see Sadiah Qureshi, *Peoples on Parade: Exhibitions, Empire, and Anthropology in Nineteenth-Century Britain* (Chicago: University of Chicago Press, 2011).
[105] See, e.g. Pamela Newkirk, *Spectacle: The Astonishing Life of Ota Benga* (New York: Amistad, 2015).
[106] Nadja Durbach, 'London, Capital of Exotic Exhibits from 1830 to 1860', in *Human Zoos: Science and Spectacle in the Age of Colonial Empires*, eds Pascal Blanchard et al. (Liverpool University Press, 2008), 84.

were preserved in large glass jars and stored in the basement of the Calcutta Museum'.[107]

Human exhibitions, which were often as much for titillating the masses as supposedly for science, at this period also started to give way to the linked preservationist projects of salvage anthropology and taxidermy, and the museumization of indigenous peoples alongside wildlife dioramas. As Franz Boas put it in 1907, 'Museums are the storehouses in which… scientific materials from distant countries, vanishing species, paleontological remains, and the objects used by vanishing tribes are kept and preserved for all future time'.[108] And as V. Pandya summarizes some hundred years later, 'Souvenirs from these dying races came to be prized in European and North American collections. The museum was the perfect theatre for witnessing the death throes of an exotic tribe'.[109] While, for many late nineteenth- and early twentieth-century thinkers, concern for the disappearance of supposedly 'primitive' cultures was primarily a scientific anxiety (a fear of lost knowledge as well as a fear of losing the human past), for Boas, this desire for scientific preservation was also coupled with an emerging liberal critique of racism.

As an institution, the American Museum of Natural History in New York City, where Boas designed one of 'the first museum exhibition to value indigenous cultures on their own terms',[110] by contrast, thoroughly embraced the scientific racism and eugenics of this period; and many of its exhibits were excellent examples of the dual projects of preserving and memorializing both endangered societies and species together for posterity. As Donna Haraway describes, the museum symbolizes 'a monumental reproduction of the Garden of Eden', whereupon exiting Olmstead's Central Park, the urban citizen, that 'over-wrought or decadent city dweller', could reflect on both the origins of species and civilizations. Transitioning seamlessly between the Hall of Asian Mammals and the Hall of Asian Peoples, for instance, the museum

---

[107] Vishvajit Pandya, *In the Forest: Visual and Material Worlds of Andamanese History (1858–2006)* (Lanham, MD: University Press of America, 2009), 82.
[108] Franz Boas, 'Some Principles of Museum Administration', *Science* 25 (1907): 920–933.
[109] Pandya, *In the Forest*, 141.
[110] As the American Museum of Natural History itself puts it, 'Northwest Coast Hall'. https://www.amnh.org/exhibitions/permanent/northwest-coast

'offers a unique communion with nature at its highest and yet most vulnerable moment, the moment of the interface of the Age of Mammals with the Age of Man'. In the museum, 'exhibition, conservation, and eugenics were all directed as coordinated medical interventions, as prophylaxis for an endangered body politic'. To Haraway, 'the three public activities of the Museum, all dedicated to preserving a threatened manhood', were 'exhibition, eugenics, and conservation'.[111] The fallout of these preservation efforts of course remains a major problem to this day. A January 2021 survey of the collections at just one other institution (Harvard), for instance, reported possessing the human remains of some 22,000 individuals.[112]

## From Genocide to Ethnocide and Ecocide

Similar to the trajectory of human endangerment and extinction discourses' preceding non-human species extinction talk (and then the two blurring together), the terms genocide and ethnocide were coined before the term ecocide. Raphäel Lemkin, the Polish-Jewish jurist, coined the term 'genocide' in 1944 and pioneered the 1948 United Nations Convention on the Prevention and Punishment of the Crime of Genocide in the wake of the Holocaust. Almost immediately upon Lemkin's popularizing of this term, a major debate about the nature of genocide arose over whether its scope included the destruction of a people's culture, as well as their outright murder. Lemkin contrasted the 'mass killings of all members of a nation' with 'actions aiming at the destruction of essential foundations of the life of national groups', and argued that 'disintegration of the political and social institutions of culture, language, national feelings, religion, economic existence of national groups and the destruction of the personal security, liberty, health, dignity, and even the lives of the individuals belonging to such groups' all equated to genocide.

---

[111] Haraway, 'Teddy Bear Patriarchy', 20–64.
[112] Lawrence S. Bacow, 'Steering Committee on Human Remains in Harvard Museum Collections'. https://www.harvard.edu/president/news/2021/steering-committee-on-human-remains-in-harvard-museum-collections/

'Genocide has two phases: one, destruction of the national pattern of the oppressed group; the other, the imposition of the national pattern of the oppressor.'[113]

As Totten et al. put it, 'It is apparent from this definition that Lemkin considered both physical and cultural genocide—or ethnocide—to be part of the general concept of genocide.'[114] Eventually, at the level of international law, Lemkin's more inclusive definition of genocide did not triumph, however. The 1948 UN convention established that while genocide might include the destruction of culture, a crime would only qualify as genocide if it included the 'killing' or 'physical destruction' with 'intent to destroy, in whole or in part, a national, ethnical, racial or religious group'.[115]

Often, with the topics of tribal endangerment and extinction, some confusion seeps in. Is it physical death that is being discussed, or is it cultural death? Some anthropologists therefore have distinguished 'ethnocide' from 'genocide' to separate the crimes of physically versus culturally exterminating a community. As stated above, ethnocide, a word closely related to genocide, in this usage refers to the intentional destruction of a people's culture, as opposed to the destruction of the people themselves. As Janet and Thomas Headland explain, 'ethnocide is when a dominant political group attempts to purposely put an end to a people's traditional way of life'.[116] Thus, Lawrence Davidson dedicates his book titled *Cultural Genocide* to 'all the victims of cultural genocide, whose destruction constitutes the slow extinction of human diversity'.[117] And Wade Davis, who has also built a career on mourning the loss of cultural diversity of indigenous

---

[113] Raphael Lemkin, *Axis Rule in Occupied Europe* (Washington, DC: Carnegie Endowment for International Peace, 1944), 79.

[114] Samuel Totten, William S. Parsons, and Robert K. Hitchcock, 'Confronting Genocide and Ethnocide of Indigenous Peoples an Interdisciplinary Approach to Definition, Intervention, Prevention, and Advocacy', in *Annihilating Difference*, 59.

[115] United Nations High Commissioner for Human Rights (UNHCHR), Convention on the Prevention and Punishment of the Crime of Genocide, *Adopted by Resolution 260 (III) A of the United Nations General Assembly on 9 December 1948*.

[116] Janet Headland and Thomas N. Headland, 'Westernization, Deculturation, or Extinction Among Agta Negritos? The Philippine Population Explosion and Its Effect on a Rainforest Hunting and Gathering Society' in *Hunters and Gatherers in the Modern Context*, vol. 1, ed. Linda J. Ellanna (Fairbanks: University of Alaska, 1994), 272–284.

[117] Lawrence Davidson, *Cultural Genocide* (New Brunswick: Rutgers University Press, 2012), v.

peoples around the world, salutes Margaret Mead 'the great anthropologist' who:

> said, before she died, that her greatest fear was that as we drifted towards this blandly amorphous generic world view not only would we see the entire range of the human imagination reduced to a more narrow modality of thought, but that we would wake from a dream one day having forgotten there were even other possibilities.[118]

With the word 'ethnocide' being coined in the late 1960s by the anthropologist Robert Jaulin, the distinction between physical and cultural genocide became even firmer in French and Spanish language scholarship. Following Sartre, who considered all colonization to be cultural genocide, Jaulin's 1970 book, *La Paix Blanche: introduction à l'ethnocide* went even further, to hold all of western culture, 'which is intrinsically criminal taken in its entirety', as accountable for ethnocide. Working with the Bari people of the Colombian Amazon, for Jaulin, it did not matter if it was democracy or fascism coming into contact with indigenous people—all are forces of 'de-civilization', since their 'object is the disappearance of other civilizations'. As Sills points out, from a legal perspective, this argument was deeply problematic, since one might find it difficult to try an entire civilization for a crime, and since, in and of themselves, 'urbanization, economic development, or modernization ... are presumably not criminal processes'.[119]

Though the term ethnocide was not widely adopted in English until the 1980s, a mere three years after Jaulin had published his book, in 1973, John Bodley introduced the term to English-language audiences at a conference in Chicago. Bodley, who is known for his wide-sweeping critique of the impact of 'progress' on indigenous peoples, defined ethnocide here as the 'forced modification of one culture by another'.[120] Usually given a

---

[118] Along with 'global warming' critics of corporate globalization often warn of 'global blanding' and participate in 'global mourning' for what is being lost. Wade Davis, 'Dreams from Endangered Cultures', TED Talks, 2003. https://www.ted.com/talks/wade_davis_on_endangered_cultures/
[119] Mark Allan Sills, *Ethnocide and Interaction Between States and Indigenous Nations: A Conceptual Investigation of Three Cases in Mexico* (PhD Diss., University of Denver, 1992), 13–14.
[120] John H. Bodley, 'Alternatives to Ethnocide: Human Zoos, Living Museums, and Real People' in *Western Expansion and Indigenous Peoples: The Heritage of Las Casas*, ed. Elias Sevilla-Casas (The Hague: Mouton, 1977), 31–51. This paper was first presented at the 'ninth World Anthropology Conference of the International Congress of Anthropological and Ethnological Sciences (ICAES), held in Chicago in 1973'. https://sites.google.com/site/bodleyanthropology/books/victims-of-progress-2

narrower, more précising, definition than Jaulin's, today the term is generally accepted as a synonym for cultural genocide. Key in most contemporary definitions of ethnocide are criminality and intentionality. This, of course, raises the issue that all cultures change, that it is in the very nature of culture to change, and not all outside influence on an indigenous community can be classified as criminally destructive.

One controversy here is that there have been some scholars who question or deny the very possibility of cultural endangerment or extinction. As early as 1979, Arthur Hippler 'argued that "culture" is an abstraction, not something that can be defended or "saved" from extinction. Thus ethnocide, the destruction of a cultural or ethnic group, could not occur'.[121] By 2001, anthropologist Stuart Kirsh had also pointed out that while 'the definition and significance of culture loss are increasingly debated in legal contexts', 'Indigenous claims about "culture loss" pose a problem for contemporary definitions of culture as a process that continually undergoes change rather than something which can be damaged or lost'.[122] And though I don't know how many anthropologists would agree with him, Graham Huggan writes, 'Few self-respecting anthropologists would now subscribe to the notion of "endangered culture"'.[123] This all suggests two opposing views of culture—one which sees culture as ever-changing and adaptable, therefore impossible of extinction, the other as something fragile and under-threat. Yet, again, to a large extent, what is most important is how indigenous peoples—in their own emic framings—themselves engage with terms such as culture loss and ethnocide.

Another problem here is the accusation that terms like ethnocide and genocide are often frivolously deployed.[124] As with the concept of endangerment, there is the danger of hyperbole and sheer mislabelling. Thus, it has been argued: 'Too often an incidence of massacre or some other

---

[121] Arthur E. Hippler, 'Comment on "Development in the Non-Western World"', *American Anthropologist* 81 (1979): 348–349; cited in Bodley, *Victims*, 21. For a rejoinder to Hippler see Gerald Weiss, 'The Tragedy of Ethnocide: A Reply to Hippler', *American Anthropologist* 83, no. 4 (Dec 1981): 899–900.

[122] Stuart Kirsh, 'Lost Worlds: Environmental Disaster, "Culture Loss", and the Law', *Current Anthropology* 42, no. 2 (Apr 2001): 167–198.

[123] Graham Huggan, 'Introduction', in *Perspectives on Endangerment*, 5.

[124] Samuel Totten, ' "Genocide", Frivolous Use of the Term', in *Encyclopedia of Genocide*, eds Israel W. Charny et al. (ABC-CLIO, 1999), 35–36. 'Frivolous use of the term 'genocide' is rampant in today's world. Well-intentioned but ill-informed individuals and groups use the term to describe a wide variety of social ills ... '

serious human rights infraction is incorrectly referred to or deemed to be genocide... As horrible as these infractions are, if they do not meet certain criteria they cannot legitimately be called genocide'.[125] The same might be said of ethnocide.

Again, following the general trend in modern intellectual history of anthropocentrism before biocentrism, and human endangerment discourse before environmental endangerment discourse, the concept of ecocide emerged as a derivative of the concepts of genocide and ethnocide, and as a label for war crimes rather than as a general critique of human impact on the environment. Unlike with the words genocide and ethnocide, however, there is some debate about who coined the term ecocide, as it seems to have first appeared in a scientific discourse community around the start of the 1970s. Was it Fernando Cesarman in his 1972 book by that same title, or was it the Yale professor of plant biology Arthur Galston two years earlier when he first discussed ecocide at a conference in the context of 'War Crimes and the American Conscience' and the Nuremberg tribunals, saying that the 'United States stands alone as possibly having committed ecocide against another country' through the use of Agent Orange in the Vietnam War?[126]

## Biocultural Diversity Conservation

> What is man without the beasts? If all the beasts were gone, man would die from a great loneliness of the spirit. For whatever happens to the beasts, soon happens to man. All things are connected. Whatever befalls the Earth befalls the sons of the Earth. If men spit upon the ground, they spit upon themselves. This we know—the Earth does not belong to man—man belongs to the Earth. This we know. All things are connected like the blood which unites one family. All things are connected. Whatever

---

[125] Samuel Totten, William S. Parsons, and Robert K. Hitchcock, 'Confronting Genocide and Ethnocide of Indigenous Peoples: An Interdisciplinary Approach to Definition, Intervention, Prevention, and Advocacy' in *Annihilating Difference*, 54–93.
[126] Fernando Cesarman, *Ecocidio: estudio psycoanalítico de la destrucción del medio ambiente*. México: Editorial Joaquín Mortiz, 1972. Erwin Knoll and Judith Nies McFadden, *War Crimes and the American Conscience* (New York: Holt, Rinehart, 1970), 71–72.

befalls the Earth—befalls the sons of the Earth. Man did not weave the web of life—he is merely a strand in it. Whatever he does to the web, he does to himself.

These words, supposedly uttered by Chief Seattle in an 1854 speech, and appearing to capture a profound sense of indigenous people's harmony with nature, as well as co-endangerment with nature, have become a sort of rallying cry of the modern environmental movement. The only problem is that they were not spoken by Chief Seattle at all, certainly not as he was resisting the annexation of the Puget Sound by the US government. They were in fact penned more than a century later, in 1971, by the environmentalist filmmaker Ted Perry; and the Chief has since then gone on to be wrongly attributed, time and again, on t-shirts and mugs, on posters for sale at national parks, and also in supposedly scholarly works on environmental and indigenous peoples' issues around the world.[127]

Again, the observation that biological and cultural diversity are linked, similarly threatened, and in need of similar or simultaneous forms of protection, in many regards is a reasonable one; but considering the bleak history of engagement with ideas of this nature aimed at indigenous peoples, including hunting analogies, people parks, and human zoos, it needs to be approached with great prudence and not just posthumously and falsely credited to wise old Indian chiefs. Today, there is a surging interest in biocultural diversity and support for its conservation, but not all contemporary advocates of this agenda have approached it with the prudence necessary to avoid repeating the prejudices of the colonial past.

J. Peter Brosius and Sarah Hitchner argue that the 'spatial and conceptual link between cultural diversity and biodiversity' is 'a seductive idea that is "good to think" of as a response to the loss of global diversity', but they also find it to be problematic in a variety of ways. In the end, they do identify homogenization as a threat to biological and cultural diversity globally, but therefore also caution against homogenizing our approaches to conservation, insisting we must acknowledge 'the complexity that characterises every conservation context'. One of the oversimplifications

---

[127] Jason Edward Black, 'Native Authenticity, Rhetorical Circulation, and Neocolonial Decay: The Case of Chief Seattle's Controversial Speech', *Rhetoric & Public Affairs* 15, no. 4 (2012): 635–645.

that they warn against is 'primordialist and essentialist ideas of culture', arguing that 'Conservation programmes guided by such notions deny communities agency and make the extension of rights contingent on adherence to externally mandated standards of what constitutes tradition'. Part of the problem, they observe, is that the biocultural diversity concept originated 'mostly from indigenous advocates who deployed this idea as a strategy for valorising indigenous people as holders of valuable knowledge and as guardians of biodiversity', i.e. it originated with western activists who often presented romanticized notions of indigenous peoples and a white saviour complex.[128]

A parallel critique of an activist discourse gone astray can be found in Lila Abu-Lughod's 'Do Muslim Women Really Need Saving?' Wary of western feminists' attempts to 'save' Muslim women, Abu-Lughod calls on readers to 'appreciate the patronizing quality of the rhetoric of saving women' and argues that 'Projects of saving other women depend on and reinforce a sense of superiority by Westerners, a form of arrogance that deserves to be challenged'. She therefore urges that, 'we should be wary of taking on the mantles of those 19th century Christian missionary women who devoted their lives to saving their Muslim sisters'.[129] Much work has similarly documented the ill effects of what has been called the 'politics of protection' and 'NGO imperialism', usually 'imposed by the west on the rest'.[130]

Though biocultural diversity conservation discourse is often framed in terms of promoting self-determination for indigenous communities, the origins of the agenda stem primarily from global policy circles. Not only has there been institutional continuity in the movement towards worldwide conservation but there has been a clear ideological continuity as well. Starting with the Swiss lawmaker Paul Sarasin's advocacy

---

[128] J. Peter Brosius and Sarah L. Hitchner, 'Cultural Diversity and Conservation', *International Social Science Journal* 61, no. 199 (2010): 141–168.

[129] Lila Abu-Lughod, 'Do Muslim Women Really Need Saving? Anthropological Reflections on Cultural Relativism and Its Others', *American Anthropologist* 104, no. 3 (2002): 789.

[130] Elizabeth G. Ferris, *The Politics of Protection: The Limits of Humanitarian Action* (Washington: Brookings Institution Press, 2011). James Petras, 'NGOs: In the Service of Imperialism', *Journal of Contemporary Asia* 29, no. 4 (1999): 429–440. Glen W. Wright, 'NGOs and Western Hegemony: Causes for Concern and Ideas for Change', *Development in Practice* 22, no. 1 (2012): 123–134. Chantal Mouffe, 'Civil Society, Democratic Values and Human Rights', in *Globality, Democracy and Civil Society*, eds Terrell Carver and Jens Bartelson (New York: Routledge, 2011), 101.

of *weltnaturschutz* including *anthropologischer naturschutz* in 1910, up through his founding of the United Nations Educational, Scientific and Cultural Organization (UNESCO) and the International Union for Protection of Nature (IUPN) in the years following World War II, and then to Raymond Dasmann's work at UNESCO towards establishing the Man and Biosphere Programme in the 1970s, as well as the International Work Group on Indigenous Affairs, founded in 1968 and based in Copenhagen, the biocultural diversity conservation agenda has firmly been in the hands of Euro-American elites and intellectuals.

Since the 1990s, the global politics of indigeneity has largely merged with the politics of environmentalism, strengthening both causes.[131] Although most observers would argue that this has been 'a good thing' for indigenous communities around the world, as well as for the environment, this book is not concerned with a simple assessment of whether this has been good or bad, nor with a cost-benefit analysis of biocultural diversity conservation or indigenous environmentalism. Instead, the goal is to contrast simple narratives with complex ones, to provide historical context for contemporary conservationist discourses, and to provide a critical reading of this past, which might provide a valuable intervention for all readers alike. Thus, perhaps the most obvious critique of the movements linking indigenous peoples and environmentalism is that they commit ecological romanticism, an appraisal that might also be made of biocultural diversity discourse.[132] As Beth Conklin rightly points out, 'the generic stereotype of native people as natural conservationists proved to be a treacherous foundation for indigenous rights advocacy because it represented native cultures in ways that did not match the realities of many native peoples' lives'.[133]

Hence, the Indigenous People's Earth Charter of 1992 is framed around 'Recognizing indigenous peoples' harmonious relationship with Nature'. Similarly, the Final Statement from the 1995 Consultation on Indigenous Peoples' Knowledge and Intellectual Property Rights in

---

[131] Beth A. Conklin, 'Environmentalism, Global Community, and the New Indigenism' in *Inclusion and Exclusion in the Global Arena*, ed. Max Kirsch (New York: Routledge, 2006), 162–163.
[132] See Archana Prasad, *Against Ecological Romanticism: Verrier Elwin and the Making of an Anti-Modern Tribal Identity* (New Delhi: Three Essays Collective, 2003).
[133] Conklin, 'Environmentalism', 162–163.

Suva, Fiji asserts: 'that *in situ* conservation by indigenous peoples is the best method to conserve and protect biological diversity and indigenous knowledge, and encourage its implementation by indigenous communities and all relevant bodies'.[134] Not only does this type of projection of indigenous peoples as natural ecologists and conservationists play to the stereotype of the 'ecological Indian' or 'ecologically noble savage', but then policy has been organized around these generalizations as well. Again, to quote Conklin,

> Funding from NGOs and governments can depend on meeting outsiders' criteria of indigenous authenticity.... causes that do not fit dominant transnational fashion will fall out of favor.... [I]ndigenous rights advocacy by NGOs has shown signs of maturing beyond ecofetishism.... Paternalistic attitudes and oppressive policies are far from disappearing, however.[135]

As Mary Hufford puts it, heritage protection has long been a field 'dominated by elite and professional constituencies', and only in recent years has there been a movement towards 'an integrated approach based on grass-roots cultural concerns and guided by ethnographic perspectives'. In cultural conservation programmes, there is the danger that the objects being preserved will 'represent cultural values belonging to professional planners more than to others with a stake in the same environment'.[136]

The 2000s was a major decade for the celebration of biocultural diversity at the United Nations. In 2001, the General Conference of UNESCO issued a Universal Declaration on Cultural Diversity where it affirmed that 'cultural diversity is as necessary for humankind as biodiversity is for nature'. In 2007 the UNEP issued a policy document stating that,

---

[134] 'The Indigenous Peoples' Earth Charter', *World Conference of Indigenous Peoples on Territory, Environment and Development*, Kari-Oca, Brazil, 25–30 May 1992, https://www.dialoguebetweennations.com/IR/english/KariOcaKimberley/KOCharter.html; United Nations Development Programme (UNDP), 'Consultation on Indigenous Peoples' Knowledge and Intellectual Property Rights', Suva Fiji, Apr 1995; Darrell A. Possey, 'Biological and Cultural Diversity: The Inextricable, Linked by Languages and Politics', in *On Biocultural Diversity: Linking Language, Knowledge, and the Environment*, ed. Luisa Maffi (Washington, DC: Smithsonian Institution Press, 2001), 380.

[135] Conklin, 'Environmentalism', 162–163.

[136] Marry Hufford, 'Introduction: Rethinking the Cultural Mission', in *Conserving Culture: A New Discourse on Heritage*, ed. Marry Hufford (University of Illinois Press, 1994), 3.

'Biodiversity also incorporates human cultural diversity, which can be affected by the same drivers as biodiversity, and which has impacts on the diversity of genes, other species, and ecosystems'.[137] And in 2010, the United Nations declared an International Year of Biodiversity.

Numerous high-level policy meetings such as the 'International Conference on Biological and Cultural Diversity: Diversity for Development—Development for Diversity' and the conference 'Sustaining Cultural and Biological Diversity in a Rapidly Changing World: Lessons for Global Policy', have stated the objective of conserving biocultural diversity. These meetings have been organized by institutions such as the IUCN (formerly called The World Conservation Union and the IUPN), the American Museum of Natural History, and the biocultural diversity conservation group Terralingua. Thus, this biocultural endangerment discourse, while often framed within the context of a support for multiculturalism and the identity politics of the oppressed, has also been primarily controlled by elite activists from Europe and North America who dually promote environmental and social causes. As declared in the plenary paper for a conference on 'Sustaining Cultural and Biological Diversity' (a title which itself dictates a policy agenda), 'a great deal still needs to be done in the international arena to strengthen this movement and to *ensure policies are filtered down to grass-roots communities*'.[138]

One aspect of the biocultural diversity conservation agenda that I have already begun to discuss in this chapter is the push to create national park-like protected areas where ecological and cultural heritage are conserved side by side. Since the 1970s, such parks have also been created under the auspices of UNESCO, which today administers the world's Biosphere Reserves as part of its Man and Biosphere Programme. UNESCO defines Biosphere Reserves as 'special environments for both people and nature ... living examples of how human beings and nature can co-exist while respecting each others' needs', spaces that foster 'the harmonious integration of people and nature for sustainable development', 'Integrating

---

[137] United Nations Environmental Programme (UNEP), *Global Environmental Outlook: Environment for Development* (Nairobi: UNEP, 2007).
[138] Jules Pretty et al., 'How Do Biodiversity and Culture Intersect?' Plenary paper for Conference on 'Sustaining Cultural and Biological Diversity in a Rapidly Changing World: Lessons for Global Policy', American Museum of Natural History, New York, 2–5 Apr 2008. My emphasis. https://www.amnh.org/research/center-for-biodiversity-conservation/convening-and-connecting/2008-biocultural-diversity

cultural and biological diversity, especially the role of traditional knowledge in ecosystem management', and 'aiming at preventing the present global trend of erosion of diversity, both biological and cultural'. Today the World Network of Biosphere Reserves 'is composed of 686 biosphere reserves in 122 countries, including 20 transboundary sites'.[139]

As with the conservation of biocultural diversity in parks, which is supposed to be enacted through the auspices of UNESCO's Man and Biosphere Programme, the project of preserving specimens of vanishing cultures is today also carried forward in various projects of global significance, the most notorious of which is perhaps the Human Genome Diversity Project (HGDP). Not to be confused with the Human Genome Project, which set its goal as mapping the entire human genome, the HGDP defined its purpose as 'the collection, preservation, management and study of a worldwide sample of human genetic variation'. The project team would achieve this by collecting genetic samples in the form of blood, saliva, or hair follicles from indigenous communities around the world, and then preserving and managing these people's 'DNA through the immortalization of cell-lines in cultures stored in centralized repositories or "gene banks"'.[140] Upon the project's inauguration, the prominent journal *Science* ran a piece on it called 'A Genetic Survey of Vanishing Peoples', declaring:

> Indigenous peoples are disappearing across the globe – victims of war, famine, disease, or simply what Cole Porter called the 'urge to merge'. As they vanish, they are taking with them a wealth of information buried in their genes about human origins, evolution, and diversity.... And time is of the essence, according to Cavalli-Sforza, who views humans as an

---

[139] The Environmental Planning & Coordination Organisation (EPCO), 'Projects: Domestic Projects: Biosphere Reserves', http://web.archive.org/web/20200720011342/http://www.epco.in:80/epco_projects_domestic_biosphere.php; The United Nations Educational, Scientific and Cultural Organization (UNESCO), 'World Network of Biosphere Reserves (WNBR)', http://www.unesco.org/new/en/natural-sciences/environment/ecological-sciences/biosphere-reserves/world-network-wnbr; UNESCO, 'Main Characteristics of Biosphere reserves', http://www.unesco.org/new/en/natural-sciences/environment/ecological-sciences/biosphere-reserves/main-characteristics/; UNESCO, 'Biological and Cultural Diversity', http://web.archive.org/web/20170512120246/http://www.unesco.org/new/en/natural-sciences/environment/ecological-sciences/biodiversity/science-and-research-for-management-and-policy/biological-and-cultural-diversity/

[140] Joanne Barker, 'The Human Genome Diversity Project: "Peoples", "Populations" and the Cultural Politics of Identification', *Cultural Studies* 18, no. 4 (2004): 574–575.

endangered species in terms of genetic diversity. He says this survey should be done within the next 5 years, or 10 at the outside. For many groups it may already be too late.[141]

With press like this, it is no surprise that the HGDP quickly came under fire from indigenous community leaders, activists, and anthropologists, who all worried that this was a thinly disguised and updated form of salvage anthropology, i.e. a salvage genomics, which would save the biological diversity of indigenous peoples in test tubes for posterity. The problem was not only that the HGDP blindly repeated the old trope of tribal endangerment and imminent extinction as the reason for urgent action. It was also that a group of geneticists had established this project almost entirely in a vacuum, without consulting indigenous peoples themselves (who for hundreds of years have been subjected to invasive, non-consensual, medical experimentation). Nor did they consult anthropologists or other social scientists who might have been able to provide valuable insight as to why the HGDP, as initially envisioned, was flawed. The project thus ignored historical and political contexts, and raised numerous ethical and pragmatic concerns.[142]

As Joanne Barker, who wrote an important critique of the HGDP for the journal *Cultural Studies*, explains:

> The discursive production of *populations* as the *endangered* people *of the world— species on the verge of* their own seemingly inevitable *extinction* against the almost predestined and certainly tragic onslaught of technological progress and cultural assimilation— is performed repeatedly in HGDP participant interviews, writings and press coverage in its early moments ... The rhetoric recalled the all-too-familiar ideologies of the Vanishing Indian ... and served to permanently situate the HGDP within the particularly American colonial and racial discourses of the nineteenth century that constituted that Indian.[143]

---

[141] Leslie Roberts, 'A Genetic Survey of Vanishing Peoples', *Science* 252 (1991): 1614–1617.
[142] Jonathan Marks, 'The Human Genome Diversity Project: Impact on Indigenous Communities', in *Encyclopedia of the Human Genome,* ed. David N. Cooper (New York: Nature Publishing Group, 2003), 1–4.
[143] Barker, 'The Human Genome Diversity Project', 584. Italics in original.

## Conclusion

All of this leads me to ponder: how different is a contemporary academic or activist's statement that cultural and biological diversity are disappearing and need to be protected from a nineteenth-century lamentation that wild men and wild beasts are disappearing and ought to be saved? Is the newer one just a more politically correct and updated version of the same old claim? Adam Kuper argues that, 'In the rhetoric of the indigenous peoples movement the terms "native" and "indigenous" are often euphemisms for what used to be termed "primitive".[144] It seems equally clear that terms like cultural and biological diversity are often used as twenty-first-century rephrasings of the wild men and wild beasts of yore.

Whereas once upon a time, the civilizing narrative of the colonialists saw the subjugation and taming of the wild and savage as necessary for progress on a unilineal scale, by the time that cultural conservationists and activists had their say, the discourse of necessary eradication and extinction of the primitive became a funeral dirge bemoaning the endangerment of the diverse and unique cultural and biological aspects of our world. The colonial violence that so extensively impacted indigenous peoples around the world in the age of empire produced feelings within the colonizers ranging from pride to revulsion. This violence was widely acknowledged, widely celebrated, but also widely lamented and resisted. Only by confronting and acknowledging the bleak history of human endangerment discourse, and carefully avoiding repeating the prejudices of the past, can advocates of biocultural diversity conservation begin to cast off this legacy and decolonize this discourse.

---

[144] Adam Kuper, 'The Return of the Native', *Current Anthropology* 44, no. 3 (Jun 2003): 389–402.

# 2
# Endangered Species & Societies in India

And now we have come to India, the land of princes and paupers, of creeds and castes, of savage men and still more savage beasts...

William T. Hornaday, *Two Years in the Jungle:*
*The Experiences of a Hunter and Naturalist*, 1885[1]

Thoughtful men of the future will inevitably charge us with the neglect of unique possibilities if we allow the last archaic civilizations of our days to vanish unrecorded. The representatives of no other discipline, except perhaps zoologists studying species threatened with extinction, are subject to such urgency

Christoph von Fürer-Haimendorf,
'Fundamental Research in Indian Anthropology', 1969[2]

I can be accused of exaggerating or going overboard and so on, but what I would like to say is that genocide is not only when you move people into concentration camps and gas them. Most of the genocide in this world is about cutting people off from their resources and letting them get thirsty or get hungry and slowly annihilate themselves. And that is happening in India

Arundhati Roy, 2013[3]

One day the hare lay under the young palm tree, idly thinking, 'If this earth were destroyed, what would become of me?' At that

---

[1] William T. Hornaday, *Two Years in the Jungle: The Experiences of a Hunter and Naturalist in India, Ceylon, the Malay Peninsula and Borneo* (London: Kegan Paul, 1885), 21.

[2] Christoph von Fürer-Haimendorf, 'Fundamental Research in Indian Anthropology', in *Urgent Research in Social Anthropology: Proceedings of a Conference*, eds, B.L. Abbi and S. Saberwal (Shimla: Indian Institute of Advanced Study, 1969), 79.

[3] Arundhati Roy interview transcript in 'India's Maoist Revolt', *Journeyman Pictures* (2013). https://www.journeyman.tv/film_documents/4103/transcript/

very instant a ripe belli fruit happened to fall and hit a palm leaf making a loud 'THUD!' Startled by this sound, the hare leapt to his feet and cried, 'The earth is collapsing!' He immediately fled, without even glancing back. Another hare, seeing him race past as if for his very life, asked, 'What's wrong?' and started running, too.... Their fear was infectious, and other hares joined them until all the hares in that forest were fleeing together. When other animals saw the commotion and asked what was wrong, they were breathlessly told, 'The earth is breaking up!' and they too began running for their lives. In this way, the hares were soon joined by herds of deer, boars, elk, buffaloes, wild oxen, and rhinoceroses, a family of tigers, and some elephants...
> Duddubha Jataka: The Sound the Hare Heard
> (Jat 322), c. 400 BCE[4]

Perhaps no category of people on earth has been the subject of more heritage conservation efforts, nor perceived as more endangered, than indigenous peoples. And in India, calls for the conservation of Adivasi culture have often reached a fever pitch, especially amongst urban middle-class activists and civil society groups. This book, then, is part of a larger global intellectual history of longstanding efforts to preserve or protect indigenous peoples, their culture, and their heritage, usually from above. It is not a history or an ethnography *of* the tribes of India, but rather a history of discourses—including Adivasis' own—about what is often perceived to be the fundamental question for nearly all indigenous peoples in the modern world: the question of their survival.[5]

In some sense, the book is essentially a study of what happens when an already problematic global discourse is (mis)applied to a unique local situation—in this case, the situation of historical change for central India's Adivasi communities. Claims of tribal endangerment and extinction in India have usually imagined the Adivasi experience to be roughly equivalent to that of indigenous peoples around the world. However,

---

[4] 'Jataka Tales of the Buddha: Part III', retold by Ken and Visakha Kawasaki. Access to Insight (BCBS Edition), 30 Nov 2013. http://www.accesstoinsight.org/lib/authors/kawasaki/bl142.html
[5] So, for example, in the next section of this chapter, I am not myself attempting to define Adivasi identity. Instead, I offer a discussion of the ramifications of various definitions that have been applied to these communities over the years.

merely proclaiming that India's Adivasis are endangered like indigenous peoples everywhere, or worse yet, that they are endangered like wildlife, is an extremely simplistic formulation of a rather complex set of problems. This critique is meant to stand in solidarity with Adivasis themselves, who are left to contend with the repercussions of such awkward formulations.

Following in the wake of a discussion of global proportions (Chapter 1), the rest of this book addresses the problems of interwoven discourses of indigenous and environmental endangerment by focusing on two major Adivasi populations in India—the Bhils and the Gonds, as well as on the transition from extermination to conservation of 'wild life' in western and central India. It seeks to significantly complicate the common perception of these people as forest communities who are disappearing along with their forests, as wild tribes that are disappearing along with wilderness, or as hunting societies that are becoming extinct along with hunted species. It is often said that traditional ecological lifestyles and livelihoods are becoming endangered or even extinct, and the comparison is frequently made with disappearing wildlife. Yet the parallel between endangered wildlife and human ways of life is as problematic as it is explanative.

There was never a serious threat of biological extinction for these communities. Gonds and Bhils long were, and today remain, two of the largest Adivasi groups in India. According to the 1941 census, out of the estimated 30 million 'aboriginals' in India, the Gonds, whose population was 3,200,405 ranked first, the Santals with a strength of 2,732,266 stood second, and the Bhils, 2,330,270 strong, ranked third.[6] Over the century, these proportions have changed only slightly, but populations have grown greatly. By the time of the 2011 census, the Gond population was 13.25 million and the Bhils 16.9 million.[7] And overall, Adivasis today represent some 8%–10% of the population of India, totalling approximately 100–130 million people.[8]

---

[6] T.B. Naik, *The Bhils: A Study* (Delhi: Bharatiya Adimjati Sevak Sangh, 1956), 3–4 (the exactitude of these figures is amusingly dubious).

[7] Census of India 2011. Home/PCA/A-11, 'Individual Scheduled Tribe Primary Census Abstract Data and its Appendix'. Office of the Registrar General & Census Commissioner, India. http://www.censusindia.gov.in/2011census/PCA/ST.html

[8] Arup Maharatna, 'How Can "Beautiful" Be "Backward"? Tribes of India in a Long-term Demographic Perspective', *Economic & Political Weekly* 46, no. 4 (Jan 2011): 42–52. Maharatna, in this demographic study finds that for 'dominant central and western tribes', such as the Bhils

Yet despite these numbers, both Gonds and Bhils, along with most other major Adivasi groups, are consistently represented as 'endangered' across nearly the full spectrum of texts about them. Thus, if 'endangerment' is to make sense as an organizing principle for understanding changes in Bhil and Gond societies, it must refer to something quite different than the threat of biological extinction. The main question, then, is what exactly, if anything, is endangered for Bhil, Gond, and other Adivasi communities of India? Is it their unique tribal cultural heritage and traditions? Is it their forest-based ways of life and livelihoods? Or, is 'survival at stake', as others have claimed, because these communities have failed to thrive in the economy and to reap the benefits of modernity?

## What's in a Name? Tribal, Indigenous, Adivasi, Forest Dweller ...

One of the major obstacles to reaching any sort of answer to this conundrum about the nature of the changes facing Bhil and Gond societies is the range of stereotypes and prejudices that get attached to them, especially when terms like 'tribe' and 'Adivasi' are used. Upon reading words like these, a lay reader might assume that these are small-scale, isolated, forest communities; perhaps this reader would also assume the cliché that since these are tribal societies, they must have lived in harmony with nature since time immemorial; and unfortunately, he or she may even attach words like primitive, backwards, or stone-age to them. For India's major Adivasi groups, the notion of the disappearing timeless tribe, who lived in harmony with nature in isolated, small-scale communities, is a myth that needs to be busted. As S.C. Dube put it as early as 1977, 'The four million Gond, the equally numerous Bhil, and the three million Santals were all regionally dominant groups and they can hardly be described as living in isolation'.[9]

---

and Gonds, 'growth of population has been above the national average and even accelerated in the post-independence period ... ' He concludes: 'The "vanishing tribes" phenomenon, of course, deserves an attention and an effective public action in its own right [sic], but it is important to keep in mind that the former does not represent the aggregate tribal situation in India'.
[9] S.C. Dube, ed. *Tribal Heritage of India*, vol. 1 (Delhi: Vikas, 1977), 3.

There is a general level of confusion and disagreement about who and what these people are. Both the Bhils and Gonds, with their massive combined populations totalling over 30 million, are not so much 'tribes' as large-scale umbrella identities, each with a wide variety of cultural ecologies and livelihood strategies. To generalize that they were all historically forest-dwelling communities that lost their forests would simply be inaccurate. In the pre-colonial and early colonial era, for instance, many Raj Gond rulers of Gondwana controlled vast kingdoms, built luxurious palaces, fortresses, and tombs, put coinage into circulation, founded cities, and were thus basically indistinguishable from neighbouring ruling elites such as Rajputs and Marathas (see Figure 2.1 and Chapter 6). Why it is assumed that the end of forest dwelling must also mean the end of Adivasi culture is the central consideration here. A standard trope in histories of independent India is that 'India has consistently defied those

**Figure 2.1.** John Edward Saché & Murray, 'Jubbulpore, Madan Mahal from the North'.

Public domain. Albumen Print, Photographer's ref. 371, 1869, 228 × 279 mm. ACP: 96.20.0553. Courtesy of the Alkazi Collection of Photography.

who make prophecies of doom for her'.[10] Why should this not be true for 'tribal' India as well?

Much as it has been argued that the very concept of the tribe is a European colonial imposition on the Indian situation,[11] I would also suggest that the idea that tribes are endangered or threatened with extinction is a concept that emerged in the global context of empire and was mapped onto the Indian subcontinent. Those fearing Adivasi endangerment and extinction often assume that the endangered object was 'fixed', i.e. there was a stable tribal/aboriginal/indigenous/Adivasi identity that the British encountered and proceeded to eradicate, an identity that is being further degraded by modernity and postcolonial development regimes. To understand why the Indian situation is so complex and unique as to render it not quite comparable to the generic metanarrative of tribal endangerment around the world, we must first of all grapple with the concept of the tribe in the Indian context.

The English word 'tribe', which has a much-disputed definition and an obscure etymology, also has no precise equivalent in any South Asian language.[12] It is thus considered a legacy of the colonial era.[13] The Bhils and Gonds went from being called 'hill and forest tribes' (1921), 'primitive tribes' (1931), 'backward tribes', and 'wild tribes' in various censuses produced by the colonial state, to being classified as 'scheduled tribes' by the 1950 Constitution of India. As forest and other hinterland communities were 'pacified' (defeated), 'agriculturalized' (peasantized), Sanskritized or Christianized, the British claimed they would erase 'wild' ways of life, yet the term 'tribe' lingers, reminding us of the continuing stigma that affects these societies. Just as the administrative designation of 'backward' implies the need to turn 'forward', it seems the term 'tribe' as deployed in India can only be understood as it corresponds to processes of detribalization. Throughout this book, when I use the term 'tribe', my intention is

---

[10] William Dalrymple, *The Age of Kali: Travels and Encounters in India* (London: HarperCollins, 1998), xv.

[11] André Béteille, 'The Concept of Tribe with Special Reference to India', *European Journal of Sociology/Archives Européennes de Sociologie* 27, no. 2 (1986): 297–318.

[12] According to the OED etymology of 'Tribe': 'L. tribus is usually explained from tri—three and the verbal root bhu, bu, fu to be. The earliest known application of tribus was to the three divisions of the early people of Rome (attributed by some to the separate Latin, Sabine, and Etruscan elements); thence it was transferred to render the Greek'.

[13] Vinita Damodaran, 'Colonial Constructions of Tribe in India', *Indian Historical Review* 30, no. 1 (Jan 2006): 44–76.

to capture, and challenge, the bias packed into this word, implicit in colonial discourse and contemporary lay language alike.

A large variety of appellations have been assigned to the Bhil, Gond, and other similar groups. Today, most Bhil and Gond communities refer to themselves as Adivasi when speaking to the outside world, and so, along with most other anthropologists and historians, I also follow suit.[14] However, the word is of relatively recent origin, becoming popular parlance only late in India's independence struggle; thus, there is the danger of anachronism in applying the word to deeper historical contexts. Literally meaning 'original inhabitants', the term Adivasi became popular as an Indic language re-appropriation of labels such as aboriginal, autochthonous, and indigenous. As Gandhi observed, 'We were strangers to this sort of classification—"animists", "aborigines", etc.—but we have learnt it from English rulers'.[15] In the 1920s and 30s, a variety of neologisms to describe these communities began to circulate, including *Raniparaj* (wild people), *Girijan* (mountain people), and Verrier Elwin's *Bhumijan* (people of the soil). The word Adivasi was then coined by 1936–1938 when political activists founded the Adivasi Mahasabha (Adivasi Grand Assembly) in Chotanagpur.[16] Considering the term's modern origins, Crispin Bates remarks that, 'The *adivasi* may thus be regarded as not so much the "original" inhabitants of South Asia but the very recent creation of colonial anthropology. Paradoxically, they might be seen as an invention rather than a victim of modernity'.[17]

Aboriginal, autochthonous, and indigenous are all rough etymological equivalents to Adivasi, but are controversial in that they all imply that these communities are the first peoples of India—this in a country where so many claim to trace their heritage back some 4,000 years, and where many ethno-nationalists insist that all Hindus are the indigenous peoples

---

[14] From field experience, I have found that Bhils and Gonds refer to themselves collectively as Adivasi, primarily when speaking to outsiders. Amongst one another on a daily basis, they rarely discuss themselves collectively using that term. Rather, they refer to specific *jati* names, e.g. among the Bhils, they will draw distinctions between Bhilala, Pawra, Padvi, Tadvi, Vasava, etc. Among the Gonds, they typically refer to themselves as Koitur meaning, 'the people', and divisions include Raj Gond, Sur Gond, Muria Gond, etc.

[15] Mohandas Gandhi, 'Discussion on Fellowship', *Young India*, 19 Jan 1928; CWMG 41, 112–115.

[16] This was probably first noted by David Hardiman, *The Coming of the Devi: Adivasi Assertion in Western India* (Delhi: Oxford University Press, 1987), 13n.

[17] Crispin Bates, 'Lost Innocents and the Loss of Innocence: Interpreting Adivasi Movements in South Asia', in *Indigenous Peoples of Asia*, eds R.H. Barnes, A. Gray, and B. Kingsbury (Ann Arbor: Association of Asian Studies, 1995): 104.

of India.[18] Ghurye thus called the term Adivasi 'divisive, undermining the unity of the Indian nation'.[19] So, while many in the international indigenous rights movement insist on calling Adivasis 'indigenous peoples', the Government of India is deeply wary of politically charged claims of Adivasi indigeneity.[20] And while the term indigenous might be useful to connote and resist Adivasis' marginalized position (as Tania Murray Li argues, 'Indigeneity is a mobile term that has been articulated in relation to a range of positions and struggles'[21]), many also wonder, as Adam Kuper does, if 'indigenous' is just a euphemistic new stand-in for older colonial terms like 'native' and 'tribal', still carrying the same old baggage, such as implications of primitivity and racial distinctiveness.[22]

This book does not seek to resolve the question of whether Adivasis were the original peoples of India. Still, it is worthwhile pointing out here that according to at least one dominant reading of ancient history— namely the reading that embraces the Aryan invasion theory and the idea of separate Aryan and Dravidian races—Adivasis are not only India's original inhabitants, of separate racial stock from the majority of Indians, they have also been India's eternally endangered minorities. Reviled as *mlecchas* (barbarians) in the Vedic era, labelled *asuras* or *rakshasas* (demons) in the *Ramayana* and *Mahabharata,* they have been driven out of the fertile plains and ever deeper into the hill and forest interiors of the subcontinent since the very beginnings of Indian history. As one advocate of this theory, Parmanand Lal, vividly described:

> The aboriginals were eventually either exterminated or they retreated, before the ever-advancing Aryan civilization, to those refugial

---

[18] In the case of the Gonds, it was long doubted that they were indigenous to Gondwana. Evidence shows that in the ninth to eleventh centuries, they migrated to the area from elsewhere and displaced other forest communities already in the area, namely the Kols and Sabaras. See B.C. Mazumdar, *The Aborigines of the Highlands of Central India* (Calcutta: University of Calcutta, 1927), 37.

[19] Ghurye cited in Suneet Chopra, 'Revolt and Religion: Petty Bourgeois Romanticism', *Social Scientist* 16, no. 2 (Feb 1988): 60–67.

[20] In 2007, 'India voted in favour of the United Nations Declaration on the Rights of Indigenous Peoples on the condition that after independence all Indians are indigenous. Therefore, it does not consider the concept of "indigenous peoples", and therefore the UNDRIP, applicable to India'. International Work Group for Indigenous Affairs, 'India', https://www.iwgia.org/en/india.html

[21] Tania Murray Li, 'Indigeneity, Capitalism, and the Management of Dispossession', *Current Anthropology* 51, no. 3 (2010): 385.

[22] Adam Kuper, 'The Return of the Native', *Current Anthropology* 44, no. 3 (2003): 389–402.

forest-fastness... Some of the weaker aboriginals preferred subjugation to extermination and exile and gradually came to be assimilated into the Aryan community, but remained outside the primary four *varnas*.... the tribal man is thus essentially vanishing relict [sic] of early man in India, confined at present to scattered and comparatively small and fast diminishing refugial areas, to which he has retreated under increasing pressure of civilization.[23]

Terms such as *janjati, janglijati, girijans,* and *vanvasi* are infrequently discussed in English language publications, perhaps because of the fact that they are problematically assumed to be coextensive with the category Adivasi. *Janjati,* a good translation for which might be 'folk caste', is a term frequently used in Hindi language academic literature to describe Bhil and Gond societies.[24] *Anusuchit janjati* is also the term used in official administrative literature in Hindi to mean 'Scheduled Tribe'. In western India, the term *janglijati* (directly translatable as 'jungle caste') is quite often used pejoratively, but with the term *janjati,* the bias in it is the assumption these peoples are indeed 'castes' or *jatis* living a 'jungly' wild life in the hills. One reason not to use the term *jati* at all is that, historically, many argue that tribes existed outside the ambit of the caste system and did not participate in it. However, these days, speaking from fieldwork experience, the majority of Bhils and Gonds, along with most other Adivasis, typically do refer to their own communities as *jatis.* While some say that *jati* should be translated as 'kind' or 'type' and not as 'caste' in this context (in some contexts, the term *jati* also means species), it does appear that by referring to themselves as *jatis,* Bhils and Gonds are situating themselves within the caste fold and broader social hierarchies of the nation.[25]

---

[23] Parmanand Lal, 'The Tribal Man in India: A Study in the Ecology of the Primitive Communities', in *Ecology and Biogeography in India,* ed. M.S. Mani (The Hague: W. Junk, 1974), 282–283.

[24] Shiv Kumar Tivari, *Madhya Pradesh ki Janjati Sanskriti* (Bhopal: Madhya Pradesh Hindi Granth Academy, 2005); Jagdish Chandra Mina, *Bhil Janjati ka Sanskritik evam Arthik Jivan* (Udaipur: Himanshu, 2003).

[25] Vinay Kumar Srivastava and Sukant K. Chaudhury, 'Anthropological Studies of Indian Tribes', in *Sociology and Social Anthropology in India,* ed. Yogesh Atal (Delhi: Pearson Education India, 2009), 76.

This point, of course, raises questions about the relationship between caste and tribe, or what has sometimes been called the caste-tribe continuum in India.[26] The line between castes and tribes has never been as clear as some colonial administrators attempted to make it. With various nineteenth and early twentieth-century definitions of the tribe in India resorting to controversial criteria such as geographical isolation, proximity to nature, statelessness, 'wildness', 'primitivity', or 'economic backwardness', the tribe concept remained nebulous. Mid-twentieth century sociologists and anthropologists attempted to explain this lack of clarity through theories such as Hinduization, Sanskritization, and Rajputization, that typically located the transition from tribe to caste in an evolutionary framework;[27] but for those fearing tribal endangerment, it was precisely those processes by which communities outside the ambit of Hinduism and the caste system were assimilated, or by which forest folk were turned into peasants and city dwellers, that endangered these communities.

Thus, a potentially appropriate term for some of the peoples this book discusses is (former) 'hill and forest dwellers'. However, it is important to note that—as in a Venn diagram—though this grouping overlaps with that of Adivasi, the categories are not coequal. Not only would it be deeply inaccurate to say that everyone now considered Bhil or Gond descended from forest or hill dwellers in the recent past, but certainly many Bhils and Gonds today also live and work in a variety of settings, including urban ones. Some may have been sedentary agriculturalists for centuries. Others led the lifestyle of *rajas* or *zamindars*, kings and feudal landlords.[28] Equally, some forest dwellers may not have been Adivasis at all, but members of other *jatis* or caste communities. Plenty of 'non-tribals' historically lived in forests, a

---

[26] Frederick George Bailey, *Tribe, Caste, and Nation: A Study of Political Activity and Political Change in Highland Orissa* (Manchester: Manchester University Press, 1960), 11 writes: 'we must see "caste" and "tribe" as opposite ends of a single line'. See also: Surajit Sinha, 'Tribe-Caste and Tribe-Peasant Continua in Central India', *Man in India* 45, no. 1 (1965): 57–83.

[27] M.N. Srinivas, 'A Note on Sanskritization and Westernization', *Far Eastern Quarterly* 15, no. 4 (Aug 1956): 481–496 originally coined the term Sanskritization to mean 'rise to a higher position in the hierarchy by adopting vegetarianism and teetotalism'. Surajit Sinha, 'State Formation and Rajput Myth in Tribal Central India', *Man in India* 42, no. 1 (1962): 36 described, 'State-formation in the tribal belt of central India is very largely a story of Rajputisation of the tribes'.

[28] Bhangya Bhukya, 'The Subordination of the Sovereigns: Colonialism and the Gond Rajas in Central India, 1818–1948', *Modern Asian Studies* 47, no. 1 (2013): 288–317.

fact acknowledged by the new Scheduled Tribes and Other Forest Dwellers (Recognition of Forest Rights) Act, at least in its title.[29]

Terms like *vanvasi*, meaning 'forest dweller', and *girijan* meaning 'mountain folk', might at first glance seem to be appropriate designations for some subjects of this book, but not for others (i.e. appropriate for people who actually live in hills and forests, but not those who do not). A major problem with calling these communities *vanvasi*, though, is that this nomenclature has been almost exclusively employed by those committed to Hindutva.[30] Because Hindu nationalists refuse to acknowledge that anyone is more indigenous to India than they are, they for long have preferred to see the *vanvasis* as 'backward' or 'primitive' Hindus who lost their way in the forest, and so must be reincorporated into the Hindu fold. G.S. Ghurye probably put it most famously in his work *The Aborigines— "So-called"—And Their Future* when he denied any fundamental difference between the tribes and mainstream Hindu civilization. Given that the Sangh Parivar organization the *Vanvasi Kalyan Ashram* to this day bills itself as 'the largest non-government organization which is working for the total development of 110 million vanvasis (tribals) of India', and states that the 'main objective of VKA is to eliminate the chasm between Hindu community and their Vanvasi brethren', it is fair to say that this perspective is very much alive today.[31]

As a descriptor of a mode of ecology, rather than an ethnic category, *vanvasi* (again, 'forest dweller') might have been useful because it can be contrasted with communities in other eco-geographical situations, such as villagers or peasants (*gramvasi*) and city dwellers (*nagarvasi*). Yet the term *vanvasi*, unfortunately, cannot escape its ideological underpinnings; it is rarely used neutrally to simply describe people living in forests. Instead, *vanvasi* is used to supplant the term Adivasi, but only by the Hindu right, to refer to the many tens of millions of people from communities such as the Bhils and Gonds, some of whom may never have

---

[29] Asavari Raj Sharma, 'The "Other" in the Forest Rights Act Has Been Ignored for Years', *The Wire*, 1 Jul 2018, https://thewire.in/rights/the-other-in-the-forest-rights-act-has-been-ignored-for-years
[30] See Vanavasi Kalyan Ashram http://web.archive.org/web/20120110143048/http://www.vanavasi.org/ and c.f. *Rettet die Naturvölker* http://www.naturvoelker.de/
[31] 'Welcome to the Vanavasi Kalyan Ashram Delhi', http://web.archive.org/web/20160327171551/http://vanvasikalyanashramdelhi.org/index.php/2-uncategorised/16-welcome-to-vanvasi-kalyan-ashram-delhi For a contemporary journalistic account of experiences in the VKA see: Sohini Chattopadhyay, 'Exclusive: Inside a Hindutva Hostel: How RSS Is Rewiring the Tribal Mind', *Catch News*, 19 Dec 2015. http://www.sacw.net/index.php?page=imprimir_articulo&id_article=12762

been forest dwellers at all, and only to imply that these communities are 'backwards' Hindus who must be turned forward and re-Hinduized. To the Hindu right, *vanvasi* life in forests is not endangered; rather, the end of forest dwelling is the policy goal.

At least partially as a result of all this muddled terminology, the debate about whether forests define Adivasi culture continues. Unlike those on the Hindu right, some more activist-oriented anthropologists believe that tribal peoples in central India are currently experiencing ethnocide or 'cultural genocide' because they are losing their forests. Felix Padel, for example, defines Adivasis as indigenous forest folk (and pairs them together with wildlife) in the first page of his book *Sacrificing People* when he writes: 'In Central India there are magnificent forests, heartland of the tiger, as well as leopards, bears, elephants, and many other creatures. The people who live in these forest areas are adivasis, India's "original inhabitants" or "aboriginals", tribal people who have evolved a way of life suited to the forest over countless generations'. Arguing that 'it is evident that there are two levels to what was killed: the physical extermination and the killing of a culture' and that 'every part of this social structure is torn apart by displacement', Padel and Das specifically list disruptions to economic systems, kinship systems, religious systems, material culture, and power structures when central India's tribes are removed from forests.[32]

In contrast to both right and left-wing activism, much recent scholarship on Adivasis stresses an understanding of these communities, where, as Sumit Guha puts it, 'Forests = tribals. This is not a dyad to which I subscribe'. The point that western and central India's Adivasis were not isolated communities, and instead were 'early integrated into the regional political economies' is an argument central to Sumit Guha's work on environment and ethnicity. He thus concludes by rejecting the simplistic notion of a 'single trajectory through historic time' that sees 'the transition from forest to field and forager to farmer' as 'continuous and irreversible' processes. Guha opens his monograph with a sentence that seems to confirm the popular narrative—'There is little doubt that forests occupy a smaller fraction of the world today than they have done for some millennia, and people living in them form an even smaller, ever-falling, proportion of the global population'. However, he then goes

---

[32] Felix Padel and Samarendra Das, 'Cultural Genocide: The Real Impact of Development-Induced Displacement', in *India Social Development Report 2008: Development and Displacement*, ed. Hari Mohan Mathur (Oxford: Oxford University Press, 2008), 109–110.

on to question what he calls the 'new global interest in and sympathy for endangered ethnicities' (which of course I have shown is by no means actually 'new'), suggesting that 'parallel concern' for endangered species and endangered cultures is 'strongest in those parts of the world (such as the Americas) where such entities have been most effectively triturated in the recent past'.[33]

Postcolonial historians working in this framework—which some have called 'revisionist'[34]—have felt the imperative to dismantle discourses that pair 'natives' with 'nature', partly because of the power dynamics involved in such constructions. Kavita Philip argues:

> Indigenous groups were *represented as* having accurate knowledge of nature due to the 'wild' or 'natural' state in which they lived... in terms that explicitly equate tribal with animal existence. 'Natives' themselves were repeatedly constructed as part of 'nature'. When we read nineteenth-century accounts of 'nature' we are invariably also reading colonial representations of 'natives'.
>
> Such a construction of locals, drawing on a nature-culture dichotomy and its attendant hierarchies, allowed colonial officials and scientists to perceive themselves as inherently superior to indigenous tribal inhabitants of colonial societies ...[35]

'Tribals' and tigers, natives and nature, peoples and parks, and wild men and wild beasts have been lumped together time and again. As have ethnocide and ecocide, and endangered species and endangered societies. One way to understand this is simply to say that this assonance and consonance is simply a language game ('The connection between the signifier and the signified is arbitrary'[36]). In fact, it is often the contemporary, academic, texts that are making up these word-combinations to caricaturize the colonial discourses they analyse. Along with Hayden White, I feel that historical explanations that rely on these linguistic

---

[33] Sumit Guha, *Environment and Ethnicity in India, 1200–1991* (Cambridge: Cambridge University Press, 1999), 1, 4, 9, 199, 201.
[34] Alan Barnard, 'Kalahari Revisionism, Vienna and the "Indigenous Peoples" Debate', *Social Anthropology* 14, no. 1 (2006): 1–16.
[35] Kavita Philip, *Civilizing Natures: Race, Resources, and Modernity in Colonial South India* (New Delhi: Orient Longman, 2003), 26.
[36] Ferdinand de Saussure, *Saussure's First Course of Lectures on General Linguistics, 1907: From the Notebooks of Albert Riedlinger/Premier cours de linguistique general, 1907: d'après les cahiers d'Albert Riedlinger* (Oxford: Pergamon, 1996), 11.

ENDANGERED SPECIES & SOCIETIES IN INDIA    83

turns are rhetorical and poetic rather than empirical.[37] However, the reason that these formulas exist is that there is an underlying empirical claim that demands to be taken seriously as well. For instance, when looking at a map of India, one can easily see a correlation between central India's last remaining forests and tiger habitats and Adivasi homelands (see Figure 2.2).

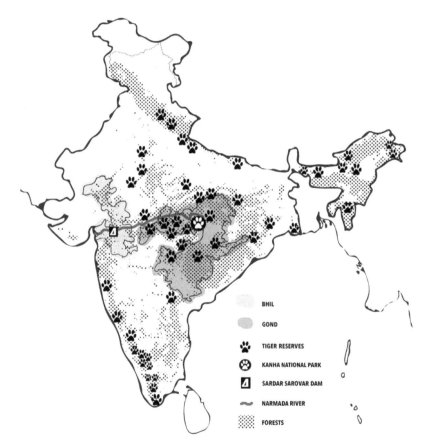

**Figure 2.2.** Tigers, 'Tribes', and Forests.
Map by Sharon Lindenfeld illustrating the *approximate* distribution and location of forests, tiger reserves, and Bhil and Gond communities in India, as well as the two main field sites covered in this book: the Sardar Sarovar Dam and Kanha National Park.

---

[37] Hayden White, *Tropics of Discourse: Essays in Cultural Criticism* (Baltimore: Johns Hopkins University Press, 1978).

Far be it from me to tell these communities how best to mobilize themselves. But it should be noted that in rejecting terms such as *vanvasi* and preferring Adivasi, or vice versa, naming has become a matter of strategic decision making about (self-) representation, rather than a neutral act of categorization. Choosing to self-identify as Adivasi or *vanvasi* might also be an act of strategic essentialism—i.e. an act of embracing seemingly positive stereotypes about oneself, such as the perception that all indigenous peoples are environmentalists—in order to use the wider society's prejudices as a tool in the struggle for land rights and political rights. As Crispin Bates puts it, 'adivasi movements in South Asia may even depend on such prejudices for their survival. Indeed, it is arguable that without such prejudices, recently as well as in the past, the adivasi as a community would not exist'.[38] Thus, the choice of whether or not to identify as endangered has major implications for Adivasi politics and for the way Adivasi identity is conceived.

## Emergence of India's Tribes as Aboriginal

> [O]ne might argue that the search for an 'essential' adivasi culture and society is itself an illusion, and that both the concept and its object have always been a political construct. Rather than ask 'who were the adivasis' therefore, it might be better to ask 'who wants to define them'
>
> Crispin Bates, 'Lost Innocents and the Loss of Innocence: Interpreting Adivasi Movements in South Asia' (1995)[39]

Bhil, Gond, and many other Adivasi societies do not fit neatly into the global indigeneity concept, or the global narrative of endangered ethnicities. And they certainly do not provide the most dramatic or extreme examples of endangerment the world has to offer. Yet the complicated nature of their transformation in the modern era is precisely why they make such suitable subjects for a study of this nature. Broad evaluative

---

[38] Bates, 'Lost Innocents', 103–104.
[39] Ibid., 117.

arguments stressing loss, destruction, decline, disappearance, vanishing, or victimhood of indigenous peoples in the modern era often appear in survey works that cover the length and breadth of the world, yet these works rarely linger on the situation in western and central India. Thus, earlier editions of John Bodley's *Victims of Progress* listed the Baigas of central India as one of its case studies on the map on its frontispiece, yet the book hardly devotes more than a page to their plight. And there is a similar lacuna in global survey works questioning the historical consensus that indigenous peoples are vanishing. Patrick Brantlinger's *Dark Vanishings: Discourse on the Extinction of Primitive Races, 1800–1930*, for example, while spanning the Americas, the Pacific islands, Europe, and Africa, barely touches on South Asia.

The reason that India's Adivasis offer such a complex case that they are rarely included in these worldwide surveys might be best understood by studying, historically, how communities such as the Bhils and Gonds were eventually incorporated into the global concept of endangered aboriginal peoples. The Latin word *aborigines* first exclusively referred to the original inhabitants of the Italian peninsula, but has been used generically in English since at least since the sixteenth century to describe the earliest settlers of any given place (and, notably, for most of that time, it was used to describe indigenous plants and animals as well as people). While 'aborigine' had been used to describe the original peoples of Australia and the South Pacific since around the time of Captain Cook's death in 1779, the idea that tribes such as the Bhils and Gonds were the aboriginal peoples of the subcontinent only began to emerge along with the development of the theory of the Aryan race and its invasion of India. In the late 1700s and early 1800s, before the development of the Aryan invasion theory, Hindus were understood to be the 'aboriginal natives' of India by British orientalists. So, for example, John Richardson in 1777 states: 'The Brahmans form the firſt tribe or caſt amongſt the Gentoos or aboriginal natives of Hindoſtan; and are ſo named from Brihma, their principal deity'. And as late as 1807, Buchanan's *Journey* defines Hindus as the 'aboriginal natives of India'.[40] By the 1830s, as the intellectual climate

---

[40] John Richardson, *A Dictionary, Persian, Arabic, and English*, vol. 1 (Clarendon Press, 1777), 392. Francis Buchanan, *A Journey from Madras Through the Countries of Mysore, Canara, and Malabar*..., vol. 3 (London: Cadell [etc.], 1807), n.p. see 'Hindu' in the general index.

in colonial India shifted away from orientalist scholarship focused on ancient Indian texts to what has been called a more 'Anglicanist' outlook focused on the civilizational superiority of the British, this shift also coincided with the rise of ethnology as a race science that came to define the hill and forest tribes of India as aboriginal remnants of an unending struggle with mainstream Hindu or Aryan civilization.

William Jones, who in 1786 famously first announced his discovery of the relationship between Greek, Latin, and Sanskrit and declared the existence of an Indo-European family of languages, himself also proposed the idea of an aboriginal 'substratum' whose language mixed with Sanskrit to form Hindi. At this point, these people were referred to as 'mountaineers' rather than aboriginals, and Jones called them 'many races of wild people with more or less of that pristine ferocity, which induced their ancestors to secede from the civilized inhabitants of the plains and valleys'. By 1807, Alexander Hamilton, the first professor of Sanskrit in Britain (at East India College), noted that 'some writers regarded [the mountaineers] as the aborigines of that country'. A year later he suggested that, 'Whether we are to consider the wild but harmless inhabitants of the mountains as a distinct race from the Hindus, must be determined by investigations not hitherto undertaken'.[41] By the 1820s, we do find that some notable texts, such as James Tod's *Annals and Antiquities* and Walter Hamilton's *East-India Gazetteer* refer to communities such as the Bhils and Gonds as the aborigines of India. However, India's tribes only became widely classified as aborigines in the wake of the establishment of the Aborigines Protection Society in 1837 and its spinoff 'student party', the Ethnological Society of London in 1843.[42]

In the 1840s and 1850s, one major player at the Ethnological Society in the establishment of the theory that India's tribes were endangered aboriginals was John Briggs. Yet Briggs, who had been instrumental in the pacification of the Bhils of Khandesh from roughly 1818 until ill health drove him to return permanently to England in 1835, only gradually

---

[41] The quotations by Jones and Hamilton in this paragraph are drawn from Thomas R. Trautmann, *Aryans and British India* (Berkeley: University of California Press, 1997), 161.

[42] Peter Pels, 'From Texts to Bodies: Brian Houghton Hodgson and the Emergence of Ethnology in India', in *Anthropology and Colonialism in Asia: Comparative and Historical Colonialism*, eds Jan van Bremen and Akitoshi Shimiz (New York: Routledge, 2013), 65.

came to believe this himself. At the beginning of his career, in 1818, Briggs doubted the Bhils' aboriginality, writing to Governor Elphinstone: 'It is difficult to say from whence the Bheels are sprung, there seems to be no good foundation for the general opinion that they are the aborigins of the soil and that they were driven into the Hill on the Hindoo invasion'.[43] Some thirty years later, he apparently had a change of heart. In 1846, John Briggs delivered a paper to the Ethnological Society where he claimed to have independently discovered that India's aborigines were from a separate racial stock from most Indians, writing that with 'the existence of the Sanskritic race in India.... the wonder is rather that any remains of the language of the aborigines should exist at all'. Now steeped in London's intellectual climate, which looked at aboriginal problems globally, and using his election as Vice-President of the Ethnological Society in 1852 as a pulpit, he begged 'to be allowed to say a few words on the present and future condition of these aborigines' of India. Arguing that he had 'shewn what is their doom according to the Hindu law, and under Hindu dominion', he asked, 'Is it fit or just that so vast a population should continue neglected under our rule? In their native forests, they are little elevated above the animals they feed upon, but still they have qualities which are highly appreciable in civil life'. It was the role of the enlightened British Indian government to protect these benighted aborigines from 'doom' as a result of 'Hindu dominion'.[44]

The idea that tribal populations of India were endangered emerged simultaneously with their identification as aboriginal; their dehumanization through animal analogy was also part of the process. Peter Pels has made an interesting case that this redefinition of Indian aboriginality was connected to what he calls colonial scholarship's transition 'from texts to bodies', i.e. from orientalist to ethnological research.[45] And he also points out that this mode of thinking about hill tribes had to do with a shift from military to scholarly logic: now that the British were no longer

---

[43] Cited in Deshpande, *John Briggs in Maharashtra*, 39. Briggs to Elp. 24.10.1818, DCI, 172.
[44] John Briggs, 'Two Lectures on the Aboriginal Race of India, as Distinguished from the Sanskritic or Hindu Race', *Journal of the Royal Asiatic Society of Great Britain and Ireland* 13 (1852): 275–309.
[45] Peter Pels, 'From Texts to Bodies', 65.

themselves threatened by predatory hill tribes, the very people who had been busy settling these tribes and recruiting military units from them now turned to describing them. Contemporaneous with Briggs, several other major scholars, such as Brian Hodgson and Max Müller, were all reaching roughly the same conclusions—that India's tribes were its aboriginal population.

After a brief and unhappy sojourn in England in 1844, where he expressed boredom making the rounds in London's scholarly societies, Brian Hodgson entered what can be described as his ethnological phase. Prior to London, his earlier scholarly work had been primarily botanical and zoological, yet Hodgson had spent much of his official energy as Resident of Nepal arguing for the recruitment of Khas and Ghorka soldiers into the British Indian Army. In the late 1840s, now free to pursue his ethnological work in Sikkim, he was also free to advocate for these 'aborigines' instead of recruiting them for the army, writing that 'these primitive races are the ancient inheritors of the whole soil, from which they were wrongfully expelled by the usurping Hindus'. Pels explains: 'As in Hodgson's plea to incorporate the Nepalese "military tribes", the ethnologist acts as both the definer, and the advocate of the people he has defined as his object. Here, however, the politics of aboriginality identifies the colonizer as the impartial arbiter defending "aboriginal" rights rather than as an employer of military labor'.[46]

At the same time that Briggs and Hodgson were writing, in 1847, the 'youthful Friedrich Max Müller not yet twenty-three gave his maiden speech in English'. Müller's paper, 'On the relation of the Bengali to the Arian and aboriginal languages of India', 'develops what we might call the two-race theory of Indian civilization'. It describes the hostile invasion of ancient India by a lighter-skinned, more civilized, race—the Aryans— who 'came as a warrior people, vanquishing, destroying, and subjecting the savage and despised inhabitants of the country'. As Müller put it: 'We generally find that it is the fate of the negro race, when brought into hostile contact with the Japhetic race, to be either destroyed and annihilated,

---

[46] Peter Pels, 'The Rise and Fall of the Indian Aborigines', in *Colonial Subjects: Essays on the Practical History of Anthropology*, eds Peter Pels and Oscar Salemink (University of Michigan Press, 1999), 96–97.

or to fall into a state of slavery and degradation, from which, if at all, it recovers by the slow process of assimilation.'[47]

By the second half of the nineteenth century, the Aryan invasion of ancient India (like Rome's relationship with the barbarians) had become a standard point of comparison when considering modern Europe's impact on tribal peoples around the world. In 1882, for example, Henry Bartle Frere, the former Governor of Bombay and High Commissioner of South Africa, wrote a paper titled 'On the Laws Affecting the Relations Between Civilized and Savage Life, as Bearing on the Dealings of Colonists with Aborigines', where he searched for a generalizable rule about colonial impact on tribes, or 'permanent laws affecting the relations between civilized and savage life' as he put it. Turning to India to establish such a law, he observed that, 'the first question ... relates to the continued existence of these races in the presence of civilization'. In India, he found that in the plains, 'The civilized Aryan immigrants have everywhere dispossessed their more aboriginal and less civilized predecessors', but that 'In the hills and forests and elsewhere, wherever the aborigines have maintained a separate national existence, the effects of Aryan contact are less visible'. Using the Aryan invasion theory to justify British colonial rule was a favourite pastime for many a colonial administrator, and so it is not at all surprising that Frere would connect this historical narrative with his contemporary situation. Suggesting that the British were just extending the age-old civilizing process to the hills, which were now accessible thanks to the advent of modern technology, he wrote: 'in many cases there has been little visible change or improvement in civilization for centuries past, till the European Aryan with his roads and railroads, his uniform codes, and his centralized administration broke into the aboriginal reserve of Warlis and Bhils, of Sonthals, or Gonds, or Koles'.

Drawing on his South African experience of the near extermination of groups such as the so-called Bushmen and Hottentots, Frere concluded his essay with a set of 'laws or invariable facts affecting the relationship between civilized and savage life' that are worth sharing in part here:

1. That it is possible for the civilized to overcome and destroy by war the uncivilized and savage race ...

---

[47] Trautmann, *Aryans and British India*, 175.

2. That simple proximity of the civilized to the uncivilized race has led, or is leading, to the extinction of the savage race ...
3. That the changes which have occurred in the native races, consequent on the proximity of European colonists, are an advance in civilization and approximation to the types of European civilization ... [48]

Whether it was with the Bhils or the Gonds, the Europeans working in western and central India in the second half of the nineteenth century were not only looking outside of India for answers but also beyond the human species. In an 1880 lecture, Colonel Davidson of the Bombay Army, for example, unfavourably compared the Bhils 'in their natural state' to 'the Bushmen of Africa, scarcely men, but rather a link between the human species and the wild creatures among whom they live'.[49] Similarly, complaining of the Gonds' 'unrestrained drunkenness', James Forsyth, in his *Highlands of Central India: Notes on Their Forests and Wild Tribes*, wrote:

> It is this unfortunate want of steadiness that has led to most of the misfortunes of the race, to the loss of their heritage in the land, and in a great many cases practically even of their personal liberty. Inferior races gave way before superior whenever they meet; and whether, as here and in America, the instrument selected be 'fire-water', or as in New Zealand, it be our own favourite recipe of powder and lead, the result is the same. The case of the Gond has hitherto little differed, whether he has preferred to cling to his rugged hills and struggle with nature, or has remained on the edge of civilisation and toiled for the superior races.[50]

Despite the deeply disturbing tone of these remarks, it was this type of thinking, at least in part, that led to the creation of the first India-wide

---

[48] H. Bartle Frere, 'On the Laws Affecting the Relations Between Civilized and Savage Life, as Bearing on the Dealings of Colonists with Aborigines', *The Journal of the Anthropological Institute of Great Britain and Ireland* 11 (1882): 313–354.

[49] 'Lecture delivered in Edinburgh to H.M.'s 78th Highlanders, by Colonel Davidson, late of the Bombay Army', cited by F.J. Goldsmid, *James Outram: A Biography* (London: Smith, Elder, 1880), 55.

[50] James Forsyth, *The Highlands of Central India: Notes on Their Forests and Wild Tribes, Natural History, and Sports* (London: Chapman and Hall, 1871), 160.

tribal protection policy in 1874, the Scheduled Districts Act. Most scholarship on South Asian environmental history points to the Indian Forest Act of 1878 as the decisive moment when India's tribes were separated from 'reserved forests'.[51] However, it is worth pointing out here that the 1870s also saw the inauguration of so-called scheduled districts—hill and forest regions to be administered especially for the care and protection of those who would come to be regarded as 'scheduled tribes'. As Uday Chandra argues, 'the Scheduled Districts Act of 1874 marked the formal inauguration of a colonial rule of difference that separated castes and tribes by law'. It also promoted 'paternalistic notions of protection' wherein 'primitive or backwards subjects' were seen as unready for liberal institutions such as democracy and self-governance. Tribes were thus consigned to what Dipesh Chakrabarty calls 'the waiting-room of history'.[52] But if they were soon to vanish, would their wait be in vain?

Not all late nineteenth-century racists subscribed to the idea that India's tribes would inevitably disappear as a result of the colonial encounter. H.H. Risley, author of the 1901 *Census of India*, probably had a better grasp of the population dynamics involved than most, though he, unfortunately, put his quantitative skills towards disturbing anthropometrics such as using the cephalic index to advance his theory that castes and tribes were defined by racial difference. In 1891, Risley outlined his position in an article titled 'The study of ethnology in India':

> Most of the barbarous and semi-barbarous tribes which come under observation in India are at the present day fairly accessible, and the inquirer can as a rule get together as many specimens of them as he wants without undergoing excessive trouble or hardship himself. Observations can thus be multiplied and repeated, and sounder general conclusions arrived at than could be derived from the study of a few specimens of a declining race. At the same time the great improvement in communications, which has brought the wilder tribes within reach of

---

[51] Ramachandra Guha, 'An Early Environmental Debate: The Making of the 1878 Forest Act', *Indian Economic & Social History Review* 27, no. 1 (1990): 65–84. Mahesh Rangarajan, *Fencing the Forest: Conservation and Ecological Change in India's Central Provinces, 1860–1914* (Delhi: Oxford University Press, 1996).

[52] Uday Chandra, 'Liberalism and Its Other: The Politics of Primitivism in Colonial and Postcolonial Indian Law', *Law & Society Review* 47, no. 1 (2013): 161.

the scientific observer, has not exposed them to that contact with colonists of European blood which has proved so destructive to the aborigines of Australia and America. Those races of India, which, for want of a better name, we may for the present call non-Aryan, show no tendency to disappear, and in some parts of the continent their numbers appear to be on the increase.

Still, Risley hedged his position. Firstly, he did note that there were a few 'tribes which are dying out, like the Lepchas, or losing their identity, like the Mech and Dhimal, by absorption into larger groups', but that by and large 'the ethnographer is by no means confined to the study of moribund types'. Secondly, he also distinguished the disappearance of tribal 'races' from the disappearance of tribal cultures. Later, in the same essay he argued that 'we find in the majority of cases that the admission of a tribe into the charmed circle of Hinduism results after a generation or two in the practical disappearance of the tribe as such', but that 'even in this extreme case the physical characteristics which distinguished the tribe tend on the whole to be preserved'.[53]

## The (Other) Ecological Indian

Labels generated with reference to indigenous communities in one part of the world have a funny way of getting applied to indigenous peoples all over the world. This probably has to do with Europeans' historical tendency to treat tribal peoples everywhere as members of the same class or category. Whether called 'indigenous' or 'tribal', these terms themselves are labels that were initially imposed by outsiders, and the communities they refer to have been linked together by this conceptualization. The idea that indigenous or tribal peoples everywhere somehow share a common identity is not what's at stake here, however. A bigger problem is that stereotypes about indigenous peoples also tend to get lazily applied all over the place.

---

[53] H.H. Risley, 'The Study of Ethnology in India', *Journal of the Anthropological Institute of Great Britain and Ireland* 20 (1891): 235–263.

As André Béteille observes, Europeans developed their concept of aboriginal or indigenous peoples based on their experiences 'in North America, in Australia, in Polynesia and Melanesia, and in sub-Saharan Africa'. Thus, when it came to deciding which groups were or were not to be classified as tribes in nineteenth-century India, colonists 'had an image of a particular kind of social formation' in mind—isolated, primitive communities living in a state of nature. India's 'communities that corresponded more or less with that image' were also labelled aboriginal and presumed to be India's first inhabitants.[54] Perhaps this process was also in some ways akin to how, in the early age of exploration, what Europeans called 'India' could be found just about everywhere and nearly any group could wind up being labelled 'Indian'. As a result, much of Asia was called the 'East Indies'; Europeans eagerly named Southeast Asia's major island chain Indonesia, meaning 'India islands' in Greek; the Caribbean was called the 'West Indies'; Native North Americans were beset with the name 'Red Indians', and the American frontier was known as 'Indian country'.

The idea that all indigenous peoples are environmentalists probably started in North America and other settler colonies and was meant to be applied to Native American 'Indians' rather than South Asians, but like many broad-sweeping claims, it has managed to grow even broader and more sweeping. Thus, when Shepard Krech III wrote his 1999 book *The Ecological Indian: Myth and History* to illuminate the Native American situation, he may as well have coined his titular 'ecological Indians' with Adivasis in mind. With innumerable parallels to the ecological Indian myth, as Krech outlines it, existing in the popular historical image of forest dwelling and peasant communities in South Asia, what might be called the (other) ecological Indian hypothesis has been nearly as pervasive in India as in the United States. As an 'antidote to the materialism' of the industrial age, the romantic image of 'the ecological Indian' has had 'simplistic, seductive appeal'.[55]

---

[54] André Béteille, 'The Idea of Indigenous People', *Current Anthropology* 39, no. 2 (1998): 187–119 points out: 'Morgan spoke of "savage" as well as "barbarous" tribes representing two distinct stages of evolution'.
[55] Clyde Ellis, 'Paradise Lost: Dismantling the Trope of Nature's Children', *Ethnohistory* 49, no. 3 (2002): 717.

Criticizing problematic 'claims that women, forest dwellers and peasants were... keepers of a special conservationist ethic', Subir Sinha et al. critique what they call the ' "new traditionalist" discourse of Indian environmentalism', which they say 'dominates the historiography of the Indian environment'.[56] Many South Asianists arguing *Against Ecological Romanticism* (to borrow another author's title) have fiercely critiqued the popular tendency to essentialize and idealize the lifestyles and values of non-industrial communities, particularly that benighted and saintly figure of environmentalist discourse around the world, 'the ecologically noble savage'.[57]

In some sense, these prejudices about indigenous peoples go all the way back to the beginnings of modern European intellectual history. There were two starkly opposing traditions of thought when it came to European views on tribal communities. One scorned them as ignoble savages, the other romanticized them as living in an Edenic state of nature. Both of these were *a priori* positions based more on dreams than reality. The divided opinion can be traced at least as far back as Thomas Hobbes who coined the term the 'state of nature' in 1651 and John Dryden who coined the term 'the noble savage' in 1672, though neither Englishman had any personal experience of any travel beyond Europe. Whereas Hobbes saw the state of nature as a 'nasty, brutish' existence, a *bellum omnium contra omnes*, a 'war of all against all', Rousseau who was long associated with Dryden's noble savage (but who never actually used the phrase himself), described the state of nature as one of idealistic harmony and saw subsequent society as a debasement. Yet Rousseau specifically stated that he was not writing a factual history, but rather what was often called a 'conjectural history': a sort of hypothetical reconstruction of the past used for philosophical reflection on the human condition. Thus, at the beginning of his *Discours sur l'origine de l'inégalité*, Rousseau urges, 'Let us therefore begin by putting aside all the facts, for

---

[56] Subir Sinha, Shubhra Gururani, and Brian Greenberg, 'The "New Traditionalist" Discourse of Indian Environmentalism', *Journal of Peasant Studies* 24, no. 3 (1997): 65–99.
[57] Archana Prasad, *Against Ecological Romanticism: Verrier Elwin and the Making of an Anti-Modern Tribal Identity* (Delhi: Three Essays Collective, 2003); Kent H. Redford, 'The Ecologically Noble Savage', *Orion Nature Quarterly* 9, no. 3 (1990): 25–29. Redford quickly retracted and apologized for the title of his article, which many found offensive, but the phrase nonetheless permeated academic discourse ever since on the question of whether or not tribal peoples live in harmony with nature.

they have no bearing on the question. The investigations that may be undertaken concerning this subject should not be taken for historical truths, but only for hypothetical and conditional reasonings'.[58] At least in this period, thinkers like Rousseau were willing to admit that their notions about men living a state of nature were based firmly in the realm of imagination. But whether they were noble or ignoble savages, whether they were ecological sinners or saints, in the European mind, they were always vanishing.

## The (Other) Vanishing Indian

> I don't care what he calls me. I call him a savage, and I call a savage a something highly desirable to be civilised off the face of the earth
> 
> Charles Dickens, 'The Noble Savage' (1853)

The ecological Indian must be paired together with another pervasive representation of indigenous peoples: the vanishing Indian. The two belong together because both represent the dominant society's view of who and what 'authentic' indigenous people are. Both the 'ecological Indian' and 'vanishing Indian' were first named and described in the North American context, but could just as easily be applied to virtually any indigenous group anywhere. As we have by now well established, the cliché that all indigenous peoples are on the path towards inevitable extinction—despite whatever evidence might be raised to the contrary—is one of the oldest canards in the colonial handbook. But just as the stereotype of 'the savage' was coupled with that of 'the noble savage', there were two sides to the vanishing Indian motif as well. In contrast to genocidal calls for the extinction of supposedly primitive races, there also existed the hope that the endangered Indian could be saved from vanishing. So, for example, while Charles Dickens was clearly not a fan of 'the noble savage', others certainly were. Writing 'he is a savage—cruel, false, thievish, murderous; addicted more or less to grease, entrails, and beastly

---

[58] Jean-Jacques Rousseau, *Discourse on the Origin of Inequality*, trans. Donald A. Cress (Cambridge: Hackett, 1992), 17.

customs; a wild animal', and referring to 'wars of extermination' as 'the best thing I know of him', Dickens found it 'extraordinary to observe how some people will talk about him, as they talk about the good old times; how they will regret his disappearance'.[59]

Ecological Indians are also vanishing Indians because they are believed to be disappearing. On the one hand, the sustained critique of ecological romanticism and the so-called ecological Indian by an ever-growing number of contemporary scholars means that fewer and fewer serious thinkers are willing to embrace naïve notions of 'ecological nobility'. And if increasing numbers of educated readers accept that the popular preconception that all indigenous peoples are natural ecologists and environmentalists is indeed a stereotype, then is the ecological Indian myth itself becoming endangered? Even the most strident indigenous rights advocates and environmentalists are willing to admit the prejudices involved. As one defender the notion of indigenous environmentalism against Redford's 'ecologically noble savage' critique writes, 'I do not assert that Indians are "ecologically noble stewards" (a ridiculous and simplistic assertion), but I do assert that Redford and others are not the ones who should set the international standards of land and resource management. It is not up to them to tell us if we are ecologically noble or not'.[60]

On the other hand, it is precisely the ecological traditions of tribal communities that are often seen as the most endangered aspects of their cultures. In the popular imagination, it is the tribe's unique relationship with nature that sets it apart from the dominant society. And if ecology is what distinguishes tribes as distinct cultural entities, then the loss of ecological traditions also signals cultural decline. Some might even go so far as to argue that as the myth of ecological nobility wanes, so does the idea of tribes as separate peoples who need to be protected as such. This is one of the dangers that come with the territory when indigenous communities strategically choose to embrace seemingly positive stereotypes about themselves—they are held up to impossibly high standards of 'authenticity', as determined by outside funding bodies such as governments and

---

[59] Charles Dickens, 'The Noble Savage', *Household Words* VII (11 Jun 1853): 337–339.
[60] K.L. Lopez, 'Returning to Fields', *American Indian Culture and Research Journal* 16 (1992): 165–174.

NGOs. If those 'criteria of indigenous authenticity' are not met, then the outside world might not recognize them as authentically tribal. As Beth Conklin puts it: 'When native people's actions contradict outsiders' expectations, support for specific indigenous causes may be diluted or withdrawn'.[61] And as Richard Lee concurs: 'While anthropologists critique the discourse of primitivism that orientalizes and distances indigenous peoples, the people themselves may be saying: "don't take that away from us. We can use it to our advantage!"'[62] Thus, the anthropologist Virginius Xaxa who himself hails from the Oraon tribe in Chhattisgarh writes: 'The identity that was forced upon them from outside precisely to mark out differences from the dominant community has now been internalised by the people themselves. Not only has it become an important mark of social differentiation and identity assertion but also an important tool of articulation for empowerment'.[63]

One example of an NGO that has often been accused of fostering this sort or primitivism—focusing on saving 'ecological Indians' from disappearing—has been Survival International. In its literature, the UK-based NGO Survival International calls itself the 'movement for tribal peoples'. But it is important to note that Survival's long-time director (now retired) Stephen Corry makes a distinction between 'indigenous peoples' generally, and 'tribal peoples', with 'tribal peoples being those who live self-sufficiently and are not integrated into the market economy and "indigenous peoples" being more mainstream and integrated'.[64] Survival International is not involved in the politics of any indigenous community in the western world or elsewhere, that is, for lack of a better word, 'modernized'. Previously called 'The Primitive People's Fund' before it changed its name in 1971, Survival was founded with a particular vision of who and what 'tribal peoples' are—small scale, isolated communities,

---

[61] Beth A. Conklin, 'Environmentalism, Global Community, and the New Indigenism', in *Inclusion and Exclusion in the Global Arena*, ed. Max Kirsch (New York: Routledge, 2006), 173–188.

[62] Richard B. Lee, 'Indigenism and Its Discontents', in *Inclusion and Exclusion in the Global Arena*, ed. Max Kirsch (New York: Routledge, 2006), 141–172.

[63] Virginius Xaxa, 'Tribes as Indigenous People of India', *Economic & Political Weekly* 34, no. 51 (18–24 Dec 1999): 3589.

[64] S. Corry, 'Interview 1: Stephen Corry, Survival International, 4 December 2007', in *The Politics of Indigeneity: Dialogues and Reflections on Indigenous Activism*, eds Venkateswar and E. Hughes (New York: Zed Books, 2011), 193–206, cited by Jonathan Woof, 'Indigeneity and Development in Botswana: The Case of the San in the Central Kalahari Game Reserve', *IDGS—Research Papers* (University of Ottawa).https://ruor.uottawa.ca/handle/10393/32750

living in the heart of nature. This has led to the accusation that Survival is yet-another, quote, 'western, twofaced and paternalist NGO half a world away' where 'it is fashionable and politically correct to criticise states that were former colonies and to romanticise "tribal peoples" as a form of wildlife that insists on keeping running around with bows and arrows and making fire with a firedrill rather than striking a match'.[65] To this, Corry responds that Survival International has nothing 'to do with "romanticism", "keeping people as they are", or "preserving cultures"'. Instead, it has to do with oppression of tribal peoples, human rights, international law, and 'fighting for justice for minorities'.[66]

Survival International is by no means alone when it comes to facing criticisms of romanticism, etc., addressed towards vanishing tribes. As Marine Carrin observes in an essay on 'Understanding Endangered Societies with Special Reference to India' in a 2017 edited volume on *Marginalised and Endangered Worldviews*:

> A number of organizations... reflect a cultural stereotype of the backward and primitive tribal whose way of life needs to be protected, or uplifted, in order to find a place in the developed world. This implies that Adivasi societies are endangered societies. But as anthropologists, we need to rethink our approach in order not to reproduce the hegemonic discourse of the power groups. We must avoid reproducing the paternalist approaches of earlier days, whether of anthropologists, NGOs or the State. How can we be of use in assisting the efforts of indigenous peoples to assert themselves?[67]

So, while Carrin does identify 'Adivasi communities as endangered societies', she brings considerable nuance to this position. Agreeing that Adivasis are '"indigenous" because they have endured a history of spoliation', she also writes that she has 'been struck, however, by the way tribal

---

[65] Ferdinand Berkhof, 'Survival International Is Paternalistic', *Sunday Standard* (Botswana), 27 Jan 2011.
[66] Stephen Corry, *Tribal Peoples for Tomorrow's World* (Alcester: Freeman Press, 2011), 301–302.
[67] Marine Carrin, 'Engaging Scholarship in Understanding Endangered Societies with Special Reference to India', in *Marginalised and Endangered Worldviews: Comparative Studies on Contemporary Eurasia, India and South America*, eds Lidia Guzy and James Kapaló (Münster: LIT Verlag, 2017), 19.

people themselves take their identity as immutable, regardless of social dynamics'. She also notes that certain Adivasis have been regionally powerful communities, e.g. Raj Gonds 'held a dominant position in former kingdoms, were generally sedentary farmers', and she points to the 'rise of a tribal middle class' in the Jharkhand movement.[68]

It is reasonable to point out that the Indian government, too, has been deeply involved in paternalistic protectionist projects which treated Adivasis as vanishing forest tribes. As discussed throughout this chapter, characteristics such as 'geographical isolation' and level of 'backwardness' have, since before independence, been used as the key indicators for determining how 'scheduled tribes' should be classified and protected by the Indian government. The Lokur Commission of 1965 described:

> the list of 1931 was of 'primitive tribes' while the list of 1935 was of 'backward tribes' and primitiveness and backwardness were the tests applied in preparing the lists of 1950 and 1956. In revising the lists of Scheduled Tribes, we have looked for indications of primitive traits, distinctive culture, geographical isolation, shyness of contact.[69]

As Selma Sonntag argues, provisions written into the Fifth and Sixth Schedules (or appendixes) of the Constitution of India played an important role in these classification schemes: 'The tribes included in the Sixth Schedule [applied in four Northeastern states] were more exotic—and, hence, seemingly more authentic—than tribes included under the Fifth Schedule'. The gist of both schedules, though, was arguably to safeguard and protect traditional cultural heritage from vanishing, i.e. 'to preserve their ethnic identity and to face the forces of assimilation squarely from their more advanced neighbours in the plains'.[70] Studying the 'bureaucratic inner workings' of what has been called 'the ethnographic state'[71]

---

[68] Carrin, 'Understanding Endangered Societies', 9–29.
[69] B.N. Lokur et al., *The Report of the Advisory Committee on the Revision of the Lists of Scheduled Castes and Scheduled Tribes* (New Delhi: Department of Social Security, Government of India 1965), 7.
[70] Selma K. Sonntag, 'Self-Government, Indigeneity and Cultural Authenticity: A Comparative Study of India and the United States', in *Indigeneity in India*, eds B.T. Karlsson and T.B. Subba (London: Kegan Paul, 2006), 190–191.
[71] Townsend Middleton, 'Scheduling Tribes: A View from Inside India's Ethnographic State', *Focaal* 65 (2013): 13.

thus visibly exposes the logics of both the 'ecological Indian' and 'vanishing Indian', which were foundational in shaping tribal policy.

## Endangered Species & Societies

Environmental history, according to one prominent scholar, is 'the story of life and death not of human individuals but of societies, and of species'.[72] The tendency in most contemporary accounts of tribal communities is to pair together the life and death of endangered species and societies into a narrative of biocultural diversity loss. Thus, standard narratives of central and western India's environmental history tend to explore the relationship between wildlife decline and concurrent changes in societies that lived in close proximity to, and once based their livelihoods on, that wildlife. These narratives paint a picture of the dramatic transformation of Bhil and Gond forest societies into sedentary, deeply impoverished, agriculturalist communities incorporated in the nation's agrarian economy. This meant the end of wildlife and forests, as much as it meant the end of wildlife-based and forest-based ways of life. The fates of wildlife species, forests, and forest societies are thus irrevocably bound together. Changing cultural and political ecologies were both a cause and a consequence of species decline. Biodiversity and cultural decline were two aspects of the same historical process.

While this biocultural narrative is in many regards convincing, one major problem is that if we cannot even agree on who Adivasis are, then how can a consensus possibly be reached as to whether they are endangered or not? Historically, were the majority of Bhils and Gonds really wildlife-based forest societies at all? This is a question still very much subject to debate. Then again, why are so many of 'us' (readers and purveyors of English-language academic texts) trying to define Adivasi identity, or for that matter, judge if they are in existential crisis? Why are so many people so eager to try to fit Adivasis into any one particular box or another? Why does almost everyone seem to want to have a clear-cut

---

[72] Richard Grove, 'Environmental History', in *New Perspectives on Historical Writing*, ed. Peter Burke (Pennsylvania: Penn State Press, 2001), 261.

answer as to how to label these communities? In order to decide if they are endangered or not?

Like the question of 'aboriginality' or 'indigeneity', or the very term 'tribe' itself, the archetypes of the Ecological Indian and the Vanishing Indian were foreign imports into India, which since the colonial period have significantly shaped Adivasi identity politics. Undoubtedly many Bhils and Gonds have lived as forest-based communities, and some ecological traditions are undoubtedly vanishing. And furthermore, many members of these Adivasi communities do share deeply held values linking environmental and social justice, which date back generations. However, the notion that writ-large these societies are ecologically noble, natural environmentalists, who have always lived in harmony with nature, and that now they and their unique ecological traditions are under threat of vanishing forever, is quite a thorny set of interlinking claims. In particular, the notion that therefore they need 'our' (read: English-language speaking, western-educated, middle-class) protection is a dangerous leap for a variety of reasons. Not only is it usually grounded in essentialism, romanticism, paternalism, and guilty conscience, it is also almost always grounded in ignorance and lack of first-hand experience. Or when suburban liberals do make it to the villages of western and central India, it is usually on embedded whistle-stop tours led by confirmed activist-believers, and they neither have the time, intellectual resources (years of historical and anthropological reading), or language skills to move beyond their preordained views.

Interestingly, many Adivasi internet activists themselves embrace this rhetoric, posting memes and videos promoting notions of both indigenous harmony with nature and tribal endangerment on their Instagram and YouTube and Twitter feeds. As one popular Adivasi Twitter feed has asked: *'Bharat me kai Adivasi samuday vilupt ho rahe hai, lekin sarkar ne Adivasi samudayon ke vilupt hone ke peeche ke karanon ka adhyayan karne ke lie koi samiti kyon nahin banai?'* ('Many tribal communities are becoming extinct in India, but why has the government not formed a committee to study the reasons behind the extinction of tribal communities?'), arguing that *'Bharat apni samrudh virasat, sanskritik aur bhashae vividhata adi ko kho raha hai'* ('India is losing its rich heritage, cultural, and linguistic diversity, etc.').[73] Soundbites such as *'Agar esa hi chala to,*

---

[73] Tweet by @Ramkeshmeena02, 5 Jun 2020. https://twitter.com/Ramkeshmeena02/status/1268740779897470978

*Adivasi vilupt ki shreni me aa jaeyega. Prakrit bachao, Adivasi bachao*' ('If things continue like this, the tribal will be categorized as extinct. Save nature, save Adivasis')[74] promote the notion of authentic Adivasi culture grounded in nature; at the same time, this content creation takes much tech-savvy, computer equipment, and a stable internet connection. It is of course easy to love nature and traditional cultural values while stuck behind a computer working in digital media production or flying across the world to attend international environmental conferences. And so, this rhetoric is often produced by educated Adivasi youths, some of whom are second-generation activists, whose parents cut their teeth in earlier social movements and had gained enough social capital to put their children through good schooling and secure them good jobs. This new generation has turned to the internet to continue the struggle for land rights, etc., and they recognize these tropes to be powerful tools in their movements.

Similarly, we find a subset of scholars of South Asia writing statements like: 'The most important point to note is that tribal cultures are now endangered', and 'We would contend that this could be considered a true apocalypse, not in a Christian understanding of the term or in the revelatory sense of its Greek roots, but rather in the common meaning of a predicted ultimate catastrophe'.[75] Here, we must not only be aware of how such rhetoric is quite literally grounded in eschatological thinking about end times, but we should also carefully consider whether it is a repetition of age-old alarmism that has been unrelenting since the colonial era. Our attention might also be drawn to how this endangerment discourse has often embraced projections of a sort of tribal Kali Yuga or dark age in order to promote the politics of tribal rescue, uplift, or even salvation.

In the end, the term Adivasi in contemporary India probably makes the most sense as a political category, rather than a historical, ecological, or even an anthropological one. As Ajay Skaria puts it, 'Being adivasi is about shared experiences of the loss of the forests, the alienation of land,

---

[74] Tweet by @rchouhan_bagh, 11 Oct 2020. https://twitter.com/rchouhan_bagh/status/1315121232757452802

[75] Stefano Beggiora, 'The End of Time in Adivasi Traditions or the Time of the End for Adivasi Traditions?' *Anglistica AION* 19, no. 1 (2015): 164, 166. Beggoria blames this crisis on coming of 'international companies worth several billion dollars, for iron and steel plants, factories, power plants, aluminum refineries and even dams or mines' as well as the fact that 'Today the tribal areas are increasingly becoming areas of.... conflict', including separatist struggles such as the Naxalite movement.

repeated displacements since independence in the name of "development projects", and much more.... the power of the word adivasi does not have to do simply with some lexical meaning—original inhabitants—but with being outside domination by surrounding plains societies".[76] Cries of Adivasi endangerment and extinction, though often exaggerated, or based on false equivalencies, or grounded in ignorance of history, ecology, anthropology, and basic demographics, are usually made with the goal of liberating these communities from ills such as economic exploitation and cultural domination. Even when such rhetoric is counterproductive, even when it stereotypes these communities, strategic or not, such cries are made as part of a political struggle against precarity, or as Vinita Damodaran puts it, 'towards transforming the balance of power in the region'.[77]

---

[76] Ajay Skaria, *Hybrid Histories: Forests, Frontiers, and Wildness in Western India* (Delhi: Oxford University Press, 1999), 281.
[77] Vinita Damodaran, 'Book Review: Environment and Ethnicity in India 1200-1991, by Sumit Guha. Cambridge: Cambridge University Press, 1999', *Journal of Political Ecology* 7, no. 1 (2000): 12-17.

# 3
# From Extermination to Conservation of India's 'Wild Life'

There is little else to be said about the tiger tribe. Unaware as we are of the place they fill in the economy of Nature, we earnestly desire their extinction in the name of our common humanity by any of the methods available to the Government. They are apparently useless. Tiger flesh is carrion, his skin has ceased to be a curiosity, or to possess a commercial value, his skull is in every surgery, or grins at the shop-window of the taxidermist. He is not even ornamental. Let him be annihilated by all means. Although in the foregoing paragraphs we have only had the royal tiger in our mind, there are many animals of the same genus, inhabitants of the Indian forest, which might, with equal advantage, be improved off the face of the earth. The lion, the leopard, the wolf, the hyaena, the lynx, the wild cat, the jackal, the wild dog, are alike the enemy of our species, and, excepting that they also prey upon the lesser *faunae* and keep down their number, are of no apparent utility.

'Field Sports in India', *The Oriental*, 1873[1]

We understand that the Secretary of State for India has sent over full instructions to the Indian Government to adopt such measures as shall seem best for the extinction of the tiger tribe. Unfortunately such has been the terror caused by the fearful depredations of solitary animals, the country population have come to regard these monsters as in some way incarnate divinities,

---

[1] Anon, 'From *The Oriental*, "Field Sports in India"', *Littell's Living Age* 119, fifth series, 4 (Oct–Dec 1873): 63.

and hence are afraid themselves of killing them. Latterly, however, prompted by the Government rewards, large numbers have been killed, but until some undetermined plan is decided upon we fear the relief will be but small. To the European officer tiger hunting is looked upon as a sport, and too often, we think, are the interests of the poorer population ignored in order that the sport may be more exciting. But while India teems with objects worthy of the greatest preservation, tigers are certainly not one of them!

'Tigers', *Journal of the National Indian Association*, 1873[2]

Alan tried to impress upon Rahman that if game became extinct it would not be long before the shikari [hunter] followed suit, and with him would disappear the numerous train of followers who now fatten on the sahib's gold. The 'man of the world' perfectly agreed with this, and pointed the moral with a little Hindustani fable bearing a striking resemblance to 'killing the goose with the golden eggs'.

Mrs. Alan Gardner, *Rifle and Spear with the Rajpoots*, 1895[3]

Tigers & tribes—the twentieth century saw massive society-wide changes of heart on both fronts. Today, tiger conservation is just about as popular as big game hunting was some hundred years ago. And, thankfully, calls for civilizing the savage are today nearly extinct in public discourse as well. This paradigm shift has been nothing less than a total reversal in values.[4] And it is this reversal that this chapter traces—from the colonial obsession with sport hunting and vermin eradication through to the beginnings of the demand for wildlife conservation that dominates public discourse today. Where other chapters in this book consider this

---

[2] W. 'Tigers', *Journal of the National Indian Association in Aid of Social Progress in India*, 14 (Oct 1873): 442.
[3] Nora Gardner, *Rifle and Spear with the Rajpoots: Being the Narrative of a Winter's Travel and Sport in Northern India* (London: Chatto & Windus, 1895), 49.
[4] See Thomas Kuhn, *The Structure of Scientific Revolutions* (Chicago: University of Chicago Press, 1962) and Robert J. Richards and Lorraine Daston, eds, *Kuhn's Structure of Scientific Revolutions at Fifty: Reflections on a Science Classic* (Chicago: University of Chicago Press, 2016) for the concept of paradigm shifts.

structural revolution as it affected so-called tribes in India, here the focus is on wildlife, primarily tigers and other carnivores.

As this chapter will show, carnivore conservation came much later than the idea of tribal protection or preservation. Before the twentieth century, calls for the protection of both tigers and tribes existed in India, but protectionist discourses emerged for tribes well before they did for tigers, even while the dominant paradigm was still focused on eradication of both. The question of what protecting tribal populations meant was a relatively complicated issue, subject to debate already at the outset of the colonial encounter. The idea that tigers might need to be protected only began to emerge towards the very end of the nineteenth century, but when it did emerge, what it meant was clear: it meant not killing tigers. This, however, was something that few colonial sportsmen and administrators were prepared to agree to until well into the mid-twentieth century.

In nineteenth-century India, tigers and other carnivores were rarely if ever seen as endangered; they were seen as endangering the lives of others. (As John Lockwood Kipling wrote in his book *Beast and Man in India*: 'In the native newspapers, as in popular talk, cases are reported in complete good faith where a Raja out hunting is endangered by a mad wild elephant or a ferocious tiger'.[5]) Anything that threatened civilization's advance into the Indian jungles was unlikely to be valued as endangered by the Victorian majority. Instead, along with recalcitrant tribes which could not be tamed, tigers and other 'dangerous beasts' were targeted for eradication. People who were perceived to threaten colonial law and order were not subject to 'protection', and neither were tigers. It was 'helpless' people such as white women and children who colonial officers felt they needed to protect, and 'predatory peoples' were compared to ravenous tigers (see Figure 3.1). Only as it became clear that certain species or peoples were no longer a threat to the colonial order would they become objects of conservation.[6]

Discursive parallels between the targeting of predatory non-human species and what were perceived to be predatory kinds of man were

---

[5] John Lockwood Kipling, *Beast and Man in India* (London: MacMillan, 1891), 355–356.
[6] See my discussion of early colonial encounters with the Bhils in Chapter 5 for an example of this transition.

**Figure 3.1.** John Tenniel, 'The British Lion's Vengeance on the Bengal Tiger' (watercolor and gouache on paper, 1870).
Public domain. Repository: Library of Congress Prints and Photographs Division Washington, D.C. http://hdl.loc.gov/loc.pnp/ppmsca.19308

common.[7] In many sources from colonial India, the language used to describe tigers and tribes overlapped and blurred. Tigers were not only referred to as a species, but as the tiger 'tribe' or 'race'. Human tribes were referred to as 'species of man', or sometimes directly, as 'savage beasts'. Whereas there was a 'war' on 'dangerous wild beasts', 'wild tribes' were often described as being 'hunted' out of their forest strongholds. Both

---

[7] Karl Jacoby reflects on the overlapping discourses of extermination facing Native Americans and wolves in the Southwestern United States, uncovering a trove of writings linking the two, and worth quoting at length here: ' "The wolf still is, he always will be, a savage; so has been, so always will be, the Apache", asserted J. S. Campion in 1878. Labeling the Apache "the wolf of the human race" served in turn to minimize the humanity of those victimized by the settlers' anti-Apache violence. Sylvester Mowry, for example, called for the "massacre of these 'human wolves' ", while John Cremony of the U.S. Boundary Survey spoke of the Apache as "a biped brute who is as easily killed as a wolf" '. This discourse cut the opposite way as well, as Jacoby further records: 'In 1818, for instance, 600 settlers in Hinkley, Ohio, launched a "war of extermination upon the bears and wolves" in which 17 wolves were killed and scalped for the local predator bounty.... Wolves had become "evil-doers... [who] deserve[d] to be destroyed", animals whose "crimes" justified the "natural right of man to exterminate" them. As the nineteenth century wolf hunter Ben Corbin put it: "The wolf is the enemy of civilization, and I want to exterminate him" '. Karl Jacoby, '"The Broad Platform of Extermination": Nature and Violence in the Nineteenth Century North American Borderlands', *Journal of Genocide Research* 10, no. 2 (Jun 2008): 255.

were sometimes described as 'vermin' to be 'exterminated'; both were eventually defended against such campaigns of eradication.

In nineteenth- and early twentieth-century British India, numerous books touted titles with the twin obsessions of empire: 'sport' and 'war'.[8] Clearly, these activities were related, not only because they both involved firing weapons at living beings, and because the same people engaged in both activities. 'Sport' was understood as an act of conquest, and colonial 'warfare', if it can be called that, was typically of the most asymmetric variety, where out-armed and out-numbered 'wild men' retreated into the hills and forests to escape the heavy hand of empire. And so we find Robert Baden-Powell, founder of the Boy Scouts, speaking of his imperial conquests in India and Africa in terms of 'man-hunting' directed 'against wild beasts of the human kind'.[9]

The term 'trophy' comes from the Greek *tropaion,* and in its original usage meant strictly, 'a monument of the enemy's defeat'. The first trophies were the spoils of war. Hunting trophies are generally interpreted as mementos from the field, memories of the defeat of the animal at hand and little else. It is a simplistic view of the hunting trophy to say that a tiger's head or skin represented nothing more than the defeat of that particular tiger.[10] As Harriet Ritvo writes, the spoils of big game hunting, 'powerfully evoked' the idea of conquest and domination of foreign territories. Parallels between triumphing over dangerous animals and restless natives were 'direct and obvious'.[11] Destroying tigers and other 'dangerous beasts'

---

[8] E.g. John Pester, *War and Sport in India 1802–1806, an Officer's Diary* (London: Heath, Cranton & Ouseley, 1913); Arthur Easdale Stewart, *Tiger and Other Game: The Practical Experiences of a Soldier Shikari in India* (London: Longmans, 1927); James Willcocks, *The Romance of Soldiering and Sport* (London: Cassell, 1925); Robert Stephenson Smyth Baden-Powell, *Memories of India; Recollections of Soldiering, and Sport* (Philadelphia: D. McKay, 1915); Montague Gilbert Gerard, *Leaves from the Diaries of a Soldier and Sportsman During Twenty Years' Service in India, Afghanistan, Egypt, and Other Countries, 1865–1885 ... With Illustrations, Etc.* (London: John Murray, 1903); Henry Germain Mainwaring, *A Soldier's Shikar Trips* (London: Grant Richards, 1920); and Stewart, *Tiger and Other Game.*

[9] Robert Stephenson Smyth Baden-Powell, *Sport in War* (London: William Heinemann, 1900), 18, 21; Also cited in Robert H. MacDonald, *Language of Empire: Myths and Metaphors of Popular Imperialism, 1880–1918* (Manchester: Manchester University Press, 1994), 22.

[10] For a study unpacking the meaning of the hunting trophy in the field symbolic studies, see: Linda Kalof and Amy Fitzgerald, 'Reading the Trophy: Exploring the Display of Dead Animals in Hunting Magazines', *Visual Studies* 18, no. 2 (2003).

[11] Harriet Ritvo, *The Animal Estate: The English and Other Creatures in the Victorian Age* (Cambridge, MA: Harvard University Press, 1987), 254.

was an important yet much-overlooked element of the colonial project. Anand Pandian has referred to this phenomenon as 'predatory care'.[12] And in Mahesh Rangarajan's words, 'the control of errant animals and of disobedient subjects was integral to the establishment of British power in the countryside'.[13] Thus, unsurprisingly, James Forsyth found already in the 1860s that most villagers felt 'the tiger himself' was 'far more endurable than those who encamp over against them to make war upon him'.[14]

The British in India often called the hunt a 'ruling passion', and at least one historian has since labelled it 'an obsession'.[15] In 1905, Colonel A.I.R. Glasfurd—huntsman, soldier, and author—calculated, 'Few subjects of such comparatively circumscribed bounds have elicited more literature than has Indian sports'.[16] Hunting books were the best sellers of the colonial literary scene. With their exotic jungle scenes, tales of 'savage men and still more savage beasts',[17] and stories of derring-do, brave white hunters captured the public imagination back home in rainy old Albion. Thus, hunters have left a prolific number of works on *shikar* to posterity. Sources for the historian of hunting in British India range from literary and artistic works, to sporting magazines, to diaries and game logs (lists of hunters, guns, and kills), besides what is available in the colonial archive. An *Annotated Bibliography of Asian Big Game Hunting Books* runs over two hundred pages long and catalogues roughly 700 volumes devoted to this rich primary source material.[18]

Technically, there was no such thing as 'wildlife conservation' in colonial India. By the end of the nineteenth century, there were bills for 'game protection', and there were forest reserves managed for resource exploitation. There was even some talk of 'preservation' of certain useful species, such as elephants. But to talk of colonial wildlife conservation, and

---

[12] Anand Pandian, 'Predatory Care: The Imperial Hunt in Mughal and British India', *Journal of Historical Sociology* 14 (2001): 79–107.

[13] Mahesh Rangarajan, *Fencing the Forest: Conservation and Ecological Change in India's Central Provinces, 1860–1914* (Delhi: Oxford University Press, 1996), 148–149.

[14] James Forsyth, *The Highlands of Central India: Notes on their Forests and Wild Tribes, Natural History, and Sports* (London: Chapman and Hall, 1871), 221.

[15] John M. MacKenzie, *Empire of Nature: Hunting, Conservation, and British Imperialism* (Manchester: Manchester University Press, 1988), 168.

[16] A.I.R. Glasfurd, *Rifle and Romance in the Indian Jungle* (London: J. Lane, 1905), v.

[17] William T. Hornaday, *Two Years in the Jungle: The Experiences of a Hunter and Naturalist in India, Ceylon, the Malay Peninsula and Borneo* (London: K. Paul, 1885), 21.

[18] Kenneth P. Czech, *An Annotated Bibliography of Asian Big Game Hunting Books, 1780 to 1980* (St. Cloud, MN: Land's Edge Press, 2003).

assume it was based on anything like the ideology of present-day conservation, would be anachronistic at best. As P.D. Stracey pointed out in his 1963 book *Wild Life in India: Its Conservation and Control,* 'In India the very term *wild life* is new. Hitherto... the emphasis has been on sport and hunting and the word commonly employed has been *game*'.[19] If the phrase 'wild life conservation' had ever been used in colonial India, which it probably was not, it might have meant one of two things. It might have meant the conservation of tribal wildness, or perhaps the conservation of the lifestyle of the European outdoorsman adventurer.

'Wild life' in the nineteenth century meant something radically different from what the word 'wildlife' means today. The term was used to describe the life of the rugged colonial pioneer. Numerous books with titles like *Wild Life in the Far West: Personal Adventures of a Border Mountain Man, Wild Life in the Interior of Central America,* and *Wild Life in the Land of the Giants: A Tale of Two Brothers,* attest to this fact. In India, for the European adventurer, 'wild life' could mean a life in the forest with the tribes and tigers, but it could also mean the wild lives of the tribes themselves. In what seems almost like a pastiche of colonial anthropology writing, in 1882, Shoshee Chunder Dutt publishing under the pseudonym Horatio Bickerstaff Rowney, wrote *The Wild Tribes of India* where he explained how 'The Assul, or unmixed Gonds are to be found most largely in the unexplored wildernesses... they live the life of wild men there and have all the virtues of the wild life in more or less degree'.[20]

It was primarily sport hunting itself that the first so-called 'fauna preservation' efforts were really aimed to preserve. The Royal Society for the Preservation of Fauna of Empire, founded in 1901, for example, was largely a club of big game hunters, or 'penitent butchers' as they have been called.[21] Yet, by the end of the 1960s this had changed. In 1969, India banned the export of tiger and leopard skins. By 1972, hunting was completely banned in India for the first time in history under the Indian Wildlife Protection Act, and hunting remains banned to this day.

[19] P.D. Stracey, *Wild Life in India: Its Conservation and Control* (Dehradun: GoI, 1963), 6.
[20] Shoshee Chunder Dutt [Pseud. Horatio Bickerstaff Rowney], *The Wild Tribes of India* (London: Thos. de la Rue, 1882), 5.
[21] R.S.R. Fitter and P. Scott, *The Penitent Butchers: The Fauna Preservation Society 1903–1978* (London: Collins, 1978).

And 1973 is also when Project Tiger, India's best-known attempt to save the Bengal tiger came into existence. Besides presumably saving the tiger and many other wildlife species from the brink of extinction, late twentieth-century India's hunting ban and conservation efforts disrupted longstanding traditions of hunting (or *shikar*) for both sport and subsistence. Although few now mourn the extinction of sport hunting in India besides a few sportsmen themselves, the hunting ban is more controversial where it impacts traditional wildlife-based livelihood systems of indigenous peoples.

Though advocates of Adivasi communities today rarely go so far as arguing for the restoration of hunting rights, there has been some notable scholarly work in this direction.[22] The theory behind such proposals is that controlled hunting, based on strict conservationist principles, might work to restore a lost sense of identity, as well as a stake in conservation efforts that allow for a sustainable rate of harvest. However, at present, the Indian state has insufficient capacity to oversee and enforce what would necessarily be a detailed and risky set of game laws, and furthermore, the political will to make such a change is virtually non-existent. Overkill could drag India's wildlife back into its pre-1972 status, or worse.

One major step towards advancing this book's claims about the parallels between the history of conservation of biological and cultural diversity in India, the chapter at hand focuses on the move from extermination to conservation, not of tribes, but of tigers and other non-human species, while also emphasizing the continuity of discourses linking wildlife decline with the fading away of forest societies. By mapping the contours of historical human impact on wildlife through hunting, through to the beginnings of carnivore conservation in India, we will see that colonial attitudes and approaches towards wildlife populations often followed those first addressed towards 'tribal' populations.[23] From early campaigns of

---

[22] See M.D. Madhusudan and K. Ullas Karanth, 'Hunting for an Answer: Is Local Hunting Compatible with Large Mammal Conservation in India?' in *Hunting for Sustainability in Tropical Forests*, ed. John Robinson and Elizabeth Bennett (New York: Columbia University Press, 2000).

[23] In the US context, commentators 'used the trope of the last Indian to help them cope with species extinction' and 'assigned to the last living representatives of a species the qualities associated with the sole survivors of a tribe'. Miles Powell, *Vanishing America: Species Extinction, Racial Peril, and the Origins of Conservation* (Cambridge: Harvard University Press, 2016), 120.

eradication and attempts to tame the wild, ultimately, there came the perception that forest dwellers of all kinds were endangered. This widespread attitude reversal now means that popular culture seeks to conserve all those things the modern experience has endangered.

## Hunting to Extinction

Despite the proliferation of historical accounts of hunting in colonial India, the quantitative impact of this 'sport' still remains an understudied subject. To date, little historical research exists either to confirm or deny that overkill was a main reason for wildlife's decline, and apparently, there is some doubt as to the argument. As an eminent South Asian wildlife historian once mused, 'The disappearance of free-ranging wildlife could simply have been a by-product of the expansion of agriculture. Greater mobility and better weapons for the hunter may have been incidental to the decline of the Bengal tiger (*Panthera tigris tigris*)'.[24] Although, globally, hunting has been found to be the second most common cause of mammal extinctions after habitat loss, accounting for 33.9% of all recorded threats (vs. 46.6% for habitat loss), it has not yet been adequately demonstrated that hunting was a major cause of endangerment or extinction for any large mammal population in colonial India.[25] In one review of 143 studies related to hunting in India, it was found that only 5.6% quantified the impact of hunting. Thus, numerous scholars have called for 'more and better' quantitative studies on hunting in India.[26]

---

[24] Mahesh Rangarajan, 'The Raj and the Natural World: The War Against "Dangerous Beasts" in Colonial India', *Studies in History* 14, no. 2 (Jul–Dec 1998). This was an early exploratory work of Rangarajan's, and so should not be taken as his definitive argument.
[25] Samantha A. Price and John L. Gittleman, 'Hunting to Extinction: Biology and Regional Economy Influence Extinction Risk and the Impact of Hunting in Artiodactyls', *Proceedings of the Royal Society B* 274 (2007): 1845–1851; G.M. Mace and A. Balmford, 'Patterns and Processes in Contemporary Mammalian Extinction', in A. Entwistle and N. Dunstone, eds, *Priorities for the Conservation of Mammalian Diversity: Has the Panda Had Its Day?* (Cambridge: Cambridge University Press, 2000), 28–52.
[26] Nandini Velho, Krithi K. Karanth, and William F. Laurance, 'Hunting: A Serious and Understudied Threat in India, a Globally Significant Conservation Region', *Biological Conservation* 148 (2012): 210–215; Thomas L. Altherr and John F. Reiger, 'Academic Historians and Hunting: A Call for More and Better Scholarship', *Environmental History Review* 19, no. 3 (1995): 39–56.

Yet, in nearly every case where mammal species considered 'game' or 'vermin' in colonial India went locally or entirely extinct, there exists documentation that the last individuals of that species were shot dead by hunters. We know this because sportsmen left proud records claiming the slaughter of the last specimens of many species to posterity. Such claims cannot always be taken at face value, but if there were contradictory claims, it is usually easy enough to resolve which is correct. For example, the 1908 *Central Provinces Gazetteer* reports that in central India, 'Lions have long been extinct, but it is recorded that a specimen was shot in Saugor in 1851'.[27] However, there is evidence that lions were shot in central India until at least the 1870s. Montague Gerard records:

> Besides four other tigers bagged in the course of two or three days' leave from cantonments, the last Central Indian lion was shot at Cheen Hill, 9 miles from Goona on Waterloo Day, 1872. Though we had frequent reports of one having been seen about—up to six or eight had occasionally been shot in a single season a few years previously—we beat on the day in question in expectation of a tiger. Towards the conclusion of the drive, I got a glimpse of what from its colour I fancied to be a *sambhur*, though it appeared to glide along more smoothly than a deer usually walks. The next moment, as its head appeared from behind the rock, I saw a fine lion with, despite its being the end of the hot weather, a very fair mane. Though he measured the same as an average tiger, he gave one the impression of being comparatively harmless, and fell to the first shot. Length, 9 feet 4 inches, of which the tail was 2 feet 11 inches, girth, 48 inches, round neck, 32 inches.[28]

I include such descriptions here in full in order to show that the authors express not an ounce of regret in the destruction of the last lion in central India. Rather, Gerard shows some degree of pride in his recounting the lion's size and how it was felled with 'the first shot'.

In Rajasthan, specifically in Mount Abu, lions were rumoured to still roam as late as 1891, but there is only positive evidence of them, by way of

---

[27] R.V. Russell, *Central Provinces Gazetteer: Imperial Gazetteer of India*, vol. 10 (Calcutta: Government Printing, 1908), 10.
[28] Gerard, *Leaves from the Diaries of a Soldier and Sportsman*, 133.

record of them being shot, until 1872.[29] Lt Col. Archibald Adams records of Rajputana:

> The lion (*Felis leo*) has now become extinct in these States, no specimen having been shot in either Marwar or Sirohi for nearly thirty years. In 1872 the Bhil Shikari of Mr. T. W. Miles brought in the skin of a full-grown Asiatic lioness which he had shot on the Anadra side of Mount Abu, and about the same year Colonel Hayland bagged four of the species near Jaswantpura, in Marwar. These were the last lions seen over the Kutch border of Marwar, and the Abu lioness was the last met with in Sirohi territory.[30]

In other areas, the lion went extinct even earlier. In the 1820s, in what is today Haryana and Punjab, wildlife historian Divyabhanusinh observes that, 'William Fraser shot 84 lions, "being personally responsible for their extinction in the area".[31]

Even in Gir (which is today the last bastion of the Asiatic lion in the world), the species was hunted down to its last few members around the turn of the twentieth century—some estimates put the number of surviving lions at the time of the species' bottleneck as low as ten, but more likely the lion population was reduced to some twenty or thirty individuals. Thanks to timely efforts started by Nawab Rasulkhanji in the mid-1890s, lions just managed to pull back from the brink of extinction. As Gerard pointed out in 1899, Indian lions 'would nowadays be quite extinct' except that they are 'to some extent preserved' in Gir. The question is why the Nawab made this effort to protect the lion. Divyabhanusinh has suggested that Rasulkhanji's conservation efforts 'were arguably the earliest in the Indian Empire for protecting a species for its own sake'. However, he then also goes on to argue that this was 'a strategy for conservation in order to ensure the survival of those hunted', i.e. lions were protected so that they could continue to be hunted.[32]

---

[29] K.D. Erskine, *Rajputana Gazetteer: Imperial Gazetteer of India*, vol. 18 (Calcutta: Government Printing, 1908), 10.
[30] Archibald Adams, *The Western Rajputana States: A Medico-Topographic and General Account of Marwar Sirohi and Jaisalmir* (London: Junior Army & Navy Stores, 1899), 163.
[31] Divyabhanusinh, *The Story of Asia's Lions* (Mumbai: Marg Publications, 2005), 122.
[32] Divyabhanusinh, 'Junagadh State and Its Lions: Conservation in Princely India, 1879–1947', *Conservation and Society* 4, no. 4 (2006): 522–540.

The interests of sport and conservation clearly conflicted in Gir (though some might say that they coincided, in that sport was the reason that lions were protected), and so one colonial officer observed that 'at no time the preservation of the lions strictly was carried out'. One of the most effective ways to continue to protect elite sporting interests while simultaneously keeping the lion population alive was to enforce hunting regulations along race and class lines. Thus, Viceroy Curzon expressed anxieties typical of his day and class, worrying 'that this noble race [the Asiatic lion] will be extinguished by the hands of common people'.[33] While most common folk were stopped from hunting lions before the turn of the twentieth century, British Viceroys and other elites continued to shoot in Gir until Lord Linlithgow's last lion hunt there in 1942, and *shikar* remained a princely prerogative until at least the mid-1950s. Still, the rise of conservation grounded in elite big game hunting interests allowed the Asiatic lion to survive the mid-twentieth century.

Cheetahs and two species of rhinoceros in India were not as fortunate. By the early twentieth century, the Indian Rhinoceros became extremely endangered, and two of its cousins, the Sumatran and Javan rhinos, went locally extinct in India. Conservationists today appear unanimous in condemning overkill via hunting starting in the nineteenth century as the major force reducing rhinoceros numbers to probably less than 200 by 1908 when Kaziranga, India's premier rhinoceros park, was first established as a reserve forest. Between 1871 and 1907, rewards were paid by the British government in Assam and Bengal for the destruction of rhinos because of the amount of damage they did to rapidly expanding agriculture. The major pressure on the species, though, came through hunting by Indian royalty and British sportsmen. During this period, the Maharaja of Cooch Behar claimed to have personally shot 207 rhinos, 'almost single-handedly sending the Greater One-Horned Rhinoceros to its doom' (this according to Vivek Menon, one of India's foremost wildlife conservationists).[34]

---

[33] The information in this paragraph, including the quotations from Viceroy Curzon and Col. Fenton, was drawn from Divyabhanusinh, 'Junagadh State and Its Lions'.

[34] Maharajah of Cooch Behar, *Thirty-Seven Years of Big Game Shooting* (Bombay: Times Press, 1908), 449. He claims to have 365 tigers, 311 leopards, 207 rhino, 438 buffaloes, 318 barasingha, among others, 'at a time when these species were being protected'. Also see Vivek Menon, *Under Siege: Poaching and Protection of Greater One-Horned Rhinoceroses in India* (Cambridge: TRAFFIC International, 1996), 11.

The first official ban on rhino hunting in eastern India was put in place in 1910, and Kaziranga was declared a game reserve in 1916. Rhinoceros hunting, however, continued in Nepal. The year following the ban in India, King George, during his Imperial Visit to Nepal in December of 1911, shot eighteen rhinos in ten days.[35] The Maharaja of Nepal continued hunting, and it is reported that between 1933 and 1940, he and his guests shot 53 rhinos. Further contributing to rhinoceros decline was endemic poaching in India. Already in 1936, the value of a rhinoceros horn was over 1,000 rupees and rising.[36]

The Asiatic cheetah, today extinct in South Asia (and surviving only in Iran), was set decisively on that path under British rule. By the end of the nineteenth century, the cheetah was disappearing across most of India. Partly, the problem was that it—like other species—was targeted specifically for its rarity. In 1887, a 'sportsman' who came across a female cheetah and her four cubs near Chhindwara, and then dispatched them with his dogs, recorded, 'It was a pretty sight, and I would have let them off scot free, but that these animals are comparatively rare in Central Provinces, and few there are, are seldom seen on account of the heaviness of the jungle'. By the 1920s, Dunbar Brander believed that 'the number of cheetah now found in the Central Province is a negligible quantity'. And by 1939, Pocock felt that the cheetah was 'now almost, if not quite, extinct in Hindustan'. Then in 1947, on the eve of Independence, the Maharaja of Korea shot the last verified cheetahs in India. Having done so, he boastingly submitted a description of the 'hunt' to the *Journal of the Bombay Natural History Society*. The journal published the account as it said, not to pander to the Maharaja's ego, but to impeach his actions.[37]

---

[35] Edgar Barclay, *Big Game Shooting Records* (London: Witherby, 1932). King George also shot 4 bear, 1 barking deer, and 39 tigers during those ten days of hunting.

[36] British Library, India Office Records (IOR) V/27/460/10, 'Proceedings of the All-India Conference for the Preservation of Wildlife' (28–30 Jan 1935) (Delhi: GoI Press, 1936); British Library, India Office Library (IOL) Mss Eur E267/20, 20b, 'Preservation of the fauna of the empire', M. Hailey to M. Seton, 6 Aug 1934. Hailey put the value of a rhino horn as high as £75.

[37] F.C. Hicks, *Forty Years Among the Wild Animals of India from Mysore to the Himalayas* (Allahabad: The Pioneer Press, 1910), 201–203. A.A. Dunbar Brander, *Wild Animals in Central India* (London: Edward Arnold, 1923), 236. R.I. Pocock, *Fauna of British India: Including Ceylon and Burma*, vol. 1 (London: Taylor & Francis, 1939), 236. E. van Ingen and van Ingen, 'Interesting Shikar Trophies: Hunting Cheetah *Acinonyx jubatus* (Schreber)', *Journal of the Bombay Natural History Society* 47, no. 4 (1948): 718–720. See Divyabhanusinh, *The End of a Trail: The Cheetah in India*, 2nd ed. (Delhi: Oxford University Press, 2002), 90–101.

## Over-Collecting

Although several contemporary scientific papers have concluded that incidents of inappropriate specimen collection are today rare, few scholars have examined the problematic history of scientific specimen collection.[38] Since this chapter considers the history of the transition from hunting to conservation, it is worthwhile observing here that supposedly scientific collecting at the end of the nineteenth century was not always well-aligned with conservation. It is often difficult to tell if the interests of sport, science, or conservation were put first in this period, but if I had to hazard a guess, I would say these interests were typically ranked in roughly that order. Problematically, scientific collectors in the nineteenth and early twentieth century specifically valued rarity. The rarer the species, the more desirable it was for museum collections. The idea that collectors would specifically seek out and kill the most endangered species they could, in order to 'preserve' them—stuffed and under glass—in museums, must strike readers as somewhat counterintuitive, at least by today's standards.

It was a paradox that at least a few collectors themselves saw. William Hornaday, for instance, who is perhaps most famous for his eventual campaign to save the American Bison from extinction in the early twentieth century, first began his involvement with bison 'preservation' as a taxidermist for the Smithsonian Museum in Washington, DC. After organizing a hunting trip for the museum, Hornaday later wrote of his experience: 'I am really ashamed to confess it, but we have been guilty of killing buffalo in the year of our Lord 1886… Under different circumstances nothing could have induced me to engage in such a mean, cruel, and utterly heartless enterprise as the hunting down of the last representatives of a vanishing race'. Repeatedly mixing the language of race and species, as well as warfare and hunting, Hornaday was deeply critical of how the bison

---

[38] Brian Henen, 'Do Scientific Collecting and Conservation Conflict?' *Herpetological Conservation and Biology* 11, no.1 (2016):13–18; David A. Norton et al., 'Over-Collecting: An Overlooked Factor in the Decline of Plant Taxa', *Taxon* 43, no. 2 (May 1994): 181–185; J.V. Remsen, 'The Importance of Continued Collecting of Bird Specimens to Ornithology and Bird Conservation', *Bird Conservation International* 5, no. 2–3 (1995): 146–180; Greg R. Pohl, 'Why We Kill Bugs—The Case for Collecting Insects', *Ontario Lepidoptera* 7 (2008): 7–15.

was brought to the brink of extinction, bemoaning: 'Could any war of extermination be more complete or far-reaching in its results!' Yet the 1886 hunting expedition was initiated by Hornaday himself. Fearing that the buffalo population was nearing extinction, Hornaday was also deeply concerned that 'the Smithsonian collections contained only a modest, motley assortment of old bison skins, skeletons, and mounted heads'. But the expedition Hornaday organized went well beyond just collecting specimens for the Smithsonian. In all, the goal was to collect up to 100 bison 'specimens', enough to supply numerous smaller museums around the United States.[39]

Given the mythos of the 'Vanishing American' (discussed in Chapter 2), as well as the US experience with the near extinction of American bison and the extinction of the passenger pigeon, among others, it is unsurprising that the early twentieth-century American scientific community was far more fixated on the problems of endangerment and extinction, both of species and societies, than many of their counterparts in India. Thus, in the 1920s, the American Museum of Natural History in New York City decided to organize a major series of expeditions to India in order to collect specimens of all of India's most endangered, fast vanishing wildlife, before it disappeared forever. As the museum's magazine reported: 'To meet this emergency the American Museum has recently completed arrangements with Colonel Faunthorpe and Mr. Arthur Vernay to secure for the new Asiatic hall some of these fine animals of southern Asia before they disappear'.[40]

From the museum's archive, Faunthorpe and Vernay come across as keen British sportsmen looking for prestige and adventure in India. Whether they truly held their American friends' concern for vanishing wildlife or were merely paying lip service to it, is less clear. Playing perfectly into the Americans' concern about endangerment, Faunthorpe

---

[39] The information in this paragraph was drawn from Mark Barrow, *Nature's Ghosts* (Chicago: University of Chicago Press, 2009), 109. For the original quotations, see William T. Hornaday, *The Extermination of the American Bison* (Washington: Government Printing Office, 1889); William T. Hornaday, 'The Passing of the Buffalo', *Cosmopolitan* 4 (1887): 85–98, 231–43.

[40] Henry F. Osborn and Harold E. Anthony, 'Vanishing Wild Life of Southern Asia', *Natural History: The Journal of the American Museum of Natural History* 22, no. 5 (Sep–Oct 1922): 402–403.

wrote to the museum director, Henry Osborn, about the urgency of their mission:

> If you wish to obtain a representative collection of the wild animals of the plains of India... I would urge that there is no time to lose. Owing to changed conditions in India, conditions which are likely to persist, game is, in many places, decreasing to the point of extinction, and it is probable that within a short period there will be very little left.... It is essential, therefore, that the collection should be made as soon as possible.[41]

As evidence of the fact that the duo very well understood their audience at the museum, it seems that Faunthorpe intentionally exaggerated the rareness of the *gaur*, or Indian Bison, in his letters to the Osborn. It is possible that he did this in order to emphasize the value of his expeditions and collections, and perhaps even to aggrandize them. In January 1923, Faunthorpe wrote: 'I think we shall have to give up the idea of obtaining the Indian Buffalo this year. These animals were almost exterminated (by rinderpest [plague]) in the Central Provinces, where they were formerly fairly plentiful, in the famine of 1896–7. They are now extremely rare in the Central Provinces and are to be found there only in very remote and unhealthy localities'.[42] Then again in May that year, he described the *gaur* as having been 'indiscriminately slaughtered by so-called sportsmen who were attracted by their rarity'. Blaming the Indian government for stepping up protection measures 'almost too late', he reported that 'Their number is now so small that another rinderpest outbreak or a slackening of forest rules, or a few poachers, might easily make the species extinct'. It was therefore 'important that the Museum should obtain good specimens of this fine animal at as early a date as possible'.[43] In contrast, numerous big game hunting texts from the same period and same region (i.e. the 1920s in the Central Provinces) are nowhere near as drastic about the status of the *guar*. Some praised increased preservation measures, but

---

[41] American Museum of Natural History (AMNH), Faunthorpe-Vernay Expedition Archive, Folder July 1922: Faunthorpe to Osborn 16 Jul 1922.
[42] AMNH, Faunthorpe-Vernay Expedition Archive, Folder January 1923: Faunthorpe to Osborn 12 Jan 1923.
[43] AMNH, Faunthorpe-Vernay Expedition Archive, Folder May–Jun 1923: Faunthorpe to Osborn.

none suggested that the *gaur* was on the verge of the extinction, even locally.[44] This exaggeration, of course, makes sense not only in the context of the near extinction of the American Bison, but specifically because characters like William Hornaday who had been so involved with saving the species, were also directly involved with the New York museum. In all likelihood, the real reason Faunthorpe failed to secure a *gaur* in 1923 was he could not be bothered to make the long journey down to the Central Provinces, preferring to secure one in Assam later in the expedition.[45]

One particularly prized specimen for the Vernay-Faunthorpe expedition would be an Asiatic Lion from the Gir forest. Apparently, in the United States, even some experts at the American Natural History Museum believed that the Asiatic lion 'might be actually extinct', bemoaned that 'there is not a specimen in this country [the USA]', and so laid 'great stress on the importance of endeavoring to get an example of the Indian Lion' into American hands.[46] It was an endeavour that would last almost a decade; after years of petitioning and exhausting every diplomatic channel available to him, Faunthorpe would finally secure permission from the Nawab of Junagadh to bag a lion in Gir in 1928.[47]

In order to get permission to hunt all of the specimens they believed they needed, especially an Asiatic lion specimen, Faunthorpe had his hopes on receiving a letter from the US president, stating that he was put on special duty to go hunting.[48] Faunthorpe specified: 'In the letter a request should be made that His Excellency, the Viceroy of India may be asked to grant special facilities to the Expedition in the way of granting shooting passes in the reserved forests and authorising the shooting of the required number of females and young of the deer tribe and others which are protected under the game law'.[49] When neither the president

---

[44] See for instance Silver Hackle [pseud.], *Indian Jungle Lore and the Rifle. Being Notes on Shikar and Wild Animal Life* (Calcutta: Thacker, 1929), 155 and W.W. Baillie, *Days and Nights of Shikar* (London: J. Lane, 1921), 70.

[45] AMNH, Faunthorpe-Vernay Expedition Archive, Folder May–Jun 1923.

[46] AMNH, Faunthorpe-Vernay Expedition Archive, Folder Aug 1922: Dr. Sanford & TA Lucas.

[47] AMNH, Faunthorpe-Vernay Expedition Archive, Folder Nov 1922: 'I find that the viceroy, even has not sufficient power to order one to be shot'. As for tiger 'Will get several and more than needed for the museum'.

[48] AMNH, [Central Archive Box 1077.8] 1921–1924, Faunthorpe-Vernay Expedition Archive, Folder Jul 1922: Faunthorpe to Osborn. 'A request from the President of the U.S.A. would receive careful attention', he wrote.

[49] AMNH, Faunthorpe-Vernay Expedition Archive, Folder Jul 1922: Faunthorpe to Osborn.

nor the governor of New York was forthcoming, eventually the museum managed to secure a letter from Secretary of State Charles Hughes.

Despite the clear emphasis on the quest to obtain all the rarest species on the brink of extinct for the museum, in a footnote to his article 'Can We Save the Mammals?' the museum president, Henry Fairfield Osborn, attempted to argue that such specimen collecting did not contribute to the extinction of these species:

> To meet the criticism which may possibly be made, namely, that museums themselves are contributing to the extermination of rare mammals, we would state that the American Museum does not sanction wholesale collecting of disappearing species. It is obvious to all that a natural history museum should be a repository of the actual facts of nature, notably the skins and skeletons of animals, and should some interesting mammal disappear from the face of the earth before such a permanent concrete record of it could be prepared and stored up for posterity, museums would have indeed been derelict in their duty.

Osborn's comment, 'that the American Museum does not sanction wholesale collecting of disappearing species' seems somewhat intellectually dishonest, however, considering that time and again in the Vernay-Faunthorpe archive, the object of their expeditions was stated to be exactly that: the collection of the last remaining specimens of 'disappearing species', whether wholesale or not. In the very same article, the president spoke of the urgency of museum collection in the face of the impending extinction crisis:

> In many parts of the world, in Australia, in northern and southern Asia and in North and South America, American Museum explorers are especially charged with the great mission of securing single specimens of these fast vanishing remnants of the Age of Mammals before it is too late. Many of the specimens which the Third Asiatic Expedition has secured will be among the last of their kind to find their way to the great museums of the world, because Mr. Roy Chapman Andrews, the leader of the expedition, has observed that their numbers are limited and that they are in near danger of extinction.[50]

---

[50] Henry F. Osborn and Harold E. Anthony, 'Can We Save the Mammals?', *Natural History: The Journal of the American Museum of Natural History* 22, no. 5 (Sep–Oct 1922): 389. Noteworthy

Another example of a species specifically targeted for its rarity, and quite possibly hunted to extinction in the period of the Vernay-Faunthorpe expedition, was the pink-headed duck (*Rhodonessa caryophyllacea*). Pink-headed ducks used to live along the Ganges, but are most likely now extinct. The last confirmed sighting of one of these ducks in the wild was in June 1935 when a hunting dog retrieved one that the naturalist Charles Inglis had shot. Yet in the 1920s, the AMNH declared it 'a disideratum of the expedition' and outlined plans to hunt and taxidermy them precisely because of their rarity.[51] Yet, rather than horror at the prospects of a hunting expedition targeting a critically endangered species, Osborn wrote to Faunthorpe that the 'capture of the pinkheaded duck with the herd of big elephants struck the American sense of humor very strongly and gave nation-wide publicity to your expedition'.[52]

As far as birds are concerned, the feather trade had long been seen as the most destructive force facing tropical avian populations, with groups like the Plumage League (now called the Royal Society for the Preservation of Birds) formed in the United Kingdom in 1889, and the Audubon Society established in Massachusetts in 1896. But scientific collecting, too, had its impact. An excellent example of an extremely endangered bird species, potentially on the brink of extinction, being nearly wiped out by an ornithologist on the very day of its scientific 'discovery' comes from Allan Octavian Hume in 1880, with his hunt for the Manipur Bush Quail (*Perdicula manipurensis*). Hume, who is at least as famous for being the founder of the Indian National Congress as he is for being one of colonial India's most prolific ornithologists, gets credit for discovering the species, but there was one 'wretched' unidentified skin in the British Museum from Bhutan many years before that. It was not known who shot it, and the locality was also not well established. Hume's encounter with the Manipur Bush Quail is worth quoting at length because it is so revealing of the attitudes of his day:

> Once, and only once, did I meet with this species, and that was near the bases of the hills in the south eastern portion of the Manipur Plain. There

---

here is the reference to the end of the Age of Mammals and the beginning of the Age of Man, antedating contemporary declarations of the rise of the Anthropocene Era by some 100 years.

[51] Today, the AMNH possesses a collection of roughly a dozen pink-headed duck specimens, all collected in the 1920s and 1930s.

[52] AMNH, Faunthorpe-Vernay Expedition Archive, Folder Dec 1922.

> were two coveys—one of six and the other of five—feeding in the very early morning in a tiny patch of ground a few yards square, thickly covered with large tufts of freshly springing elephant grass.... I did not see the birds myself, as I was a few yards to the right, but two of my people, on whom I could rely, saw them distinctly as they ran into the high grass.

His men described it as being of an unknown kind, and so Hume desperately wanted a specimen of this bird. But it seemed hopeless, given the long grass, as they had no elephants and no dogs. So, Hume made his entire contingent wait for two hours. When the birds didn't reappear, he eventually tried to burn the tall grass, but to no avail. He wasted another hour that way, and eventually had to abandon the attempt. Hume continues:

> Naturally I was not going to move until I did get a specimen, so my whole camp, soldiers and sailors (we had a lot of boatmen), camp followers, and all the inhabitants of the village were turned out.... Although we had fully one hundred men working with their heavy hatchet-swords (*dahs*, as the Burmese call them)... it was some hours before we had got the ground into shape, and fully three o'clock before the beating commenced. At dusk, by dint of our united endeavours, I had knocked over six, of which we had failed to retrieve one. The first bird had convinced me that the species was new to me, and what still more surprised me was that the villagers one and all denied having ever previously seen the bird. We were one and all exhausted... But I had been very lucky. I had dropped every bird that rose, some of them very difficult shots. They had risen singly and at long intervals.
>
> Next day I let every one have a long sleep, a good breakfast and a good smoke, and by 10 am, we were again in the grass. By three o'clock I had knocked down five more, of which, however, we failed to find one. After that we saw no more, and I fully believed that these were only the two coveys of six and five respectively seen and counted by my people. I have had many hard days' shooting in my life, but never any harder than these two.[53]

---

[53] A.O. Hume, 'Perdicula Manipurensis, Sp. Nov', *Stray Feathers* 9 (1880): 467–471.

In the name of science, not only did Hume pursue these birds until every last one he could find was shot dead, but he also destroyed their entire habitat in the process. Hume not only personally discovered this species of birds, but may have also brought them to the brink of extinction. Thought to be extinct for more than eighty years, this species was only recently rediscovered by experts working in Manipur in 2006.[54] Like in the famous case of the Forest Owlet and other Lazarus taxa in India, this rediscovery and ones like it are beams of light and hope in a dark and looming sky of extinctions. Still, Hume, late Victorian India's most famous ornithologist, was never particularly concerned with the problems of rarity, endangerment, or extinction.[55]

## Impact on the Tiger

The tiger is one of the few South Asian wildlife species for which there exists a considerable amount of primary source material from the colonial era describing the causes, circumstances, and consequences of its decline. It is also perhaps the only South Asian species, besides the lion, for which we have historical estimates of its population size dating back at least one hundred years. E.P. Gee's 1964 estimate that there were 40,000 tigers in India circa 1900 has been taken as axiomatic by much of the conservation community. However, asked by Sankhala what the basis for this estimate was, Gee replied: 'Some estimate is better than none, and it should hold good until it is improved'.[56] Sankhala's inquiry as to the basis of Gee's figures raises the crucial point that we may never be able to precisely determine the actual sizes of past wildlife populations. By 1947, Jim Corbett, in conversation with Viceroy Wavell, estimated that the tiger population in India was 3,000 to 4,000, or less than 10% of the 1900 population. On hearing this, Wavell wrote in his journal that he was, 'rather

---

[54] BirdLife International, '*Perdicula manipurensis* (amended version of 2016 assessment)', *IUCN Red List of Threatened Species 2017*. https://dx.doi.org/10.2305/IUCN.UK.2017-1.RLTS.T22679012A112384972.en

[55] Tring Natural History Museum, MSS Hume. In Hume's 9-volume diary in the Tring Archive, he nearly never discusses the problem of extinction. Thanks to Alison Harding, Ornithology Librarian, and Robert Prys-Jones, head of the Bird Group at the Natural History Museum, for guiding me through the Tring collections.

[56] Kailash Sankhala, *Tiger! The Story of the Indian Tiger* (Delhi: Rupa, 1978), 177.

surprised at the smallness of this estimate'.[57] In 1964 Gee then also estimated that there were only 4,000 tigers alive in India. This figure could well have been accurate, because in 1972, an official census found positive evidence of fewer than 1,900 tigers in the land.[58]

Some of the records for most tigers killed include the Maharaja of Surguja who by most accounts shot 1,150 tigers, villagers of a town called Jattygaon who were said to have killed 1,053 tigers for rewards paid by the British between 1821 and 1828, and an Englishman named George Palmer who reportedly hunted over 1000 'Royal Bengals' between 1832 and 1862. Adding together all of the tigers killed by hunters who publicly claimed large bags between the mid-nineteenth and mid-twentieth centuries, this gives us a tally of tens of thousands of tigers killed (see Appendix 3.1).

As a class, India's Maharajas hold the majority of records for most tigers killed. Yet Maharajas seldom hunted alone. With hundreds, sometimes thousands, of beaters (employees used to drive the hunted creatures to the sportsmen to kill) closing in on a single tiger, the 'Royal Hunt' writ large was often less concerned with sportsmanship, and more with the pomp and circumstance of the undertaking. Major W.T. Johnson described one particularly unsporting episode while out hunting with the Maharaja of Baroda, 'with all his retinue of elephants and horses' and 'about three thousand beaters' as the Raja 'sits on one the elephants with a silk umbrella, eating betul-nuts'. Writing that he 'was so glad when the poor deer escaped' that he once forgot himself 'and halloa'd out "hurrah" when a poor hare, with about five hundred people of every description after it, with dogs, etc., escaped unhurt, much to other disgust of the Maharajah' (see Figure 3.2).[59]

Maharajas often entertained Viceroys and other elite guests, and every sort of precaution was taken, not only to protect the gentleman *shikari*, but also to ensure that he got his bag. As James Best tells us, tigers shot by elites were 'popularly known as "Viceroy's tigers"; beasts that have been

---

[57] D.C. Kala, *Jim Corbett of Kumaon* (Delhi: Ravi Dayal, 1979), 67. Mahesh Rangarajan also believes this to be a low estimate. (Pers. comm.)

[58] Sankhala, *Tiger!*, 177; Karan Singh and Indian Board for Wild Life, *Project Tiger: A Planning Proposal for Preservation of Tiger (Panthera tigris tigris Linn.) in India* (New Delhi: Government of India, Ministry of Agriculture, 1972).

[59] W.T. Johnson, *Twelve Years of a Soldier's Life* (London: A.D. Innes, 1897), 21.

**Figure 3.2.** Typical odds.
Public domain. Source: Bernard C. Ellison, *H R H the Prince of Wales's Sport in India* (London: William Heinemann, 1925), 29.

driven over time-honoured ground to a place where they are certain to come out for the brass hat to massacre'.[60] Godden and Godden record: 'If an important guest is invited to shoot he should see, if not shoot a tiger. To make sure he does, the kill to which the tiger returns, and the drinking holes, may be doctored with opium. Tigers can become opium addicts'.[61] British sportsmen often criticized India's Rajas for being overly destructive towards game and for lacking a British sense of fair play, yet they also sometimes criticized their own elite. In a move vaguely reminiscent of Dadabhai Naroji's *Poverty and un-British rule in India,* Matt Cartmill remarks how when the Prince of Wales in 1876 flushed out a cornered tiger by pelting it with used mineral-water bottles, this must have been viewed

---

[60] Matt Cartmill, *A View to a Death in the Morning: Hunting and Nature Through History* (London: Harvard University Press, 1993), 136. J.W. Best, *Forest Life in India* (London: John Murray, 1935).
[61] Jon and Rumer Godden, *Shiva's Pigeons: An Experience of India* (New York: Knopf, 1972).

as 'un-British' by many serious sportsmen. Still, even while criticizing, most of these same sportsmen were eagerly competing with each other to hunt with the 'princes' and to enjoy their hospitality. Tigers were highly valued prizes for Indian royalty to bestow on visiting dignitaries, and as the species became increasingly scarce, vigorous steps were taken to ensure a bag. As one shikari recorded as late as 1963:

> If you want to be dead certain of bagging your tiger, domesticate him first! When the tiger makes a kill, let him go and give him another one after three or four days, and go on in this manner until five or six baits have been consumed. When the tiger gets easy food and becomes lethargic eating more than it requires, it will remain in the area and become careless.[62]

Another author records, 'Native chiefs are beginning to realise that to "cement friendship" with any great man who has the power to do them good or evil a tiger is a very valuable asset. Chiefs have been known even to trap and purchase tigers for a "State Function".'[63] For royalty to go to such lengths to impress an important guest shows precisely how valuable tigers were to those rulers. Such anecdotes also hint at how far reduced the tiger population had become, so as to necessitate such duplicitous measures.

Still, most early wildlife conservationists maintained that the elite hunt was acceptable until hunting in India was banned entirely in 1972. Even in 1961, many public figures, including conservationists, considered it *de rigueur* that Queen Elizabeth and the Duke of Edinburgh should go tiger hunting in Rajasthan and Nepal.[64] As one commentator wrote:

> Some people in England started an agitation that the Queen should not shoot a tiger in India and a few individuals in India also joined hands with them in order to come into the limelight. Whenever I read these reports I used to laugh at the ignorance of those agitators who, I believe,

---

[62] Khan Saheb Jamshed Butt, *Shikar* (Bombay: Rusi Khambatta, 1963), 47.
[63] Felix [pseud.], *Recollections of a Bison & Tiger Hunter* (London, 1906), 47.
[64] British Film Institute, Newsreel Highlights of 1961 (UE61019), *Queen Elizabeth Visits Nepal in Time for a Massive Tiger Hunt*: 'Britain's Queen Elizabeth and Prince Philip, visiting Nepal, are guests of King Mahendra on a mammoth tiger hunt, in which 325 elephants take part in the round-up of the big cat'.

did so merely to show their intelligence and importance. There was nothing wrong in the Queen's accepting to shoot a tiger when the world knows that offering a tiger-shoot to a distinguished guest is traditionally a part of Indian hospitality. I am very glad that when this question was referred to Mr. E.P. Gee by the Fauna Preservation Society of London he replied, 'that the tiger is not a protected species in India, and that the shooting of a tiger by the Royal Party would be just the same as shooting a stag in Scotland, and therefore it should not be frowned upon'.[65]

## Vermin Eradication

Species targeted in the 'war on dangerous beasts' in British India included predators such as the tiger,[66] lion,[67] cheetah,[68] bear,[69] wolf,[70] wild dog,[71] and venomous snakes.[72] Rewards were also sometimes paid

---

[65] Kesri Singh, *Hints on Tiger Shooting* (Bombay: Jaico Publishing House, 1969), xiv.

[66] The Bengal Tiger (*Panthera tigris tigris*) is listed as 'Endangered' in the IUCN Red List. There are estimated to be approximately 3,000 tigers alive in India today, a number that represents well over half of the worldwide tiger population. Of eight traditionally classified subspecies of *Panthera tigris*, three have gone extinct since the 1940s. 'India tiger census shows rapid population growth', BBC, 29 Jul 2019. https://www.bbc.com/news/world-asia-india-49148174

[67] The Asiatic Lion (*Panthera leo persica*) is listed as 'Critically Endangered' by the IUCN Red List. Once ranging across central and western India, the only wild population is now located in and around Gir Forest National Park in Gujarat. There were approximately 674 individuals around Gir in 2020, roughly doubling from 327 in the year 2000. Mahesh Langa, 'Gujarat's pride grows as it now hosts 674 Gir lions', *The Hindu*, 11 Jun 2020. https://www.thehindu.com/sci-tech/energy-and-environment/gujarats-pride-grows-as-it-now-hosts-674-gir-lions/article31799404.ece

[68] The Asiatic Cheetah (*Acinonyx jubatus venaticus*) is extinct in India and is elsewhere listed as 'Critically Endangered' by the IUCN. It is believed that fewer than 100 individuals exist in Iran. M.S. Farhadinia, et al., 'Status of Asiatic cheetah in Iran: a country-scale assessment' (Tehran, Iran: Iranian Cheetah Society, 2014), 4. https://ptes.org/wp-content/uploads/2015/01/Iran-cheetah-population-final-report-fall-2014.pdf

[69] The Indian Sloth Bear (*Melursus ursinus*) is listed as 'Vulnerable' by the IUCN Red List.

[70] The Indian Wolf (*Canis lupus pallipes*) is listed as 'Critically Endangered' by the IUCN Red List. Today, most studies report approximately 2,000–3,000 wolves in India. Monit Khanna, 'With Less Than 3,000 Alive, Indian Wolf Is Most Endangered Wolf Species: Study', *India Times*, 4 Sep 2021. https://www.indiatimes.com/technology/science-and-future/indian-wolf-endangered-species-study-548691.html

[71] The *Dhole* or Asiatic Wild Dog (*Cuon alpinus*) is considered 'Endangered' by the IUCN Red List.

[72] The 'big four' venomous snakes in South Asia are the Indian cobra, *Naja naja*; the Common krait, *Bungarus caeruleus*; the Russell's viper, *Daboia russelii*; and the Saw-scaled viper, *Echis carinatu*.

EXTERMINATION TO CONSERVATION  129

Table 3.1. Number of 'Dangerous Wild Beasts' Killed Annually, 1875–1927

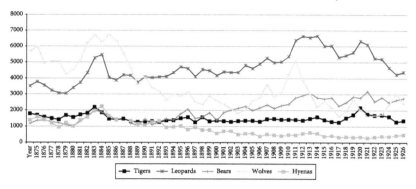

Table 3.2. Amount Paid Annually for the Extermination of 'Wild Beasts'

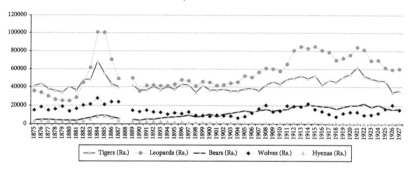

for the destruction of elephants. Mahesh Rangarajan has estimated the numbers of animals killed for reward in British India in the fifty years between 1875 and 1925, finding that, 'over 80,000 tigers, more than 150,000 leopards and 200,000 wolves were slaughtered'.[73] Previous to this, he also published that the number of tigers exterminated was about 65,000 in the same period.[74] In contrast, the records I have located, though roughly comparable to Rangarajan's estimates, indicate that 'precisely' 79,299 tigers, 248,738 leopards, 102,695 bears, 186,890 wolves, 43,968 hyenas, and at least 6,934,170 snakes were slaughtered for reward from 1875 to 1927. Tables 3.1–3.2 provide a pair of graphs depicting a

---

[73] Mahesh Rangarajan, *India's Wildlife History: An Introduction* (London: Permanent Black, 2001), 32.
[74] Rangarajan, 'The Raj and the Natural World'.

year-by-year breakdown of the number of animals killed and amount paid for reward by species in British India between 1875 and 1927, which I have collated from Government of India, Home Department, files located in the India Office Records, London, and the National Archives of India, Delhi.

Annually, one to two million rupees were spent paying for this scheme. Yet these figures represent only a fraction of the total number of animals killed. Rewards data were only collected in British India, i.e. roughly two-thirds of the area of the subcontinent at the empire's peak. In most cases, a reward required turning in the hide of the animal, and so if the hide could not be recovered, or if it was incomplete or damaged, no reward might be paid.[75] Furthermore, 'officials recorded *only* those cases where they paid out a sum of money. A delay in claiming the bounty [for instance] meant the killing went unrewarded and unrecorded'.[76]

Though not centrally regulated, rewards paying for the destruction of 'vermin' had been instituted in many districts already in the 1790s and had become standard practice across British territories by the middle of the nineteenth century. It was only in 1870, however, that these rewards were systematized across British India. The impetus for this systematization at the all-India level began in August of 1869 when Captain B. Rogers submitted a proposal to Lord Mayo, outlining a plan of using spring guns along forest paths to kill what he called 'noxious wild beasts'. The idea of rigging spring guns throughout the land was almost 'universally condemned... as dangerous to human beings and cattle'.[77] But the issue was brought up before a committee in the Government of India, where 'H.W. Freeland said that whether we agreed with Captain Rogers'

---

[75] This was largely enforced along class lines. It was reported in the Central Provinces, 'European and Native gentlemen are, as a matter of course, allowed to retain the skin of the animals they kill... On the other hand, as in the case of native shikaree, where there is a chance of the skins being fraudulently reproduced for the payment of the reward a second time, the district authorities are in the habit of taking possession of the skins'. National Archives of India (NAI), Home-Public (H(P)) A, September 1871, nos. 43–72.

[76] Rangarajan, *India's Wildlife History*, 32.

[77] SOAS, pamphlet CWML T71, Brudenell Rogers, 'The Destruction of Human Life and Property in India by Noxious Wild Animals' (London, 1873), 1, 14; also NAI, H(P) A, September

proposal or not, it must be admitted that he had done a good service in ventilating the subject'. Freeland, among others, also suggested 'that the best mode of getting rid of such animals was by the system of rewards'.[78] As quoted in the epigraph to this chapter, it was in this context that groups such as the National Indian Association now advocated in all earnestness that 'the Indian Government to adopt such measures as shall seem best for the extinction of the tiger tribe', writing that 'while India teems with objects worthy of the greatest preservation, tigers are certainly not one of them!'[79] And it was at this point that the bounty scheme for the destruction of predators was standardized across all of British India.

To understand the impetus for this systematic slaughter, it must be appreciated that the destruction of life and property by wild animals and poisonous snakes was perceived as an incessant scourge in colonial India. According to Home Department statistics, between the years 1882 to 1908, tigers alone killed over 900 people per year in British India. Adding the death toll from other wild animals as well, the number of dead averaged 2,725 per year. Adding snakes, over 24,100 persons per year were being killed. Perhaps indicative of escalating human–wildlife conflict, by the 1920s, the number of people killed annually by tigers increased to an average of 1,275. However, the number killed by other wild animals and snakes dropped slightly, so that 'only' about 22,500 people were being killed each year.[80] When the reward system for the destruction of these 'vermin' species was first instituted at the all-India level in 1870, policy makers believed it to be the most effective way of dealing with this

---

1871, nos. 43–72. One officer in the Central Provinces went so far as to say to Rogers suggestion: 'A short time since I would have scorned the idea of killing a tiger or other beast by stratagem, and would have felt the most supreme contempt for any English sportsman doing so ... I now look upon it in the light of a question involving the lives of hundreds of persons yearly, and ... as affecting the loss of cattle'.

[78] Rogers, 'The Destruction of Human Life', 18.

[79] W., 'Tigers', 442.

[80] NAI, H(P) 'Statement Showing the Results of the Measures Adopted in British India with the View of Exterminating Wild Animals and Venomous Snakes' (1882–1894); NAI, H(P) 'Number of Persons Killed in Each Province of British India by Wild Animals and Snakes' (1895–1927).

endangerment of human life and property.[81] Ironically, perhaps, it was also during 1869–1872 that the question of 'legislating for the protection of game animals' was considered by the Government of India for the first time, but it was decided 'that such legislation was neither necessary nor desirable.'[82] It was argued at that time that existing customs of 'tribal' populations were 'in themselves sufficiently restrictive and apt' for the preservation of 'game animals.'[83]

Rangarajan also argues that the declaration of 'war' on the subcontinent's 'dangerous beasts' during the colonial period was a European cultural export, and indeed he provides convincing evidence of the European origins of the British vermin eradication program.[84] As early as 1428, James I ordered his Barons to destroy not only wolves but also their pups. 'Seek quhelpes of Wolves and gar slay them', dictated a royal command.[85] Under the Tudors, the wolf had a close season for three months in the winter, but probably as early as 1500 CE, wolves were wiped out in England.[86] They persisted for a further two and a half centuries in the Scottish highlands and Ireland. One hunter in 1614 Ireland recorded that 'wolves and woodkernes were commonly bracketed together.'[87] (Relevantly, woodkernes were semi-nomadic outlaws of Ireland who were subjugated by the English military at this time.) Still grants were given to Englishmen to go to Ireland to destroy wolves as late as the seventeenth century, with rewards for their destruction going up to £6 depending on age and sex. Relatively early in terms of historical anthropogenic impacts on wildlife, in England, human presence caused the extinction of many species. The brown bear, hunted for meat and fur, disappeared around 900 CE. The beaver, hunted to extinction for its pelt, was last seen in Wales in 1188. In 1676, the last wild boar in England and Scotland was killed. Boar only managed to survive as long

---

[81] NAI, H(P) A, Sep 1871, nos. 43–72.
[82] NAI, H(P) A, Nov 1886, no. 34–61, 'Preservation of Game Birds and Animals in India', 1; see also NAI, R&A, Aug 1872, no. 5–11.
[83] NAI, H(P) A, Nov 1886, no. 34–61, 'Preservation of Game Birds and Animals in India', 26.
[84] Rangarajan, 'The Raj and the Natural World'.
[85] James Ritchie, *The Influence of Man on Animal Life in Scotland: A Study in Faunal Evolution* (Cambridge: Cambridge University Press, 1920), 117.
[86] Ibid., 120. Also see D. Evans, *History of Nature Conservation in Britain* (London: Routledge, 1992), 14–15.
[87] Eileen McCracken, *The Irish Woods since Tudor Times: Distribution and Exploitation* (Newton Abbot: David & Charles, 1971), 28–30.

as they did because for 400 years, their survival had been encouraged through a practice of providing them food during the winter.[88] And yet, somehow, the majority of scientific-minded Europeans continued to disbelieve in the concept of extinction of species until the nineteenth century.[89]

## The Preservation of Privilege

Before the mid-twentieth century paradigm shift towards carnivore conservation, there was conservation of a sort: the conservation of colonialism, and the preservation of privilege, by means of laws out of which contemporary wildlife conservation policies have grown. Efforts to guard elite sporting interests and ensure commercial forestry during the high noon of empire in India may have served as a form of wildlife conservation, but this was not the intent. The past politics of carnivore conservation are easily summarized as selfish attempts to protect sportsmen's pleasure. Here, I am to some extent responding to Richard Grove's argument in *Green Imperialism*, where he suggests that the intellectual legacy of 'environmentalism' can be traced as far back as seventeenth-century discourse on colonial forestry.[90] Grove accurately notes that a small minority of Europeans—scientific observers on isolated islands in the Indian Ocean, or Alexander von Humboldt on his travels through Latin America, for instance—worried about dwindling forests and occasionally species decline as early as the 1700s. However, in terms of popular sentiment, the wildlife conservation movement that included carnivores, and advocated for their protection due to fear of their extinction, emerged only in the mid to late twentieth century, and must be understood as a *volte-face* from earlier attitudes.

Before that 180-degree shift, elite efforts to guard their own sporting interests arguably had ecologically beneficial effects but were emphatically *not* a form of intentional carnivore conservation. Perhaps the best example of a game law in colonial India based on the preservation of privilege was

---

[88] Evans, *History of Nature Conservation*, 14–15.
[89] See Chapter 1 for the evolution of the extinction concept.
[90] Richard Grove, *Green Imperialism: Colonial Expansion, Tropical Island Edens, and the Origins of Environmentalism, 1600–1860* (Cambridge: Cambridge University Press, 1995).

Rule XIV of the 'Shikar Rules of Shimla Hill States'. The law made it a criminal offense for local Pahari people to hunt in their own homeland with a simple statement: 'Shooting in Dhami State near Ghanna-ki-Hatti is prohibited. All forests here are preserved for the use of His Excellency, the Viceroy'.[91] Rule XIV did not develop in a vacuum, however. Game laws in the colonies replicated those in England, where hunting for centuries had been the prerogative of the elite, and also found precedent in traditions of the Royal Hunt in India as preserved by the Maharajas.

With the reservation of hunting for the nobility and gentry came the criminalization of poaching, which bred much animosity among the lower orders. There was so much class-based animosity over poaching in England, that at least one historian has argued that the struggle over poaching was tantamount to warfare.[92] As G.M. Trevelyan wrote in his classic text *English Social History*, 'there was never a truce in the poaching war in old England'.[93] By the late medieval period, killing royal deer was a crime punishable by death. The infamous 'Black Act' of 1723 went so far as to make it a felony (read: a hanging offense) to appear in a park with your face painted black, a common method of disguise used by poachers in that period.[94] There was a widely held view in the general public that poachers were morally innocent, but in some elite circles they were seen as highly criminal[95] (see Figure 3.3).

By the nineteenth century, opponents of privileged access to game frequently bemoaned 'that terrible Code called the Game Laws which has been growing harder and harder all the time that it ought to have been wearing away'.[96] The Scottish novelist and poet Robert Buchanan fumed:

> The Game Laws are the tribute paid by the overworked and over-taxed people of England to the Lords of the Bread—to the predatory classes

---

[91] J.C. Coldstream, 'Shikar Rules of Shimla Hill States' (1924); cited in Roshni Johar, 'Stepping into a World of Charm', *Tribune* (India), 27 Nov 1999. https://www.tribuneindia.com/1999/99dec04/saturday/head7.htm

[92] Harry Hopkins, *The Long Affray: The Poaching Wars, 1760–1914* (London: Papermac, 1986).

[93] G.M. Trevelyan, *English Social History* (London: Longmans, Green, 1942); cited in Hopkins, *The Long Affray*, 1.

[94] E.P. Thompson, *Whigs and Hunters: The Origin of the Black Act* (London: Allen Lane, 1975).

[95] Michael J. Carter, *Peasants and Poachers: A Study in Rural Disorder in Norfolk* (Suffolk: Boydell Press, 1980), 60.

[96] William Cobbett, *Cobbett's Weekly Register* (London: J.M. Cobbett, 1822); cited in Hopkins, *The Long Affray*, 12.

**Figure 3.3.** 'The Game Laws—or the Sacrifice of the Peasant to the Hare'. *Punch* 7 (1844): 197. Public domain.

who have appropriated the land and depopulated the hills and valleys, to increase their own selfish pleasures. The destruction of the Game Laws is as inevitable in the long-run as was the destruction of Slavery, the repeal of the Corn Laws, the overthrow of an alien Church in the sister isle; but the fight will be a stiff one between the freemen of this country and our savage or only semi-civilised aristocracy and plutocracy.[97]

---

[97] Quoted in Henry S. Salt, ed., *Killing for Sports* (London: G. Bell, 1915), 69.

It is in this context that colonial India's game laws have been understood as extensions of their English forbearers. By the last quarter of the nineteenth century, the British attempted to impose game laws to regulate local *shikaris* throughout their Indian empire. This change to local hunting patterns occurred remarkably quickly in places like the Central Provinces considering that the British established their Raj there only in 1861. Wakefield, publishing his memoirs in 1878 worried, 'There are no game-laws in India, and no particular close time is observed, the natives killing everything all the year round—a proceeding not calculated to increase the game in the country'. He predicted that this situation, 'sooner or later will have to be stopped by the aid of legislation'.[98] 1878 was also the year the Indian Forest Act was passed.

The Indian Forest Act represented a dramatic expansion of government powers over the subcontinent's forests, wildlife, and peoples. It is not uncommon for scholars to present a picture of European forestry in this era being primarily concerned with exploitation and expropriation of forest wealth. The Forest Department in India achieved this end by trifurcating forests into Reserve Forests where people had no rights, Protected Forests where people's rights were typically restricted, and Village Forests for local usage.[99] In reference to wildlife, the Act defined most small animals as well as skins and furs as minor 'forest-produce' controllable by the state, in an attempt to limit hunting by local people.[100]

To C.F. Amery, Baden-Powell, and the creators of the 1878 Indian Forest Act, people's access to forests in India was seen as a 'privilege', and 'privilege' was defined as a 'concession granted by the government'.[101] Thus administrators were horrified to learn when 'Government forests' were 'actually burdened with rights or privileges of third parties'.[102]

---

[98] W. Wakefield, *Our Life and Travels in India* (London: Sampson Low, 1878), 351.

[99] Madhav Gadgil and Ramachandra Guha, *This Fissured Land: An Ecological History of India* (Berkeley: University of California Press, 1993), 123–134.

[100] GoI, *Indian Forest Act* (Act VII of 1878), 56 states: '"Forest-produce" includes the following.... skins, tusks, bones and horns'.

[101] C.F. Amery's comments published in B.H. Baden-Powell, *Report of the Proceedings of the Forest Conference, 1873–74* (Calcutta: Office of the Superintendent of Government Printing, 1874), 125; Dietrich Brandis, *Memorandum on the Forest Legislation Proposed for British India, Other Than the Presidencies of Madras and Bombay* (Simla: Government Press, 1875), 112; points drawn from an unpublished conference paper by V.M. Ravi Kumar, 'Multiple Voices: Evolution of Colonial Forest Policies in Madras Presidency, an Enquiry into Ideas and Legal Discourses, 1800–1882', Conference on Livelihoods, Environment, and History at Calcutta University, Mar 2005.

[102] NAI, R&A, Forests, Apr 1875, no. 20–22.

The Indian Forest Act was designed to systematically limit the rights of people dependent on the forests for their livelihoods and sustenance requirements.

Call it 'selfish conservation': there were clear British administrative attempts to preserve wildlife *from* subaltern encroachments, only to conserve game *for* sportsmen to kill. In one perhaps not so uncommon example, E.F. Burton records an incident where a 'civil officer would not grant [gun] licenses for fear that the villagers would shoot [a] tiger, which he wanted for himself, and as he *did shoot all* the tigers (such greediness was a great mistake), the other and peaceful animals destroyed the cultivation at their leisure'.[103] By the 1890s, game laws, in the proper sense, had been enacted locally in many areas throughout India. In general, these laws were prejudiced against the poor as they required the purchase of licences. They were also prejudiced against subsistence hunting as opposed to sport, and outlawed practices such as trapping and snaring. In the 1887 debates leading up to a bill for 'Game Preservation', it was argued that 'the object in view has always been not the protection of private property in game, but the protection of the wild creatures themselves from destruction in their breeding season... This Bill... is in no way designed to pursue the unlicensed sportsman on his shooting grounds'.[104] But the fact that legislators had to claim the law was not out against the poor rural hunters, suggests that exactly the opposite was perceived to be true. Inevitably, dominant groups would use their power to suppress weaker ones and preserve their privilege.

Game laws were written by and for British sportsmen. As one sportsman in Central India wrote while drafting the law to protect a particularly threatened species of bird, the Likh Florican (*Sypheotides indicus*), 'These are only found here in the breeding season. If they are shot then, they will probably become extinct. If they are not to be shot, they might as well, for our purpose be extinct. This is not a sportsman-like doctrine, but still—I would suggest a compromise'.[105] Administrators readily displayed elite bias against 'the *phansi pardees* or Native game-snarers and few Native shikaris' who were said to be a class, 'so small and

---

[103] E.F. Burton, *An Indian Olio* (London: Spencer Blackett, 1888), 287.
[104] IOR L/PJ/6/216 f.2062 of 1887, 'Abstracts from the Proceedings of the Council of the Governor General of India', Viceregal Lodge, Simla, Wed 8 Jun 1887.
[105] NAI, CIA, Shooting, file no. 760 of 1898–1902, 'Game Laws', 4.

insignificant that it may reasonably be required to give way to the convenience of the majority'[106]—the majority being British sportsmen.

Those officials who supported the rights of local hunters did so mainly in the interests of agriculture and protecting crops from herbivores. Yet the category of colonial administrator was not a monolith. As one district judge objecting to the 1887 Game Protection Act put it, 'some of the wild tribes depend mainly upon game for livelihood. It is very hard that they should in any way be fettered in their search for such means of livelihood. Their condition is already hard enough'.[107] Also, not every Englishman subscribed to the view that subaltern *shikaris* were exclusively to blame for the diminution of game. As R.W. Burton wrote in his 1953 book, *The Preservation of Wild Life in India*, 'It must be admitted that up to that time—that is till the beginning of this century—the main agent of destruction was the "European sportsman".... Neither the indigenous "shikari" nor the wild dog—two kinds of "poacher" frequently accused—can properly be blamed for it'.[108] Nonetheless, numerous acts that simultaneously served to protect game and alienate local peoples were passed across British India. And even though Burton believed that 'poachers' were not to blame for the loss of wildlife, he still believed it imperative to reduce their impact. Echoing the general prejudice of mid-twentieth century Europeans against local hunting traditions, Burton wrote:

> The time has long past when snarers of indigenous game birds should be allowed to continue to earn a livelihood in that way; in any case all markets should be denied them, and public opinion should recognize that flesh of such wild creatures [as opposed to domesticated animals] is not in these days at all necessary for human existence and should ban the killing of them for food alone. Properly regulated sport may be allowed during the seasons prescribed by local governments in respect to each species.[109]

---

[106] IOR L/PJ/6/212 f.1633 of 19 Aug 1887, 'Papers relating to the Bill for the Protection of Game', from W.H. Horsley, Esq, CS, to Acting Under Secretary to Government, Bombay (15 Jul 1887).
[107] Ibid., from District Judge, Sholapur–Bijapur, to Under Secretary to Government, Bombay (11 Jul 1887).
[108] R.W. Burton, *The Preservation of Wild Life in India* (Bangalore: Bangalore Press, 1953), 52.
[109] R.W. Burton, 'Wild Life Preservation in India', *Journal of the Bombay Natural History Society* 47, no. 4 (1948): 101.

Hunting for survival was perceived as 'not... at all necessary' and should be banned, yet trophy hunting should 'be allowed'. Whereas local people suffered continual erosion of their forest rights or 'privileges', as evidenced by a 1914 proposal to allot 'special areas of forest lands near cantonments for British soldiers to shoot in', British soldiers and sportsmen were continually granted more shooting privileges in the late colonial period.[110]

Based on the logic that natural prey was in decline because of subaltern *shikaris*, the British, in turn, also blamed them for the increasing depredations caused by tigers and other carnivores. For according to a prevalent theory of the time, tigers turned to attack domesticated animals and people when their natural prey and habitat diminished. In his 1892 'tour of Jubalpur and Narmada', the Chief Commissioner of the Central Provinces observed: 'No doubt native shikaris are rapidly clearing out the deer; and this decrease of the natural prey of the tiger and panther must have a good deal to do with the heavier loss of cattle'.[111] Those that held the view that 'blame' should be more evenly distributed found themselves in the minority position. Still, some did voice their opinion. As James Best put it, it was not only the 'native *shikari*' that was responsible. 'Every man's hand is against the noble tiger', he wrote.

> He has no close season and no protection for his females or young; a reward is on his head and he is the target for the native shikari sitting safely in a tree with a weapon which often inflicts pain but seldom kills. The unfortunate beasts can never approach their food without fear of a treacherous shot, for despite their enormous strength and speed they are often hard put to find food and when hunted are driven from one retreat to another in the hottest part of the day.[112]

Yet, while not every European author blamed subaltern *shikaris* for the destruction of wildlife, most certainly did. The British were typically unified in blaming 'the natives' for the diminution of game in their Indian

---

[110] NAI, R&A, Forests, May 1914, nos.1–15, 'Allotment of special areas of forest lands near cantonments for British soldiers to shoot in'.
[111] IOR L/PJ/6/362/f.2275, Judicial and Public Annual Files, 'Reports from local Governments and Administrators on the action taken for the destruction of wild animals and venomous snakes during 1892'.
[112] J.W. Best, *Shikar Notes for Novices* (Allahabad: The Pioneer Press, 1920), 17–18.

Empire. Henry Seton-Karr, an early sportsman-conservationist, wrote in 1908: 'Your true sportsman is always a real lover of nature. He kills, it is true, but only in sweet reasonableness and moderation, for food if necessary, but mainly for trophies. Wholesale and unnecessary slaughter are abhorrent to him'.[113] Quite paradoxically, it seems to have been a widely held belief that killing for subsistence was 'unnecessary slaughter' whereas killing for sport and trophies was a matter of, as Seton-Karr put it, 'sweet reasonableness and moderation'.

## Towards Carnivore Conservation

As already established, the phrase 'colonial wildlife conservation' is a misnomer. The colonial approach to tigers, leopards, bears, wolves, wild dogs, and snakes was embodied in the colonial love for sport hunting as well as the reward system that paid handsomely for their destruction. Until the very end of the Raj, hardly anybody who was anybody could possibly care about saving tigers and other dangerous wild animals from extinction.

From as early as the 1870s, a few voices did ring out against the reward system, but a perspicacious and precocious minority is seldom powerful enough to stop widespread destruction. In 1877, the officer in charge of catching elephants for the government of Mysore, G.P. Sanderson, already regretted the British 'war of extermination against tigers'. As Sanderson perceptively put it, 'Cultivation would recede in many parts of the country were there no tigers. The balance of nature cannot be interfered with impunity'.

> The tiger is no unmitigated evil in the land.... It is a pity to see the tiger proscribed and hunted to death by every unsportsmanlike method that can be devised, in response to popular outcries chiefly in England without foundation in fact, about his destructiveness. Trace out and slay every man-eater by all means possible, and at any expense; but ordinary tigers are exceedingly inoffensive, and have their uses. May the day be far distant when the tiger shall become practically extinct!

---

[113] Henry Seton-Karr, 'The Preservation of Big Game', *Journal of the Society for the Preservation of the Wild Fauna of Empire* 4 (1908): 26.

Yet for all his defence of the tiger, Sanderson was still a keen sportsman and a staunch defender of sport hunting, like many others of his day. And he clearly expressed this cognitive dissonance when he wrote: 'Of course all tigers are fair game to the sportsman; they can never be unduly reduced by shooting.'[114] Similarly, in 1888 E.F. Burton remarked, 'Fair and moderate shooting is all that is wanted, not poisoning and otherwise "improving" [tigers] off the face of the earth,'[115] but few seemed to listen.

In 1906, J.D. Rees raised the 'question of the indiscriminate offer of rewards for the slaughter of tigers' before the House of Commons. Rees argued that, simply in order to gain rewards, 'professional slaughterers destroy these animals'. When Rees wrote to the Secretary of State, asking whether this matter could be brought up with the Government of India, the Secretary's answer was brief, perfunctory, stating only 'I am afraid that I cannot promise to address the Government of India in the sense suggested by the honourable Member, nor should I expect them to share his views on the subject of the preservation of tigers'.[116] Thus the reward system would stay in place for decades to come. The sportsman James Best also argued against the reward system, but not until its end was already nigh. 'There is no necessity to offer a reward of a sovereign for the killing of a tiger', he published in 1920; 'no European sportsman needs this inducement, and indeed would be prepared to pay more than such a sum into the Government treasuries for the privilege of shooting one'.[117] By the mid-1920s, rewards for the destruction of tigers and other predators were finally abandoned in many areas of India, and they generally ceased being paid by the early 1930s, though they continued to be paid in several locations even through independence. Partly this may have been due to a rising conservationist consciousness, but largely it seems it had to do more with economics, and with questions over the effectiveness of the reward system.[118]

---

[114] G.P. Sanderson, *Thirteen Years among the Wild Beasts of India: Their Haunts and Habits* (London: Wm. H. Allen, 1878).
[115] Burton, *An Indian Olio*.
[116] IOR L/PJ/6/769 f.2175, 19 Jul 1906, 'House of Commons question on the indiscriminate offer of rewards for the slaughter of tigers'.
[117] Best, *Shikar Notes for Novices*, 18.
[118] IOR L/E/7/1352, File 3178: 'Annual Returns of destruction of and persons killed by wild animals', 8 Jan 1934, letter to Count John de Salis: 'I have been asking about mortality from wild animals and I find that we used to have figures up till some five or six years ago when they were

Remarkably, even in 1936, during the All-India Conference for the Preservation of Wildlife 'Item no. 1' on the agenda included: 'the destruction of such wild animal, [sic] such as wild dogs, as tend to decrease other and more important game'.[119] During the conference, when item no. 1 was raised, the chairman quickly moved on to the next part of the agenda, saying, 'There is really not very much to be said on the point. The Forest Department already issues rewards for the destruction of such wild animals'. Nobody thought it important enough to suggest that carnivores too ought to be protected. Early twentieth-century conservationists still perceived carnivores as a threat to humanity.[120] When sanctuaries were proposed in Central India, they were intended as places where, 'harmless and interesting creatures could live and breed in peace'.[121] Though the naiveté of this ecological vision should be readily apparent today, it is one that only began to be seriously challenged in the 1930s.

Previous to this, most conservationists and preservationists around the world held that carnivores needed to be destroyed. Even many of the most famous early conservationists, the very people credited with laying the groundwork for modern environmentalism, Americas like William Hornaday and Aldo Leopold, for example, not only began their lives as keen sportsmen and their careers by promoting and encouraging the eradication of carnivores, but their ideas also often reeked of the racial anxieties of their time, place and class. William Hornaday, who is famous for quotations such as, 'The wild things of this earth are not ours… They have been given to us in trust', believed so strongly in his paternalist duty towards preserving 'the wild things of the earth', that he oversaw the installation Ota Benga, a Congolese 'pygmy' man, in the Primate House of the Bronx Zoo. And in his 1913 book titled *Our Vanishing Wild Life*, he made an exception to his preservationist crusade for 'mountain lions and gray wolves', writing that they 'should be shot out of the entire Grand

---

discontinued as it was found that they were notoriously inaccurate and practically worthless. I believe that one or two Provinces still collect figures for their own purposes, but we do not get them and there is no figure for India as a whole. I am sorry therefore that I am not able to supply the information you asked for'.

[119] IOR V/27/460/10 'Proceedings of the All-India Conference for the Preservation of Wild Life, 28–30 Jan 1935' (Delhi: GoI Press, 1936), 1.

[120] Ibid., 15.

[121] Nagpur Archives, Berar Forest Department, 242 of 1903, 'Orders prohibiting the shooting and snaring of certain wild animals and game birds within the Chikalda Station Block… Except… tigers, panthers, and other dangerous animals', R.D. Hare to Sec. for Berar, 14 Apr 1903.

Canyon National Forest'.[122] Similarly, Aldo Leopold, who in the 1930s eventually emerged as one of the world's first ecological advocates for carnivore conservation, is far more widely known for his environmentalist quotations than for his racist and speciesist ones. He had several inspirational adages such as these:

> Like winds and sunsets, wild things were taken for granted until progress began to do away with them.
>
> Man always kills the thing he loves. And so we the pioneers have killed our wilderness. Some say we had to. Be that as it may, I am glad I shall never be young without wild country to be young in.[123]
>
> For one species to mourn the death of another is a new thing under the sun.[124]

But it is also important to be aware of his more problematic aphorisms:

> The erasure of a human subspecies is largely painless—to us—if we know little enough about it. A dead Chinaman is of little import to us whose awareness of things Chinese is bounded by an occasional dish of chow mein. We grieve only for what we know.[125]
>
> The Biological Survey is making splendid progress in eradication work... It is going to take patience and money to catch [read: kill] the last wolf or lion in New Mexico. But the last one must be caught.[126]

---

[122] William Temple Hornaday, *Our Vanishing Wild Life: Its Extermination and Preservation* (New York: C. Scribner's sons, 1913), 7, 343. Hornaday's 1898 report, *The Destruction of Our Birds and Mammals: A Report on the Results of an Inquiry*, framed the parallel between wolves and men this way: 'Unless man is willing to accept a place on the list of predatory animals which have no other thought than the wolfish instinct to slay every living species save their own, he is bound by the unwritten laws of civilization to protect from annihilation the beasts and birds that still beautify the earth'. And except to include this quotation, a recent biography of Hornaday (perhaps better called a hagiography) entirely ignores the problem of predators in lauding the man's conservation ethos. See: Stefan Bechtel, *Mr. Hornaday's War: How a Peculiar Victorian Zookeeper Waged a Lonely Crusade for Wildlife That Changed the World* (Boston: Beacon Press, 2012).
[123] 'Foreword' and 'The Green Lagoons' in Aldo Leopold, *A Sand County Almanac and Sketches Here and There* (New York: Oxford University Press, 1949), vii, 148.
[124] 'On a Monument to the Pigeon' in Leopold, *Sand County*, 110.
[125] Leopold, *Sand County*, 49. In some versions, the word 'dislike' was substituted for 'dish'.
[126] Aldo Leopold, 'The Game Situation in the Southwest', *Bulletin of the American Game Protective Association* 9, no. 2 (1920): 3–5.

Leopold was one of the first public intellectuals in the twentieth century to eventually come around to the understanding that wolves and other carnivores were integral to ecosystems as top predators, and should not be completely exterminated. But as Mike Powell has documented, it appears Leopold never lost his racist edge. What Powell calls 'race peril' was deeply linked with extinction fears, not only in the United States but all around the world in the early twentieth century.[127]

In colonial India, there never was a major campaign to protect the tiger or any other animal species from humans, besides the cow. One might expect that nationalist leaders, or the leaders of the cow protection movement, would also want to protect tigers or other wildlife considered to be 'vermin' or 'wild beasts' by the British, as a form of resistance to colonialism. This was not the case, however. Even Swami Dayananda, who wrote the foundational text on late nineteenth-century cow protection, *Gokarunanidhi*, did not make an argument for protecting wildlife. In fact, his commentary on the Vedas speaks against the protection of carnivores, writing: 'Let no one kill animals that are useful to all but protect them... But the wild animals who cause injury to the animals and to the cultivation of the villages and their inhabitants may be killed or driven away by the rulers'.[128]

Gandhi's attitude towards tiger hunting was also more complicated than one might deduce from universally applying the concept of non-violence, or even from reading the proliferation of environmentalist articles that have been written about 'the Mahatma' in recent years.[129] Tigers did not fit neatly into Gandhi's *weltanschauung*. True, in most cases, Gandhi condemned hunting, especially hunting for sport or pleasure; but when it came to dangerous animals such as tigers, he seems to have believed that it was the government's duty to protect people from the ravishes of these beasts. He once criticized the 'inhumane' and 'barbarous *shikar* laws of Jaipur State' where tigers were 'protected under pain of heavy fines' and where people were endangered. Jaipur's tigers, said

---

[127] Powell, *Vanishing America*, 158–185.
[128] Dayananda Saraswati, *Gokarunanidhi: Ocean of Mercy for the Cow* (Lahore: Virajanand Press, 1889), p. viii.
[129] E.g. Thomas Weber, 'Gandhi, Deep Ecology, Peace Research and Buddhist Economics', *Journal of Peace Research* 36, no. 3 (May 1999): 349–361.

Gandhi, were free to 'eat men and animals with impunity'.[130] In this sense, Gandhi, like almost all his early twentieth-century peers, was not a wildlife conservationist. To Gandhi, tigers were the example *par excellence* that nature could be cruel and violent. Rather than interpreting the tiger as some nationalists did, as a native symbol for a powerful India, Gandhi repeatedly equated the British with predatory tigers.[131] On one occasion, Gandhi remarked:

> Living amidst tigers and wolves, we can do only two things. True courage lies in absence of fear of wild animals. Tigers and wolves too have been created by God, and we should view them without any ill-will. This can be practiced only by saints... There is a second type of courage which consists in facing tigers and wolves with weapons. This also involves risk to one's person. Such is the plight of those living in the midst of whites.[132]

This chapter constitutes further evidence that only what is valued can be perceived as endangered. The awareness of the value of living carnivores, as I have documented, came about as a result of several factors: one was the eventual scientific recognition of their vital role in maintaining healthy ecosystems; another was the dawning realization that their disappearance was part of a broader global extinction crisis. Only after the trigger-happy colonists had departed—and with them, their compulsions for vermin eradication and trophy sport—were concerted efforts made at carnivore conservation. Unlike efforts at saving tribes, however, it was not until well into the post-independence period, around the time of the emergence of the modern environmental movement of the early 1970s, that the value of India's tigers and other large carnivores would come to be widely appreciated. At that point, issues surrounding tiger conservation and tribal survival would merge once again in many practical ways.

---

[130] *The Collected Works of Mahatma Gandhi*, vol. 76 (31 May 1939–15 Oct 1939), 209. http://www.gandhiserve.org/cwmg/VOL076.PDF

[131] See Ruth Vanita, 'Gandhi's Tiger: Multilingual Elites, the Battle for Minds, and English Romantic Literature in Colonial India', *Postcolonial Studies* 5, no. 1 (2002): 95–110.

[132] *The Collected Works of Mahatma Gandhi*, vol. 7 (15 Jun 1907–12 Dec 1907), 203. http://www.gandhiserve.org/cwmg/VOL007.PDF

## Coda: The Extinction of Hunting

> The first challenge for hunting is simply to survive in a modern society. However, considering the importance of hunting for 250 million indigenous people [worldwide] and the importance of hunting to cultural diversity or to rural industries or traditions, this challenge becomes bigger. To us the challenge of hunting in the modern world will be to prove itself as a major force for conservation and cultural survival for minorities and for the survival of a way to secure an important part of our protein demand which is not restricted to the clearing of tropical rainforests to ranch cattle for McDonald's hamburgers and for the replacement of the world's wild marine and freshwater fish stocks by fish farms.
>
> Bauer and Giles, 2002

Hunting culture disappears with the extinction of hunted species. Partly because *shikar* is very much out of fashion in contemporary India, its history seems to be something the former ruling families would rather hide than eulogize. Some of the princely families, or those in control of their estates, are hoarding historical documents and blocking access to their archives, which they fear may prove embarrassing. When I interviewed the current Maharaja of Rewa, for example, without raising the subject myself, he specifically had me quote him as saying that there was 'no tradition of killing 109 tigers' in his family, and that writers who claimed there was such a tradition were doing so 'to glorify their own texts'.[133] It was made impossible for me to find any relevant documents in the Rewa Palace Library. In fact, the most interesting thing I encountered in this library was a large, frightened bat. Later, in the Rajasthan State Archives, Bikaner, I discovered this passage in the *Rewa State Administration Report* of 1913–1914, which told a different story:

> *The number of tigers shot by His Highness the Maharaja…* Seven tigers were shot during December 1913 and first two weeks of January 1914.

---

[133] Interview with the Maharaja or Rewa, in Rewa, Madhya Pradesh, 29 Nov 2005.

The total number of tigers shot by that time was... 109. One hundred nine is an auspicious Hindu number, as the standard number of beads in a garland, including the head bead, is 109. The event was, therefore, fittingly celebrated in the State. The celebrations included the following items, namely:

1) A salute of 17 guns was fired to celebrate the event.
2) Ten prisoners were to be released from the Jail.
3) The officials and servants with His Highness the Maharaja were given an extra privilege leave of one month—all others in the State fifteen days' extra leave.
4) Officials and servants with His Highness the Maharaja received one month's extra pay as reward.
5) Brahmans were fed, and those performing Puja at the Chirahula temple were given Rs. 15 each as charity.
6) All public offices were closed for two days.
7) Khasgi servants were paid their 'Nichhabar', which was stopped previously.

The number of tigers shot by His Highness the Maharaja during the year was 9, and the total number to the end of the year was 111.[134]

When I spoke to the Trustee in charge of the Maharaja Ganga Singhji Archive in Lallgarh Palace in Bikaner, I encountered similar resistance. In 2005, one palace custodian who wished to remain anonymous complained about the large number of 'so-called researchers' who come to the palace only interested in *shikar* and nothing else. Fearing that opening the records of the Maharajas would be 'an embarrassment to the family', the handwritten manuscripts of the Maharaja Sadul Singh's big game and bird shooting diaries are sitting in a glass case that has been nailed shut. The Maharaja's diaries contain a detailed account of how he shot 68,434 head of game including 24,838 Imperial Sand Grouse, 22,847 ducks, and 266 tigers between 1891 and 1942.[135] It is partially because these numbers

---

[134] Rajasthan State Archive (RSA), *Rewa State Administration Report, 1913–1914*, 2.
[135] RSA, Maharaja Sadul Singh, *His Highnesses' General Shooting Diary*, vol. 2 (Bikaner: Government Press, 1941).

148   THE NATURE OF ENDANGERMENT IN INDIA

sound so accusatory that the trust refuses to open its collections to researchers. The irony, though, is that these brutal statistics are already in the public domain in the Rajasthan State Archives and can even be found on the internet. Any further research into the qualitative history of hunting with the Maharajas might in contrast serve to emolliate the disturbing picture that these numbers paint.[136]

Similar resistance to discussing the history of hunting with outsiders came from many rural villagers. Two personal experiences should suffice to make this point. In a village in the buffer zone of Kanha National Park, I was speaking to an elderly Baiga gentleman, when I saw he had some *chital* antlers hidden in some leaf cuttings sitting by the door to his hut. He told me the antlers were collected from the forest floor, which I am sure was true. But then I asked him about whether he or his father had ever hunted in the past. '*Nahi, nahi*' (no, no!) he exclaimed in horror, and held his arms up in an 'X' above his head to show he would surely go to jail, not for hunting, but even if we continued to talk about this sensitive topic. I pressed, saying 'These days hunting is illegal, but before it was not. When you were a child you never played hunting?' (*Aaj kal shikar karna gerkanuni hai, lekin pahele nahi tha. Bachpan me, aap kabhi nahi shikar khelte the?*) Still, he denied ever having lifted the bow and arrows he had hung up on his wall against a wild animal—'we have never gone hunting', he said ('*ham kabhi nahi shikar gaye*'). It was only on getting to know Adivasi elders a bit better over time that most would begin to open up with stories from their youth about hunting. But still, the most commonly related tales would involve being employed as subaltern *shikaris* and beaters in elite hunts, rather than about independent hunting practices.

On another occasion, I visited the ancestral home of Limba Ram, India's Olympic medal-winning archer, who hails from the Jhadol district of Rajasthan. There I met and interviewed his mother. When I asked her how Limba Ram had learned archery, she denied that he, his father, or anyone else in the family, ever hunted. According to her, the government had taught Limba how to use a bow, not his father. This, even though an Adivasi-style wooden bow hung above the doorway to the traditional mud-built home. We talked a bit about the past, and about how many

[136] Thanks to an anonymous collaborator, I received a photocopied version of the descriptive portion of Sadul Singh's Big Game Diary, and an index of the hunting records in Lalgarh's archive. However, the Bird Shooting Diary remains unread and under glass.

animals there once were, and how vast the jungle once was. She then told me that a tiger used to come around the village. When I asked what happened to it, she pointed towards the horizon at some huts on neighbouring hills and said, 'those people over there killed it'. Thus, 'elites' and 'subalterns' alike would often deny, and erase, their histories of hunting.

Perhaps the greatest irony in the story of extinctions relating to hunting in India, however, is not the extinction of hunted species themselves, which was, unfortunately, to be expected. The irony is that, despite the fact that the modern conservation regime largely developed out of elite sporting interests, it is the elite tradition of the big game hunt involving thousands of men and elephants that can be said to be largely 'extinct' in India, whereas subaltern forest-based livelihoods involving hunting to some extent linger on in poor rural communities. Not only do numerous texts refer to 'the extinction of the British Raj' in 1947, but many also observe that this was a period of 'the extinction of the Princely Order itself', and call India's princes 'a doomed tribe'.[137] As Salman Rushdie evocatively describes in his story 'The Firebird's Nest':

> Now his father is dead, the tigers are extinct, and the birds have all gone, except one, which never sings a note and, in the absence of trees, makes its nest in a secret place that has not been revealed... There are no princes now. The government abolished them decades ago. The very idea of princes has become, in our modern country, a fiction, something from the time of feudalism, of fairy tale... In this place, the prince has become plain Mr. Maharaj. He is a complex man... In his youth he was a mighty sportsman, but since his retirement he has had no time for games. He heads an ecological institute... [138]

Does this mean that forest cultures have in some sense succeeded in the struggle for survival where empires and elites have failed? Hardly. Whereas the very existence of forest societies and cultures are perceived

---

[137] For books using the language of extinction in reference to the British Raj and the Princely Raj, see: Lionel James Trotter, *The History of the British Empire in India: From the Appointment of Lord Hardinge to the Political Extinction of the East-India Company, 1844 to 1862* (London: W.H. Allen, 1866), and D.R. Mankekar, *Accession to Extinction: The Story of the Indian Princes* (Delhi: Vikas, 1974), ix.

[138] Salman Rushdie, 'The Firebird's Nest', *New Yorker*, 23 Jun 1997, 122 cited in Ann Grodzins Gold and Bhoju Ram Gujar, *In the Time of Trees and Sorrows: Nature, Power, and Memory in Rajasthan* (Durham N.C.: Duke University Press, 2002), 1.

to be endangered, lineages of wealth and power are, in general, alive and well some seventy-five years after the end of the Raj. Though feudal and colonial power structures have in some sense ended, it can hardly be said that the first have become the last.[139] Whereas many have long framed the 'extinction' of oppressive political forces as a desirable goal (one stray example would be that the preamble to the 1956 Egyptian Constitution under President Gamal Abdel Nasser proclaimed as its objectives: 'the eradication of imperialism, the extinction of feudalism, the destruction of capitalistic influence ... '), thankfully few today, in contrast, would expressly argue for the eradication of forest-based cultures. Instead, elite efforts have repeatedly been addressed at saving tribes, much as since the middle of the twentieth century, they have been addressed at saving wildlife. This is because, in the words of Patrick Brantlinger, thinkers from all political perspectives have long been aware that indigenous people around the world faced, 'if not outright extermination, then ... transformation'.[140]

The question of responsibility for the destruction of India's wildlife, which preoccupied colonial sportsmen and forms the background for today's conservation policies, was never as simple as polemicists wanted it to be. The endangerment of wildlife was not primarily the fault of forest dwellers, but it went hand in hand with the decline of forest dwelling as a way of life. Sport hunting was as much a pursuit of 'wild lives'—simultaneously a chance for 'civilized' sportsmen to experience the wild thrill of the forest, and an act of conquest and subjugation of everything wild—as it was a pursuit of animal 'wildlife'. The ultimate irony of the hunt was that, as the sportsman pursued both wildlife and wild lives, he destroyed the very things he loved.[141]

---

[139] To paraphrase *Mathew* 20:16—'So the last will be first, and the first will be last'. This was also Frantz Fanon's famous definition of decolonization in *The Wretched of the Earth*: 'Dans décolonisation, il y a donc exigence d'une remise en question intégrale de la situation coloniale. Sa définition peut, si on veut la décrire avec précision, tenir dans la phrase bien connue: "Les derniers seront les premiers"'. Frantz Fanon, *Les Damnés de la Terre* (Paris: F. Maspero, 1961), 2.

[140] Patrick Brantlinger, *Dark Vanishings: Discourse on the Extinction of Primitive Races, 1800–1930* (Ithaca: Cornell University Press, 2003), 36.

[141] For an article of mine on the colonial sportsman's pursuit of the 'wild life' see: Ezra Rashkow, 'Wilding the Domestic: Camp Servants and Glamping in British India', *The Indian Economic & Social History Review* 58, no. 3 (2021): 361–391. For other scholarly sources considering the concept of being 'loved to death', see: Marilyn Lawrence, 'Loving Them to Death: The Anorexic and Her Objects', *The International Journal of Psychoanalysis* 82, no. 1 (2001): 43–55; and Ben Daley and Peter Griggs, '"Loved to Death": Coral Collecting in the Great Barrier Reef, Australia, 1770–1970', *Environment and History* 14, no. 1 (2008): 89–119.

Appendix 3.1. Tigers Killed 'Hall of Fame'*

| Names | Number Killed | Description | Date | Source |
|---|---|---|---|---|
| Van Ingen and Van Ingen (taxidermists) | 10,000+ | Performed taxidermy on over 10,000 tigers | | P.A. Morris, Van Ingen, and Van Ingen, *Artists in Taxidermy* (Ascot: MPM, 2006). |
| Maharaja Ramanuj Saran Singh Deo of Surguja | 1,707 | '1,707 tigers during his lifetime' | | Kailash Sankhala, *Tiger! The Story of the Indian Tiger* (Delhi: Rupa, 1978), 131. |
| Maharaja Ramanuj Saran Singh Deo of Surguja | 1,150 | "The Maharaja of Surguja wrote to me in a letter dated April 6, 1965: "My total bag of Tigers is 1,150 (one thousand one hundred and fifty only.)"' | 6 Apr 1965 | George Schaller, *The Deer and the Tiger* (Chicago: University Press, 1972), 226. |
| Maharaja Ramanuj Saran Singh Deo of Surguja | 1,116 | "The Maharajah of Surguja, who is still alive, holds the record with 1116 tigers' | | Stracey, *Wild Life in India*, 2; Valmik Thapar, *Battling for Survival: India's Wilderness Over Two Centuries* (New Delhi: Oxford University Press), 218. |
| Maharaja Ramanuj Saran Singh Deo of Surguja | ~1,100 | 'around 1,100' | | Valmik Thapar, *Tiger: Portrait of a Predator* (London: Collins, 1986), 14. |
| Licensed sportsmen | 1,074 | 'A total of 1,074 tigers were shot on license in government forests of the state between 1929 and 1939... and if the number of animals shot on private lands and illegally without license were added to this figure, the actual kill would probably be twice as high' | 1929–1939 | Schaller, *The Deer and the Tiger*, 227. |

*(continued)*

Appendix 3.1. Continued

| Names | Number Killed | Description | Date | Source |
|---|---|---|---|---|
| Villagers in Jattygaon | 1,053 | 'in Jattygaon Khandesh… the slaughter of tigers in 1821-8 amounted to 1053; bounty was claimed on this number as "vermin" and many others must have been killed but were unrecorded' | 1821–1828 | Sankhala, *Tiger!*, 90. |
| 'Maharja [sic] of Udaipur' | 1,000+ | 'The Maharaja [sic] of Udaipur shot at least 1,000 tigers during his lifetime.' This is likely inaccurate. Not only is the title incorrect (it should be Maharana), Julie Hughes who has studied Udaipur extensively, provides detailed estimates below. | | Schaller, *The Deer and the Tiger*, 226; Thapar, *Tiger*, 14. |
| George Palmer | 1,000 | Killed 1000 'Royal Bengal Tigers' between 1832 and 1862 | 1832–1862 | Sankhala, *Tiger!*, 90. |
| In Madras Presidency | 932 | 'The Presidency of Madras paid Rs. 50 per head for 932 tigers between 1879 and 1883' | 1879–1883 | Mohd Momin Khan, *The Malayan Tiger* (Kuala Lumpur: Institut Terjemahan & Buku Malaysia, 2014), 8. |
| Maharaja Scindia of Gwalior and guests | 900 | '700 by 1911.' 'Guests accounted for a further 200' | 1911 | Shuja ul Islam and Zohra Islam, *Hunting Dangerous Game with the Maharajas in the Indian Sub-Continent* (New Delhi: Himalayan Books, 2004), 169; Sankhala, *Tiger!*, 133. |
| Maharaja Gulab Singh of Rewa (r. 1922–1946) | 900 | 'shot about 900 in the early 1920s' | 1920s | Divyabhanusinh, 'Junagadh State and its Lions', 532. |

| | | | |
|---|---|---|---|
| Mangal Khan | 900 | 'seen over 900 tigers killed' | 1922 | Edgar Barclay, *Big Game Records* (London: Witherby, 1932), 110; John Prescott Hewett, *Jungle Trails in Northern India: Reminiscences of Hunting in India* (London: Methuen, 1938), 66–70. |
| Maharaja of Datia | 780 | | | Vijaya Ramadas Mandala, *Shooting a Tiger: Big Game Hunting and Conservation in Colonial India* (New Delhi: Oxford University Press, 2019), 252. |
| Maharaja of Rewa | 616 | | | Stracey, *Wildlife in India*, 2; Thapar, *Battling*, 218. |
| Nawab of Tonk | 600+ | 'crossed the 600 mark' | Early 20th century | Rangarajan, *India's Wildlife History*, 38; Thapar, *Battling for Survival*, 31. |
| Wazir Khan | 600 | A mahout, 'been at the death of over 600 tigers' | | Nigel Woodyatt, *My Sporting Memories: Forty Years with Note-book & Gun* (London: Herbert Jenkins, 1923), 23–24. |
| F.B. Simson AKA 'Hogspear' | 500–600 | 'author of "Sport in Eastern Bengal" shot five to six hundred tigers in twenty one years in India, towards the end of the last century'; 'literally some thousands of boars… If the pigs knew what a formidable enemy has ceased to slay their race, they would rejoice exceedingly' | – ret. 1872 | F.B. Simson, *Letters on Sport in Eastern Bengal* (London: R.H. Porter, 1886); Stracey, *Wild Life in India*, 2; "The Month", *Oriental Sporting Magazine* 5 (May 1872): 238. |

*(continued)*

Appendix 3.1. Continued

| Names | Number Killed | Description | Date | Source |
|---|---|---|---|---|
| Maharana of Mewar, nobles, and guests | 565 | 'If we assume the percentage of kills made by the Maharana, his nobles, and guests remained constant from 1884 through 1930, then the grand totals shot by all parties in the state from 1921 through 1930 would be 565 tigers, 1,312 leopards, and 3,927 boar' | 1921–1930 | Julie E. Hughes, 'Royal Tigers and Ruling Princes: Wilderness and Wildlife Management in the Indian Princely States', *Modern Asian Studies* 49, no. 4 (2015): 1230. |
| Maharaja Jung Bahadur of Nepal | 550+ | 'Maharaja Jung Bahadur, after he became Prime Minister in 1903 (A.D. 1846), was able to indulge in his passion for big game hunting, and during the next 31 seasons he made many cold weather shikar trips to the Terai, and is said to have killed over 550 tigers' | 1846–1877 | Evelyn Arthur Smythies, *Big Game Shooting in Nepal* (Calcutta: Thacker, Spink, 1942), 38. |
| Maharana Fateh Singh of Mewar | 500+ | 'Maharana Fateh Singh of Mewar (r. 1885–1930) shot over 500 tigers during his reign' | 1885–1930 | Divyabhanusinh, 'Junagadh State', 512. |
| Maharaja of Gauripur | 500+ | | 1884–1940 | Thapar, *Tiger*, 14; Rangarajan, *India's Wildlife History*, 38; Sankhala, *Tiger!*, 133. |
| Maharaja of Rewa | 500 | | | Thapar, *Tiger*, 14. |
| Sir Percy Wyndham | 500 | 'he thinks that he has seen about five hundred shot' | 1890s–1930s | Hewett, *Jungle Trails*, 66–70. |
| 'The *duffedar*, Old Hursar Singh' | 500 | 'probably been present at the death of over 500 tigers' | | Gerard, *Leaves from the Diaries*, 130. |
| Shikari of F.B. Simson | 400–500 | 'the most experienced tiger-shooter in my own service… I know he killed between four and five hundred tigers' | | Simson, *Letters on Sport*, 116. |

| | | | | |
|---|---|---|---|---|
| Juddha Shamsher Jang Bahadur Rana | 433 | Total bag in seven seasons: 433 tigers, 53 rhinos, 93 leopards, 22 bears, 20 crocodiles, 1 wild buffalo, 3 elephants (captured), and many wild dogs, hyena, deer, etc. | 1933–1940 | Smythies, *Big Game Shooting*, 36; Schaller, *The Deer and the Tiger*, 226. |
| Maharana Fateh Singh of Mewar | ~421 | 'Between 1884 and 1921, Maharana Fateh Singh of Mewar (r. 1884–1921, d. 1930) and his nobles and guests killed at least 82 tiger, 220 leopard, 1,186 wild boar, 65 sambar, 21 chinkara, and 8 chital in Mewar.... for the period between 1921 and Fateh Singh's death in 1930 [, a]veraging the somewhat disparate numbers provided by Tanwar in his two published memoirs, the prince killed 339 tiger, 853 leopard, and 1,178 wild boars during the last decade of his life' | 1884–1930 | Hughes, 'Royal Tigers', 1229–1230. |
| George Yule | 400+ | 'he stopped counting after his tally had reached 400' | 1860s–1880s | Thapar, *Tiger*, 13; Rangarajan, *India's Wildlife History*, 38. Sankhala, *Tiger!*,132. |
| Sir Edward Braddon | 400+ | 'Braddon says, in his "Thirty Years of Shikar", that his heroic friend George Yule had killed more tigers than any man who ever lived. But we have been told by the late Sir George Chesney that Braddon, who was his brother-in-law, had destroyed more tigers than any man now living.' | | Anon, "Two Great Shikaris", *Blackwood's Edinburgh Magazine* 157, no. 956 (Jun 1895): 949. |
| Frederick C. Hicks | ~400 | 'I kept count up to 200, then stopped.... It may be 400, or more or less, I don't know'. 'I have a vague idea of trying on occasions to count up and accounting for something over 200 tigers which I have shot; but whether those were all of them, or only half, I could not say in the least'. | 1910 | Stanley Jepson, ed., *Big Game Encounters: Critical Moments in the Lives of Well-Known Shikaris* (London: Witherby, 1936), 189; Hicks, *Forty Years Among the Wild Animals*, 13. |

*(continued)*

Appendix 3.1. Continued

| Names | Number Killed | Description | Date | Source |
|---|---|---|---|---|
| Maharaja Nripendra Narayan of Cooch Behar and guests | 370+ | 'no less than 370 tigers, 208 rhinoceroses, 430 buffaloes and 324 barasingha deer' | 1871–1907 | Thapar, *Battling for Survival*, 218; Stracey, *Wild Life*, 2. |
| Maharaja Nripendra Narayan of Cooch Behar | 365 | 365 tigers, 311 leopards, 207 rhino, 438 buffaloes, 318 barasingha, among others. 'More than a dozen tigers of record size (over ten feet)' | 1871–1907 | Barclay, *Big Game Shooting*, 109; Stracey, *Wild Life in India*, 2; Sankhala, *Tiger!*, 133. |
| In Rewa | 364 | 'in three years (1924–6) 163 tigers were shot, and over the period 1923–69 the total was 364'. | 1923–1964 | Sankhala, *Tiger!*, 133. |
| In Central Provinces | 349 | '349 tigers were killed… in the Central Provinces of India over a six month period in 1864' | 1864 | Khan, *The Malayan Tiger*, 8. |
| In Kotah | 334 | '334 tigers were bagged in … Kotah' | 1920–1965 | Sankhala, *Tiger!*, 90. |
| Maharajkumar of Vizianagaram | 325+ | 'Over 325 in forty years'. Cf. Maharajkumar of Vijayanagaram | | Thapar, *Tiger*, 14. |
| Maharajkumar of Vijayanagaram | 323 | 'the Maharajkumar of Vijayanagaram … has shot 323 tigers to date (letter, April 5, 1965)'. Cf. Maharajkumar of Vizianagaram | 1965 | Schaller, *The Deer and the Tiger*, 226. |
| Gen. Mulligatawny | 300+ | 'You are doubtless acquainted with General Mulligatawny, who has shot his three hundred tigers, and Sir John Spearshaft, late of the Bombay Civil Service, who can count his first spears by the hundred' | | James Moray Brown, *Shikar Sketches, with Notes on Indian Field-Sports* (London: Hurst & Blackett, 1887), 1. |
| Col. Geoffrey Nightingale | ~300 | 'More than 300'; Thapar; 'Nearly 300', Sankhala | -1868 | R.W. Burton, *Preservation of Wild Life*, 82; Thapar, *Tiger*, 13; Sankhala, *Tiger!*, 132. |

| | | | | |
|---|---|---|---|---|
| Lt Col. John Champion Faunthorpe | 300+ | 'Exactly how many tigers he killed does not appear to be known, but it is believed to be over 300'. | 1892–1929 | Barclay, *Big Game Shooting*, 111. |
| Lt Col. A.E. Ward | 300+ | 'enormous numbers … believed to be over 300' | | Barclay, *Big Game Shooting*, 111, 116. |
| Col. Martin | 300+ | 'The Central India Horse, of which the best known tiger-hunters were Colonel Martin and Sir Montagu Gerard, shot many hundreds during the time that the jungles of the Gwalior and Rewa States were their happy hunting-grounds'. | | Hewett, *Jungle Trails*, 66. |
| E.B. Baker | 300+ | 'shot several hundred tigers in Bengal and Assam, measured his largest 10 feet 4 inches' | | Hewett, *Jungle Trails*, 69. |
| W.P. Okeden | 300+ | 'shot several hundreds' | | IOR Mss Eur A.210 'Diary and Sporting Journal of William Parry Okeden', India, 1821–1841; Hewett, *Jungle Trails*, 55, 66–70. |
| Khan Saheb Jamshed Butt | 300+ | 'While his own account stands at over 150 tigers, he has supervised hunting arrangements with other sportsmen which account for more than double this number' | | Khan Saheb Jamshed Butt, *Shikar* (Bombay: Rusi Khambatta, 1963), 12. |
| Sir Henry Ramsay | 300 | 'Probably several hundreds and he never sat up for a tiger, if he could help it' | | Woodyatt, *My Sporting Memories*, 16. |
| Prime Minister of Nepal | 295 | 'The former Prime Minister of Nepal shot 295 tigers in seven years (1933–9)' | 1933–1939 | Sankhala, *Tiger!*, 131. |
| Maharaja of Bikaner Ganga Singh | 266 | 266 tigers, 7 lions, and 61 leopards | 1942 | Ganga Singh, *His Highness' General Shooting Diary*, vol. 2, From 21st July 1920 to 20th July 1942 (Bikaner: Gov't Press, 1941). |

*(continued)*

Appendix 3.1. Continued

| Names | Number Killed | Description | Date | Source |
|---|---|---|---|---|
| Digby Davies | 250+ | | | Charles Elphinstone Gouldsbury, *Tiger Slayer by Order: Digby Davies, Late Bombay Police* (London: Chapman & Hall, 1915), 35n. |
| M.D. Chaturvedi | 250, 50+ | 'witnessed' 250, shot 50+ | Retired 1954 | Sankhala, *Tiger!*, 132; Valmik Thapar, *Saving Wild Tigers, 1900–2000: The Essential Writings* (New Delhi: Permanent Black, 2001), 157. |
| Lt Gov. Sir John Prescott Hewett and army officers | 247 | 247 'seen shot myself', but 'my own contribution to this bag is nothing very wonderful... at least half the bag must have been got by officers of His Majesty's army'. | | Hewett, *Jungle Trails*, 66–70. |
| Lt Gen. Sir James Outram | 235+ | 'He has noted that, during ten years, or from 1825 to 1834 inclusive, he himself and associates in the chase, killed no fewer than 235 tigers, wounding 22 others; 25 bears, wounding 14; 12 buffaloes, wounding 5; and killed also 16 panthers or leopards. Of this grand total of 329 wild animals, 44 tigers and panther or leopard were killed during his absence by gentlemen of the Khandesh hunt; but Outram was actually present at the death of 191 tigers, 15 panthers or leopards, 25 bears, and 12 buffaloes' | 1825–1834 | Frederic John Goldsmid, *James Outram: A Biography* (London: Smith, Elder, 1880), 112. |
| Sir Montague Gerard | 227 | 227 by 1903 in Central India and Hyderabad | 1903 | Rangarajan, *India's Wildlife History*, 38; Thapar, *Battling for Survival*, 31. |

| | | | |
|---|---|---|---|
| 'British Royals' | 218 | 'British royals killed 218 tigers, 84 rhinoceroses, 63 leopards and 33 bears on five different occasions between 1876 and 1938' | 1876–1938 | Yogesh Dongol, 'Cultural Politics of Community-Based Conservation in the Buffer Zone of Chitwan National Park, Nepal' (PhD Diss., Florida International University, 2018), 134. |
| Sir Sainthill Eardley-Wilmot | 200+ | 'seen at least two hundred dead tigers' | | Sainthill Eardley-Wilmot and Mabel Eardley-Wilmot, *Forest Life and Sport in India* (London: E. Arnold, 1910), 95–96; Hewett, *Jungle Trails*, 66–70. |
| Sir John Campbell | <200 | 'Sir John Campbell, who has seen nearly 200 tigers killed, of which he has shot at least 60' | | Barclay, *Big Game Shooting*, 116; Woodyatt, *My Sporting Memories*, 15. |
| Col. Baigre | 195 | 'Sir Edmund Loder, in the course of a letter written in 1875, refers to Colonel Baigre, who, he says, has killed 195 tigers' | 1875 | Barclay, *Big Game Shooting*, 116. |
| Col. Maynard | 167 | | | J.S. Edye, *Sport in India and Somali Land* (London: Gale & Polden, 1895), 116. |
| Lt William Rice | 158 | Sankhala says 'during summer vacations 1850-4, killed and wounded 93 tigers in open forests near Nimach Cantonment… including 31 cubs' | 1850–1854 | William Rice, *Tiger-Shooting in India: Being an Account of Hunting Experiences on Foot in Rajpootana, During the Hot Seasons, from 1850 to 1854* (London: Smith, Elder, 1857); Sankhala, *Tiger!*, 132. |
| Gen. Sir Bindon Blood | 150 + | Seen more than 150, killed 52. | | Barclay, *Big Game Shooting*, 116–121. |
| Anon. | 147 | 'one hundred and fortyseven by another in the Central Provinces during a service life which ended in 1930' | 1930 | Stracey, *Wild Life in India*, 2. |

*(continued)*

Appendix 3.1. Continued

| Names | Number Killed | Description | Date | Source |
|---|---|---|---|---|
| Rana of Nepal and guests | 120 | 'Single season bag: In one season, covering 68 days, the total bag included 120 tigers, 38 rhinos. 28 leopards. 15 bears, 11 crocodiles and 1 elephant (captured)'; '120 tigers, 27 leopards and 15 sloth bears in one hunt in Nepal in 1919' | 1919 | Smythies, *Big Game Shooting*, 36. |
| Viceroy Linlithgow | 120 | '120 tigers in ten weeks [1938–1939] in the Chitawana Valley of Nepal' | 1938–1939 | Thapar, *Tiger: Portrait of a Predator*, 14. |
| Maharaj Ganga Singh | 104 | '104 including 17 in ten days in March 1920' | March, 1920 | Sankhala, *Tiger!*, 133. |
| Macpherson | 100+ | 'killed his hundred tiger and more' | | Woodyatt, *My Sporting Memories*, 26. |
| Raja Bahadur of Banali, Kirtyanand Sinha | 100+ | 'at least 100' | | Kirtyanand Sinha. *Shikar in Hills and Jungles* (Calcutta: Newman, 1934). |
| Tom Innes of Balrampur | 100+ | 'My dear, I shot my hundredth tiger 15 years ago and then I stopped counting' | | D.C. Kala, *Jim Corbett of Kumaon* (Delhi: Ravi Dayal, 1979), 93. |
| 'District Officials' | 100+ | 'It is not uncommon for District Officials in India, as a public duty in the course of their career, to kill a hundred tigers by organized drives, young buffaloes being tied up at likely spots for bait; on the principle of sacrificing one for all; and tigers so localized are driven out by a line of elephants and shot from the howdah'. | | Barclay, *Big Game Shooting*, 116–121. |
| Maharana of Udaipur | 100 | 'centuries include' | | Sankhala, *Tiger!*, 133. |

| | | | | |
|---|---|---|---|---|
| Maharaja of Kota | 100 | 'centuries include' | | Sankhala, *Tiger!*, 133. |
| Maharaja of Jaipur | 100 | 'centuries include' | | Sankhala, *Tiger!*, 133. |
| Nawab of Tonk | 100 | 'centuries include' | | Sankhala, *Tiger!*, 133. |
| Maharaja of Vijanagaram | 100 | 'centuries include' | | Sankhala, *Tiger!*, 133. |
| 'Nathu, Shikari' | 100 | 'Another faithful friend was Nathu, shikari, looking old at forty, but active and untiring, who had been with my father at the death of a hundred tigers, many of whose striped skins adorned the walls and floor of our bungalow' | | R. G. Burton, *The Tiger Hunters* (London: Hutchinson, 1936), 22. |
| John Broun, ICS | 100+ | 'probably shot a hundred' | 1887–1923 | Woodyatt, *My Sporting Memories*, 15. |
| 'Mr. —' | 100+ | 'Has shot over a hundred tiger to his own rifle… What a selfish old swine he must be' | | Woodyatt, *My Sporting Memories*, 15. |
| Capt. Caulfield | 93 | 'Approved tiger slayer', '93 poisoned in 1874' | | Sankhala, *Tiger!*, 132. |
| Lt-Col. Sir William A. Gordon-Cumming | 83 | 'Shot 73 tigers in one district along the Narmada River in 1863 and 1864, and he once shot 10 tigers in 5 days along the Tapti River' | 1863–1872 | Schaller, *The Deer and the Tiger*, 226; Sankhala, *Tiger!*, 132. |
| Jahangir | 86 | 'Jahangir killed over 17,000 animals. These included as many as 889 nilgai, 86 tigers and lions and 1,670 gazelle and antelope' | | Rangarajan, *India's Wildlife History*, 14. |
| Deputy Collector at Mymensing | 40–80 | 'A deputy collector who had long been stationed at Mymensing, a most experienced sportsman, noted for having killed more bears in that district than any one else, and who had been at the death of hundreds of buffaloes and scores of tigers' | | Simson, *Letters on Sport*, 173. |

*(continued)*

Appendix 3.1. Continued

| Names | Number Killed | Description | Date | Source |
|---|---|---|---|---|
| Sir Sainthill Eardley-Wilmot et al. | 40–80 | 'In those days we were in the habit of spending a fortnight of the month of May in Nepal . . . The average bag, with fifteen or twenty elephants, was about twenty tigers, panthers, and bears, and as many deer as one cared to shoot' | | Eardley-Wilmot, *Forest Life and Sport*, 29. |
| Badrul ul Islam | ~60 | 'In his lifetime, my father [Badrul ul Islam] shot three times as many tiger as Corbett bagged' | | Islam, *Hunting Dangerous Game*, 19. |
| Capt. James Forsyth | 40–50 | 'for many a man has killed his forty or fifty tigers who has never succeeded in bagging, by fair stalking, a single bull bison or a stag sambar' | | Forsyth, *Highlands of Central India*, 266. |
| C.J. Shorey | 50 | 'I have shot about 50 tigers and leopards' | | C.J. Shorey, 'Shikar Tales', *Journal of the Bengal Natural History Society* 20, no. 3 (Jan 1946): 87. |
| Sahibzada Abdul Shakur Khan of Tonk | 47 | At forty-three years: 'I have so far shot 47 tigers, 158 panthers, and 71 bears over and above most numerous other wild quadrupeds—the biggest ones in India. The list would, it is hoped, greatly swell if only Providence spared my life for a decade or two more.' | | Khan, *Shikar Events*, i, 1. |
| G.F. Pearson | 46 | | | G.F. Pearson, "The Degeneration of Tigers", *Indian Forester* 35 (1909): 273. |
| A cavalry officer of the 7th Hussars | 42 | 'A cavalry officer of the 7th Hussars', '42 in two summer vacations.' | | Sankhala, *Tiger!*, 132. |

| | | | | |
|---|---|---|---|---|
| Herky Ross and party | 40 | 'champion rifle-shot of India.' Shot 40 tigers in a single trip in the Terai, 'a record that has never been touched'. | | Edward Braddon, *Thirty Years of Shikar* (Edinburgh: William Blackwood, 1895), 211. |
| King George V | 39 | 'The total bag had been thirty-nine tigers, eighteen rhinoceroses, and four bears'; 'on the occasion of His Majesty the King's visit to Nepal' | 18–28 Dec 1911 | Charles Hardinge, *The Historical Record of the Imperial Visit to India 1911* (London: Murray, 1914), 320–327; Barlay, *Big Game Shooting*, 107. |
| Prince of Berar | 37 | Nizam of Hyderabad's son, shot in thirty-five days | 1937 | Mandala, *Shooting*, 251. |
| William and Mr. A | 36 | 'William arrived yesterday; he looks uncommonly well … He and Mr. A have killed 36 tigers, the largest number ever killed in this part of the country by two guns' | 1839 | Thapar, *Battling for Survival*, 4. |
| Prince Azan Jah Bahadur and party | 35 | 'in the course of 33 days shooting killed 35 tigers,' around Hyderabad | 1935 | Burton, *Preservation of Wild Life*, 82; Sankhala, *Tiger!*, 133. |
| Sainthill Eardley-Wilmot and Abdul Razak | 35 | 'Thirty-five tigers and an unrecorded number of panthers and bears we killed together … when he fell a victim to dysentery' | | Eardley-Wilmot, *Forest Life and Sport*, 138. |
| John Kerr | 30 | | | Pearson, 'Degeneration of Tigers', 273. |
| Jung Bahadur Rana of Nepal | 30 | 'killed 30 tigers in a single hunt' | 1850 | Yogesh Dongol, 'Cultural Politics of Community-Based Conservation in the Buffer Zone of Chitwan National Park, Nepal' (PhD Diss., Florida International University, 2018), 134. |
| Edward VII, Prince of Wales, and party | 28 | | 1875–1876 | Mandala, *Shooting*, 254. |

(*continued*)

Appendix 3.1. Continued

| Names | Number Killed | Description | Date | Source |
|---|---|---|---|---|
| Col. Garbott, et al. | 27 | 'in the Chitawan Valley.... party, which consisted of Colonel Garbott, C.O. of the 2nd Bengal Lancers; Major Ellis, R.E.; Major Bewicke-Copley (Sir Baker's military secretary); Major Smith-Dorrien, Derbyshire Regiment; and Capt. Browne Clayton, 5th Lancers, were lucky enough to secure twenty-three tigers, four cubs, and four leopards in fourteen days' | 1897 | Barclay, *Big Game Shooting*, 108. |
| Brig. Gen. R.G. Burton | ~27 | 'I have twice shot from thirteen to fourteen tigers during expeditions lasting six weeks each in particular tracts of country' | | Burton, *The Tiger Hunters*, 156. |
| Edward VIII, Prince of Wales | 27 | 'his expedition seems to have been lucky enough to secure twenty-three tigers, four cubs, and four leopards in fourteen days, besides a large quantity of various kinds of deer and birds' | 14–21 Dec 1921, Feb 1922 | Sankhala, *Tiger!*, 132. |
| 'A hunting party' | 23 | | Apr 1897 | Barclay, *Big Game Shooting*, 108. |
| Paul | 23 | 'Paul * (A Dutch sportsman, and not the Apostle) ... in about a week killed twenty-three royal tigers, besides several leopards' | | Edward B. Baker, *Sport in Bengal: And How, When, and Where to Seek It* (London: Ledger, Smith, 1887), 75; Burton, *The Book of the Tiger*, 95. |
| Samuel Baker | 22 | 'In the course of his many visits to the Central Provinces he shot 22 tigers and everyone that he fired at he bagged' | | Barclay, *Big Game Shooting*, 57. |

| | | | | |
|---|---|---|---|---|
| Forsyth | 21 | 'Forsyth (1911) shot 21 tigers in 31 days in Uttar Pradesh' | 1911 | Schaller, *The Deer and the Tiger*, 226. |
| Col. Jim Corbett | 19 | 'Between 1907 and 1938, Corbett tracked and shot a documented 19 tigers and 14 leopards—a total of 33 recorded and documented man-eaters' | 1907–1938 | Corbett National Park, 'About Edward James Jim Corbett'. http://www.corbett-national-park.co.in/About-Edward-James-Jim-Corbett.html |
| 'A scion of the Hearsey family' | 17 | '17 tigers in ten days in the Kheri forests of UP' | | Kala, *Jim Corbett of Kumaon*, 93. |
| 'British soldiers on foot' | 17 | 'during a short summer leave near Booranpur' | 1830 | Sankhala, *Tiger!*, 132. |
| Capt. J.H. Baldwin | 12+ | 'Baldwin spoke of the good old days when one could bag a dozen tigers in a fortnight' | ~1882 | Thapar, *Saving Wild Tigers*, 157. |
| R.P. Cobbold | 11 | 'A notable bag to one rifle was made by Mr. R.P. Cobbold in the Central Provinces in 1897. Between 1 March and 1 June, Mr. Cobb old shot 11 tigers, 3 panthers, 4 buffaloes, 2 bison, 4 bears, 2 sambhur and cheetah, making a total of 26 head of big game' | 1897 | Barclay, *Big Game Shooting*, 110. |
| Mrs Atkinson | 11 | Daughter of John P. Hewett | | Woodyatt, *My Sporting Memories*, 15. |
| Kenneth Anderson | 7–20 | 'He is officially recorded as having shot 8 man-eating leopards (7 males and 1 female) and 7 tigers (5 males and 2 females) on the Government records from 1939 to 1966 though he is rumored to have unofficially shot over 18–20 man-eating panthers and over 15–20 man-eating tigers' | 1939–1966 | Monish [pseud.], 'Kenneth Anderson (1910–1974)', 27 Apr 2010. https://www.africahunting.com/threads/kenneth-anderson.2771/ |

\* Notes: (1) When the same data point was provided by multiple sources, I have attempted to credit the first several sources to mention it. (2) Where there may be some discrepancy between data points—for example, where multiple sources provide conflicting statistics—I list each separately. Therefore, some individuals appear here more than once with several different totals. (3) Dates have only been provided when they were explicitly stated and when the differed from the publication date of the source.

# 4
# 'The Tribal Problem'

How does it feel to be a problem?
W.E.B. DuBois, *The Souls of Black Folk*, 1903

My general views on the subject of protection of the aboriginals are that it is absolutely essential, that without it he will continue to lose his lands, his own type of village life and what is left of his tribal culture and customs. To be effective this protection will have to be very much more positive than anything hitherto contemplated... No area is now too remote, too inaccessible or too unprofitable for the non-aboriginal malguzar, trader or adventurer.

E.S. Hyde, 1941[1]

Nearly 15 million inhabitants of India have been preserved in a state of semi-barbarism, denied education, medical facilities and other amenities of civilised life so that they may never develop a consciousness of their political and economic rights and learn to struggle in an organised and systematic manner against their innumerable wrongs... British Imperialism divides to rule. It has not only attempted to foster and perpetuate communal differences but has also divided the entire territory of the country in such a way as to confine the operation of democratic forces within as narrow limits as possible... The argument that the primitive people would be best off if allowed to remain in their natural isolation under the protective arm of British law is a pretence to hide the innumerable

---

[1] Cambridge Centre for South Asia Archive (CCSA), Letter to W.V. Grigson from ESH about aboriginal reserves, 14 Jan 1941. Hyde to Grigson: Camp Gwara, 14 Jan 1941.

economic wrongs which are inflicted on these people by British administration.

Ahmad, 'Excluded Areas Under the New Constitution', 1937[2]

The so-called primitives should retain the naturalness, health and physical beauty of primitive life and environment, and they should take to civilisation without its neurosis and its unhappiness, its intolerance and its bigotry, its violence and its ruthlessness, its selfishness and its cruelty and its tendency to seek prosperity and success of the few through the exploitation of the many.

B.H. Mehta, 'The Problem of the Aborigines', 1949[3]

In mid-twentieth century India, politicians, administrators, anthropologists, activists, and others spent tremendous time and energy in discussing solutions to the so-called 'tribal problem'. Yet, fascinatingly, in the massive paper trail they left behind, nobody ever seemed to quite put their finger on exactly what the 'tribal problem' actually was. In one sense, it came down to the question of the very 'existence' or 'survival' of the 'tribes', i.e. the fear of tribal endangerment and extinction. In another sense, the central issue was what the anthropologist Christoph von Fürer-Haimendorf once called 'a passionate controversy about the policy to be adopted vis-à-vis the aboriginal tribes'.[4] Following this logic, 'the tribal problem' has most often been characterized as a policy debate between mid-twentieth century anthropologists and administrators, a policy debate that was often boiled down to three competing ideological approaches to these communities: isolation, assimilation, and integration.

Whereas 'isolationists' were accused of being 'no-changers' who wanted to 'preserve the aboriginals in a museum' or 'a zoo' as specimens to study, the 'assimilationists' were lambasted for attempting to eradicate tribal culture and religion, and for seeing the tribes merely as

---

[2] Z.A. Ahmad, 'Excluded Areas Under the New Constitution', *Congress Political and Economic Studies* 4 (Allahabad: Ashraf, 1937), 6.

[3] B.H. Mehta, 'The Problem of the Aborigines', in *Thakkar Bapa Eightieth Birthday Commemoration Volume,* eds T.N. Jagadisan and Shyamlal (Madras: Diocesan Press, 1949), 244.

[4] Christoph von Fürer-Haimendorf, 'The Tribal Problem in All-India Perspective', in *Tribes of India: Struggle for Survival,* ed. Christoph von Fürer-Haimendorf (Berkeley: University of California Press, 1982), 313.

'backward Hindus' who ought to be incorporated into 'the mainstream'. 'Integrationists' appeared in the 1950s as the consensus camp, attempting to reconcile these two positions. While claiming they would protect tribal culture, integrationists were often difficult to distinguish from assimilationists in that they were usually most concerned with economically and politically integrating the tribes into the nation in the name of national unity.

Noteworthy here is that whether these administrators and anthropologists supported isolation, assimilation, or integration, all three positions were deeply paternalistic: all three presented tribes as needing to be cared for because they could not care for themselves. Rarely in the literature do we ever find any suggestion of asking the tribes what they themselves wanted, and there never was an official policy of consulting the communities in question. Furthermore, though often portrayed as a 'debate', the period of outright debate between isolationists and assimilationists was rather short-lived. Reaching a 'solution' to 'the tribal problem' was less of a debate and more of a broad consensus progressing away from what was seen as a colonial policy of isolationism and towards a framework of national integration under Congress leadership. While the 'isolationist' approach dominated up until the 1940s, and there was a relatively brief moment of substantive debate between colonial administrators and Indian nationalists from roughly 1937 to 1947, by the start of the independence period, with the old colonial guard out of power, a national integrationist policy towards the tribes took hold. While there was of course some level of disagreement even at this time, following independence nearly all major participants in the development of tribal policy expressed shades of views in favour of tribal integration or assimilation into the nation. This 'solution' to the 'problem' had emerged almost as if a Hegelian dialectic—colonial thesis: isolation, anti-colonial anti-thesis: assimilation, independence era synthesis: integration. Shades of integrationism then persisted virtually unchallenged, as the dominant approach to the tribal problem in India, until the mid-1980s. At this point, with the growth of the international indigenous rights movement, along with the rise of Adivasi social movements such as the Narmada Bachao Andolan (the Save the Narmada Movement), the old outlook that tribal ways of life in the hills and forests were endangered—specifically that tribal ways of life were threatened by the mainstream and by development—again started to gain popularity among many in the emerging Indian middle classes, especially on the left (see Chapter 5).

In recent decades, the only major study of the tribal problem in mid-twentieth century India has been Ramachandra Guha's biography of Verrier Elwin.[5] The entirety of the problem is personified by Elwin, 'through whose work and reception', Guha writes, 'we can track the shifting fashions in twentieth-century anthropology'.[6] Thus, Guha is focused on Elwin as 'quite possibly the most influential anthropologist to work in India, and certainly the most prolific', and to a lesser extent on his best-known interlocutors, namely G.S. Ghurye and A.V. Thakkar. Yet as brilliant as Guha's writing undoubtedly is, there simply is no way to encapsulate the entire gamut of voices weighing in on the tribal problem through a single biography. In Guha's wake, Elwin-studies has gone through something of a renaissance, but as two later biographers of 'the philanthropologist' put it: 'The tribal question in India obviously does not begin or end with Elwin. It is both broader and more complex than what Elwin had been able to experience, write about and advocate. But the efforts made so far by anthropologists and administrators alike have tended to iron out all naunce [sic] from our understanding...'[7] While Elwin was one of the most eloquent writers in mid-twentieth century India to put pen to paper on the subject of defending tribal ways of life, he was but one of numerous colonial anthropologists and administrators to be pigeon-holed as isolationist.

This chapter situates itself in mid-twentieth century India between approximately 1930 and 1980, as many hundreds of individuals were deeply involved in publishing and working on this 'problem', and as Indian administrator-anthropologists were supplanting European ones. So, while a single chapter like this cannot possibly give voice to every historical actor who engaged with 'the tribal problem', my hope here (as throughout the book) is to let these sources speak for themselves as they

---

[5] Ramachandra Guha, *Savaging the Civilized: Verrier Elwin, His Tribals, and India* (Chicago: University of Chicago Press, 1999).
[6] Ramachandra Guha, 'Between Anthropology and Literature: The Ethnographies of Verrier Elwin', *Journal of the Royal Anthropological Institute* 4, no. 2 (Jun 1998): 325–343.
[7] T.B. Subba and Sujit Som, eds., *Between Ethnography and Fiction: Verrier Elwin and the Tribal Question in India* (Delhi: Orient Longman, 2005), 8. Still, Subba and Som's volume focuses on Elwin in much a similar way, even borrowing the title and theme of their book from Guha, 'Between Anthropology and Literature'.

express their fears of tribal and national endangerment. It might at first seem paradoxical that it was mainly the British who were advocating saving endangered tribal culture through 'protection' and 'isolation', and Indian nationalists who were pushing to 'civilize' these 'primitives' through assimilation, national integration, and economic development. However, it must be remembered that by this time, many educated Indians had internalized not only the English language but also English values, especially imperialist notions of race, civilization, and progress. Furthermore, there seems to have been genuine fear that the British were threatening to divide and rule the nation, attempting to separate the tribes from the mainstream through isolationist tactics that involved scheduled districts, possibly separate electorates or separate states, or even an Adivasistan akin to Pakistan. Therefore, while some anthropologists were deeply committed to preserving the tribal cultures they felt were threatened, this concern was subordinated to the feeling harboured by the majority of nationalists that the unity of India itself was endangered and needed to be preserved.

## Colonial Tribal Policy: From 'Improvement' to 'Isolation'

There was a clear consensus amongst early twentieth-century colonial administrators and anthropologists: the tribes of India were endangered and needed protection. In some ways, this was not very different from late nineteenth-century approaches to tribes in India. Past administrators also saw tribes as threatened and believed in various forms of tribal protection. Previously, however, so-called 'protection' through 'improvement' with an eye towards 'civilizing the savage' was the dominant colonial approach, and this might arguably constitute ethnocide, despite what colonists believed. By the *fin de siècle*, the general feeling was emerging that most tribes had been so subdued, and forest areas had been so far reduced, that so-called 'wild tribes' now needed to be sheltered—as one of the most famous statements of the problem put it—from an 'over-hasty and unregulated process of "uplift" and "civilization" '.[8]

---

[8] Verrier Elwin, *The Baiga* (London: J. Murray, 1939), 511.

One of the big questions here is motive. It seems that most of the colonists believed in their own good intentions. Those who advocated the civilizing mission certainly believed that this would benefit the tribes, and arguably even those who advocated for the extinction of barbarism and primitivity believed that this was in the tribes' best interests. The difference was that by the late nineteenth century, calls for the extinction of 'savage tribes' were fading, and fear of tribal endangerment was now emerging as a prevailing colonial anxiety. As the 1908 *Imperial Gazetteer of India* put it, for 'forest tribes', 'the advance of civilisation must mean either extinction or absorption into a population possessing stronger vitality. The policy of the Government of India is to permit no sudden imposition...'[9]

The British may have genuinely believed in their good intentions towards the tribes, but by the 1930s, British motivation was being questioned at every turn by Indian nationalists. Some nationalists were now becoming sceptical of the colonial logic behind any form of tribal protection, especially when it involved keeping the tribes isolated from other Indians. The first concerted efforts at challenging colonial tribal policy thus came about during nationalist protests to the much-hated Simon Commission or Indian Statutory Commission Report of 1930 and the subsequent 1935 Government of India Act with its provisions for Excluded and Partially Excluded Areas for India's tribes.

At first, the level of rhetoric stating the difference between the British and the Congress view of the tribal problem was relatively subdued. In 1930, a *Report on the Depressed Classes of Bombay* authored by several prominent Indian nationalists, including A.V. Thakkar, explained that 'the problem of the Aboriginal and Hill Tribes... arises from the fact of isolation from the main body of the community' and called for greater economic integration.[10] But by 1937, there erupted an all-out war of words between Congress and colonial positions on tribal policy. Responding directly to Thakkar's 1930 report suggesting that the problem was 'isolation', Symington wrote: 'This is a view with which, if it is to be taken at its face value, I profoundly disagree... Actually, the problem of the aboriginal

---

[9] James Sutherland Cotton and William Stevenson Meyer, *Imperial Gazetteer of India*, vol. 3, ch. 2 Forests (Oxford: Clarendon Press, 1908), 124.
[10] British Library, India Office Records (IOR) V/26/803/5, *Report of the Depressed Classes and Aboriginal Tribes Committee, Bombay Presidency* (Bombay: Govt. Central Press, 1930).

and hill tribes lies not in their isolation from but in their contacts with the main body of the community'.

Symington thus promoted a paternalistic position towards the tribes, writing that 'at any rate for the next generation, we must regard the aboriginal as being in the nursery. Like a child—he must be protected from outside interference and victimization, and like a child he must be taught how to hold his own. In short, the State's attitude must be paternal'.[11] This type of patronizing rhetoric led the Congress to publish a scathing critique of the colonial excluded areas policy, which can be seen in the epigraph to this chapter by Z.A. Ahmed when in 1937 he accused the government of India of attempting to preserve 'nearly 15 million inhabitants of India… in a state of semi-barbarism, denied education, medical facilities and other amenities of civilised life'.[12]

To W.V. Grigson, one of the main proponents of the colonial policy, the nationalist reaction was a good thing because it 'stimulated Indian public opinion for the first time to a realization of the existence of the aboriginal problem'.[13] In private conversation in 1936, Verrier Elwin gave a more cynical response to the Hindu Congressmen who opposed colonial tribal policy, saying that, 'This company of vegetarians and teetotallers would like to force their own bourgeois and Puritan doctrines on the free and wild people of the forests'.[14] Grigson defended the policy, claiming that there was 'political prejudice against anthropologists', and worried: 'There is now a danger of constitution-makers dropping the present constitutional safeguards, forgetting the aboriginals and leaving them again to *laisser faire*'. Others British officials argued that Congress wanted to remove protections such as excluded areas because they feared losing power over tribal regions.[15]

By 1941, A.V. Thakkar observed the broad contours of what has ever since been styled the tribal problem 'debate': 'Among those interested in the welfare of the aborigines there are two schools favouring two different

---

[11] IOR V/27/803/1, D. Symington, *Report on the Aboriginal and Hill Tribes of the Partially Excluded Areas in the Bombay Presidency. For official use only* (Bombay, 1938), 1–2.
[12] Ahmad, 'Excluded Areas', 6.
[13] 'The lively controversy that followed stimulated Indian public opinion for the first time to a realization of the existence of the aboriginal problem'. W.V. Grigson, 'The Aboriginal in the Future India', *Man in India* 46 (Jan–Feb 1946): 16–17.
[14] Elwin to William Paton, 1936; quoted in Guha, *Savaging the Civilized*, 105.
[15] Grigson, 'The Aboriginal in the Future India', 16–17.

policies, which are generally called "Isolationism" and "Intervention".[16] Indeed at this point, British and Indian anthropologist administrators were by and large divided into two rival schools; yet a short six years later, the isolationist approach had largely gone extinct along with the colonial regime, giving way to a nationalist policy of 'intervention', as Thakkar called it. Furthermore, despite the Congress critique of colonial tribal policy, it was not only European administrators who advocated tribal protection through isolation prior to 1947. Not all Englishmen supported isolationism and not all Indians advocated for tribal assimilation or integration. By the 1960s, T.S. Wilkinson would look back on the 1930s and ridicule 'well-meaning anthropologists' who 'in their attempts to save the tribals from the evil consequences of culture-contacts advocated the "separationist" or "isolationist" view-point'.[17] He also cited D.N. Majumdar and S.C. Roy as two examples of Indians who favoured isolationism.

S.C. Roy, often regarded as the father of Indian ethnography, was perhaps the first Indian anthropologist. He also was a clear critic of colonial contact with the tribes. 'With the opening of the country by roads and railways under the British rule', according to S. C. Roy, 'and the gradual deforestation of the country and even the increasing restrictions on the use of forests, these forest tribes (the Birhors and Korwa of Bihar) are slowly and surely dying out, partly from famine and partly from loss of interest in life'.[18] Visiting other tribes of Chota Nagpur such as Mundas and Oraons, as well as the Birhor and Korwa, Roy wrote of their suffering, and in his 1925 monograph *The Birhors*, he expressed his fear of tribal extinction as a result of colonial modernity:

> I have been endeavouring to record, as faithfully as possible, the 'primitive' culture,—the rapidly disappearing customs and institutions, ideas and beliefs,—of the different 'aboriginal' tribes of Chota-Nagpur. As for

---

[16] A.V. Thakkar, 'The Problem of the Aborigines' (Poona: R.R. Kale Memorial Lecture, Gokhale Institute of Politics and Economics, Sep 1941), 23.
[17] T.S. Wilkinson, 'Isolation, Assimilation and Integration in Historical Perspective', *Bulletin of the Tribal Research Institute, Chhindwara, M.P.* 2, no. 1 (Jun 1962): 23.
[18] Sarat Chandra Roy, 'The Effect on the Aborigines of Chotanagpur of Their Contact with Western Civilization', *Journal of the Bihar and Orissa Research Society* 17, no. 4 (1931): 359; S.C. Roy, 'The Aborigines of Chota Nagpur. Their Proper Status in the Reformed Constitution of India', *Man in India* 26, no. 2 (1946): 120–136.

the Birhors, it is not only their 'primitive' customs and institutions, ideas and beliefs, that are fast decaying, but the people themselves would appear to be gradually dying out.[19]

In contrast to Roy, D. N. Majumdar who in 1937 wrote his book *A Tribe in Transition* on the Hos of Singhbum may have begun his career advocating isolation as the best way to save tribes, but by 1950 he expressed ambivalence about the direction of national tribal policy, writing for UNESCO:

The two axioms of cultural rehabilitation should be: (1) we cannot be civilized unless everyone of us is civilized, and (2) every people, however primitive or civilized, has a right to its own way of life, and to the development of its traditional culture. To reconcile these two requires a complete grasp of the details, and a sympathetic understanding of the realities of tribal aims and aspirations.

This rare nod to tribal self-determination—paying attention to the tribes' own 'aims and aspirations'—was probably only lip service. Majumdar had his own position on what should become of the tribes. While embracing the aspirations of national integration and economic development for all, he still wrote of 'detribalization' with some concern, discussing various tribes that had either been 'assimilated' or 'acculturated'. He thus supported the work of the Backward Class Department, advocating economic improvement, but also said 'economic improvement may not be the solution for tribal ills today... Under the prevailing economic conditions, disintegration of tribal life is as real today as the lack of social solidarity in community life in the villages... The pattern of tribal life everywhere has been disturbed... and unless tribal cultures can be readapted to tribal dynamics, the future of the tribal people cannot be assured'.[20] Majumdar observed that 'The influence of Hinduism on the tribal cultures has certainly been great', and feared that 'many of the tribes like the Korwas could preserve their cultural heritage only at the expense of their

---

[19] S.C. Roy, *The Birhors: A Little-known Jungle Tribe of Chota Nagpur* (Ranchi: Mission Press, 1925), iv.
[20] D.N. Majumdar, 'Tribal Rehabilitation in India', *International Social Science Bulletin: Documents on South Asia* 3, no. 4 (Winter 1951): 811.

tribal vitality, and to-day, like many other primitive tribes, they are faced with extinction'. Arguing that the 'free life in the forests' was something that 'protected them from cultural invasion', Majumdar celebrated the tribe that 'lives a wild life'.[21]

Similarly, Tarak Chandra Das, an early anthropologist from Calcutta University, referred to Adivasis as 'children of nature' and to their lands as 'their habitat'. Full of anger towards missionaries, he wrote that 'Christianity has destroyed beliefs'. But it was not just missionaries that he blamed.

> In India, the aboriginal tribes have to face two sets of exploiters: there are the foreigners to whom every Indian, whether savage or civilized, is equally exposed, and besides them there are the advanced Indians, who have established themselves in various capacities in the midst of the aboriginal population and are advancing their own interest at the expense of the savage. The Indian aborigines thus require double protection—protection from both internal and external exploiters.[22]

Das took his arguments for cultural preservation to the extreme and argued for the protection of even those practices 'which seem in terms of human suffering most cruel', e.g. human sacrifice and witch burning. Whereas most liberal humanitarians shirked at the notion of preserving manners and customs they themselves found abhorrent, he suggested that it was not the place of outsiders to eradicate such practices as these too, 'have some place in the maintenance of the society'.

Towards the end of his life, in the early 1960s, Das became more circumspect about the nature of the transformation in tribal India, though. Rather than writing about disappearing tribal culture, he talked about social change, writing: 'Society is dynamic; it is never static. Human groups change slowly or rapidly under the pressure of internal and/or external forces'. Still, he railed against all forms of external missionary pressure on tribal life—Christian, Muslim, and Hindu—saying: 'The ordinary

---

[21] D.N. Majumdar, *The Fortunes of Primitive Tribes* (Lucknow: Universal Publishers, 1944), 1, 4.
[22] Tarak C. Das, 'Cultural Anthropology in the Service of the Individual and the Nation: Presidential Address Delivered in the Section of Anthropology', in *Proceedings of the Twenty-Eighth Indian Science Congress* (Benares, 1941), 24.

converted tribal looks with wistful eyes on the free and frolicsome life of his non-converted brethren'.[23]

For J.H. Hutton, Commissioner for the Census of 1931, the question seemed to be how to slow the rate of change in tribal India, and the answer was clearly 'isolation'. 'For centuries before the British', changes 'were slow' and so tribes were 'therefore capable of gradual and proper adaptation'; now colonial modernity was 'rendering the tempo of change too swift for the tribes to accommodate themselves to it properly'. Thus, for example, Hutton had mixed feelings on the subject of tribal education, calling it 'a doubtful blessing'. On the one hand, he felt that it would 'unfit them' for traditional forest-based lifestyles, but on the other, that 'it is probably a necessary weapon of defence' in the face of modernity. Hutton was clear that, to him, 'the real solution of the problem would appear to be to create self-governing tribal areas with free power to self-determination', and he also proposed special separate electorates for tribes on these grounds.[24] Similarly, W.G. Archer, a friend to Hutton and Elwin, also supported isolation, and wrote in 1941:

> In Ranchi District, the Uraons, Mundas and Kharias have been exposed to two forms of moral uplift—one from the Christian Missions, the other from Hindu reformers. Each has produced its own type of 'moral' tribesman—a type that is puritanical in outlook, is afraid of life, and is on the whole much less happy than the unadulterated tribesman. Moral uplift in this sense is a poison.[25]

It is difficult to find any evidence that British anthropologists and administrators intentionally tried to harm the nationalist movement by dividing the tribes from the mainstream. Rather, they seemed to earnestly express a romantic, nostalgic outlook on a tribal life that could only suffer further cultural loss through contact with civilization. And perhaps the irony that it was now Indians themselves who were

---

[23] Tarak C. Das, 'Nature and Extent of Social Change in Tribal Society of Eastern India', *Sociological Bulletin* 11, no. 1–2 (1962): 221–238.
[24] Hutton quoted in Thakkar, 'The Problem of the Aborigines', 26.
[25] IOR MSS Eur F236/11, Papers of W.G. Archer, 'On the proposal of Mr. Thakkar to found an "All India Society for safeguarding aboriginal interests" to be named Indian Aborigines Friends Society', 171.

extending the old colonial civilizing discourse was not lost on them. Only once in my extensive archival research did I ever find an explicit statement of British self-interest in keeping the tribes separated from the larger Hindu population. In the file dating back to 1881, Robert Needham Cust, a somewhat famous colonial administrator and judge, active in the orientalist movement and also in evangelical circles, was writing to W.W. Hunter:

> It is of moment to the maintenance of our rule that they [the tribes] should not be absorbed into their Hindu neighbours, but maintain an existence, as a counterpoise to the Brahminical and Moahometan elements, and this can best be done by arresting, as far as an equitable system of government permits, the decay of their language, the extinction of their lawful customs, and the destruction of their national existence. 'Divide et Impera' was the great maxim of our Roman predecessors, and masters, in the art of ruling Subject Nations.[26]

## Assimilation, Mainstreaming

In the pre-independence era, A.V. Thakkar and G.S. Ghurye had some unlikely bedfellows in their campaigns to incorporate India's tribes into the mainstream. While it might seem counterintuitive, heavy hitters such as Mahatma Gandhi and Babasaheb Ambedkar were both supporters of assimilationist or integrationist policies and rejected isolationism for Adivasis. Despite the fact that Gandhi's *Hind Swaraj* was 'a severe condemnation of modern civilization', rejecting railroads and telegraphs in favour of a republic of villages, he vigorously supported A.V. Thakkar who sought to integrate, modernize, and otherwise 'civilize' India's tribes. Writing of Thakkar's efforts, Gandhi proclaimed: 'Who can deny that all such service is not merely humanitarian but solidly national, and brings us nearer to true independence?'[27]

---

[26] IOR L/PJ/6/72, File 691 of 1881, Robert Needham Cust, Hon Sec to RAS to Hn Dr WW Hunter, President of Edu Comm of Brit India.
[27] M. K. Gandhi, *Constructive Programme: Its Meaning and Place* (Ahmedabad: Navajivan, 1941), 23–24. Gandhi here also incorrectly suggested that the term Adivasi 'was coined, I believe, by Thakkar Bapa'.

Per Ram Guha, 'adivasis never figured seriously in the Mahatma's programmes of social reform'.[28] Yet by the close of the 1930s, Gandhi began to worry that 'Adivasis might follow the example of the Muslim League and launch a series of campaigns for separate states'.[29] This is probably why Gandhi stood by Thakkar even when he proclaimed, 'The aborigines should form part of the civilised communities of our country'. Thakkar argued that this was:

> not for the purpose of swelling the figures of the followers of this religion or that, but to share with the advanced communities the privileges and duties on equal terms in the general social and political life of the country. Separatism and isolation seem to be dangerous theories and they strike at the root of national solidarity. We have already enough communal troubles, and should we add to them instead of seeing that we are all one and indivisible? Safety lies in union not in isolation.[30]

As opposed to Gandhi's overtly political and pragmatic reasons for supporting national integration for the tribes, it seems that Ambedkar earnestly believed that tribalism and primitivity must be purged from the earth, just as he believed untouchability should be eradicated. In Ambedkar's 1936 book *The Annihilation of Caste,* he called it a 'shameful state of affairs' that 'aborigines have remained in their primitive uncivilized State in a land which boasts of a civilization thousands of years old'. 'Thirteen millions of people living in the midst of civilization are still in a savage state and are leading the life of hereditary criminals!', he exclaimed. Asking, 'Why has no attempt been made to civilize these aborigines', he answered, 'that the aborigines have remained savages because they [the Hindus] had made no effort to civilize them'. The key to Ambedkar, as to why this should be, was the caste system. Ridiculing *savarnas* as too

---

[28] R. Guha, 'Lost in the Woods', *Hindustan Times,* 23 Oct 2008. https://www.hindustantimes.com/india/lost-in-the-woods/story-gbX8spVkWcqrgjhzuLDHnO.html
[29] David Hardiman, *Gandhi in His Time and Ours: The Global Legacy of His Ideas* (New York: Columbia University Press, 2003), 151.
[30] Thakkar, 'Problem of the Aborigines', 26; quoted in R. Guha, 'Savaging the Civilised: Verrier Elwin and the Tribal Question in Late Colonial India', *Economic & Political Weekly* 31, no. 35/37 (Sep 1996): 2380.

anxious to preserve their own caste to get their hands dirty working with 'tribals', he wrote: 'Caste is, therefore, the real explanation as to why the Hindu has let the savage remain a savage in the midst of his civilization.'[31]

Elite nationalists in the early twentieth century such as Gandhi and Ambedkar were deeply steeped in an English-medium educational system that embraced concepts of civilizational and racial hierarchies. It is thus somewhat unsurprising yet sad that at the same time most Indians were rejecting prejudice about their own primitivity, the idea that the tribes were 'backward' featured prominently in mainstream thought. Tribes were to be 'brought up' to the level of the general population. As Pooja Parmar puts it, 'To be a tribal person meant to be living in a state of social, cultural, and economic primitiveness, and once a person shed that status one also shed one's tribal identity'. Thus during the Constituent Assembly debates preceding independence in 1947, one Congress member 'declared that the Scheduled Tribes "sub-human state of existence" was "a stigma on our nation just as the existence of untouchability is a stigma on the Hindu religion"'.[32]

There was a strong right-wing chauvinistic tendency at work when it came to assertions of Hindu superiority over tribal culture, as well. We can see this kind of thinking, in particular, in the case of M.S. Golwalkar—a man dubbed the 'guru of hate' by Ram Guha, and called 'Shri Guruji' by the RSS. Golwalkar once wrote:

> The non-Hindu people of Hindustan must either adopt Hindu culture and language, must learn and respect and hold in reverence the Hindu religion, must entertain no idea but of those of glorification of the Hindu race and culture... In a word they must cease to be foreigners, or may stay in the country, wholly subordinated to the Hindu nation, claiming nothing, deserving no privileges, far less any preferential treatment—not even citizens' rights.[33]

---

[31] B.R. Ambedkar, 'Annihilation of Caste with a Reply to Mahatma Gandhi' (1936), in *Writings and Speeches*, vol. 1 (Bombay-Education Department: Government of Maharashtra, 1944).
[32] Pooja Parmar, 'Undoing Historical Wrongs: Law and Indigeneity in India', *Osgoode Hall Law Journal* 49, no. 3 (Summer 2012): 512–513.
[33] Madhav Sadashiv Golwalkar, *We, or, Our Nationhood Defined* (Nagpur: Bharat Publications, 1939), 104–105.

Siding with the British government in its earlier efforts to sedentarize the tribes, he was also angered that the 'Government has classified all the "non-Christians" and "tribals" as distinct from Hindus'. Complaining of 'the problem of the wandering habits of the tribals', Golwalkar asked: 'How can they be given any training or samskars when they do not stay at one place at all for any length of time? ... If we could domesticate even the wild animals roaming in the jungles, can we not persuade our own people to take to better and more refined ways of life?'[34]

Golwalkar's views on 'the tribal problem' are particularly problematic in light of the fact that he defended the rights of the 'German race' to 'keep up the purity of the Race and its culture' by 'purging the country of the Semitic Races—the Jews', and felt it was the right of the 'Hindu race' to do so as well, saying that what the Nazis were doing in 1939 was 'a good lesson for us in Hindusthan to learn and profit by'. While some would certainly see it as less controversial to advocate for the rights of Adivasis to 'keep up the purity of the Race and its culture', others might be equally concerned about any expressions of preserving racial purity—even that of marginalized groups. Golwalkar argued that, 'Germany has also shown how well-nigh impossible it is for Races and cultures, having differences going to the root, to be assimilated into one united whole.'[35] Nonetheless, he argued for assimilation of the *girijans*, as he called them, into the national mainstream, since they were merely 'backward Hindus' and—according to him—not members of a distinct race.

Taking this opportunity to reflect on the Nazi holocaust and its extermination discourses in comparison to those at work in India, I think it is worthwhile turning to the writing of Zygmunt Bauman who argues that Nazi racism mobilized 'anti-modernist sentiments and anxieties' in its campaign against the Jews. According to Bauman, National Socialism proposed an 'ideal *volkisch* society of the future', and Nazis such as Joseph Goebbels 'identified modernity as the rule of economic and monetary values, and charged Jewish racial characteristics with responsibility for such a relentless assault on the *volkisch* mode of life and standards of human worth'. This position is diametrically opposed to the assimilationist attitude taken by self-ascribed 'mainstream Hindus' towards

---

[34] M.S. Golwalkar, *Bunch of Thoughts* (Bangalore: Vikrama Prakashan, 1966).
[35] Golwalkar, *We, or Our Nation Defined*, 86–87.

'THE TRIBAL PROBLEM' 181

modernizing and civilizing the tribes, and perhaps explains why even the British largely bemoaned the extinction of India's tribes during their colonial heyday. Again to quote Bauman:

> In a world that boasts the unprecedented ability to improve human conditions by reorganizing human affairs on a rational basis, [Nazi] racism manifests the conviction that a certain category of human beings cannot be incorporated into the rational order, whatever the effort... that certain blemishes of a certain category of people cannot be removed or rectified—that they remain beyond the boundaries of reforming practices, and will do so for ever.... To summarize: in the modern world distinguished by its ambition to self-control and self-administration, [this genocidal] racism declares a certain category of people endemically and hopelessly resistant to control and immune to all efforts at amelioration. To use the medical metaphor: one can train and shape 'healthy' parts of the body, but not cancerous growth. The latter can be 'improved' only by being destroyed.[36]

While both Jews and Adivasis were subjected to dehumanizing discourses, according to this racist logic, Jews were targeted for extermination because Nazis believed they could not be reformed; in contrast, Adivasis were targeted for improvement, because it was believed they could be. And whereas Jews were not accepted as part of the folk culture or *Volkskultur*, Adivasis were seen as its quintessence. For these reasons, the 'Jewish problem' and the 'tribal problem' had fundamentally different solutions.[37]

In part, this comparison is important because of firmly established Nazi-Hindu nationalist alliances emerging in the late stages of India's independence struggle.[38] For instance, Savitri Devi née Maximiani Portas,

---

[36] Zygmunt Bauman, *Modernity and the Holocaust* (Cambridge: Polity Press, 1989), 62, 65.

[37] Very few authors seem to have ever teased out this parallel. One recent article to do so was Murzban Jal, 'Historical Materialism and a Relook at the "Tribal Question" in India', *Mainstream Weekly* 55, no. 1 (24 Dec 2016). Jal asks: 'The "Jewish Question" gave birth to Nazism and Zionism, what would the "Tribal Question" give birth to?'

[38] Benjamin Zachariah, 'A Voluntary Gleichschaltung? Indian Perspectives Towards a Non-Eurocentric Understanding of Fascism', *Journal of Transcultural Studies* 5, no. 2 (2014): 63–100 and Benjamin Zachariah, 'At the Fuzzy Edges of Fascism: Framing the Volk in India', *South Asia: Journal of South Asian Studies* 38, no. 4 (2015): 639–655.

who embraced both Nazism and Hinduism, and believed that Adolf Hitler was akin to an avatar of Vishnu, had this to say about the incorporation of tribes into the Aryan community:

> As long as the hill-tribes of India (the so-called 'animists' etc.) do not feel that *their* primitive forms of worship are one of the innumerable aspects of manifold Hinduism, and that *they* are a part and parcel of manifold Hindudom, their strength is lost to the cause of Hindudom. And it is a pity, for they are sturdy fighters. But they will never feel themselves Hindus unless the Hindus make them feel so, through their behaviour towards them; unless they are treated as Hindu.[39]

It is also worthwhile exploring these Nazi-Hindutva connections because by the outset of the independence era, the Hindu right had dominated the debate on the tribal problem; their position was not very far from what became national policy. One individual who was both personally connected to Golwalkar and was in a position to shape right-wing tribal policy was Ramakant Keshav AKA Balasaheb Deshpande, a member of the RSS. According to the RSS *Organizer*, Deshpande attended Nagpur's Hislop College where he came into contact with Golwalkar in the 1920s. To further quote the *Organizer*:

> After independence Balasaheb was appointed by the then Ravi Shankar Shukla Government to work in tribal dominated Jashpur area as 'Regional Officer' of the 'Tribal Development Scheme' ... This particular area had gone into the iron grip of the Christian missionaries who had converted the simple tribal people to their religion by using all means fair and foul. Their conversion to Christianity had alienated them from the cultural and national moorings... Balasaheb took up this daunting challenge and succeeded in establishing 100 government schools in Jashpur area in 1948.... Thakkar Bappa visited Jashpur as promised and praised Balasaheb and his efforts. As a token of appreciation he gave him Rs 251/- as prize for his accomplishment. He showered praises on him in his article in the magazine of Adim Jaati Sevak Sangh

---

[39] Savitri Devi, *A Warning to the Hindus* (Calcutta: Brahmachari Bijoy Krishna, Hindu Mission 1939), 94.

wherein he wrote: 'Shri Balasaheb Deshpande is an able and competent activist in eastern India'.[40]

In 1952, Deshpande established the Vanvasi Kalyan Ashram in Jashpur in present-day Chhattisgarh, 'with six children of the Oraon tribe'.[41] (The organization itself claims that Deshpande was inspired by A.V. Thakkar to do so.[42]) According to Jafferlot, 'the Ashram grew rapidly and a permanent office was established in 1963, inaugurated by the RSS chief M.S. Golwalkar'.[43] While prior to the 1970s, the Ashram appears to have had only a single branch, it 'grew exponentially between 1978 and 1992. Today, the VKA says they run a total of 17,808 projects across 28 states and 2 union territories in India. They claim to have made contact with 51,763 tribal villages in the country'.[44] As discussed in Chapter 2, all of this is worth observing because the organization's avowed mission is to assimilate the tribes into the Hindu mainstream.[45]

In 1952, the sociologist M.N. Srinivas coined the term 'sanskritization': a process 'by which a "low" Hindu caste, or tribal or other group, changes its customs, ritual, ideology, and way of life in the direction of a high, and frequently, "twice-born" caste'.[46] While usually understood as a neutral description of a sociological phenomenon, 'sanskritization' was also the Hindutva prescription for what *should* happen to India's tribes. As Carol Upadhya puts it, 'Sanskritisation has become a rather dangerous hegemonic idea not only within Indian sociology but also in public discourse, for it implies that absorption into Brahminical culture and social order is a natural outcome of upward socioeconomic mobility'.[47] In his first-ever usage of the term, Srinivas expressed the Hindutva agenda quite

---

[40] Virag Pachpore, 'The Legend Called Balasaheb Deshpande', *The Organizer*, 23 Dec 2013.
[41] Sohini Chattopadhyay, 'Exclusive: Inside a Hindutva Hostel: How RSS Is Rewiring the Tribal Mind', *Catch News*, 19 Dec 2015. http://www.sacw.net/index.php?page=imprimir_articulo&id_article=12762
[42] Vanvasi Kalyan Ashram, 'About Us'. https://vanvasi.org/about-us/
[43] Christophe Jaffrelot, *The Hindu Nationalist Movement and Indian Politics: 1925 to the 1990* (London: C Hurst, 1996).
[44] Chattopadhyay, 'Inside a Hindutva Hostel'.
[45] Vanavasi Kalyan Ashram Delhi, 'Welcome to the Vanavasi Kalyan Ashram Delhi'. http://web.archive.org/web/20160327171551/http://vanvasikalyanashramdelhi.org/index.php/2-uncategorised/16-welcome-to-vanvasi-kalyan-ashram-delhi
[46] M. Srinivas, *Social Change in Modern India* (Bombay: Allied Publishers, 1966), 6.
[47] Carol Upadhya, 'The Hindu Nationalist Sociology of GS Ghurye', *Sociological Bulletin* 51, no. 1 (2002): 27–56.

clearly: 'A low caste was able, in a generation or two, to rise to a higher position in the hierarchy by adopting vegetarianism and teetotalism, and by Sanskritizing its ritual and pantheon'. Relevantly, Srinivas happened to be the student of G.S. Ghurye, the most famous advocate of raising the tribes into Hindu civilization.

Munshi in 1979 suggested that whereas Srinivas was committed to Brahminism, N.K. Bose was committed to national unity.[48] Bose, who between 1967 and 1970 was Commissioner for Scheduled Castes and Tribes, had written a famous article as early as 1941 on 'the Hindu method of Tribal absorption'.[49] Arguing against 'protectionism' on the grounds that it represented 'a latent two-nation theory', Bose suggested that Hindus were culturally *laissez-faire,* and described a 'Brahminical way of acculturation' that he believed was fundamentally different from western forms of cultural imposition. Supposedly, the tendency 'was not to displace the original social and religious culture of the tribes, but rather to preserve it'. Calling Hinduism a 'federation of faiths' (yet also referring to the 'culture of the conquerors' and the 'vanquished culture'), Bose believed that the aim of Brahminism was to keep 'lower' castes from rising 'high', i.e. to keep them in their place, so that they would not aspire to upper-caste status. Still, something had to be done 'to bring the tribal cultures in line with Brahminism'. 'Brahmins modified the old culture [of the tribes] when it went against the grain of their own ideas and left the rest intact'.[50]

To summarize, following the 1935 Government of India Act, which established 'totally and partially excluded areas' for tribes, most educated Indians emerged 'firmly in favour of a policy of assimilation', largely on nationalist grounds. Critiquing the long-term impact of this assimilationist policy on India's tribes, historian Crispin Bates describes the 'wholesale expropriation of their forest reserves by eager [Hindu] settlers from the lowlands' and 'the sheer destitution that resulted'. Reflecting on the tribal problem as a whole from the perspective of 1988 when he was writing, Bates morosely observes, 'the problem itself is beginning

---

[48] Surendra Munshi, 'Tribal Absorption and Sanskritisation in Hindu Society', *Contributions to Indian Sociology* 13, no. 2 (1979): 293.
[49] N.K. Bose, 'The Hindu Method of Tribal Absorption', *Science and Culture* 7, no. 2 (1941): 188–194.
[50] Munshi, 'Tribal Absorption and Sanskritisation in Hindu Society', 293–297.

to disappear. The tribals are being assimilated. In many cases the only vestige that remains of once powerful tribal kingdoms is a scattering of sometimes violent proto-nationalist movements'.[51]

## Towards National Integration

It was Jawaharlal Nehru, the first Prime Minister of independent India and adept statesman that he was, who did more than anyone else to bridge the gap between the isolationists and assimilationists and to move tribal policy towards economic and national integration. In a series of speeches in the early 1950s, Nehru outlined his vision for 'the tribal people' or 'the tribal folk', as he sometimes called them. Nehru was fond of saying he attached 'the greatest importance' to a great variety of things, but when in 1952 he said before parliament, 'I attach the greatest importance to the tribal people of India and I hope that this House will consider the matter more fully', his words ring true with a sense of urgency. 'The tribal folk', according to Nehru, 'have a very special culture which should be protected and encouraged to advance along the lines of its own genius. I do not want the tribal culture of India to be overwhelmed or exploited just because the people to whom it belongs happen to be simple folk'.[52]

Nehru, who was friends with Verrier Elwin, expressed similarly romantic sentiments in his vision of tribal life, to the point where even Elwin jokingly acknowledged this, writing that Nehru's speeches were 'as far from reality as I am'.[53] Nehru declared that long before he became Prime Minister, he had always 'felt very strongly attracted to the tribal people of this country', and that he was 'alarmed' whenever he saw people trying 'to shape others according to their own image or likeness and to impose on them their particular way of living'. Comparing 'civilized' and 'tribal' life, he reflected, 'I am not at all sure which is the better way of living. In some respects I am quite certain theirs is better'. Speaking before an audience of

---

[51] Crispin Bates, 'Congress and the Tribals', in *The Indian National Congress and the Political Economy of India*, eds Mike Shepperdson and Colin Simmons (Aldershot: Avebury, 1988), 231.
[52] Jawaharlal Nehru, 'Looking Back' (Speech in Parliament, New Delhi, 22 May 1952), *Speeches*, vol. 2 (Delhi: Government of India Publications Division, 1954), 17.
[53] Cited by Guha, *Savaging*, 222.

social workers, he went on to make a passionate case for the value of tribal life as he imagined it:

> My own predilection is for the mountains rather than for the plains, for the hill folk rather than the plains people.... Above all, they are a people who sing and dance and try to enjoy life; not people who sit in stock exchanges, shout at one another and think themselves civilized. I would prefer being a nomad in the hills to being a member of stock exchanges.... Is that the civilization we want the tribal people to have? I hope not. I am quite sure that the tribal folk, with their civilization of song and dance, will last till long after stock exchanges have ceased to exist.

'Therefore', Nehru concluded, 'it is grossly presumptuous on our part to approach them with an air of superiority or to tell them what to do or not to do. There is no point in trying to make of them a second rate copy of ourselves'. Yet despite these feelings of fondness, Nehru still had his eye on national politics, and he clearly saw 'tribal folk' as key voting blocks in rural India. Thus, he envisioned the 'basic problem of India, taken as a whole' as 'one of integration and consolidation', and called for 'psychological integration' as well as political consolidation. 'India must build up for herself a unity'.[54]

Looking back on the decade of debate pitting isolation against assimilation before independence, Nehru reflected: 'We have approached the tribal people in one of two ways. One might be called the anthropological approach in which we treat them as museum specimens. The other approach is one of ignoring the fact that they are something different requiring special treatment and of attempting forcibly to absorb them into the normal pattern of social life'. Critiquing those who 'may talk day after day about development', but would seek improvement through assimilation, he pronounced, 'We must let them feel that we come to give and not to take something away from them'. His solution must have appeared pragmatic and balanced to his contemporaries: on the one hand, tribal

---

[54] J. Nehru, 'The Tribal Folk: Speech at the Opening Session of the Scheduled Tribes and Scheduled Areas Conference' (New Delhi, 7 Jun 1952), *Speeches*, vol. 2 (Delhi: Government of India Publications Division, 1954), 576–583.

lands and forests should receive 'a measure of protection', on the other hand, 'Obviously, there is need for schools, for health relief, for cottage industries and so on'. However, it was important to always keep in mind, 'that we do not mean to interfere with their way of life but want to help them live it'.

By 1958, in the foreword to Verrier Elwin's *A Philosophy for NEFA,* Nehru would put forward his definitive statement of 'Tribal *Panchsheel*'—his five fundamental principles for tribal development in India:

(1) People should develop along the line of their own genius and we should avoid imposing anything on them. We should try to encourage in every way their own traditional arts and culture.
(2) Tribal rights in land and forest should be respected.
(3) We should try to train and build up a team of their own people to do the work of administration and development. Some technical personnel from outside will, no doubt, be needed, especially in the beginning. But we should avoid introducing too many outsiders into tribal territory.
(4) We should not over-administer these areas or overwhelm them with a multiplicity of schemes. We should rather work through, and not in rivalry to, their own social and cultural institutions.
(5) We should judge results, not by statistics or the amount of money spent, but by the quality of human character that is evolved.[55]

While these may have sounded like lofty ideals, their impact turned out to be rather problematic. In effect, by envisioning tribes as in need of economic and national integration, it also marked them out as primitive or backwards peoples to be 'developed' and, despite rule #4, subjected them to massive state-driven intervention under a series of five-year plans. Nehru, who described big dams as 'the temples of modern India', might have had a romantic view of tribal life, but he was also a believer in what James Scott once called 'authoritarian high modernism'.[56] As the

---

[55] J. Nehru, 'Foreword', in Verrier Elwin, *A Philosophy for NEFA*. Elaborated in: *Report of the Committee on Special Multipurpose Tribal Blocks* (New Delhi: Government of India, Ministry of Home Affairs, 1960), 13.

[56] James C. Scott, *Seeing Like a State: How Certain Schemes to Improve the Human Condition Have Failed* (New Haven: Yale University Press, 1998), 87.

nation rushed towards industrial modernity, many have argued that it left countless Adivasis as 'victims of progress' in its wake.

Nehru was by no means alone in his views about preserving tribal culture while simultaneously promoting integration and development. K.P. Chattapadhyay, for instance, who was amongst the first Indians to study anthropology in London in 1919–1920 and was the first chair of anthropology at Calcutta University, delivered a paper in 1949 that anticipated Nehru's position.[57] Writing that 'the tribal problem in our country is as serious as the communal problem', he nonetheless argued that 'one essential point has been overlooked. The culture of most tribal folk contain [sic] valuable elements which should be conserved'. Saying that 'There is unfortunately an influential school of thought which has been responsible for the view that the tribal folk are culturally part of the Hindus, and should be absorbed', he further argued that, 'We have no right to inflict on the tribals, the kind of domination through political power which our former imperial masters inflicted on us in our colonial stage'. Chattapadhyay thus took a nuanced position that while on the one hand 'economically they need both teaching of improved methods of production as well as safeguards against exploitation', on the other, 'We have not enough land to spare or adequate areas for poorly productive shifting cultivations as the No-changers have suggested for preserving old ways of life'.[58] Similarly, in 1949 S.C. Dube, a product of the University of Nagpur, expressed sentiments much along the lines of Nehru's:

> Socio-cultural integration of the tribes in the main stream of Indian Society must be our ultimate ideal, but transition of the tribes from primitiveness to civilization should be planned with care and caution so as to ensure the survival of the still vital elements in the tribal cultures and save them from decay, degradation and disintegration.[59]

---

[57] Gerald Gaillard, *The Routledge Dictionary of Anthropologists* (London: Routledge, 2004), 272.

[58] K.P. Chattapadhyay, 'The Tribal Problem and Its Solution', *Eastern Anthropologist* 3, no. 1 (Sep 1949): 20.

[59] S.C. Dube, 'The Kamars and Some Problems of Tribal Adjustment', *Eastern Anthropologist* 2, no. 4 (Jun 1949): 192.

B.H. Mehta, also writing in 1949, declared: 'National Isolation Impossible—Assimilation Imperative', but then argued for what in retrospect can be identified as a clearly integrationist position. Reflecting back on the recently ended colonial era, he described the origins of tribal protectionism:

> As imperialism and all forms of exploitation came to be exposed in the nineteenth century and the present century, and colonial rule and capitalism were found to be ruthlessly exterminating the primitive races, humanitarians the world over found a sincere interest in the well-being and welfare of these unfortunate neglected peoples.

To some extent, Mehta was sympathetic with this type of 'humanitarianism', writing 'the aborigines must primarily be approached in a spirit of service and not domination'. He was also mindful of 'ancient heritage' and its preservation. However, he argued that protection through isolation was a lost cause:

> The idealistic approach of leaders like Malinowski can be appreciated and understood, but India has to realise that it is no longer possible to create cultural islands and to isolate natural human groups to their own way of development... It is futile now to plead for isolation, segregation and reservation. They can no longer be left alone, and left to themselves they will not desire to be alone.[60]

Post-1947, in one sense, the Congress backtracked somewhat on its avowed hatred of Scheduled Areas. Following the Constituent Assembly debates, the Constitution of 26 January 1950 not only continued the existence of Scheduled Areas but also included the first use of the term 'Scheduled Tribes'.[61] However, the policies now taken towards these areas and peoples were anything but isolationist; they were thoroughly developmentalist. 'Primitiveness' and 'backwardness' were the tests applied to populations to see if they fit into the lists of scheduled tribes—the

---

[60] Mehta, 'The Problem of the Aborigines', 236–240.
[61] Government of India (GoI), *Constitution of India*, Articles 341 and 342—giving the president of India and governors of the states a mandate to compile a full listing of scheduled castes and tribes.

more primitive and backward, the more in need of integration. As the Indian Statutory Commission paternalistically put it, 'We know that the tribes are backward and we know for centuries past they are backward; but our approach should be not what the tribes would do for themselves, but what we should do for them'.[62]

Through a series of five-year plans following the Soviet model starting in 1951, Tribal Development Blocks (third plan), Tribal Development Agencies (fourth plan), and Tribal Sub-Plans covering Integrated Tribal Development Projects (ITDPs) (fifth plan) became the order of the day. As Katherine Charsley points out, 'even under the more flexible model for Tribal development in the fifth five-year plan, project designers were told to keep in mind the underlying aim: "to arrest the nomadic character of the 'tribes' and provide them wherewithal to lead a settled life".'[63] And as B.K.R. Burman perceived in 1960:

> According to the Backward Class Commission, lack of 'assimilation in the main body of the people' and 'kind of life lead by them' are the two main diagnostic features for determination of the Scheduled tribes. In other words there are two ways to look at the tribals, one as primitive folk, who have remained backward in the scale of civilization; the other as minority population who have not been assimilated in the main body of the population.... So long as this image of 'being primitive' and 'being different' continues, they will undoubtedly continue to be regarded as tribals.[64]

Paradoxically, integrationists called for protecting tribal culture while simultaneously economically integrating the tribes into a burgeoning industrial economy. Since many of these same people felt that it was precisely 'wildness', 'backwardness', 'primitivity', proximity to nature, etc.,

---

[62] John Allsebrook Simon, *Report of the Indian Statutory Commission,* vol. 1 (London: His Majesty's Stationery Office, 1930), 158.

[63] Katharine Charsley, '"Children of the Forest" or "Backwards Communities"? The Ideology of Tribal Development', *Edinburgh Papers in South Asian Studies* 7 (1997), 5; S. Sanyal, 'Primitive Tribes of Bihar: Strategy for Development', *Man in India* 68, no. 4 (1988): 359.

[64] B.K. Roy Burman, 'Basic Concepts of Tribal Welfare and Tribal Integration', *Journal of Social Research* 3, no. 2 (1960): 17–18. Burman clearly rejected the notion that tribes were the 'indigenous peoples' of India, going so far as to launch a hunger strike at an international conference because they were being treated as such by the participants.

that defined tribal culture, it is difficult to understand how both cultural preservation and economic integration might be simultaneously feasible.

The Communist Party of India took much the same sort of evolutionary and developmentalist approach to the tribes as the Congress. As late as 1973, their publications argued that 'Backwardness is the hallmark of the tribals' existence' and locked the tribes into the classic trope of timelessness, saying that, 'for tribal people in India time has stood still for many centuries'.[65] Nonetheless, communists made fun of the 'Gandhian workers' like 'Thakkar Bapa' for their 'liberal-democratic approach' and 'missionary zeal', and critiqued the Congress-wallahs saying they 'hardly realise and appreciate the revolutionary potentialities of the tribal'. A.B. Bardhan, who authored a 1973 Communist Party publication titled *The Tribal Problem in India*, argued with the Congress that the 'British imperialists kept the tribal people and the areas they inhabit deliberately isolated from the rest of the Indian people', because they 'did not wish them to become a part of the national movement'. 'The areas inhabited by the tribal people were converted by the imperialists into excluded areas— in an effort to keep them as exclusive preserves of the foreign administration and the christian [sic] missionaries'. But Bardhan also criticized the authors of the constitution:

> when they sat down to frame the constitution of India, they took great care to liberally intersperse it with articles and schedules purporting 'to promote with special care the educational and economic interests of the weaker sections of the people and, in particular, of the scheduled castes and the scheduled tribes', 'to protect them from social injustice and all forms of exploitation', and so on.

But the communist position was that these liberal protections had little or no effect and missed the opportunity for 'bringing about a radical socioeconomic transformation'. Bardhan felt the key was to 'harness the initiative of the tribal masses themselves'. ' "More than anything else a cadre of people committed to tribal uplift is needed".... from where else can the tens of thousands of cadres come, if not from amongst the tribal people themselves?' But again here, it is important to note that communists

---

[65] A.B. Bardhan, *The Tribal Problem in India* (Delhi: Communist Party Publication, 1973), 17.

were not calling for consultation with tribes to form their development agenda. Their agenda was set—it was communist. But they wisely calculated that there was no one better to pit against the Indian bourgeoisie than the tribals. They seemed like the perfect candidates to join in 'the revolutionary struggle against all forms of exploitation' because 'the tribal people are the worst and most helpless victims' of 'the tentacles of the capitalist market economy'.[66] When the tribal problem was understood to be the problem of poverty, the logical solution was 'development', and development was paired irrevocably with integration into the economy.

Present-day ecological Marxists would argue that tribal peoples have suffered capitalist alienation from labour, undergoing both estrangement from themselves and their cultures as well as alienation from nature and their lands (*entfremdung* and *entäußerung*), detached from traditional life through dehumanizing market-based relationships. Questions of how 'tribes' have been stripped of their so-called species-being (*Gattungswesen*) or species-life (*Gattungsleben*) would also be examined.[67] However, in historical practice, Marxist regimes have rarely taken such 'ecological' approaches to supposedly tribal populations. Thus, Marx's legacy has been deeply problematic for the so-called 'pre-industrial' peoples of the world. The materialist conception of history and dialectical materialism rested on the same nineteenth-century evolutionist dreams of progress as that of the colonial administrators, and in the twentieth century, these were still often being paired together. Lenin, for example, consistently railed against what he called 'stagnation and Asiatic backwardness'.[68] As he once wrote, communism 'will put an end to the division between town and country, will make it possible to

---

[66] Ibid., 8.
[67] In doing so, they draw directly on Marx's own writings on estranged and alienated labour: 'Die äußerliche Arbeit, die Arbeit, in welcher der Mensch sich entäußert, ist eine Arbeit der Selbstaufopferung, der Kasteiung'. 'Indem die entfremdete Arbeit dem Menschen 1. die Natur entfremdet, 2. sich selbst, seine eigne tätige Funktion, seine Lebenstätigkeit, so entfremdet sie dem Menschen die Gattung; sie macht ihm das Gattungsleben zum Mittel des individuellen Lebens'. 'Die entfremdete Arbeit macht also: 3. das Gattungswesen des Menschen, sowohl die Natur als sein geistiges Gattungsvermögen, zu einem ihm fremden Wesen, zum Mittel seiner individuellen Existenz. Sie entfremdet dem Menschen seinen eignen Leib, wie die Natur außer ihm, wie sein geistiges Wesen, sein menschliches Wesen'. Karl Marx, 'Die entfremdete Arbeit', *Ökonomisch-philosophische Manuskripte* (1844). https://www.marxists.org/deutsch/archiv/marx-engels/1844/oek-phil/1-4_frem.htm
[68] Vladimir Ilyich Lenin, 'The Heritage We Renounce', in *Lenin's Collected Works*, vol. 2 (Moscow: Progress Publishers, 1972), 491–534. http://www.marxists.org/archive/lenin/works/1897/dec/31c.htm

raise the level of culture in the countryside and to overcome, even in the most remote corners of land, backwardness, ignorance, poverty, disease, and barbarism'.[69] Similarly, under Mao, the ideology of China's Cultural Revolution explicitly called for the destruction of the 'four olds': Old Customs, Old Culture, Old Habits, and Old Ideas.[70] Where in this vision is there any room for a forest-based or supposedly 'tribal' way of life?

After colonial 'isolationism' was defeated by virtue of India gaining its independence, and 'integrationism' became the order of the day, there was only one relatively major public figure in mid-twentieth century India who advocated a radical alternative for India's 'Adibasis', as he called them. Jaipal Singh, an Oxford-educated Olympic field hockey-playing member of the Munda tribe from what is now Jharkhand state, stood in the Constituent Assembly of India between December 1946 and January 1950 as the representative of 'the aboriginal tribes of Chhota Nagpur'. And as Parmar puts it, Singh 'considered himself the representative of the thirty million original inhabitants of India, a point he emphasized over and over again'.[71]

Jaipal Singh's most famous speech in the Constituent Assembly debates is worth quoting at length here, not only because of its eloquence, but also because it reveals so much both about his position and the vast array of prejudices and hurdles lined up against him and his community:

> Mr. Chairman, Sir, I rise to speak on behalf of millions of unknown hordes—yet very important—of unrecognised warriors of freedom, the original people of India who have variously been known as backward tribes, primitive tribes, criminal tribes and everything else. Sir, I am proud to be a Jungli, that is the name by which we are known in my part of the country... What my people require, Sir, is not adequate safeguards as Pandit Jawahar Lal Nehru has put it. They require protection from Ministers. That is the position today. We do not ask for any special protection. We want to be treated like every other Indian. There is the problem of Hindusthan. There is the position of Pakistan. There is the problem of Adibasis. If we all shout in different militant directions,

[69] Ibid., 'Report on Work of the All-Russia C.E.C. and C.P.C.', vol. 30, 335.
[70] Xing Lu, *Rhetoric of the Chinese Cultural Revolution: The Impact on Chinese Thought, Culture, and Communication* (Columbia: University of South Carolina Press, 2004), 61–68.
[71] Parmar, 'Undoing', 504.

feel in different ways, we shall end up in Kabarasthan. The whole history of my people is one of continuous exploitation and dispossession by the non-aboriginals of India punctuated by rebellions and disorder, and yet I take Pandit Jawahar Lal Nehru at his word. I take you all at your word that now we are going to start a new chapter, a new chapter of Independent India where there is equality of opportunity, where no one would be neglected ... [72]

Singh tried taking back the term 'jungli' much the same way the LGBTQ community has now re-appropriated the term 'queer'—but his colleagues in the constituent assembly would have none of it. They maintained that the goal was to civilize the savage, and that Jaipal was the perfect example of the civilizing mission's success. During the constituent assembly debates, on the cusp of independence in April 1947, Vallabhbhai Patel who would become India's first Deputy Prime Minister under Nehru, made this clear when he said: 'I think that it should be our endeavour to bring the tribal people to the level of Mr. Jaipal Singh and not keep them as tribes, so that, 10 years hence... the word "tribes," may be removed altogether when they should have come up to our level.'[73]

Singh, in contrast, had a radically different agenda. Focused on the centrality of land rights and the trauma of dispossession, he advocated for nothing less than the resurrection of 'tribal republics' in India. 'The aboriginals' land must be inalienable', he proclaimed. When he mentioned 'the problem of Hindusthan' and the 'position of Pakistan' in the same breath as the 'problem of Adibasis', he was careful not to say 'the problem of Adibasistan'. However, many in the Congress party still feared that after Singh took control of the Adivasi Sabha (Adivasi Assembly) and renamed it the Adivasi Mahasabha (Adivasi Grand Assembly) in 1939, that he was dabbling in anti-national politics.

After the Muslim League formally adopted Pakistan as its goal following the Lahore Resolution of 1940, there was a real fear that other minorities such as Dalits and Adivasis would also try to form breakaway republics. Thus, R.S. Shukla wrote to Vallabhbhai Patel expressing his

---

[72] GoI, *Constituent Assembly Debates (Proceedings)*, vol. 1, 19 Dec 1946. https://www.constitutionofindia.net/constitution_assembly_debates/volume/1/1946-12-19
[73] Vallabhbhai Patel on 30 Apr 1947, quoted by Ghurye, *The Scheduled Tribes*, 349. Also quoted in Bates, 'Congress', 21.

concern that 'The Adivasi Mahasabha also came closer to the Muslim League during the war period... The Muslim League thought of carving out an independent Adivasistan which would form a corridor between East and West wing of the proposed Pakistan'.[74] Other sources report that cries of 'Pakistan Zindabad' were heard along with those of 'Adibasistan Zindabad' in mid-1940s Bihar, and that the Muslim League claimed that 'a confederation of Adibasistan and East Pakistan will be practical, defensible, solvent and self sufficient'.[75] At least some contemporary oral histories agree, with one Jharkhand-born member of the All India Momin Conference recalling: 'Jinnah had told the Adivasis that they should ask for Adivasistan and he would demand Pakistan. He told Jaipal Singh he himself desired Assam and he would give Bengal to the Adivasis'.[76]

Reflecting on this situation from the late 1950s, M.S. Niyogi in his *Report of the Christian Missionary Activities Enquiry Committee* also argued that the push for 'Adiwasisthan', as he called it, arose along with the demand for Jharkhand state, and that Singh was 'commonly described as the father of the Jharkhand movement'. However, Niyogi blamed Christian missionaries along with the Muslim League for propagating the movement. 'Adiwasisthan', according to the Niyogi report, 'was approved by the Aboriginals, local Christians and Muslims'—the 'demand for Adiwasisthan was accentuated along with the one for Pakistan'—but it was 'missionaries', he argued, who 'sought to keep it under their influence by excluding all the nationalists elements from this movement'. The report contends that following independence, 'the agitation for Adiwasisthan was intensified, with a view to forming a sort of corridor joining East Bengal with Hyderabad, which could be used for a pincer movement against India in the event of a war between India and Pakistan'. Yet again, Christian missionaries were to blame for promoting

---

[74] R.S. Shukla to Sardar Vallabhbhai Patel, 20 Jan 1948, letter no. 435; Durga Das, ed., *Sardar Patel's Correspondence 1945–50. Vol. 7 Integrating Indian States, Police Action in Hyderabad* (Ahmedabad: Navajivan, 1973), 525.
[75] Mahesh Kumar Deepak, 'Communal Politics and the Role of Various Political Ideologies in Bihar: 1940–45', *Scholarly Research Journal for Interdisciplinary Studies* 4, no. 30 (Mar 2017): 5021 quotes S.S. Pirzada, *Select Speeches of M.A. Jinnah*, 306. However, no book with this exact title appears to exist. http://www.srjis.com/pages/pdfFiles/1497252864Mahesh%20Kumar%20Deepak.pdf
[76] Kathinka Sinha-Kerkhoff, 'Voices of Difference: Partition Memory and Memories of Muslims in Jharkhand, India', *Critical Asian Studies* 36, no. 1 (2004): 113–142.

an 'isolationist doctrine'; they came 'ostensibly to do social work, but in reality to propagate the Adiwasi movement'.[77]

## Urgent Anthropology

Claud Lévi-Strauss's elegy to a dying world could perhaps be given credit for relaunching tribal endangerment discourse again in 1960s India. In *Tristes Tropiques*, first published in France in 1955, Lévi-Strauss dedicated an entire chapter to describing a single sunset, and many more to disappearing cultures around the world. By 1965 he would deliver a keynote address discussing the future direction of the discipline in response to this sense of loss. 'It is precisely because the so-called primitive peoples are becoming extinct that their study should now be given absolute priority', he insisted. 'With the high rate of extinction afflicting primitive tribes the world over', Lévi-Strauss forecasted that 'within a century or so, when the last native culture will have disappeared from the Earth ... our only interlocutor will be the electronic computer'.[78] The movement that would arise around these fears was dubbed 'urgent anthropology'.

Following Lévi-Strauss, the Wenner-Gren Foundation, which publishes the journal *Current Anthropology* took the lead on pioneering the field of urgent anthropology, proclaiming: 'There should be no single world center for urgent research, other than *CA*'. The journal claimed that urgent anthropology was a new approach, but in response, Jacob Gruber authored an article describing a long history of what he called 'salvage anthropology' dating back at least to the nineteenth century.[79] One critic thus labelled 'urgent anthropology' a 'conceptual fallacy which has dogged us for over a century' and noted that, 'Each generation seems to pass through the same throes of wanting to "preserve last remaining vestiges"'. Another had, 'very mixed feelings about this "salvage" program'.[80] The Austrian

---

[77] Niyogi, M. Bhawani Shankar et al., *Report of the Christian Missionary Activities Enquiry Committee, Madhya Pradesh 1956* (Nagpur: Government Printing, 1957), 120–121.

[78] Claude Lévi-Strauss, 'Anthropology: Its Achievements and Future', *Current Anthropology* 7, no. 2 (Apr. 1966): 124–127; *Tristes Tropiques*. (Paris: Plon, 1955).

[79] Jacob W. Gruber, 'Ethnographic Salvage and the Shaping of Anthropology', *American Anthropologist*, New Series 72, no. 6 (Dec 1970): 1289–1299.

[80] Priscilla Reining, 'Urgent Research Projects', *Current Anthropology* 8, no. 4 (Oct 1967): 362–416.

Anna Hohenwart-Gerlachstein also wrote to *Current Anthropology* to outline how its programme was by no means new: as early as '1952, at the International Congress of Anthropological and Ethnological Sciences in Vienna, that [Robert von] Heine-Geldern arranged a symposium under the heading "An S.O.S. of Anthropology"', and subsequently 'in Philadelphia in 1956, the problem of working on disappearing culture phenomena was discussed in a meeting of the International Union of Anthropological and Ethnological Sciences'.[81]

During the first conference on urgent anthropology held in Washington, DC in 1966—co-sponsored by the Smithsonian and the Wenner-Gren Foundation—'The conference kept returning to the "image of anthropology" held by administrators and government officials' in certain areas of the world, and it was noted that 'There are places where anthropologists are thought to be hostile toward social and cultural change; sometimes anthropological field research is viewed as a form of exploitation'.[82] This was almost certainly a reference to India. By 1968, India held its own spinoff conference on urgent anthropology in the old Viceregal Lodge at the Simla Institute of Advanced Studies, but attitudes were deeply divided. The editors of a volume produced from the conference's proceedings began by noting that, historically, 'social anthropologists with only a few exceptions have been mainly concerned with the social customs and institutions of "black" peoples subject to "white" rule', and one of the early papers observed how some Indians felt 'that anthropology was nothing but a means to satisfy the idle curiosity of Europeans'.[83]

There were at least a few serious detractors to the idea that India's tribes and their cultures urgently needed to be saved. Niharranjan Ray, for example, in his 'Introductory Address' to the conference, argued that 'social anthropology in India, to my mind, is not so much a study of vanishing as of changing communities and cultures, changing in a

---

[81] Anna Hohenwart-Gerlachstein, 'The International Committee on Urgent Anthropological and Ethnological Research', *Current Anthropology* 10, no. 4 (Oct 1969): 376–377.
[82] 'Smithsonian-Wenner-Gren Conference', *Current Anthropology* 8, no. 4 (Oct 1967): 355–361.
[83] B.L. Abbi and S. Saberwal, 'Introduction', in *Urgent Research in Social Anthropology: Proceedings of a Conference*, eds B.L. Abbi and S. Saberwal (Simla: Indian Institute of Advanced Studies, 1969), 1; A. Aiyappan, 'Urgent Anthropology for Southern India', in *Urgent Research in Social Anthropology: Proceedings of a Conference*, eds B.L. Abbi and S. Saberwal (Simla: Indian Institute of Advanced Studies, 1969), 35.

relatively slow or fast pace, but changing nevertheless', and then went on to say that: 'As a student of Indian history I know of hardly any caste or tribal group that has vanished or is vanishing'. Ray then compared the argument that India's tribes are vanishing to the claim that 'Buddhism has vanished altogether from India, as many knowing people even do, without realising how most of the ideas and institutions of the religion have passed into what is called Hinduism'. I. Karve put it particularly strongly:

> The question of the tribes is linked up with our national unity and security. At no point can we stress tribalism so as to give a separate group identity to these people. They can keep their names and customs without interference. But they must be rapidly assimilated to the rest of the Indian population, and by the rest of the population I mean the linguistic region within which they find themselves.

Many anthropologists seemed particularly interested in preserving so-called primitive cultures. But to Karve, 'primitiveness' was 'but a passing phase':

> Most of the Khasis, Mundas, Santhals, some Gonds and Bhils have already passed that stage and live a life comparable to the life of the peasants. As to their picturesque customs, other castes have customs and festivals no less picturesque. They want to take part in national life on terms of equality. They deserve protection like that guaranteed to the backward, but not deliberate isolation.[84]

Given the volume's various critiques of urgent anthropology as a European preoccupation, it is somehow unsurprising that one of the main advocates for urgent anthropology emerging from the proceedings was Christoph von Fürer-Haimendorf. Haimendorf, who had been deeply influenced by Heiner-Geldern who began the urgent anthropology craze in post-World War II Austria, now also revealed himself as

---

[84] I. Karve, 'The Tribals of Maharashtra', in *Urgent Research in Social Anthropology: Proceedings of a Conference*, eds B.L. Abbi and S. Saberwal (Simla: Indian Institute of Advanced Studies, 1969), 96, 99.

a great supporter of Verrier Elwin, following Elwin's death in 1964. In an interview, Haimendorf once described Elwin as 'the greatest sort of anthropological idealist I'd ever met'. Still, Haimendorf clearly sympathized with Elwin, who he described as believing 'we must protect tribal people, they must not be totally assimilated to the advanced population'. And discussing Elwin's anti-assimilationist stance, he suggested that Elwin 'exerted very healthy influence' on the tribal problem debate.[85]

Making an explicit animal analogy to endangered species, Haimendorf declared at the 1968 Simla conference (as cited in the epigraph to Chapter 2): 'thoughtful men of the future will inevitably charge us with the neglect of unique possibilities if we allow the last archaic civilizations of our days to vanish unrecorded. The representatives of no other discipline, except perhaps zoologists studying species threatened with extinction, are subject to such urgency'. Yet Haimendorf did not call for tribal conservation, nor did he make the comparison to wildlife conservation. His main interest, along with most promotors of urgent anthropology, was not saving tribes themselves, but rather saving endangered anthropological data. 'Considering the incipient disintegration of tribal life' he had witnessed all over India, he worried 'whether within a few years such a study could still be undertaken'.[86]

In William Sturtevant's report from the 1966 Washington, DC conference inaugurating the field of urgent anthropology, this point about the preservation of cultural data was made excessively clear. 'Anthropology is in danger of losing the largest portion of its laboratory just at the time when it becomes able to use it effectively', the report in *Current Anthropology* claimed. 'A main purpose of their field investigations' was therefore, the 'recording of data on cultures undergoing change'. While the extinction of tribal cultures might now be inevitable, 'The purpose of the conference was to explore the proposition that, late as it is, a concerted international effort may yet recover a very significantly greater amount of data than would be preserved without such an effort'.[87] This, however,

---

[85] A. Macfarlane, 'Interview with Professor Christoph von Fürer-Haimendorf' [Video file] (2003), http://www.dspace.cam.ac.uk/handle/1810/28
[86] Christoph von Fürer-Haimendorf, 'Fundamental Research in Indian Anthropology', in *Urgent Research in Social Anthropology: Proceedings of a Conference,* eds B.L. Abbi and S. Saberwal (Simla: Indian Institute of Advanced Study, 1969), 79.
[87] 'Smithsonian-Wenner-Gren Conference', 355–361.

was again a point of criticism by Indian administrators who disapproved of India being treated as a 'laboratory' for Europeans to experiment in, of India's peoples as sources of cultural 'data' for foreign anthropologists, and of the exoticization they saw as going along with all of this. After all, the 1960s was the era of hippie romantic sensibilities, redolent with primitivism, directed towards a supposedly mystic east.

In his 1969 report to *Current Anthropology*, L.P. Vidyarthi provided a rather conservative write-up of the results of the Urgent Anthropology conference in Simla. Writing that 'the problem of urgency' had to be viewed with an eye towards 'national development', he argued that in India, there was a 'coexistence of diverse styles of life, from the very primitive to the most technologically advanced' and did not seem particularly concerned that 'The former are likely to be radically transformed in the near future in the context of the vast programme of planned economic development'.[88] However, within just a few short years, Vidyarthi seems to have come around to the cause of urgent anthropology in a less reluctant way. In 1971 he wrote again to *Current Anthropology*, stating that those who ignored the study of 'nomadic tribes and other primitive tribes facing demographic and cultural extinction' and preferred to study tribes in the northeast engaging in separatist struggles 'will fail to perform the proper task of Urgent Anthropology'. And by 1976, as President of the Indian Anthropological Association, Vidyarthi acknowledged, 'In general... tribes in different parts of India are passing through an accelerated phase of transformation and the equilibrium in the traditional society has definitely been greatly disturbed. A phase of transition marking the meeting of the two worlds, traditional and modern, in in the process'. Still, 'the identity and variety of the tribal culture, of course in changed form, will be maintained'.[89]

Despite Vidyarthi's optimism, just as in earlier colonial days, it was not only European anthropologists who sided with the notion that tribal cultures must be protected, or at least that data about them had to be preserved before it was lost forever. At the 1968 Simla conference, S.C. Dube, for example, described his long-time concern for India's vanishing tribes:

---

[88] Lalita Prasad Vidyarthi, 'Conference on Urgent Social Research in India', *Current Anthropology* 10, no. 4 (Oct 1969): 377–379.
[89] L.P. Vidyarthi and Binay Kumar Rai, *The Tribal Culture of India* (Delhi: Concept, 1976), 472.

Sixteen years ago, at the invitation of Professor Heine-Geldern, I attended one of the earliest symposia on Urgent Tasks of Anthropology held in Vienna during the Fourth International Congress of Anthropological and Ethnological Sciences. On re-reading the condensed version of my oral presentation published four years later (Dube 1956), I find that in a large measure I shared with the other participants a concern for studying vanishing tribal cultures and rare institutional forms. In the developing countries there has been a noticeable shift in their conception of what is urgent: rather than studying quaint and exotic little groups they would have their anthropologists concentrate on social and cultural phenomena relevant to nation building. But I am still oldfashioned enough to believe that the wonder that permeates mankind is worth exploring. As such, I would not accord too low a priority to what is known as salvage anthropology.[90]

## Indigenous Rights Movements Since the 1970s

Starting in the 1970s and 1980s, the national consensus on the tribal problem was starting to wane. Much of this shift in view can likely be related to the rise of international indigenous rights movements in that period. It was at that time that many global tribal rights organizations such as Survival International and Cultural Survival were founded, and international law first started to address the rights of indigenous peoples.[91] As summarized in the *Duke Law Journal*:

> Since the 1970s, in international human rights forums around the world, indigenous peoples have contested the international legal system's continued acquiescence to the assertions of exclusive state sovereignty and jurisdiction over the terms of their survival. Pushed to the brink of extinction by state-sanctioned policies of genocide and ethnocide,

---

[90] S.C. Dube, 'Five Research Proposals', in *Urgent Research in Social Anthropology: Proceedings of a Conference*, eds B.L. Abbi and S. Saberwal (Simla: Indian Institute of Advanced Study, 1969), 61.
[91] Theodore Macdonald, Jr., 'Introduction: 25 Years of the Indigenous Movement in the Americas and Australia', *Cultural Survival Quarterly*, Jun 1997. https://www.culturalsurvival.org/publications/cultural-survival-quarterly/introduction-25-years-indigenous-movement-americas-and

indigenous peoples have demanded heightened international concern and legal protection for their continued survival.[92]

In another law review special issue titled *Endangered Peoples: Indigenous Rights and the Environment,* a critique of mid-twentieth century policies towards indigenous peoples globally could just as easily read as a critique of India's integrationist tribal policy specifically:

> The experience of indigenous populations from the mid-1940s through the mid-1980s was such that international development programs were seen as a means of depriving them of their lands and natural resources. This was particularly true of large-scale hydroelectric projects, agricultural programs, mining and petroleum extraction activities, and development programs aimed at assisting nonindigenous peoples to settle in the territories of indigenous peoples.[93]

We thus seem to have come back full circle to earlier twentieth centuries views of non-interference with tribal cultures. However, in this new iteration, paternalism was out; indigenous peoples themselves were finally playing a significant role in their own affairs; and self-determination and sovereignty, along with land rights and environmental rights, were the name of the game. In this context, many South Asian anthropologists and administrators were also coming around in their views—not to the idea of tribal independence or separatism, but at least to acknowledging the negative impacts of the last thirty years of tribal policies. Integrationism was now viewed as having an extremely deleterious impact on endangered tribal cultures. Suranjit Kumar Saha, for example, complained of a 'paradox' between 'commitments by the state to protect tribals from exploitation and social injustice on the one hand and of the worsening conditions or exploitation and repression of the tribals on the other'. Saha would claim that government programmes 'have had very little effect in

---

[92] Robert A. Williams, Jr., 'Encounters on the Frontiers of International Human Rights Law: Redefining the Terms of Indigenous Peoples' Survival in the World', *Duke Law Journal* (1990): 665.
[93] Robert K. Hitchcock, 'International Human Rights, the Environment, and Indigenous Peoples', *Colorado Journal of International Environmental Law and Policy* (special issue: *Endangered Peoples: Indigenous Rights and the Environment*) 5, no. 1 (1994): 10.

stemming the worsening immiserisation of the tribal people', and that the government itself acknowledged the 'ineffectiveness of the government sponsored tribal development programmes' in its own planning documents.[94] The problem, according to Saha, was that, 'The state as well as the academic community in India regard the country's tribal problem as one of integrating a geographically isolated and economically backward section of its population into its national mainstream of society and economy', entirely missing 'the problem which is the exploitative nature of the integrative process itself'. Economic integration had been a bust, according to Saha: 'The elite of the broader society begin to dominate the production process of the tribal areas' and 'the tribal society loses its economic autonomy'. Cultural integration was, too: 'Any suggestion that … [sanskritization] will secure any economic or social advantages to the tribals therefore seems to be a logical as well as an historical absurdity'. Thus, Saha again raised the fear that 'the Hindu elite' will 'use the rhetoric of national integration to break down or dilute the sense of separate ethnic identity and pride of the tribals'. To Saha, 'postcolonial Indian scholarship' was aimed at 'facilitating and accelerating the process of incorporation of the tribal communities into an elite controlled pan-Indian political economy at unequal and progressively deteriorating terms'.

> To visualise India's tribal problem as one of breaking down the current social isolation of the tribal people and of integrating them into the national mainstream under the existing conditions is to cause extreme violence to their immediate as well as long term interests. The national mainstream is the Hindu-Muslim social formation, and the historically determined relations of exploitation which bind it with the tribal society are precisely the reasons of the latter's destitution and immiserisation.[95]

Similarly, towards the end of his life in 1981, B.H. Mehta, who had been a firm integrationist in the 1940s and 1950s, also seemed to question what decades of this nationalist policy had accomplished. He began his two-volume magnum opus *Gonds of the Central Indian Highlands* by asserting

---

[94] Suranjit Kumar Saha, 'Historical Premises of India's Tribal Problem', *Journal of Contemporary Asia* 16, no. 3 (1 Jan 1986): 275.
[95] Ibid., 291, 311.

the urgency of his work: 'there will be little chance in the future to study the traditions and background of Gond society even after one decade'.[96] By the mid-1980s, public opinion in India seems to have returned full circle to the view that Adivasis were losing their unique forest-based cultures and traditions as a result of economic and political integration. And even the Government of India in its 1989–1990 *Report of the Commission for Scheduled Tribes and Scheduled Castes* now acknowledged that 'colonisation of tribals carried out in the name of development', has challenged the very survival of Adivasi communities; stating that 'their conditions come to the close of [sic] ethnocide'.[97]

Again, we see that India's so-called tribal problem, though often framed as a debate, usually reached a consensus policy position that evolved according to the times. All along, the fundamental concern was indigenous survival in the modern world. But the solution to the problem continued to shift with historical circumstances. With the emergence of major social and environmentalist movements since the 1980s, such as the Save the Narmada movement (the *Narmada Bachao Andolan*, discussed in Chapter 5), the fear of parallel biological and cultural endangerment for tigers and tribes, forests and forest-based ways of life, again surfaced in late twentieth-century India as a dominant discourse.

---

[96] B.H. Mehta, *Gonds of the Central Indian Highlands*, vol. 1 (Delhi: Concept, 1984), xxx. Mehta goes on to say that 'The study reveals that the present progress of tribal welfare and community development in tribal areas may prove effective to achieve regional and economic development and national integration. But greater and deeper attention will have to be given to the problems of the real welfare of the people'.
[97] *Report of the Commission for Scheduled Tribes and Scheduled Castes* (Delhi: Government of India, 1990).

# 5
# *Narmada Bachao, Manav Bachao*

They [the Bhils] seem, in their natural state, like the Bushmen of Africa, scarcely men, but rather a link between the human species and the wild creatures among whom they live. Robbers and marauders by natural descent, for long their hand was against every man and every man's hand against them. Hunting, varied by plundering and cattle-lifting, was their normal trade. There was something noble in them too; they were in fact the Rob Roys of India and, like our Rob Roy, they for a long time actually levied black mail [sic] from the inhabitants of the open country. Proscribed by Government and hunted down, they were killed by hundreds, but never subdued.

David Davidson, 1880[1]

Our introduction of the Bhil to the rule of law instead of the rule of force, previously his real element, has been like trying to teach a child to swim by throwing it in the middle of a pond. The Bhil has not been quite drowned; he can feel the bottom—rock bottom—with his feet. But he will never learn to swim that way; and meanwhile he is suffering many ill-effects from too long immersion in a strange element. He does not know how to master that element; instead it masters him.

David Symington, 1938[2]

---

[1] 'Lecture Delivered in Edinburgh to H.M.'s 78th Highlanders, by Col. Davidson, Late of the Bombay Army'; F.J. Goldsmid, *James Outram: A Biography* (London: Smith, Elder, 1880), 55.
[2] British Library, India Office Records (IOR) V/27/803/1 David Symington, 'Report on the Aboriginal and Hill Tribes of the Partially Excluded Areas in the Bombay Presidency. For official use only' (Bombay, 1938).

Whether or not these people are truly tribal in terms of World Bank definitions is of great significance to the Bank, the people, and the three Indian states. Bank policy on involuntary resettlement makes special provision for tribal people. The 1982 Operational Manual Statement urges that every effort be made to 'safeguard the integrity and well-being' of tribal peoples, and at the minimum to 'prevent or mitigate harm.' Both the 1982 and 1991 policy directives emphasize the importance of detailed research into the social, economic, and cultural implications of projects that impinge on tribal peoples' lives and lands. If the people of the Narmada valley are not merely 'backward Hindus'—a term that has been used to characterize the link between Scheduled Tribes and mainstream Indian society—then the Bank and governments are burdened with a greater responsibility. It is no wonder that the status of the peoples of the Narmada valley has been the subject of many arguments.

Bradford Morse and Thomas Berger, 1992[3]

Dear Friends, The 17 years long struggle in the Narmada valley has now reached it's [sic] peak. And what lies ahead is an unprecedented challenge. It has been established that the height of the demonic Dam 'Sardar Sarovar' will be raised... It is a State sponsored 'massacre by water', as it is bent upon drowning the adivasi and farmers, there is no idea of the exact number of the endangered people and without any possibility of their just resettlement with alternate land. This will be the man-made flooding and submergence of the people.

NBA Press Release, 15 June 2002[4]

Starting in the 1980s, the Narmada River Valley in central India became the site of one the most famous anti-dam movements in the world. The struggle to save the Narmada River from being dammed, which raged over the course of some thirty years, has largely been lost. The Sardar

---

[3] Bradford Morse and Thomas Berger, *Sardar Sarovar: Report of the Independent Review* (Ottawa, Canada: Resource Futures International, 1992), 63.
[4] 'Narmada Satyagraha 2002—A Call to the Conscience of the Nation', NBA Press Release, 15 Jun 2002. https://www.wussu.com/roads/r02/r0206281.htm

Sarovar Dam alone, which according to the Indian media in 2017 became the second largest dam in the world in terms of volume of concrete (7,320,000 cubic meters), by most accounts has displaced approximately 240,000 people, over 57% of whom were scheduled tribes, mainly Bhil Adivasis.[5] And the Sardar Sarovar is not alone. In all, 30 major, 135 medium, and some 3000 small dams have been planned along the Narmada and its tributaries. According to the World Commission on Dams, large dams in India have displaced 16–38 million people. Around the world, somewhere between 40 and 80 million people were displaced by the 45,000 large dams built in the twentieth century.[6]

The Narmada Valley has not only been the site of one of India's most protracted environmentalist and tribal rights struggles. It has also been the most prominent site of Bhil endangerment discourse since the 1980s. As to be expected with any contentious state-sponsored project in India where the lives of hundreds of thousands of people are being impacted, the level of rhetoric in the Save the Narmada Movement (*Narmada Bachao Andolan*) has sometimes been polemical to the extreme. Voices in opposition have often reached a crescendo, with cries of endangerment and extinction frequently being heard. Labelled as ecocide, ethnocide, and even genocide, the construction of the Sardar Sarovar Dam in particular was said to threaten to destroy not only the Bhils' way of life but the Bhils themselves.[7] Time and again, in attempts

---

[5] Peter Bosshard, 'New Independent Review Documents Failure of Narmada River Dam', *World Rivers Review: Special Focus on River Restoration*. Oakland, CA: International Rivers, 15 Dec 2008. http://web.archive.org/web/20140910090656/https://www.internationalrivers.org/resources/new-independent-review-documents-failure-of-narmada-river-dam-1806; IANS, 'PM Modi to Inaugurate World's Second Biggest Dam on September 17', Indian Express, 14 Sep 2017. https://indianexpress.com/article/india/pm-narendra-modi-to-inaugurate-worlds-second-biggest-sardar-sarovar-dam-on-september-17-4843132/; Parag Dave, 'Concrete Used in Narmada Dam Can Build a Road Around Equator', *Rediff News*, 29 Sep 2006. https://www.rediff.com/news/2006/sep/29dam.htm.

[6] World Commission on Dams, *Dams and Development: A New Framework for Decision-Making: The Report of the World Commission on Dams* (London: Earthscan, 2000), 17, xxx.

[7] One problem here is that the term Bhil itself is an ethnonym that acts as a large umbrella category covering a wide variety of people. Examples of Bhil groups may include Vasava/Vasave, Paura/Padvi, Bhilala, Dangi Bhil, Dungri Bhil, Garasia, Bhil Mewasi, Meena, Bhil Mina, Rawal Bhil, Bhil Rajput, Tadvi, Dholi, etc. Yet there is no consensus on who is/is not a Bhil, or what precisely defines Bhil identity. Some of these groups might reject the term Bhil themselves, yet still be labelled as such by surrounding communities. Some might self-identify as Bhil on some occasions but not others. Some might have historically transitioned into or out of this category. Some might self-identify as Rajput or Kshatriya, others as Adivasi or tribal. While some maintain that they have a discrete religious identity, others self-identify as either Hindu or Muslim. There is a wide variety of Bhil languages and dialects as well, including but certainly not limited

to save the Bhils, they have been compared not only to indigenous peoples around the world ('The construction of large dams on the Narmada river exemplifies the crises facing indigenous peoples'[8]) but also to endangered species ('It is almost as if these people were an endangered species of wild life whose habitat had to be shut away from ordinary society'[9]).

It is worth documenting how pervasive this trope of Bhil endangerment and extinction in the face of the dam has been. Already in July of 1983, half a decade before the famous *Narmada Bachao Andolan* (Save the Narmada Movement, or NBA for short) coalesced in 1989, the renowned Gandhian activist Baba Amte wrote to Indira Gandhi to protest the dam. In his letter to the prime minister, he equated tribes with trees and endangered species, described the Bhils as living in a 'natural habitat' almost like a variety of wildlife, and spoke of their impending 'ethnocide':

> At least 40,000 tribal persons will be uprooted along with the loss of millions of trees. Of course, it is intended to transplant these people elsewhere... But nothing can compensate the wrench they would suffer in leaving their traditional cultural environment for an alien Marathi speaking setting... To remove the tribal people from their natural habitat would be cultural 'ethnocide' apart from adding to their adversity. I need hardly mention the many endangered species of rare and precious animals. I would earnestly request you to intercede on behalf of Man and nature, and reaffirm the national policy of protecting forest wealth and tribal culture.[10]

By 1990, Baba Amte would step up as a leader of the Save the Narmada *andolan*, and write an anti-dam pamphlet called 'The Case Against the

---

to: Bauria, Wagdi, Bhilori, Magari, Bhili, Bhilali, Chodri, Dhodia, Dhanki, Dubli, Kalto, Palya, Pauri, Pardhi, Rathwi, Vasavi, etc.

[8] Angana Chatterji, 'Commentary: Anthropology and Cultural Survival', *Anthropology News* 45, no. 3 (Mar 2004): 7–8.

[9] M.N. Buch, 'Is Verrier Elwin Still Relevant? A Study of the Bhils of Jhabua', *Centre for Governance and Political Studies, Vivekananda International Foundation*, 17 Oct 2012. https://www.vifindia.org/article/2012/october/17/is-verrier-elwin-still-relevant-a-study-of-the-bhils-of-jhabua

[10] Hans Staffner, *Baba Amte: A Vision of New India* (Delhi: Popular Prakashan, 2000), 43.

Narmada Project'. He would again call the project 'Large-Scale Cultural Ethnocide', saying 'Finally, and above all, I oppose the NSP and SSP for the large-scale cultural ethnocide they will perpetrate. I refer to the 3 lakh [300,000] people living in the submergence zones who will be rendered homeless by the two projects. Already, more than 50,000 people living in the submergence zones of the Tawa and Bargi projects on the Narmada have had to flee with nowhere to go'.[11] In 1991, along with Medha Patkar, Baba Amte would win the prestigious Right Livelihood Award, the Save the Narmada movement would be propelled to international fame, and this discourse of ethnocide and tribal extinction would set the tone for years to come. In their acceptance speech for that award, Patkar and Amte would declare: 'Not just green, but green and red ideas together can lead us to the right livelihood. The seeds of this are still alive in many tribal societies which cannot be allowed to be extinct'.[12] A 1995 *Atlas of Endangered Peoples* would subsequently list the people of the Narmada Valley as critically endangered, describing 'an ambitious scheme to build 3,000 dams' and saying 'The local people, including members of the Bhils and Tadavis tribes, will lose land and home if the project goes ahead'.[13] Similarly, in a chapter titled 'confronting the genocide and ethnocide of indigenous peoples', a major edited volume on the anthropology of genocide from 2002 would list the Narmada as a site of genocide.[14]

Although, as discussed in Chapter 1, the term ethnocide has come to be distinguished from genocide as the intentional destruction of culture as opposed to the actual murder of entire populations, numerous authors continue to refer to what has happened in the Narmada as 'cultural genocide' rather than ethnocide. For example, Felix Padel, in a 2009 updated edition of his book *Sacrificing People: Invasions of a Tribal Landscape*,

---

[11] Baba Amte, 'Narmada Project: The Case Against and an Alternative Perspective', *Economic & Political Weekly* (1990): 811–818.

[12] 'Acceptance speech—Medha Patkar and Baba Amte/Narmada Bachao Andolan', Right Livelihood Award, 31 Dec 1991. https://www.rightlivelihoodaward.org/speech/acceptance-speech-medha-patkar-and-baba-amte-narmada-bachao-andolan/

[13] Steve Pollock, *Atlas of Endangered Peoples* (New York: Facts on File, 1995), 44–45. This book lists the Gonds as an 'Endangered People', as well.

[14] Samuel Totten, William S. Parsons, and Robert K. Hitchcock, 'Confronting Genocide and Ethnocide of Indigenous Peoples an Interdisciplinary Approach to Definition, Intervention, Prevention, and Advocacy', in *Annihilating Difference: The Anthropology of Genocide*, ed. Alexander Laban Hinton (Berkeley: University of California, 2002), 71.

continues to refer to this phenomenon as 'cultural genocide'. And likewise, in 2018, Debasre De wrote:

> I have already talked about the physical genocide that is the indiscriminate killing and raping of the tribals.... The other form of genocide is cultural genocide.... Since cultural genocide means psychic death for the adivasis.... 'A Bhil may brave a tiger in forest, but is afraid to face even an insignificant outsider.' Another crucial aspect is the 'linguistic genocide' or 'rape of language'....[15]

Language pairing ethnocide and ecocide would become a defining feature of the anti-dam movement. One of the most famous slogans for the Narmada Bachao Andolan (NBA) was *'Narmada Bachao! Manav Bachao!'* literally meaning *'Save the Narmada! Save the Humans!'* This motto made its way into countless signs, stencilled onto the sides of houses, silkscreened onto flags and t-shirts (see Figure 5.1). Again and again, wildlife, forests, and tribal peoples are lumped together in this discourse: 'The submergence is devastating wildlife and precious ecosystems. The people, treated with contempt by the state, have nowhere to go'.[16] As are people and fish: 'Across the world, dams and diversions are the primary cause of endangerment or extinction for one-half of the world's freshwater fish, contribute substantially to the decimation of marine fisheries, and have displaced tens of millions of people in the name of projects built to benefit distant cities and agricultural producers'.[17] The activist Rahul Banerjee put the link between people and forests particularly starkly: 'These life-giving forests stand to disappear if the project is eventually completed. Also slated to disappear is the tribal whose identity is intricately linked with this forest. They will be lost, as statistics, a displaced population.... If the forests disappear, so do the people who depend on it'.[18]

In the campaigns to ' "save" the Bhils and the forest', the Bhils are said to be 'struggling for survival' and that 'survival is at stake'. Sometimes

---

[15] Debasree De, *A History of Adivasi Women in Post-Independence Eastern India: The Margins of the Marginals* (Delhi: Sage, 2018), xxxiii.
[16] Chatterji, 'Anthropology and Cultural Survival', 7–8.
[17] Barbara Brower and Barbara Rose Johnston, eds. *Disappearing Peoples? Indigenous Minorities in South and Central Asia* (Walnut Creek, CA: Left Coast Press, 2007), 14.
[18] Rahul Banerjee, 'The Forests of Shisewadi: Facing Displacement', http://anar-kali.blogspot.com/2013/05/mumbais-water-needs-versus-livelihoods.html

**Figure 5.1.** The Narmada Bachao Andolan Logo.
*Narmada Bachao, Manav Bachao* Translation: 'Save the Narmada, Save the Humans'. Fair use.

publishing only under his first name, Rahul (thereby avoiding the use of his Brahmin surname), the self-identified anarcho-environmentalist Rahul Banerjee wrote in *Economic & Political Weekly*, 'As modern development threatens to displace tribal populations from their last fastness in the hills and forests, they have begun all over the world to fight for survival using modern means and methods'. Referring to the Bhils as 'nature's children' and their lands as 'their habitat', Banerjee tells us how 'Old men recall with tears in their eyes the golden days' and that 'the Sardar Sarovar Project (SSP), a multipurpose dam now under construction on the river Narmada in Gujarat will finally seal the fate of the bhils [sic] of Alirajpur'. 'A process which had started with the decimation of the bhils' forests will culminate in loss of their ancestral lands'.[19]

Sometimes it was peoples' lives that were said to be endangered, but other times it was only livelihoods. Banerjee, who has published works with titles such as 'The Bhils: A People Under Threat' writes that 'The Bhils have traditionally depended on shifting agriculture for their

---

[19] Rahul, 'Reasserting Ecological Ethics: Bhils Struggles in Alirajpur', *Economic & Political Weekly* 32, no. 3 (Jan 18 1997): 87–91. Banerjee subsequently returned to publishing works using his surname, and lists this article as his own on his website.

livelihoods.... any encroachment on their habitat and obstruction to their style of living seriously endangers their livelihood'. But there is also a clear pairing of forest-based livelihoods with an argument that the Bhils' culture itself is forest-based. Banerjee goes on to say that 'the Bhils have been caught in between the destruction and alienation of their traditional habitats on the one hand and the improper functioning of modern government services on the other' and 'the culture of the Bhils has come under pressure with the destruction of their resource base'.[20]

Bhil culture is said to have been 'drowned out' or 'submerged' alongside their villages in the Narmada Valley.[21] As Angana Chatterji would write in a commentary on 'anthropology and cultural survival': 'If history chronicles that the people of the Narmada were indeed drowned out, with them will die ways of being, languages, spiritualities, and memory precious to sustaining our world'.[22] And as Medha Patkar, leader of the NBA, would say in a video produced by the Right Livelihoods Foundation after she won her award from that organization in 1991: 'everything would go underwater with the lives and livelihoods'.[23] By 2015, a fact-finding commission would produce a major report on the Narmada titled *Drowning a Valley: Destroying A Civilization*.

The rhetoric of 'vanishing' or 'disappearing' culture was also frequently deployed. Describing a field trip he took to the Narmada as a young and impressionable student with an anthropology professor in the mid-1980s, Yoginder Sikand recounted: 'it was clear even at that time that their ancient religious tradition would soon disappear'. Now writing in 2012, Sikand imagined all that must have been lost: 'And for all I know, with the dam now firmly in place, their village might now have been completely wiped off the map of the world, sunk deep in the swirling waters of the Narmada, its denizens being reduced to manual labourers in some dusty, nondescript Indian town'.[24] Yet Sikand never mentions actually following up with this village and speaking with its (presumably) former residents.

---

[20] Rahul Banerjee, 'The Bhils: A People Under Threat', *Humanscapes* (Sep 2001).
[21] See the documentary, *Drowned Out*, dir. Franny Armstrong. Spanner Films, 2002. https://spannerfilms.net/films/drownedout
[22] Chatterji, 'Anthropology and Cultural Survival', 7–8.
[23] Right Livelihood Award Laureate Medha Patkar and the Sardar Sarovar Dam, 1991, 3:54–57, https://youtu.be/he0oXpq5gS4
[24] Yoginder Sikand, 'Simple Ways of Life', *Deccan Herald*, 23 Dec 2012. https://www.deccanherald.com/content/300193/simple-ways-life.html

Displacement and resettlement are seen as particular evils within this framework. Thus, a 2000 World Commission on Dams report titled *Sharing Power: Dams, Indigenous Peoples and Ethnic Minorities* produced by Marcus Colchester of the Forest Peoples Programme included a section titled 'Resettlement as Ethnocide'. It begins: 'As numerous commentators acknowledge, involuntary resettlement is a traumatic process, regardless of one's social or economic background'. This is not mere cultural change, however; to Colchester and others, resettlement is literally fatal: 'Even where planning is effective, some (especially the aged) will never come to terms with their new homes. For them the transition period ends only with death'.[25] Similarly, under the heading 'Displacement and cultural genocide', Felix Padel writes:

> Adivasi rootedness to the land exists through what is in effect an invisible umbilical cord. Displacement for these communities means a severing of this cord: a psychic death that few non-tribals have any conception of, since most families in mainstream society have had no roots on land they have worked, for some generations. This is the sense in which Adivasis, through invasions of their land by dam and mining projects, face a situation of genocide: every aspect of their social structure is severely disrupted, and people witness the death of the communities, cultural security and ecosystems that they and their ancestors had always carefully maintained. Adivasis often say 'we cannot eat money'.[26]

Tribal extinction is seen as the inevitable result of development-induced displacement. The Bhils, like tribal people all over the world, are described as having a special relationship with a specific piece of land, and once this relationship is severed, it is like cutting, as Padel puts it, 'an invisible umbilical cord'. This is the common perspective: 'Once indigenous peoples are displaced, their lives will be destroyed; they will have to create a new community and their culture will become extinct'.[27]

---

[25] World Commission on Dams, *Dams and Development*, 17.
[26] Felix Padel, 'How Best to Ensure Adivasis' Land, Forest and Mineral Rights?' *Institute of Development Studies Bulletin* 43, no. S1 (Jul 2012): 51.
[27] William N. Holden and R. Daniel Jacobson, 'Ecclesial Opposition to Nonferrous Metals Mining in Guatemala and the Philippines: Neoliberalism Encounters the Church of the

As explained in the situation in eastern India: 'The fear of being dominated by "plains culture" through the influx of "outsiders" rests on the belief that the culture of non-tribals will dominate tribal culture and make it extinct. This is an understandable fear'.[28] Since fear of cultural death is thus framed in relation to land loss, the politics of land rights and cultural rights also go hand in hand. As the famed Adivasi scholar and policy maker Ram Dayal Munda put it: 'To separate the Adivasi from his land is to stop his breathing. If you want to see an Adivasi's extinction, take him away from his land—as it is happening at present'.[29]

It was perhaps the Booker Prize-winning author and activist Arundhati Roy who has taken these Narmada rhetorics to their greatest extreme, comparing the impact of development-induced displacement to that of a nuclear holocaust. In a 1999 essay titled 'The Greater Common Good', she writes: 'I feel like someone who's just stumbled on a mass grave… The millions of displaced people in India are nothing but refugees of an unacknowledged war… Big Dams are to a Nation's "Development" what Nuclear Bombs are to its Military Arsenal. They're both weapons of mass destruction' (see Figure 5.2).[30]

When people feel passionately about an issue such as the Narmada, when they are desperate to garner public attention and rally people to action, and when all other avenues have failed, it is fathomable why they then might resort to such deeply disturbing claims of genocide, mass destruction, and extinction. And, of course, claims of genocide are made all the time these days over far less significant troubles.[31] One problem,

---

Poor', in *Engineering Earth: The Impacts of Mega Engineering Projects*, ed. Stanley D. Brunn (London: Springer Dordrecht Heidelberg, 2011), 400.

[28] Duncan McDuie-Ra, 'Civil Society and Human Security in Meghalaya: Identity, Power and Inequalities' (PhD Diss., University of New South and Wales, 2007), 103.

[29] Ram Dayal Munda, Adi-Dharam, https://www.goodreads.com/quotes/8540290to-separate-the-adivasi-from-his-land-is-to-stop

[30] Arundhati Roy, 'The Greater Common Good', *Outlook India*, 24 May 1999. For a critique of the statistics presented in Roy's article, see: Hartosh Singh Bal, *Waters Close Over Us: A Journey Along the Narmada* (Delhi: Harper Collins, 2013).

[31] As one scholar tweeted in context of the Russian invasion of Ukraine: 'As a genocide scholar I am an empiricist, I usually dismiss rhetoric. I also take genocide claims with a truckload of salt because activists apply it almost everywhere now. Not now. There are actions, there is intent. It's as genocide as it gets. Pure, simple and for all to see'. Tweet by @eugene_finkel, 4 Apr 2022. https://twitter.com/eugene_finkel/status/1510922348899315716. Matthew Kupfer and Thomas de Waal, 'Crying Genocide: Use and Abuse of Political Rhetoric in Russia and Ukraine', Carnegie Endowment for International Peace, 28 July 2014, documents how 'within a decade of being coined and codified by the United Nations, the word genocide had

**Figure 5.2.** 'Damned! Doomed! Drowned!'
Photo owned by International Rivers, 'Narmada River Dams Protest: Arundhati Roy, Medha Patkar protest against dams on India's Narmada River'. Creative Commons Licence CC BY-NC-SA 2.0. https://www.flickr.com/photos/internationalrivers/3439550054/in/album-72157630547218220/

though, is that such heightened rhetoric may very well have alienated some moderates from the Save the Narmada movement. For sceptics, it becomes seen a bit like the children's parable of Chicken Little or the Jataka tale of 'The Sound the Hare Heard'. Critics will inevitably ask: is the sky really falling? This endangerment discourse has been latched onto as blatant exaggeration by at least one proponent of big dams, B.G. Verghese, as an argument for why the anti-dam voices might easily be ignored and why the Sardar Sarovar should be raised 'to its full height'. In 1999, Verghese gloated that the completion of the dam 'now seems assured with the Supreme Court rejecting glib talk of what has sometimes been termed "ethnocide" and an unprecedented environmental disaster'. Expressing particular distaste for Roy, he wrote that 'Arundhati's

already degenerated into a term of political abuse'. https://carnegieendowment.org/2014/07/28/crying-genocide-use-and-abuse-of-political-rhetoric-in-russia-and-ukraine-pub-56265

idealisation of the tribal lifestyle reeks of glorification of the noble savage. This is what she ordains for them: grubbing for roots, deprived, impoverished, and "protected" by the NBA... The poetry was charming; the facts wrong; more rhyme than reason'. Calling the anti-dam movement 'total irresponsibility by neo-Luddites who fear the future and would live in a make-believe romantic past', over his years of advocating for the dam, Verghese not only produced plenty of his own polemical pro-dam rhetoric, but clearly identified the rhetoric at work in the anti-dam movement as well.[32]

In contrast to Verghese, my own goal here is certainly not to argue in favour of the dam. There is no denying that displacing hundreds of thousands of people by inundating their land has been a life-shattering experience for affected communities of the Narmada, and that peoples' suffering is real. Nor is there any denying that there have been major problems relating to the way that resettlement and rehabilitation have been carried out. Much has been lost with the flooding of the Narmada Valley, no doubt. Still, it is worthwhile asking whether such extreme claims of endangerment and extinction, ethnocide, and even genocide, are accurate, justified, or even productive, in the case of the Bhil communities of the Narmada. None of this discussion of endangerment discourse in the Narmada Valley should be read as a defence of big dams, nor as a condemnation of activism writ-large. There has been a tremendous amount of excellent, no-nonsense, environmental, and social activism in the Narmada that has not resorted to flagrant sloganeering from above to achieve its ends.[33] Instead, this critique of endangerment discourse might be considered within the context of the vast field of literature on effective risk assessment and communication, much of which criticizes the media and activists for emphasizing drama over facts and for sensationalizing stories.[34] The example of Verghese does seem to highlight the fact that,

---

[32] Boobli G. Verghese, 'Sardar Sarovar Project Revalidated by Supreme Court', *International Journal of Water Resources Development* 17, no. 1 (2001):79–88. B.G. Verghese, 'A Poetic License', *Outlook India*, 5 Jul 1999. https://www.outlookindia.com/magazine/story/a-poetic-licence/207723

[33] For some richly nuanced oral histories of activists in the Narmada that move beyond the rhetoric discussed in this section, please see Nandini Oza's: https://oralhistorynarmada.in/early-history-of-the-movement/

[34] Ranjit Dwivedi, 'Displacement, Risks and Resistance: Local Perceptions and Actions in the Sardar Sarovar', *Development and Change* 30, no. 1 (1999): 43–78.

while risk perception is to some extent always subjective, wildly exaggerated claims of extinction will not always be viewed as benign hyperbole, and might actually undermine attempts to redress more legitimate grievances.

Furthermore, the Verghese example also points to the fact that the issue of risk assessment is one of conflicting values. When it comes to a subject as controversial as the Narmada, or the so-called tribal problem in India, the question of what's at stake is fiercely contested and what's in danger is a matter of perspective. Many people sincerely believe that tribes such as the Bhils are fundamentally hill and forest communities whose unique cultural traditions will become extinct when they are removed from natural landscapes. Others take the standpoint that trying to keep the Bhils isolated in the forests is nothing but a primitivist pipedream that will condemn these people to lives of romanticized poverty. Such a view holds that in order to survive, these communities must be integrated with the nation, and that economic development does not necessarily mean cultural endangerment.

Alas, people on both sides of this debate often come to it with preexisting notions of who and what Adivasi communities are, and what the best path forward is for them. Much of the extinction rhetoric used in the Narmada probably holds entirely true in certain other situations of development-induced displacement facing indigenous peoples in other parts of the world, so the Narmada may very well represent another case of (mis)applying global discourses of indigenous peoples and biocultural diversity endangerment to the very specific situation of central India. External activists coming from middle class, urban backgrounds, often steeped since youth in romanticist ideas about tribal life, and dreams of 'saving' innocent victims, carried that logic with them into the Narmada valley.[35]

Similarly, modern India's policy makers, who by and large have tended to have integrationist and developmentalist leanings, and who have long loved massive development projects, often carried forward their agendas

---

[35] Already in 1997, Brosius examined 'the ways in which Western environmentalists' in Sarawak drew on scholarly work to constructed Penan indigenous peoples as 'endangered' in order to deploy their image in media campaigns. See J. Peter Brosius, 'Endangered Forest, Endangered People: Environmentalist Representations of Indigenous Knowledge', *Human Ecology* 25, no. 1 (Mar 1997): 47–69.

with nearly colonial levels of paternalism towards project-affected communities.[36] Thus, the offensive claim that Bhil communities would be 'better off' being displaced from their 'un-developed villages' so as to guarantee their 'gradual assimilation in the mainstream of the society' was literally espoused in the Indian Supreme Court judgement of 18 October 2000, which paved the way for the completion of the dam:

> It is not fair that tribals and the people in un-developed villages should continue in the same condition without ever enjoying the fruits of science and technology for better health and have a higher quality of life style. Should they not be encouraged to seek greener pastures elsewhere.... The displacement of the tribals and other persons would not per se result in the violation of their fundamental or other rights. The effect is to see that their rehabilitation at new locations they are better off than what they were [sic]. At the rehabilitation sites they will have more and better amenities than which they enjoyed in their tribal hamlets. The gradual assimilation in the mainstream of the society will lead to betterment and progress.[37]

Still, by the 1980s, even the most polemical voices on both sides of this debate at least played lip service to the idea of consulting local stakeholders, with elite activists often claiming to represent 'tribal voices'; and this surely represents some improvement over earlier periods when Adivasis' own perspectives were entirely ignored in 'the tribal problem debate'. In the end, though, both sides continued to push the agendas they entered the field with, despite changing conditions on the ground, and despite what local people had to say. The state certainly never capitulated to social movements and activist demands to stop the dam, fighting every setback in turn. But similarly, even after the construction of the Sardar Sarovar Dam was a *fait accompli,* the NBA's celebrity activist leaders and

---

[36] Many 'post-development theorists' bemoan the mid-twentieth century monolithic modernity building project embodied by Nehru who called big dams the 'temples of modern India' and asked the poor to sacrifice for the good of the nation. See Vinay Gidwani, 'The Unbearable Modernity of Development? Canal Irrigation and Development Planning in Western India', *Planning and Progress* 58 (2002): 1–80, for a good reflection on this general critique of development.

[37] Lakshmi Chand Jain, *Dam Vs Drinking Water: Exploring the Narmada Judgement* (Delhi: Parisar, 2001), 12–13.

Figure 5.3. Medha Patkar, Domkhedi Satyagraha, Maharashtra, 21 Sep 1999.
Photo owned by International Rivers. Creative Commons Licence CC BY-NC-SA 2.0. https://www.flickr.com/photos/internationalrivers/7646765266/in/album-72157630547218220/

external middle-class environmental activists failed to adapt to this reality. They continued to fight against the already existing dam, when at this point, many Bhil communities themselves were pushing to ensure adequate resettlement and rehabilitation (see Figure 5.3). And when some Bhil leaders did strike their own deals for resettlement, they were ostracized or portrayed as traitors to the movement, rather than receiving support during the resettlement process.

## Popular Misconceptions

Chronologically, anyway, the first major problem with the endangerment discourse in the case of the Narmada is that it is based on fundamental misunderstandings of Bhil history and identity. A romanticist and orientalist construction of 'the tribal Bhil' has been popularized since the resurgence of indigenous rights movements of the 1980s. It holds that the Bhils were, until relatively recently, isolated, hunter-gatherer communities, who were living in harmony with nature, and whose first encounter with the outside world was through colonialism, followed by modern capitalism, which destroyed their age-old way of life. To translate one author writing in Hindi on the Bhils: 'Adivasis and forests complement each other. In the past, the forests raised the Adivasis, and the Adivasis also protected the forests'.[38] Thus, writings specifically on Bhils contain the same tropes of tribal extinction and endangerment common to survey works on indigenous peoples around the world. Typical of works in the popular genre, *Fighting for Survival: the Bhils of Rajasthan* is a brief, 48-page, oversized picture book recording the impressions of the authors' journey into hills of western India in the 1990s. The book describes the ecological and economic transformation of the Bhils in emotive form, and the suggestion of endangerment is strong. We read:

> Like tribal communities throughout the world their lives have been dramatically changed since they came into contact with outside influences... They were not an agricultural or farming community. The Bhil were hunters and gatherers. Their survival depended on the forests, which were thick with wildlife and medicinal products.... The Bhils source of food and shelter was taken away from them with the new laws of forest ownership. The British Government sold timber rights to logging companies which logged vast areas of land. When the Bhil cut down trees for themselves they were imprisoned. To survive, they were forced to work for a very small wage, cutting and carrying timber for the big companies. Their lifestyle of hunting and gathering was being changed to one where the people had to work for cash which they then would use to buy what they needed.... As their lifestyle was changed, the Bhils increasingly came into contact with the rest of Indian society.... The national government's earlier aim was to encourage tribal communities to blend into the main society of India. It wanted people like the Bhil to be absorbed.[39]

---

[38] 'Adivasi aur van ek dursre ke purak hai. Atit me jahan vanon ne adivasiyon ka poson kiya hai vahi adivasiyon ne bhi vanon ka sanrakshan kiya hai'. Ashok Patel, *Bhil Janjivan aur Sanskriti* (Bhopal: Madhya Pradesh Hindi Granth Academy, 1998), 17. My translation.

[39] Liz Thompson and Simon Coate, *Fighting for Survival: The Bhils of Rajasthan* (Melbourne: Reed Education, 1997), 4, 6, 8, 11.

According to the popular historical narrative, the Bhils were isolated, pre-capitalist hunter-gatherers, who were forced through colonialism to become peasant agriculturalists and servants of the forestry industry. They are said to have fallen victim to the market, and prey to assimilation. For what it lacks in accurate details, the narrative makes up through an elaborate evocation of loss and decline, painting history as tragedy.

Many would-be tribal reformers on the Hindu right also imagine Bhil history as a unilinear move from hunter-gatherer to agriculturalist, except rather than tragedy, they see the transformation of *vanvasi* (forest folk) into good Hindu peasants as their mission. As one septuagenarian Brahmin living amidst the Bhils in Jhadol District, south of Udaipur in Rajasthan, told me in March 2006, 'Everything has changed here. These people can read. They celebrate this [Hindu] festival like you saw now. They used to kill the animals and eat the meat. Now their lives are different. Now there are no [wild] animals. Everything is changing. Development. The government is trying to change the people—every day they are trying'.[40] Earlier that day, the headmaster of a local school for Bhil students, who was also upper caste, took me to a Holi *mela* sponsored by the Krishna *mandir* in a nearby village. All of the local Bhils came through the temple to do *puja* before commencing with their traditional *dhol* drumming and circle dance.

That the Bhils transformed from hunter-gatherers to sedentary agriculturalists is oft repeated in the literature. In the words of Prakash Chandra Mehta in *Changing Face of the Bhils*, 'The Bhils were a tribe of foodgathers and hunters in the post [sic]. Later they cultivated millets on hills slopes by slash and burn method... The introduction of settled cultivation brought significant change in their economic as well as social development. Bhils are now no more nomadic in nature'.[41] Judith Whitehead, writing in a volume titled *Disappearing Peoples*, also agrees that the name Bhil 'meaning—bow and arrow in Dravidian languages—indicates that they were hunter-gatherers who migrated from south India'.[42] Christoph

---

[40] Interview in Hindi, 19 Mar 2006.
[41] Prakash Chandra Mehta, *Changing Face of the Bhils* (Udaipur: Shiva, 1998), 78.
[42] Judith Whitehead, 'The Bhils', in *Disappearing Peoples? Indigenous Groups and Ethnic Minorities in South and Central Asia,* eds Barbara Brower and Barbara Rose Johnston (Walnut Creek, CA: Left Coast Press, 2007), 73.

von Fürer-Haimendorf writing in the 1980s also did not stray much from the main features of this story.

> Much speaks for the assumption that the Bhils, who had traditionally close links with forest areas, were hunters and gatherers, but today none of the numerous Bhil groups persists on that economic level. Though some of them continue to carry bow and arrows, and supplement their diet by digging for roots and tubers, nearly all Bhils are now settled plow cultivators. But traditions of a nomadic forest life are strong and the Bhils' archery and prowess in hunting were famous even a hundred years ago. Indeed Bhils are among the few hunter-gatherers who used to be depicted as such in Indian works of art. An extensive ethnographic literature covers the conditions of many Bhil groups as they prevailed at various times during the 20th century, but only casual remarks in historical sources refer to the nomadic lifestyle of Bhil forest-dwellers.[43]

The myth that the Bhils transformed from hunter-gatherers into sedentary agriculturalists in the modern era plays into the politics of mourning hunter-gatherer extinctions around the world. As Sutapa Chattopadhyay writes in her PhD dissertation on *Involuntary Migration and the Mechanisms of Rehabilitation: The Discourses of Development in Sardar Sarovar, India*: 'At present, all Adivasis are depending mainly on agriculture and different livelihood mechanisms. For all practical purposes, hunter-gatherers are extinct on the Indian subcontinent.'[44] In *This Fissured Land,* a seminal work in South Asian environmental history, Ram Guha and Madhav Gadgil also have a section connecting species extinction and tribal decline that begins with the heading 'Hunter-Gatherers: The Decline Towards Extinction'. Hunter-gatherer extinction has been a persistent trope in anthropological literature around the world at least since 1966 when Lee and DeVore held their famous Man the Hunter symposium. The resulting book opened with the following remarks:

---

[43] Christoph von Fürer-Haimendorf, *Tribal Populations and Cultures of the Indian Subcontinent* (Leiden: Brill, 1985), 24–25.

[44] Sutapa Chattopadhyay, 'Involuntary Migration and the Mechanisms of Rehabilitation: The Discourses of Development in Sardar Sarovar, India' (PhD Diss., Kent State University, 2006), 29.

Cultural Man has been on earth for some 2,000,000 years; for over 99 per cent of this period he has lived as a hunter-gatherer.... To date, the hunting way of life has been the most successful and persistent adaptation man has ever achieved. Nor does this evaluation exclude the present precarious existence under the threat of nuclear annihilation and the population explosion. It is still an open question whether man will be able to survive the exceedingly complex and unstable ecological conditions he has created for himself.... The time is rapidly approaching when there will be no hunters left to study.[45]

In contrast, much important recent work done by historians, who might be said to occupy a revisionist camp, largely rejects the claim that the Bhils were for most of their history isolated hunter-gatherers who rarely interacted with other communities and did not participate in markets in the subcontinent. This work demonstrates that in cultural, political, and economic terms, Bhil history was far more complex than the popular understanding allows. David Hardiman, for example, makes it a point to challenge the popular view of the Adivasis as autochthonous and isolated societies, described by Fürer-Haimendorf in his book *Struggle for Survival*, as persisting 'until recently in an archaic and in many respects primitive lifestyle'.[46] In each of the narratives of transformation quoted above, the change in modes of production/subsistence is the central feature, but they only tell of a simple transition from a primitive hunter-gatherer lifestyle to an impoverished peasant livelihood system. Hardiman rejects such a simple bifurcation, arguing:

> They [Bhils] have been characterized as hunters and gatherers or rudimentary agriculturalists using slash-and-burn methods... [but] it is wrong to define 'adivasi' in terms of a particular form of agricultural production.... While a few adivasis are nomads or hunters and gatherers, the large majority have for centuries been settled agriculturalists,

---

[45] Richard Lee and Irene Devore, 'Problems in the Study of Hunters and Gatherers', in *Man the Hunter: The First Intensive Survey of a Single, Crucial Stage of Human Development—Man's Once Universal Hunting Way of Life*, eds Richard Lee and Irene Devore, (Chicago: Aldine, 1968).
[46] Christoph von Fürer-Haimendorf, 'The Tribal Problem in All-India Perspective', in *Tribes of India: Struggle for Survival*, ed. Christoph von Fürer-Haimendorf (Berkeley: University of California Press, 1982), 1.

cultivating land in a wide range of ways. Some have practised slash-and-burn, using only hand tools, while others have used a plough drawn by bullocks.[47]

That 'the equivalence of tribal and aboriginal' in central India 'originates, in fact, in nineteenth-century racial theory' is an argument central to Sumit Guha's book, *Environment and Ethnicity in India*, as well. Relying on a rich panoply of mediaeval texts across multiple local languages, Guha documents in marvellous detail how the Bhils were less a hunter-gatherer community and far more a self-identified group of 'kings of the forest', establishing quasi-state formations in the highlands. Guha demonstrates how the name Bhil does not even emerge in the annals of the subcontinent's history until the mediaeval period, and by the 1700s, it is clear that these groups are primarily identified as 'as forest-dwelling warriors and antagonists of Brahmanical civilisation'. The Bhil Chiefs formed a regime that collected taxes from the neighbouring peasantry, traded forest produce widely with surrounding merchants, were dependent on said peasants and merchants for maintaining their lifestyle, formed large armed followings, controlled the movement of goods and people through their hills, and participated in most the early modern period's key military campaigns (see Figure 5.4). Thus, as Guha puts it, 'The Bhils, it must be evident, were not isolated remnant populations savagely defending themselves against an inexorably encroaching civilization—rather, they were determined to share in the goods that civilisation could yield and to establish their dominance over the peasantry who toiled to produce the harvests that fed Bhil and Brahman alike'.[48]

To give the popular narrative the benefit of the doubt, perhaps calling the Bhils 'hunter-gatherers' was meant as shorthand for a range of ecological practices contrasting with those common to modernity. Perhaps the issue could simply be one of nomenclature. What, after all, is a 'hunter-gather'? The orthodox view of hunter-gatherers does not acknowledge that they could simultaneously practice other modes of subsistence. Yet as Nurit Bird-David shows, especially in the South Asian context,

---

[47] David Hardiman, *Coming of the Devi: Adivasi Assertion in Western India* (Delhi: Oxford University Press, 1995), 11–12.
[48] Sumit Guha, *Environment and Ethnicity in India, 1200–1991* (Cambridge: Cambridge University Press, 1999), 6, 199.

**Figure 5.4.** Parley with the Bheels in the Beechwara Pass.
Public domain. Source: Robert Brown, *The Peoples of the World: Being A Popular Description of the Characteristics, Condition, and Customs of the Human Family*, Vol. 4 (London: Cassell, 1892), frontispiece.

'hunter-gatherer' is a far more fluid category than commonly understood. To quote Bird-David, 'It is now clear that for centuries, even millennia, so-called hunter-gatherers have pursued a variety of additional subsistence activities, consuming—sometimes even growing—agricultural and pastoral products', and that 'current debate concerning the status of modern hunter-gatherers has so far ignored a critical question, namely, how they carry out their "other" subsistence activities and combine them with hunting and gathering'.[49] Some Bhils hunted and gathered, but they also farmed the forests, collected tribute from the surrounding peasantry, traded goods and services with surrounding communities, formed armies, waged armed struggles against encroaching empires in order to protect their domain, and built state formations of their own.

---

[49] Nurit Bird-David, 'Beyond "The Hunting and Gathering Mode of Subsistence": Culture-Sensitive Observations on the Nayaka and Other Modern Hunter-Gatherers', *Man* 27, no. 1 (Mar 1992): 19–22.

Already in 1968, Richard Fox rejected the notion that so-called hunter-gatherers in India were 'cultural leftovers or fossils', an 'assumption' he argued, which was 'made within the framework of antique cultural evolutionism'. Rather, Fox suggested, 'Indian hunters-and-gatherers represent occupationally specialized productive units similar to caste groups such as Carpenters'. These 'professional primitives', as he called them, nurtured an ecological niche on the margins of mainstream civilization wherein they traded forest goods for products made by neighbouring agriculturalists and townspeople.[50] Unfortunately, some early environmental historians carried Fox's notion of this niche forward in a rather perverse way, with Madhav Gadgil and K.C. Malhotra in 1983 equating castes and tribes to non-human species: 'With its reproductive isolation and hereditary mode of subsistence, *a caste population can be considered an analogue of a biological species* and assigned an ecological niche... One may then view the Indian society as being analogous to a biological community made up of a number of "cultural species" or endogamous caste groups'.[51]

If anything, the ecological niche that the Bhils occupied in the sixteenth through early nineteenth century was one of rulers of forest regions. As Eric Beverley maintains, Bhil power at the margins of empire acted as an alternative source of law and sovereignty rather than a zone of lawlessness.[52] Similarly, Alf Nilsen argues for the 'partial integration and liminal position of Bhil forest polities', which he calls 'tributary states' that 'were neither wholly autochthonous nor wholly subordinated to Rajput and Maratha states'.[53] Many Bhils claimed Kshatriya or Rajput warrior status, and according to many scholars, there is actually precious little difference between who was a Bhil and who was a Rajput. Marco Fattori, for example, describes the 'Rajput Bhil connection as nebulous' and argues that Bhil identity was a 'loose category'.[54] Likewise, Benjamin points out that the 'term "Bhils" was often applied to all those who led a lawless

---

[50] Richard Fox, '"Professional Primitives": Hunters and Gatherers of Nuclear South Asia', *Man in India* 49 (1969): 139–160.

[51] Madhav Gadgil and Kailash C. Malhotra, 'Adaptive Significance of the Indian Caste System: An Ecological Perspective', *Annals of Human Biology* 10, no. 5 (1983): 465–477.

[52] Eric Lewis Beverley, 'Frontier as Resource: Law, Crime, and Sovereignty on the Margins of Empire', *Comparative Studies in Society and History* 55, no. 2 (2013): 241–272.

[53] Nilsen, Alf Gunvald, *Adivasis and the State: Subalternity and Citizenship in India's Bhil Heartland* (Cambridge: Cambridge University Press, 2018), 60–61, 63.

[54] Marco Fattori, 'The Bhils and the Rajput Kingdoms of Southern Rajasthan', in *Narratives from the Margins*, eds Sanjukta Das Gupta and Raj Sekha (Delhi: Primus Books, 2012), 128.

life and resided in the deep jungles'.[55] Here, Benjamin means to suggest that the term Bhil was often used quite generically to refer to anyone perceived to be beyond the pale of civilization.

Supposedly 'wild' Bhils were contrasted with Rajputs who were seen as having settled kingdoms. Yet there is plenty of archival evidence of cases where as soon as a Bhil chief legitimized himself with a proper kingdom, he would then start to be labelled as a Rajput. Often this transformation was completed through Charan bards who would recast lineages, thereby literally rewriting history. Similarly, a Rajput group that fell out of power and retreated into the hills and forests would be branded as Bhil and have its lineage redefined accordingly. The implication is that there had historically, for centuries, been a revolving door between Bhil and Rajput identity. If the difference between Bhil and Rajput is really as minimal as this perspective suggests, and historically the distinction has been more geographical than genetic or even cultural, then it is hard to imagine the Bhils to be an endangered ethnicity.[56]

None of this is to say that the Bhils did not hunt, however. Certainly, they did. Yet as self-declared rulers of the hill and forest tracts, hunting was a supplementary livelihood activity. The primary source of income for Bhil chiefs and their followers was the collection of 'taxes' levied on villages (*tanka* and *haq* payments) and 'tolls' on travellers (*rakhwali*). From the outset of the colonial encounter, these payments were perceived by the British to be illegal excises, or more clearly—extortion and plunder.[57] They were also compared to *shikar* or hunting. In the words of Captain William Hunter, the first commander of the Mewar Bhil Corps:

> [P]lunder to a Bheel has hitherto been the charm of his existence; plundering they designate 'Shikar', and the prospect of driving off a few bullocks, possessing themselves of the property of travellers or of a field

---

[55] N. Benjamin and B. B. Mohanty, 'Imperial Solution of a Colonial Problem: Bhils of Khandesh up to c. 1850', *Modern Asian Studies* 41, no. 2 (2007): 344.

[56] Fattori, 'The Bhils and the Rajput Kingdoms', 133–136.

[57] 'He is often called in old Sanskrit works like Venápúka, Child of the Forest; Pál Indra, Lord of the Pass—these names well describe his character; his country is approached through narrow defiles—Pál or Nal (a causeway). Through these none can pass without his permission. In former days he always levied "rakhwáli" or black-mail [sic], and even now native travelers find him quite ready to assert what he deems his just rights'. T.H. Hendley, 'An Account of the Maiwár Bhíls', *Journal of the Asiatic Society of Bengal* 44, no. 4 (1875): 358.

of ripe grain, has hitherto in the estimation of this strange people been found to outweigh all the advantages, which have at different times been held out to them, by the offer of regular employment.[58]

Parallels between hunting and 'plunder' (i.e. tribute collection through raiding) were often drawn, but so-called plunder was always the primary livelihood, and hunting a distant secondary one. A report on the Mewar Bhil Corps from 1856 confirms this, saying that 'in bad seasons it [hunting] appears to be almost the only means the Bheels have of supporting themselves without plunder.'[59] Another officer in the field with James Outram continued this metaphor of Bhil *shikar*, reporting: 'they are heaven-born hunters. They must always be hunting something— money-lenders when other quarry fails. During the aftermath of 1857, they hunted the mutineers.'[60] To the Bhils as well as the British, hunting was the sport of kings. By making *shikar* (of animals and men) the centrepiece of their livelihood system (rather than labour-intensive sedentary agriculture), the Bhils maintained a sense of royal identity as kings of the forest. As I have shown elsewhere, however, by the late nineteenth century, the British interpreted hunting for food as evidence of quintessential tribal primitivity.[61]

If anything is extinct for the Bhils, it is not their status as huntergatherers, it is their sovereignty; their status as kings of the hills of western-central India has long since passed. Nobody is denying that there has been great social, ecological, economic, or political change in western India over the last few hundred years. The Maratha Empire collapsed after the third Anglo-Maratha war in 1818. And admittedly, some Shiv Sena *bakhts* do mourn the loss of the great Maratha power of yore. In this sense, we can also identify a celebration of the Bhils' former power and mourning for its loss in the political clamour for a separate Bhilistan

---

[58] National Archives of India, New Delhi (NAI), FD, 6 Sep 1841, 33–35, FC, Capt. Hunter's report on the rights, privileges and usages of Grassia and Bhil Chiefs, Kherwara, 20/7/1841. (Section II General remarks regarding the Bheel tribes). Thanks to Marco Fattori for pointing me towards this quotation.
[59] *Papers Relative to the Meywar Bheel Corps under the Command of Major Wm. Hunter* (London: EIC, 1856), 14; Also cited in Guha, *Environment and Ethnicity*, 44.
[60] Goldsmid, *James Outram* (1880), 265.
[61] Ezra Rashkow, 'Making Subaltern Shikaris: Histories of the Hunted in Colonial Central India', *South Asian History and Culture* 5, no. 3 (2014): 292–313.

state or Bhil Pradesh on the borders of Gujarat, Rajasthan, Maharashtra, and Madhya Pradesh, a movement which has been gaining some strength recently.[62] As one Bhil Pradesh activist recently tweeted in Hindi: '*Agar apni sanskriti sabhyata ko bachana hai, to Bhilpradesh ko banvana hai*'— 'If our culture is going to be saved, Bhil Pradesh has to be made'.[63] Yet this entails a very different vision of Bhil culture and its past from the primitivist position of environmental activists who portray the Bhils as simple forest folk and wish to restore them to that imagined state.

## Colonial Endangerment Discourse

Another major problem with the endangerment discourse outlined in the introduction to this chapter is that it in many ways echoes the colonial past. If external NBA activists had considered their own claims in historical context, they would have found that, at least since the beginning of the nineteenth century, the Bhils were projected as threatened with 'extermination' and as in need of 'protection'; they may then have realized that their own perception of 'tribal' culture and fear for its loss are in many ways are part of a much longer and broader history of predictions of tribal endangerment and extinction. Such self-reflexivity might also have led to the recognition that they were joining in a long line of those who have inserted themselves into these communities in order to protect and to save.

Indigenous rights advocates since the 1980s have completely reimagined the Bhil past in conformity with their understanding of who and what indigenous peoples are supposed to be. The view of the Bhils as isolated and primitive tribes in the past whose only interactions were with the natural world around them is clearly contradicted by the

[62] Sangeeta Pranvendra, 'Bhil Tribals Forge Political Unity, Give BJP, Congress Jitters in Several States; Community Alleges Neglect from Govt', *Firstpost*, 4 May 2019. https://www.firstpost.com/politics/bhil-tribals-forge-political-unity-give-bjp-congress-jitters-in-several-states-community-alleges-neglect-from-govt-6572111.html. Aarefa Johari, 'In Gujarat's Adivasi Belt, BJP has to Contend with Bhilistan Separatists, Boycotts and "Big People"', *Scroll*, 6 Nov 2017. https://scroll.in/article/856382/in-gujarats-adivasi-belt-bjp-has-to-contend-with-bhilistan-separatists-boycotts-and-big-people
[63] Tweet by @GeetaTribal (30 May 2021). https://twitter.com/GeetaTribal/status/1398866714587123712

historical record. At the turn of the nineteenth century, when the British first ventured into the hills of western and central India, they encountered the Bhils not as isolated tribes living in harmony with nature, but rather as supposedly 'predatory' and 'warlike' people who they perceived to be engaged in banditry, terrorizing the peasants in the plains, and posing a serious impediment to the dream of extending their *Pax Britannica* into the Indian interior (see Figure 5.4). As Graham described them, the Bhils were 'a peculiar race of barbarians, subsisting chiefly on plunder', a people 'whose sole occupation was pillage and robbery, whose delight alone consisted in the murderous foray, and whose subsistence depended entirely on the fruits of their unlawful spoil'.[64] Some of the first records in the colonial archive to mention the tribe described various military engagements with 'Bhil Chieftains'—some of whom were 'rewarded' for helping the British, while other 'rebel chiefs who had committed depredations' were subject to 'pacification'.[65] The Bombay Government's policy to 'counteract the depredations of the Bhils of Khandesh' in order to 'control and pacify' them was solidly in place immediately following the Anglo-Maratha wars, by 1818.[66]

From the outset, colonial discourse was riddled with inconsistencies in how Europeans approached 'remote districts, which are much infested by the predatory tribes of Bhils'.[67] The majority of British voices claimed to want to 'protect' the Bhils from 'extermination' while simultaneously waging military campaigns against them; British calls for the Bhils 'to reform' under their civilizing influence were often accompanied by animal analogies of extermination.[68] Yet nowhere in this early nineteenth-century archive does it describe the Bhils as isolated hunter-gatherers;

---

[64] IOR V/27/910/35 D.C. Graham, 'A Brief Historical Sketch of the Bheel Tribes, Inhabiting the Province of Khandesh' (Bombay, 1843), 2; cited in Nilsen, *Heartland*, 74.

[65] IOR F/4/306/7026, Jan–Apr 1809, 'The Bhil chief Raja Bhim Singh is rewarded for his help in securing the capture of Holkar's rebel chiefs who had committed depredations in the territories of the Peshwa and the Nizam'.

[66] IOR F/4/1022/28050, Dec 1819–Jun 1825, 'The Bombay Government defend the measures they took to control and pacify the Bhil tribes of Khandesh—corrupt conduct of some of the Company's native servants in that province—question of the conduct of Captain John Briggs, the Political Agent in Khandesh'; IOR F/4/720/19550–F/4/722/19555, vol. 1–6, Dec 1817–Mar 1822, 'Measures taken to counteract the depredations of the Bhils in Khandesh'.

[67] W.H. Sleeman, *Rambles and Recollections of an Indian Official* (1844; London: Archibald Constable, 1893) vol. 1, 357–358.

[68] IOR F/4/1026/28138 'Affray between a Party of Local Horse & the Bheel Inhabitants of Burree', Political Letter from Bengal Dated 27 Jul 1826.

rather they were called 'a wild, savage, ferocious race of robbers'.[69] John Malcolm, who was placed in military and political charge of the region, recorded that when the British army entered Malwa in 1818, the country was not safe for troops to pass. Then within the span of two years, by 1820, Malcolm reported progress—'the vicious and depraved part of the community... has become sensible to the blessings of a better course of life... the spirit of industry and improvement has been spread'.[70] Similarly, James Outram, who founded the Khandesh Bhil Corps, held out hope for improving the Bhils, writing in 1825: 'It is not unreasonable to hope this hitherto degraded race finding protection under our mild rule where no distinction is drawn between Bheel and Brahmin, may become gradually habituated and attached to the change'.[71] Reflecting back from the position of the 1880s when protecting the Bhils was even more *en vogue*, according to Goldsmid, the Lieutenant Governor of Bombay Mountstuart Elphinstone also wanted to 'reclaim rather than exterminate' the Bhils.[72]

In contrast, some early nineteenth-century British sources clearly called for wiping out the Bhils, and this rhetoric reached disturbing genocidal proportions at times. So, for example, in 1821, William Chaplin wrote to Elphinstone that, 'Nothing but a war of extermination can put an end to these troubles for the race of these marauders [the Bhils of Khandesh] is evidently not to be reclaimed by any measures of indulgence'.[73] Despite plenty of examples like Chaplin's where colonial officials dehumanized the Bhils and called for their extermination, East India company officials usually maintained that their true purpose was to protect the Bhils, and that it was really homegrown empires such as the Marathas and various Rajput kingdoms which had sought to exterminate them. The British seemed to revel in describing how much more humane

---

[69] G. Poulett Cameron, *The Romance of Military Life* (London: Houlston and Wright, 1858), 94.

[70] John Malcolm, *Report on the Province of Malwa, and Adjoining Districts* (Calcutta: Government Gazette Press, 1822), 644.

[71] J. Outram, Durrungaum, 1 Sep 1825. Lt Commanding Bheel Corps to Lt Col. Robertson, Collector in Candeish; cited in Goldsmid, *James Outram* (1880), 67; Arthur Henry A. Simcox, *A Memoir of the Khandesh Bhil Corps, 1825–1891: Compiled from Original Records* (Bombay: Thacker, 1912), 60. K.D. Erskine, *The Mewar Residency* (Ajmer: Scottish Mission Industries, 1908), 79, similarly reports that the Mewar Bhil Corps 'was raised between 1840 and 1844 with the object of weaning a semi-savage race from its predatory habits'.

[72] Goldsmid, *James Outram*, 59.

[73] Chaplin cited in K. Ballhatchet, *Social Policy and Social Change in Western India, 1817–1830* (London: Oxford University Press, 1957), 214.

their administration was, in comparison to 'native states'. Examples of this sort of talk are numerous. For instance, in Dhar, south of Udaipur, in 1832, the East India Company resident reported that:

> Instead of endeavouring to reclaim the Bheel population of its territories from their wild and barbarous habits, and of encouraging, by mild and equitable treatment, the cultivation of an intercourse with them... the Dhar administration appear to be in the habit of regarding them, not in that light of men, whose dispositions are susceptible of improvement by the efforts of a benevolent policy systematically connected to that purpose, but as wild beasts, whose savage propensities are only to be repressed by violence and who are only to be subdued by total extirpation.[74]

Similarly, in 1832 James Tod described the history of the Rajput takeover of what had formerly been a Bhil kingdom or chiefdom in Kota: 'This indigenous race, whose simple life secured their preservation amidst all the vicissitudes of fortune... were dispossessed and hunted down without mercy'. Yet it is hard to know how Tod could reconcile his description of 'the savage Bhil' as living in a state of nature, 'like the beasts, subsists upon the wild-fruits of the jungles', with his assertion that a 'Bhil chief, styled Raja' had ruled this region since its earliest days and had built the 'ancient fortress of Ekailgurh, five coss south of Kotah'.[75] Regardless, Tod, like most of his contemporaries, blamed Rajputs and other neighbouring powers for exterminating the Bhils, while arguing that the British were there to protect the tribes and ameliorate their position. 'Had the wild tribes been under the sole influence of British power, nothing would have been so simple as effectually, not only to control, but to conciliate and improve them; for it is a mortifying truth, that the more remote from

---

[74] NAI, For, Pol, 31 Dec 1832, no. 67, 68, 'proceeding to establish, on a permanent basis, the future tranquility of the Dhar possessions, as far as that tranquility may be affected by the turbulent disposition of the Bheel inhabitants'.

[75] James Tod, *Annals and Antiquities of Rajasthan: Or the Central and Western Rajput States of India*, vol. 2 (1832) 2nd ed. (Madras: Higginbotham, 1873), 469, 591. *Coss* or *kos* is a now 'endangered' unit of measurement, which originated in ancient India, and which 'signified "a call," hence the distance at which a man's call can be heard'. Henry Yule and Arthur Coke Burnell, *Hobson-Jobson: Being a Glossary of Anglo-Indian Colloquial Words and Phrases and of Kindred Terms Etymological, Historical, Geographical and Discursive* (London: John Murray, 1886), 202.

civilization, the more tractable and easy was the object to manage, more especially the Bhil'.[76]

In 1838, John Bax, Resident at Indore, gleefully reported that the 'states of Malwa are too weak and unenlightened to restrain the Bheels residing within their respective limits', and that 'application of force' was 'the only method which ever occurs to them and which has never yet succeeded'.[77] He then went on to say that native states like Malwa:

> have been so long in the habit of receiving this poor and wretched race as wild animals rather than men that it is only by bringing before their eyes the fact that Bheels are capable of being civilized and of becoming useful subjects that they will ever be brought to believe...

Bax thus encouraged 'that their pacification and civilization be attempted by means similar to those which have been so successful in Candish'.[78]

As Captain Goldsmid recounted, 'The following anecdote may illustrate the kind of treatment the Bhils used to receive from their Mahratta rulers': a high-ranking Brahmin in the Maratha government in Khandesh purportedly argued that 'these kind of people', i.e. Bhils, 'would go on

---

[76] James Tod, *Annals and Antiquities of Rajasthan: or the Central and Western Rajput States of India*, v. 1 (1829) 2nd ed. (Madras: Higginbotham, 1873), 434. In general, Tod has often been contrasted with liberals such as James Mills as having a more 'romantic, conservative' disposition, than some of his fellow countrymen. For Tod: 'The forces that served to destroy the ancient customs of the world were "evils [which] are inseparable from the age, and the inevitable results of an ever-progressing civilization." Progress, in and of itself, produced inescapable evils. Modernity was an evil, for Tod, for it represented exactly the opposite of the ancient social forms and customs that he was most actively interested in protecting. In this, Tod was wholly consistent with the Romanticism that embraced the Orient as a protest against contemporary English society'. Jason Freitag, *Serving Empire*, 99.

[77] The same situation was recounted in Barwani, on the southern bank of the Narmada river. According to a British officer by the name of Spears, the 'Dewan of Badwani' promoted a policy of 'destroying [Bhils] as one would destroy vermin wherever they could be caught', because 'plunder was in their blood and they could not be reformed'. Since the Dewan 'did not entertain hopes of being able to totally root out and exterminate' the Bhils, he calculated that 'severe examples... would terrify' them 'into eventual forbearance from plunder'. Letter dated 27 February 1820 from Malcolm to Metcalfe. Deccan Commissioner Records, vol. 343, Poona Archives. Cited in Shashank Kela, *A Rogue and Peasant Slave: Adivasi Resistance, 1800–2000* (Delhi: Navayana, 2012), 71–72. And again, a British political department memo claimed that the Marathas viewed the Bhils as 'outcasts from society and any measures for their extermination were considered justifiable'. Maharashtra State Archives, Bombay, Political Department, 1873.Vol 87. Comp 1551. Cited in Ajay Skaria, 'Shades of Wildness: Tribe, Caste, and Gender in Western India', *Journal of Asian Studies* 56, no. 3 (1997): 726–745. (Archival source cited here by Kela & Skaria not seen personally).

[78] NAI, For, Pol, 20 Jun 1838, 3 & KW, 17. To Bax, esq. Indore.

thieving as long as there was anything to steal, and that formal trial, and civilised punishments were altogether misapplied in their case'. Therefore, he ordered 'troops who had been in concealment to fall upon them, and they were all exterminated'. Goldsmid continued:

> In answer to my expressions of horror at such a proceeding, my visitor informed me 'that it would doubtless have been wrong had they been reasonable beings, but they were little better than monkeys, and had all the attributes of wild beasts, and could only be dealt with by measures similar to those necessary for exterminating beasts of prey'—and he left me with evident pity for the philanthropic weakness which prevented a young Englishman from agreeing to the lessons of age and experience.

Goldsmid thus concluded that, 'Such had been the treatment to which the Bhils had been used under our predecessors'.[79] In contrast to what East India Company officials claimed that native states were inflicting upon the Bhils, by 1832, the British described their own mission:

> [to] confirm this class of people in their incipient habits of submission and obedience, to inspire them with confidence in the efficiency of the British protection, to encourage the freedom of their intercourse with the inhabitants of the plains, and to introduce among them the cultivation of those dispositions and propensities, which were necessary to qualify them for appreciating the advantages and relishing the pursuits of civilized society.[80]

Thus, calls for preserving so-called predatory tribes such as the Bhils came significantly earlier than the parallel shift in rhetoric which transformed carnivores such as tigers from 'verminous wild beasts' into objects of conservation (see Chapter 3). What's fascinating in the case of the Bhils is how they were firmly converted in the colonial imagination from a wild and dangerous presence in the hills of the early nineteenth century into a childlike and beleaguered minority—endangered and in need of protection—within the course of roughly fifty years. Since these two

[79] Goldsmid, *James Outram* (1880), 392–393.
[80] NAI, For, Pol, 31 Dec 1832, no. 67, 68.

forms of 'wild life', i.e. 'wild men' and 'wild beasts', had long been linked in colonial discourse through dehumanizing animal analogies, there is a clearly discernible movement from awareness of endangered peoples to concern for endangered nonhuman species. By the last decades of colonial rule, most observers in western India would assert that both 'wild men' and 'wild beasts'—the early twentieth century of equivalents of biological and cultural diversity—were endangered.

Domesticating the 'wild Bhils', their 'wild forests', and what we now call wildlife species would have to go hand-in-hand. Thus, in 1819, Mountstuart Elphinstone wrote that 'I shall if possible induce the Mohammedan Bheels, who are of a more civilized description than the Hindoos, to settle [down]... but it will be necessary to make some advances to them, to cut down the Jungles, and to cultivate the ground'.[81] Following the third and last Anglo-Maratha War, ending in 1818, Elphinstone described, 'The greater part of Candeish' as 'covered with thick jungle, full of tigers and other wild beasts, but scattered with the ruin of former villages'.[82] In this power vacuum—as the Marathas had retreated and the British were yet to establish their command—the 'wandering and predatory' Bhils were pronounced as having 'infested the neighbouring country'.[83] In 1825 William Chaplin agreed: 'The tigers which swarm in every part of this half desolate Province, are indeed infinitely less baneful to its prosperity than these outlaws whom it is more difficult to reclaim from their savage nature than those wild animals'.[84] The British now attempted to 'tame' the Bhils and their hills, by establishing their own monopoly on power in the countryside.

---

[81] IOR F/4/721 (1823–1824) Bombay Political, no. 821, vol. 3 'Relative to the arrangements adopted in consequence of the depredations of the Bheels in Candeish', Extract Bengal Political Consultations, 2 March 1819, John Briggs to the Hon'ble Mount Stuart Elphinstone, 590. Grant, in the Central Provinces Gazetteer refers to 'Mohammadan Bhils' as 'another instance of the ill-effects which the strong meat of civilization has upon primitive races ill-prepared to receive it'. P.cxviii.

[82] David Arnold, 'Disease, Resistance and India's Ecological Frontier, 1770–1947', in *Issues in Modern Indian History: For Sumit Sarkar*, ed. Biwamoy Pati (Delhi: Popular Prakashan, 2000), 5. Also cited in Ballhatchet, *Social Policy*, 25. See also Sumit Guha, 'Forest Polities and Agrarian Empires: The Khandesh Bhils, c. 1700–1850', *Indian Economic & Social History Review* 33, no. 2 (1996): 133–153.

[83] Walter Hamilton, *The East-India Gazetteer*, vol. 1, 2nd ed. (London: Parbury, 1828), 97, 143.

[84] Letter dt. Poona, 18 Apr 1825 to Newnham (no. 93 of 1825). Political Dept., 1825. Vol. 29/192, Maharashtra State Archives, Mumbai. Cited in Benjamin and Mohanty, 'Imperial Solution', 345.

This linking of the Bhils and their hills, as well as tigers and tribes, continued throughout the colonial era. Rudyard Kipling, with his usual chauvinist verve, wrote that the Bhils 'seemed to be almost as open to civilization as the tigers of his own jungles'.[85] We can see it again in an 1898 land settlement survey that recommended: 'The best chance for the Bhil is that he should be improved and civilised along with the opening up of the country'.[86] Independence era historical scholarship, too, has not always avoided repeating this parallel construction. We find it again, for instance, when the historian Arvind Deshpande describes Khandesh as 'full of wild jungle that abounded in wild life', while all in a single paragraph mentioning that 'the wild hill tribes reigned' and 'the chief wild animal found in Khandesh was the tiger'.[87]

To Colonel John Briggs, who served as political agent in Khandesh under Elphinstone in the early nineteenth century, a large part of the debate over whether the Bhils could be 'domesticated' or had to be 'eradicated' came down to the question of their underlying ethnic or racial identity. If the Bhils were a 'wild race' at their core, there would be no way they could be reclaimed as productive members of society, but if their 'race' was not fundamentally 'wild' and they were just people who had broken off from the mainstream to lead a 'wild life' in the hills during a time of political turmoil, then they could be reclaimed.

Asserting that only 'two or three Chiefs of Bheels… have been born in the Hills', and that the rest 'of the Chief[s] and Bheels now in those fastness were born in villages on the plain and have been driven by the State of the country into their present haunts', in 1819 John Briggs insisted that the 'Satpoora Bhils are by no means a wild race of people, their language and their habits are the same as those of the towns who resemble the ordinary inhabitants of the country'. Since Briggs believed that the Bhils were not a 'wild race' and instead resembled 'ordinary inhabitants' of India, he also believed that 'elevating them from thieves to soldiers' was possible, and that an 'irregular corps of Bheels would answer the purpose of

---

[85] Rudyard Kipling, 'The Tomb of his Ancestors', *McClure's Magazine* 10, no. 2 (Dec 1897): 100.
[86] IOR V/23/295 No. 8 of 1898, p. 37. From the Survey Commissioner and Director, Land Records and Agriculture, Bombay; to the Chief Secretary to Government, Revenue Department. Poona, 12 Feb 1898.
[87] Arvind M. Deshpande, *John Briggs in Maharashtra: A Study in District Administration under Early British Rule* (Delhi: Mittal, 1987), 27–28.

civilising and of providing for them'—thus, Briggs laid the foundations for the Khandesh Bhil Corps, which was eventually established in the mid-1830s, after his departure from India. The goal was 'drawing them from the Hills and ... rendering them useful members of society'.

However, Briggs also believed that his view conflicted with that of the local Maratha and Rajput rulers, writing, 'the Bheels are for the most part look't on as robbers constitutionally rather than from habit and the inhabitants generally have an inveterate hatred against them'. Furthermore, the 'enmity of the inhabitants against the Bheels' was 'carried to such lengths that they would rejoice and join heartily in any plan for their extrapation [sic]'. Nonetheless, 'the Bheel shall be reclaimed', Briggs insisted, 'and return[ed] to that state of society to which he originally belongs'.[88]

Often this protectionist discourse was resignedly pessimistic; those who believed the Bhils were a 'primitive race' also believed they could not be saved, and that their extinction was inevitable. As a Baroda state official put it: 'They must die out'.[89] Their extinction was understood to be part of an unstoppable global process. Comparisons to the so-called Bushmen of southern Africa, another supposedly vanishing race, were particularly prevalent. Already in the 1840s, we find this comparison cropping up in the writing of Lieutenant Colonel John Sutherland who was Secretary to the Governor General of India, Charles Theophilus Metcalfe. After moving to Knysna, South Africa in 1845, Sutherland wrote of the Bhils:

> They are a wilder and far more savage people than the Bosjemans of Africa—and the endeavours of the British Government to reclaim the Bheels, by giving them lands near their mountain fastnesses, cattle, and implements of husbandry—to turn them from a predatory to an agricultural people—have in many places been attended with only partial success.[90]

---

[88] John Briggs, Political Agent in Candeish to M. Elphinstone, D.C.F. 174, Letter no. 367, Dhoolia, 8 Jan 1819; the full text of this letter appears in Deshpande, *John Briggs in Maharashtra*, 215–223. Thus, 'each Bheel watchman should receive monthly two Rupees, a sum which in Candeish will not support more than one person of the very lowest order with food, it is still sufficient to induce the Bheels to relinquish their predatory habits'.
[89] Hardiman, *Coming*, 69; citing K.B. Jadhav, *Opinion on the Revision Settlement Report of Mahuva Taluka* (Baroda: Government Press, 1914), 19, 21.
[90] John Sutherland, *Original Matter Contained in Lt. Col. Sutherland's Memoir on the Kaffers, Hottentots, and Bosjemans, of South Africa* (Cape Town: Pike & Philip, 1847).

Following the Darwinian revolution, comparisons to other 'dying races' would remain, as would metaphors of hunting these people down like 'wild creatures', but now evolutionary language would start to feature prominently in such descriptions as well. As in the speech by Colonel Davidson cited as an epigraph to this chapter, the Bhils were seen as a potential missing link between man and ape.[91] Yet when colonial writers did admit that the British themselves were the agents of Bhil extinction, they framed extermination as a policy that had been pursued in the past, but not any longer. Simcox, in his 1912 *Memoir of the Khandesh Bhil Corps*, thus recounts of older colonial days:

> The Bhils had come to be regarded, not as mere criminals, but as creatures without human feeling, as dangerous wild beasts or noxious vermin, from whom no good could be hoped. It was the desire, and was considered the duty of all good citizens to hunt them, trap them, and destroy them at sight.[92]

Comparisons to 'dangerous wild beasts' and references to 'hunting out' the Bhils were common in earlier periods of colonial conflict and expansion in the Bhil homeland. Now, by the late nineteenth century with the Bhils largely subjugated, the evolutionary language of equating the Bhils to apes, as well as other species lower on the totem pole of animal existence, was more prevalent. As the Collector of Surat, W. R. Pratt wrote in 1876: 'The condition of the people is about as low as it is possible to conceive human beings to be in a land that acknowledges the supremacy of British rule. The cultivators from whom a mass of revenue is derived are little higher than monkeys in the gradation list of animated nature. They wear very little more clothing, and beyond keeping body and soul together, have no idea of bettering their condition or moving at all upon the scale of civilization'.[93]

In March 1896, E. Maconochie, Survey Settlement Officer of Taloda Taluka in Khandesh District, made a similarly disturbing statement of the

---

[91] Lecture delivered in Edinburgh to H.M.'s 78th Highlanders, by Colonel Davidson, late of the Bombay Army cited by Goldsmid, *James Outram*, 55.
[92] Simcox, *Memoir of the Khandesh Bhil Corps*, 62.
[93] IOR V/10/747, Report by W. R. Pratt, 28 Aug 1876; also cited in Hardiman, *Coming*, 68.

case that the Bhils were inexorably doomed, also along social Darwinist lines of the struggle for survival:

> That the Bhils and Maochis can by any amount of nursing be brought to the permanent level of well-being of the better classes of cultivators I do not believe. Like every other primitive race they are bound to give way before the hardier survivors of a more complex struggle for existence. But I do believe, on grounds of expediency no less than of humanity, in the policy of giving them a fair chance, to use the cant phrase, of letting them down gently. A certain number will prove exceptions to the general rule of absorption and extinction, and to the remainder the inevitable will be less cruel.[94]

His opinion seems to have pervaded the settlement literature of the time, for two years later, in 1898, we find it repeated that: 'Like aboriginal populations all over the world they would have to make way. The process, however, sentiment may rebel against it, is inevitable. The question is how far a paternal Government ought to retard it'.[95]

Portraying the Bhils as wild animals being eradicated and as members of dying races served not only to dehumanize but also to primitivize these peoples. Now that their power had been crushed, defining them as primitive meant that they did not have to be reckoned with as legitimate native states on the same level as Rajputs and Marathas. Instead, they could be easily subjugated, not through anything like a symmetrical military conflict, but merely by hunting them like wild animals out of their forest strongholds. By the late nineteenth century, any semblance of genuine political power had been eradicated and long since forgotten. Their communities fully marginalized, they were now deemed to be primitive tribes truly in need of stern paternalistic protection. Why such protection was needed was utterly clear to most *fin de siècle* administrators—along with all that was fundamentally 'wild', the only options for the Bhils were to

---

[94] IOR V/23/295, No. 24 of 1896. E. Maconochie, Survey Settlement Officer, Deccan Revenue Survey, to The Collector of Khandesh, Camp Pimparpada, Taloda Taluka, Khandesh District, 6 Mar 1896. *Papers Relating to the Original Survey Settlement of 148 Government Villages of the Nandurbar Taluka (Including Navapur Petha), Shirpur and Shahada of the Khandesh Collectorate*. Selections from the records of the Bombay Government; new ser. no. 424. (Bombay: Government Central Press, 1904), 9–10.

[95] IOR V/23/295, No. 8 OF 1898, p. 37.

be either tamed or face extinction. If these were truly 'wild tribes'—then like 'primitive people' around the world who were bound to nature—the only way to save them was to isolate them from the dominant society and allow them to continue their 'rude existence' in the hills and forests. However, most administrators would eventually argue that forests were rapidly disappearing and that it was no longer possible to sustain such vast populations in a state of nature. Thus, these communities had only two options—either assimilate into the wider population and become at least semi-civilized, or physically die out. Either way, according to the late colonial imagination, forest cultures were soon to become extinct.

## From Extermination to Preservation

> I see no reason why there should not be reserved lands for the Bhils as there are reservations for the Red Skins in America and aborigines in Australia
> H.T. Ommaney, Acting Collector and Political Agent, Khandesh, 1883[96]

By the late nineteenth century, paternalism dominated the British attitude towards the Bhils. The Bhils were projected not only as wild animals but also as wild children. Again, this dramatic shift in thinking meant there were no longer calls for exterminating the Bhils, but rather for protecting and preserving them, especially since many now believed that their extinction was imminent. Paternalism was necessary because if the Bhils were not protected—being virtually infants, new to civilization—they would be cheated and abused by merchants, money lenders, and native rulers. Again, it was other Indians to blame for the Bhils' beleaguered state, not the British. For many, the best way to protect the Bhils and other so-called primitive tribes was to keep them and their lands isolated from the deleterious outside influences of their fellow Indians. As per the 1904

---

[96] IOR V/24/2410 Annual report on the working of the Western Bhil Agency, Khandesh, 1883, H.T. Ommaney, Acting Collector and Political Agent, Khandesh, Dhulia, 28 Sep 1883, to E.P. Robertson, Commissioner, C.D., p. 17.

Nandurbar Settlement Report, 'The two objects of all protective schemes should be... (a) to ensure that the wild tribes shall not be disturbed and their lands exploited by outsiders, and (b) that they shall not fall into the hands of the usurer and the legal harpies'.[97] But as Ajay Skaria rightly observes, in the colonial imagination, 'Protection was needed not only against others: the Bhils also had to be protected from their own more deplorable traits'.[98]

'The Tomb of his Ancestors', a short story Rudyard Kipling published in December 1897, gives us a clear sense of the paternalism afforded to the Bhils. The story follows the lives and careers of multiple generations of colonial officers from the same family, two of whom served in the same district in central India, both named John Chinn. As one of the Chinns reassures his men, 'The Bhils are my children. I have said it many times'. The story begins by tracing the career of the elder John Chinn who began the process of civilizing the Bhils. Chinn, 'went into his country, lived with him, learned his language, shot the deer that stole his poor crops, and won his confidence, so that some Bhils learned to plow and sow, while others were coaxed into the Company's service to police their friends'. Kipling tells us, 'Centuries of oppression and massacre made the Bhil a cruel and half-crazy thief' and 'the wildest of them still clung to the Satpura ranges'. These colonial officers dedicated their lives to their mission of taming the wild ways of the Bhils and turning them into a military police force, the Bhil Corps. Although the Bhils 'were, and at heart are, wild men', Chinn, of course, succeeded in this task of bringing in the colonial order, and Kipling writes that, 'When they understood that standing in line did not mean instant murder, they accepted soldiering as a cumbrous but amusing kind of sport, and were zealous to keep the wild Bhils under control'. With the Bhil Corps, one part of the Bhil community was used to police the other. To Kipling, it was the ideal colonial situation: 'The officers talked to their soldiers in

---

[97] IOR V/23/295 *Papers Relating to the Original Survey Settlement of 148 Government Villages of the Nandurbar Taluka (Including Navapur Petha), Shirpur and Shahada of the Khandesh Collectorate.* Bombay: Printed at the Government Central Press, 1904. Selections from the records of the Bombay Government; new ser. no. 424. No. 314 OF 1896, from the Superintendent, Deccan Revenue Survey; To the Collector or Khandesh.
[98] Ajay Skaria, 'Shades of Wildness', 726–745.

a tongue not two hundred folk in India understood; and the men were their children, all drawn from the Bhils, who are, perhaps, the strangest of the many strange races in India'.[99]

The debate about how to save/protect the Bhils usually came down to whether it was best to 'improve' their nature or keep them 'in nature'. At the end of the nineteenth and beginning of the twentieth century, we see that some efforts were being put in place, 'in order that Bhils may be preserved in their savage simplicity', but overall as one Revenue Department official put it, it was believed, 'that on the whole Bhils will gain more than they lose by being in contact with more advanced classes'.[100] As C.E. Gouldsbury described Khandesh, its hills were 'teeming with wild animals, especially tigers and panthers, and peopled by a once savage race of men, the Bhils, whom Government gradually weaned from savagery by the wise policy of free grants of land, seed and cattle, which induced them to settle down as cultivators'.[101]

But by the World War I era, and certainly during the interwar period, the majority of colonial officials had shifted their preference towards isolationism. In the words of one 'sahib who loved India': 'Above all, we were running a great campaign to protect the Bhils from the depredations of their moneylenders, who were amongst the worst in India, I suppose partly because the Bhil was a somewhat unsatisfactory debtor'.[102] Believing that the Bhils were too easily exploited by the 'more advanced classes', and they themselves were at least partly to blame, these sahibs would now push to segregate the 'hill tribes' from the general population. As Ajay Skaria astutely observes: 'if the difference between the colonizers and the colonized was erased, so was the justification for colonial presence. The civilizing mission thus never could be about erasing wildness: it always had to be about subordinating the wild, constructing the

---

[99] Kipling, 'The Tomb of His Ancestors', 100.
[100] IOR V/23/295, No. 500. Bombay Castle, 24 Jan 1902. Revenue Department, P.J. Mead, Under Secretary to Government, 84.
[101] Charles Elphinstone Gouldsbury, *Tiger Slayer by Order: Digby Davies, Late Bombay Police* (London: Chapman & Hall, 1915), 27.
[102] Maurice Zinkin, 'From Revolt to Love', in Khushwant Singh, *Sahibs Who Loved India* (2008), 131. IOR V/24/2410, Bombay. Western Bhil Agency: Annual report on the working of the Western Bhil Agency, Khandesh, 1876, p. 3. Major Probyn, Western Bhil Agent, Khandesh reported that Bhils going into debt often 'absconded', but that it was 'not worth while to hunt them out for a debt they are unable to pay'.

colonized as wild, and sustaining that construction'.[103] For some colonists, 'wildness' itself was eventually perceived as endangered and in need of protection.

One of the most famous statements of the late colonial isolationist policy came in David Symington's 1938 report on 'Measures for improvement of conditions of Bhils and other Aboriginal and Hill Tribes in Partially Excluded Areas in the Bombay Presidency'. Disagreeing 'profoundly' with the position that 'the problem of the aboriginal and hill tribes arose from their isolation from the main body of the community', Symington was absolutely clear that he favoured quarantining the Bhils for their own protection:

> Where their geographical position keeps them beyond the reach of the outside world, as in the Akrani mahal [current Maharashtra side of the Narmada River], they are happy and independent; but in the places, now all too many, where they are in constant contact with more educated people, they are degraded, timid and exploited.

Thus, not only for Symington, but for the bulk of colonial officials of the 1920–1940s, it might have been more accurate to say they advocated 'secluded areas', rather than 'excluded areas', for India's scheduled tribes. Still, Symington's goal was not to keep the tribes as they were. For example, he certainly did not express any concern for saving endangered languages. Symington believed that 'aboriginal education' should be in Hindi, and he was 'not in favour of giving instruction in any of the Bhili, Varli or other aboriginal dialects'. This was because, 'These dialects besides varying from taluka to taluka, are so far as I can ascertain merely corruptions of good speech and unworthy of survival'. Symington, like many other colonial administrators of his day, believed that the Bhils could best be 'improved' while in a state of social isolation, writing that what the Bhils 'need above all things is strong Government action to protect them from exploitation, and to supply in as full a measure as possible for their educational, social and economic needs thus gradually bringing

---

[103] Ajay Skaria, *Hybrid Histories: Forests, Frontiers, and Wildness in Western India* (Delhi: Oxford University Press, 1999), 193.

them up to the general level of their neighbours'.[104] At any rate, whether protecting the Bhils through integration or isolation (a debate discussed at length in Chapter 4), the approach was always self-avowedly paternalistic. As an Indian Civil Service officer described of a fellow district collector in 1926, he 'hunted his tigers, spanked his wild children with paternal hand and ruled with untrammelled authority'.[105]

The World Bank's independent review of the Sardar Sarovar Project argued that 'the reality of isolation played an immense part in tribal groups' continuing distinctive identity' and that 'the remoteness of many regions where tribal groups continued to live (or to which they withdrew in order to maintain their ways of life) has meant that many groups maintain distinct tribal identities'.[106] However, this remoteness and isolation, which was often remembered in oral histories that I have collected in the region as well, was largely a creation of the late colonial era. While some elders who are alive today vividly remember a time of relative 'isolation' in the early to mid-twentieth century, these memories are of a specific historical moment for these communities when their segregation was probably at its historical peak. Yet this certainly does not mean that isolation has historically always been a defining feature of these communities. Instead, the belief in tribal isolation was an orientalist and primitivist late colonial invention which not only rewrote Bhil history but also attempted to redefine Bhil identity.

Indian nationalist tribal policy of the mid-twentieth century tended to accept colonial notions of tribal primitivity at face value, and to set at its task the elimination of this primitivity and its replacement with progress by ending the Bhils' age-old isolation and incorporating them into the mainstream. By the 1930s, one Indian nationalist proudly reported this change: 'The Bhils... are gradually giving up their former modes of

---

[104] IOR V/27/803/1 David Symington, 'Report on the Aboriginal and Hill Tribes of the Partially Excluded Areas in the Bombay Presidency. For official use only' (Bombay, 1938). See also: IOR Mss Eur D1156, Papers of David Symington, Indian Civil Service, Bombay.

[105] Evan Maconochie, *Life in the Indian Civil Service* (London: Chapman and Hall, 1926), 36. Cited in Ajay Skaria, 'Shades of Wildness'.

[106] Morse and Berger, *Sardar Sarovar*. As Thakur points out, the bulk of fieldwork for this report was carried out by anthropologists whose primary areas of expertise were in indigenous communities of the western hemisphere, such as Inuit communities. Anthropologists like Hugh Brody transposed their understanding of indigenous peoples in North America into the central Indian situation when they wrote their report on the Narmada.

living... They are now not afraid to leave their native places and go outside for their livelihood. They have now realised the benefits of education'.[107] To Majumdar in 1951, the Bhils were a tribe 'who have become partially Hinduized' and their 'tribal name' was 'on the way to becoming a caste name'.[108] Naik's view in 1956 was 'that Bhil economics are not much different from the general Indian rural economics' and so the goal was to 'help to preserve the Bhil and guide his emergence from primitiveness to a full-statured national life'.[109] And describing the Bhils in 1974, P. Lal writes: 'Some of the weaker aboriginals preferred subjugation to extermination and exile and gradually came to be assimilated into the Aryan community'.[110] All of this explains the mainstream (developmentalist, assimilationist) Indian perspective that indigenous rights activists of the 1980s encountered when they began their anti-dam movement. It also goes some way towards explaining why the NBA activists ended up recycling what was essentially an early twentieth-century colonial perspective—namely that the Bhils were isolated forest communities whose very existence was endangered by the Sardar Sarovar Dam and related projects.

## 1980s Social Movements

To understand the rise of Bhil endangerment discourse with the Narmada, as well as the late twentieth-century emergence of the idea that the Bhils, until relatively recently, were isolated hunter-gatherer communities, it is worthwhile situating ourselves in the 1980s in India when neo-Gandhian social movements began to gain momentum, especially on the left. At this point, the so-called tribal problem in India, which appeared to have been largely settled, apparently was not (see Chapter 4). Integration, often indistinguishable from assimilation, had been the widely accepted

[107] IOR L/PJ/9/240, 'Excluded and Partially Excluded Areas Order in Council', 1936.
[108] D.N. Majumdar, 'Tribal Rehabilitation in India', *UNESCO International Social Science Bulletin* 3, no. 4 (1951): 802–812.
[109] Thakorlal Bharabhai Naik, *The Bhils: A Study* (Delhi: Bharatiya Adimjati Sevak Sangh, 1956), 71.
[110] Parmanand Lal, 'The Tribal Man in India: A Study in the Ecology of the Primitive Communities', in *Ecology and Biogeography in India*, ed. M.S. Mani (Dordrecht: Springer, 1974), 281–329.

public policy for the last thirty years since independence. But now, the children of the 1960s and the 1970s, who had been raised on a diet of hippie idealism and who had witnessed the birth of environmentalism, were becoming a force to be reckoned with in the 1980s. It was at this point that a couple of other factors coincide as well: a new global indigenous peoples' rights movement emerged as a powerful moral voice on the world stage, and at the same time, environmentalist NGOs started to be recognized as powerful actors capable of taking on nation-states.[111] This coalescing of forces changed the way mainstream India and the world would think about Adivasis, rekindling fears of endangerment and igniting movements for their protection.

As Judith Whitehead argued, 'neo-Gandhianism represented adivasis through a discourse of ecological romanticism that did not reflect existing realities and tended to privilege urban, middle-class perspectives'. At the peak of the Save the Narmada movement, literally thousands of influenceable young activists from urban centres such as Pune, Bombay, and Delhi would come pouring into the valley, only to be joined by globetrotting international celebrities and activists from abroad. Thus, warning of 'submerged and submerging voices', Whitehead outlined, 'the everyday practices by which a middle-class group organized, managed, and controlled media images of adivasis'. She documented how NBA activists who acted as 'intermediaries between adivasis and the wider world often came from middle-class backgrounds' and carried with them 'urban worldviews, which were typically laced with romantic images of honest and simple "tribal" peoples'. For example, she recounted how in 1999, during the Rally for the Valley, when hundreds of journalists arrived along with celebrity-activists like Arundhati Roy, it was the first time she 'saw groups of male adivasis attired in "traditional" lungis and turbans, some playing long flutes and ready for the photographers'. And at one point she was even asked by a photographer 'to move', as she puts it, 'because I was spoiling his photograph of "authentic" adivasi culture'. One NBA worker argued that a resettlement village 'was not a "real" Adivasi village because the resettlement process had "ruined them" and

---

[111] Although the term NGO was coined c.1945 by the UN, post-WWII, we can both antedate the term to show the existence of NGO-like entities at work well before this date, yet also maintain that NGOs arose as particularly powerful non-state actors in the late twentieth century.

'"authentic" tribal community was juxtaposed with modernized and corrupted "tribes" of today'.[112]

Similarly, Baviskar documents how in 'the case with the anti-dam movement in the Narmada valley... adivasis self-consciously perform stereotyped roles, pandering to hegemonic cultural expectations, in order to gain their own ends, usually with some prompting from backstage non-adivasi activists'. She then goes on to describe how 'During one political meeting, an influential supporter of the anti-dam struggle (a very senior bureaucrat) gave a speech in which the audience was told that, as adivasis, they were "mother earth's children" and that the dam would tear them from their mother's breast', before telling us that, 'As a rule, adivasis do not use this metaphor, preferring more prosaic descriptions of the threat to their land and livestock'.[113] An Adivasi leader who eventually split with the NBA, Uday Singh Bonda, has been frequently quoted in the literature putting it this way:

> We have realised that we are expected to fight against the dam, remain naked and keep performing our traditional dances. We are being deliberately encouraged to remain like this, so that our photographs can convince the world to halt the dam. We don't care if the dam is built or not. We want a good deal for our children. We have fought for the activists for years, but have got nothing in return.[114]

---

[112] Judith Whitehead, 'Submerged and Submerging Voices: Hegemony and the Decline of the Narmada Bachao Andolan in Gujarat, 1998–2001', *Critical Asian Studies* 39, no. 3 (2007): 339–421.

[113] Amita Baviskar, 'The Politics of Being "Indigenous"', in *Indigeneity in India*, eds Bengt Karlsson and Tanka Subba (London: Kegan Paul, 2006), 41. This, interestingly, seems to represent a shift from Baviskar's earlier position as expressed in her first book where she 'identified' the anti-dam movement 'as resistance to culturally destructive development' (6), and eventually became an activist. In that book she describes how 'I formulated my research hypothesis after being influenced' by the likes of Vandana Shiva and 'American Deep Ecologists' who believe 'that adivasis in forests everywhere are conservationist' and 'expected' to find 'alienation of their natural resource base and their subsequent cultural impoverishment'. Despite admitting that 'On going to the Narmada valley, I discovered a somewhat different reality' (46–48), Baviksar still repeats a number of unfounded historical and cultural stereotypes about the Bhils in subsequent chapters, calling them 'segmentary tribal societies' (56) and arguing 'that the geographical isolation of Bhils and Bhilalas in the "fastnesses of the Satpuras" and Vindhyas has played a major role in enabling them to hold their own vis-a-vis the modern state and the caste system' (88). Amita Baviskar, *In the Belly of the River: Tribal Conflicts over Development in the Narmada Valley* (Delhi: Oxford University Press, 1995).

[114] Dwivedi, 'Displacement, Risks and Resistance', 68.

Vikramaditya Thakur also documents how many urban 'tourist activists', as he calls them, travelled to the Narmada 'for short visits lasting two – four days' ever since 'the NBA-led movement had been extensively covered by the Lonely Planet's volume on India'.[115] These tourist-activists, many of whom lacked the language skills necessary to communicate with the people in the valley, could be shown what the movement wanted them to see, and played a vital part in spreading the movement's message to the English-language media and global NGOs. Thakur opens his PhD dissertation with a retelling of the standard narrative of the impact of the dam on the Bhils of the Narmada given to him by a middle-class female Brahmin social activist when he first arrived in the valley: 'The Bhils have been living in the Narmada valley for thousands of years. They have their own distinct religion and are not Hindus. Till the British captured the area, there was dense forest all around that no one had penetrated. The Bhils lived around their forest happily till the dam intervened and destroyed their lives….' In his study, he points out 'several stereotypical ideas prevalent in both academic studies and media coverage about the Bhils': 1) that the Bhils are 'totally distinct from the communities around them', 2) that the Bhils are 'indigenous to the Narmada valley', and 3) that they lived 'undisturbed in the midst of thick forests happily till the dam rudely interrupted their lives'. According to Thakur, rather than succeeding in their construction (or supposed 'preservation') of the Bhils as ecologically noble savages, 'what the elite external activists inadvertently do by organizing the Bhils against the state is to facilitate state formation in the marginal hill area'. Local Adivasi leaders, now trained in dealing with the government by the environmentalist movement, take 'an independent course' and split 'away from the elite external activists to pursue what is most crucial for the Bhils'. They start negotiating for good agricultural land 'while they also bargain for modern facilities like roads and schools'.[116]

---

[115] Vikramaditya Thakur, 'Merchants of Mobilization: Representing Anti-dam and Resettlement Claims in Western India', *Agrarian Crisis Conference*, Cornell University, 5–6 Apr 2013 (unpublished paper).

[116] Vikramaditya Thakur, 'Unsettling Modernity: Resistance and Forced Resettlement Due to a Dam in Western India' (PhD Diss., Yale University, 2014), 37, 55, 70. Thakur, who began his tenure in the Narmada Valley as an activist, quickly became jaded by certain aspects of the movement and returned to the field in subsequent years as an academic. See also: Vikramaditya Thakur, 'Learning and Leading: Resistance, Subaltern Leadership and the Making of Two Bhil

Roxana Hakim, working with a Vasava hill community in Gujarat which at the time of her article (1996) had been recently displaced and resettled by the Sardar Sarovar Project, also concludes 'they do not perceive a threat to their identity'. Some members of the community did joke with Hakim that she 'would no longer recognise them' when she 'returned at a later date'. However, Hakim notes that the Vasavas she worked with did not see this as an issue of 'giving up their culture' in exchange for mainstream culture in the plains. 'They acknowledge the differences, but have never viewed these differences as resulting in a clash and the subsequent victory of one culture over another'. Instead, Hakim suggests that most Vasavas would point to examples of unique customs as evidence that they are keeping their cultural traditions alive. For example, instead of a dowry where a girl's family pays to marry off their daughter, as is traditional in many Hindu castes, Vasavas maintain a bride price system, where a boy's family pays for him to marry the girl (this custom was still in practice in the resettlement colony where I lived as well). Hakim's conclusions are relevant here, finding that:

> The Vasavas voice many concerns with regard to resettlement and rehabilitation (R and R), but they do not conceive of the move to the new land as resulting in the 'death' of their people (genocide), rhetoric that is found in much of the NGO literature especially with regard to the Amazonian tribes.... Most Vasavas have simply not thought, and often don't want to think of the implications that constant exposure to a deshi way of life will have on their own culture. The reason is simply that the community does not regard their current way of life as a 'static' one that represents a 'traditional' lifestyle, that resettlement will change and therefore 'destroy'.[117]

## A Tale of Two Leaders

Over the course of the last fifteen years, between 2005 and 2020, I have repeatedly returned to central India to conduct oral history fieldwork

Community Leaders from the Narmada Valley, Western India', *South Asia Multidisciplinary Academic Journal* 21 (2019): 1–19. http://journals.openedition.org/samaj/5661

[117] Roxanne Hakim, 'Vasava Identity in Transition: Some Theoretical Issues', *Economic & Political Weekly* 31, no. 24 (15 Jun 1996): 1492–1499.

with Adivasi communities facing conservation and development-induced displacement. What I have consistently found is that people on the ground, people themselves facing eviction or having already gone through it, rarely if ever spoke of their own experience in terms of metanarratives of endangerment and extinction. Instead, they usually focused on everyday forms of precarity and the many struggles in their lives. Local activists (*karyakarta*) would sometimes resort to categories of cultural endangerment and extinction, but when they did, it seemed that they were adopting an imported discourse, rather than extemporaneously explaining their situation based on personal experience. Deeper discussion nearly always tended to give way to more nuanced and complicated narratives, no matter who the interlocutor.

In the hot season of 2015, thanks to the generous arrangements of an anthropologist friend of mine, Vikramaditya Thakur, I was lucky enough to have been invited to live in the homes of two former NBA Adivasi leaders in Nandurbar district of Maharashtra. One of these leaders, A-bhai Vasave had accepted rehabilitation, and led his community to re-settlement in 2004. The other, B-ji Padvi, had never left the movement, and at the time of my visit, continued to live on a hillside directly above the submergence zone. Neither they, nor any of the many Bhils and other Adivasis, either activist or not, who I have lived with and extensively interviewed over the years, took endangerment and extinction discourse to the heights I just outlined in the introduction to this chapter. Rather, they come to this situation bearing many different perspectives on issues of cultural change and loss, the impacts of displacement, and resettlement.

Since 2004, A-bhai Vasave and his family have lived in a resettlement colony, which was essentially a suburb of a town in the plains of Nandurbar. The family shares a large multiroom house, which was actually their original home from their village in the hills, and which had been transported down to the plains by truck as part of their resettlement package. Sometimes referred to by outsiders as huts, these homes are in fact worth a small fortune, since they are built out of large amounts of the finest teak in Khandesh. Constructed in the traditional Bhil manner, teak poles are knitted together with bamboo strips, giving the house natural ventilation so crucial especially in the hot season without air

**Figure 5.5.** Interior of a home in a resettlement colony in Nandurbar District, Maharashtra, during a wedding.
Photo by author.

conditioning. These handsome traditional homes have earthen floors but are topped with terracotta (*kaul*) tiled rooves (see Figure 5.5).

A-bhai and his whole family were extremely welcoming and regaled me with tales of their days fighting against the dam with the *andolan*, a chapter occupying decades of their lives. Though A- had unfortunately lost one of his legs due to gangrene several years before my visit, he was still a very proud man and a strong leader for his people. He was very clearly used to receiving visitors and meeting foreign activists and academics. He had even travelled abroad himself in his youth, visiting Stockholm with NBA leaders including Medha Patkar in 1991 to receive the Narmada Bachao Andolan's Right Livelihood Award, and touring throughout Europe to promote the anti-dam movement.

But in 2004, A-bhai split with Medha Patkar and led his people to resettlement. He was not the first village leader to do so, and he would not be the last. This was a traumatic moment for A-, his family, and his whole village. And A- more than once spoke mournfully of his loss, saying that for someone who hasn't experienced it, it would be impossible to understand what it feels like to have your entire village and the landscape of your youth taken away from you forever. But A- still felt he did the right thing in eventually embracing resettlement. One sweltering hot afternoon during my several-week-long stay at his home, I remember asking him, 'So, despite all of your best efforts, and many victories along the way, the dam was eventually built. Does this mean that you lost?' 'No', he said, 'we didn't lose. We won. Medha's fight was to stop the dam and save the environment. Ours was for land, to make sure we could have a decent life'. His people received a good resettlement package. Rather than having his village split apart, and rather than being pushed to live in Gujarat, receiving only one hectare of land as initially offered by the settlement officer, or accepting bribes that would benefit only him and not his community, A-bhai managed to secure a site of his choosing on the Maharashtra side of the river, where he was from and where he knew the language. Other villages were split apart and resettled piecemeal, moving only the lowest houses in the village as the water level approached.[118] Instead, A- demanded to move his entire village all together into the same resettlement colony. Following those who had gone before them, they were also able to move their original houses from the hills, and they received two hectares of good farmland per family. A- said they had begun fighting for resettlement initially, in the 1980s, before the *andolan* became a purely anti-dam movement. A- then joined the *andolan* fighting against the dam for some twenty years, facing many *lathi* charges and arrests (going to jail in Delhi, Bombay, Nandurbar, Dhulia, etc.), before leaving the movement and finally achieving his initial goal of resettlement for his community.

Life in the resettlement colony, by most accounts, was relatively good. Overall, it was the younger generation who preferred it most, saying there was nothing for them up in the hills but poverty. While some people, elders especially, clearly held nostalgia for the old days, most still admitted that they appreciated the benefits of life near town, with roads,

---

[118] Referred to as the *pari passu* approach to resettlement, this was used during the initial resettlement process already in 1991, following consultation with the World Bank.

hospitals, shops, schools, etc. Hearing this for me was all relatively unsurprising, since I had encountered similar perspectives in many other communities affected by conservation and development-induced displacement throughout the region. Yet every time I hear these perspectives, I still find it jarring, since they contrast so starkly with the activist belief that displacement equals death for indigenous peoples.

My anthropologist friend was furious one day because a coworker had produced an abstract for his work that oversimplified the situation in the colony, calling it 'apartheid' and saying that the Adivasis there were 'condemned to cotton production'. 'Condemned?!', he demanded repeatedly. 'These people are not condemned. Cotton production is massively successful. Do you see the motorcycles they are driving, the tractors they are buying, and that they have satellite TV, water filters, refrigerators, etc.?' While I was living there, workers were burying cables along the roadside to bring highspeed internet to the area. One night in the colony there was a wedding. Crowds of young people were out, circle dancing or sitting in small groups singing folk songs, and everyone generally having a great time under the starry sky. As we strolled down the road, greeting revellers as we passed, Vikram turned to me and said: 'See! Here are your endangered tribals'.

One afternoon, sitting inside in the shade, trying to keep cool in the blazing 115°F (46°C) degree heat, A-bhai put it this way: 'Our culture (*sanskriti*) did not drown in the dam. We still have our way of life (*rahansahan*) and our traditions (*parampara*) here'. Then, A- and I spoke about history, and he related his understanding of his community's past. 'In the sixteenth century we were pushed into the hills by Marathas and Mughals. We were Rajput. Now we call ourselves Vasave—same thing. In the nineteenth century, forests were captured by the British. In the twentieth century we lost the forests too. But we won in our fight with the NBA—we got resettlement, land, etc.'

On language change, A- has his own perspective, too. 'We learned Marathi a bit late. At first in the village, we just spoke Pavri [the local Bhil dialect]. Hindi came much later. Around the time the movement started 150–200 kids went to school. There was a school before that too, but barely active. We needed Hindi and Marathi to translate for the movement, speak to activists, journalists, etc. We had no English though'. To

A-, there was little concern for language loss. Instead, his fight has been to learn more languages, so that he could negotiate with the state and fight for his community. On clothes: 'of course in the old village we just wore *langoti*' (a cloth wrapped around the waist, *khoita* in Pavri/Bhili). He offered no clear answer why he now prefers western wear even in the sweltering heat. In the resettlement colony, A- and his family always slept with all the lights on all night, a phenomenon not altogether uncommon in newly electrified areas.[119] Eventually, I found it much more comfortable to move my cot outdoors and sleep in the dark, relatively cooler summer night air.

I spoke with Ranjana Kanhere, the founder of a well-respected NGO based in the nearby city of Shahada. She put it this way: 'We came here well before the dam came. Moving people from their homes is difficult, but there's lots of benefits to be had'. 'So, everything is OK in resettlement?' I asked a bit incredulously. 'No, people are poor, lots of problems still. Nothing is perfect anywhere in the world. But people in America think the tribals just live in forests and dance. People here see Bollywood movies and think that way too. People think Adivasi culture has been destroyed [in resettlement]'. 'Has it been?' 'No', she answered reflectively, 'I don't think so'.[120]

Heading into the hills on the Maharashtra side of the Narmada in the scorching heat one day towards the end of May, I was going to meet B-ji Padvi in his home on the banks of the SSP submergence zone. The last stretch of road going through the hills of Akkalkuwa was long and hard (this also happened to be the first road constructed in the early 1990s to move Bhil families into resettlement colonies in the plains). The SUV packed with over 20 people and their market goods, a Mahindra

---

[119] Thakur in a personal communication remarked to me that: 'I have noted that lights not switched off in many rural houses even in rural Bihar that has non-ST population. The practical reasons: [a] to supply water to fields, electricity would alternate between 7–9 days during day and then night, so people know the cycle by keeping it on. Home and farm supply was finally split by the state supplier MSEB in 2017 so now it is 24-hours at home but still the same cycle in the fields [b] can spot snakes and other vermin entering house or issues with cattle since they too are tied nearby [c] convey that they are home so protection from thieves [d] women who get up before sunlight to answer nature's call often in the open, find it convenient to move [e] high ceiling, dark bamboo walls so light not that intense as our homes'.

[120] For more on Ranjana and her husband Vikram Kanhere and how they came to Nandurbar in the 1970s as founders of the labour organization *Shramik Sanghatana*, see Amrita Basu, *Two Faces of Protest: Contrasting Modes of Women's Activism in India* (Berkeley: University of California Press, 1994).

Commander, climbed the steep winding roads with some difficulty. Women and children sat inside the cabin. Men piled onto every available surface outside the vehicle. Several times the engine overheated and had to be cooled with water from a roadside ditch. Other times the driver made the passengers sitting on the roof and engine and hanging off the sides of the vehicle get off and walk for particularly precipitous stretches of the rough dirt track. The lack of good transport up here certainly is a challenge for the communities still living in the hills (see Figure 5.6).

After the packed car ride, the hike the rest of the way to the village was relatively easy, especially since B-ji had his boat waiting for us halfway there. On the boat, which was large enough to ferry some 30 people (or 60 by rural Indian standards), but held just a handful of us now, B-ji explained how his village had been split in two by the dam. More than half of it had been drowned, and those who remained moved uphill on either side of the submergence zone. He himself had had to rebuild twice,

**Figure 5.6.** In the searing heat, the jeep engine needed to be cooled down several times along the way.
Photo by author.

being twice displaced by the rising waters when the government raised the height of the dam.

If anybody should have embraced endangerment discourse, it was B-ji. He believed that A-bhai made a mistake in accepting resettlement in the plains. 'Now he just has a little square of land, without the possibility of getting any more. He has a car [I don't correct him that A-bhai doesn't actually own a car], tractor, etc. He can go to town. But what will he do there? He doesn't have the mountains anymore, their air and wind, sunshine and sunset over the Narmada. He's lost the jungle which was his patrimony (*virasat*)'. Watching that first stunning sunset over the hills and the reservoir from his home, I understood what he was saying. 'Yes, it's beautiful', B-ji agreed. But it's a sad and beautiful place. It's hard not to feel that something was lost here. Having your land drowned, your village drowned, your jungle drowned, your shrines and temples destroyed.

One day, B-ji and I sat together looking at the old district planning maps that I had brought from the New York Public Library. They showed the state lines from the 1950s that divided Madhya Bharat from Bombay State. The Narmada flowed between them. As I read aloud the names of all the old villages, we noted how many were either misspelled or completely mislabelled. And how many villages, especially on the riverbanks, had drowned. This all might have seemed like a tragic example of cultural endangerment.

Unprompted, though, B-ji pointed out some benefits of the dam. Now with the massive reservoir, you can actually use a boat to get to your neighbours faster. Now people in the Vindhyas are just a quick trip from the Satpuras. And with all the resettlement, the population is very small, so this feels like a very rural area again. It struck me that, in some sense, perhaps he actually liked it better this way. B-ji had established a bit of a fiefdom for himself up here, living like a peasant king on his promontory. He had one wife in this house on the hill above the submergence zone where I was staying, another in town.[121] B-ji's house on the side of the Narmada was the biggest, nicest, and best situated in the immediate area, with beautiful guineafowl wandering through the yard and his own

---

[121] Although polygyny is against the law, and this custom is fading, over the course of many years of fieldwork, I have encountered several instances of Adivasis informally retaining the practice. Again, what might be called an endangered tradition by some is considered a scourge to be eradicated by many others.

**Figure 5.7.** A home above the Narmada submergence zone, and an NBA *Jivanshala*.
Photo by author.

boat docked below. B-ji also oversaw the NBA-run *Jivanshala* school that was situated right next to his house. If this were America, this real estate would be worth a fortune. As it is, this is officially forest department land, and if the authorities really wanted to, they could come and evict him (see Figure 5.7).

I went out on a walk one morning with B-ji's seven-year-old son. We visited the neighbouring huts, not half the size of B-ji's, with only thatched or half-thatched roofs, no solar panels like his, no boats docked below, just one room, not three, made of bamboo and mud, not teak beams, and only small children at home alone, their parents out working. The only teenagers I met on our walk were making some bamboo walls for a hut. These teenagers—they would have loved to move out of the hills to a resettlement colony. They barely remembered a time before the dam. It was just their parents who wanted to stay here. 'There's nothing here', they told me. 'The only problem is the fields aren't good down there'. 'You want to work in the fields?' I asked. 'Yes, well, I've studied too, and my brother works in town'. B-ji's older children, meanwhile, were in boarding school and had secured good government jobs down in the plains.

While in the hills, I often met with a young man named D-, a social worker, who caused quite a stir in the village, when he married the Sarpanch's sister, since he wasn't Padvi ('tribal'). Talking to D- one night, he told me he thought that the resettlement colony I had been living in down in the plains was nicest, because it was one of the first. 'H-colony has electricity, outhouses, decent land, etc. Others have none of that. The worst was G-pur'. I didn't contradict him at the time. But as far as I know, this information is not necessarily correct. H- was not the first resettlement colony by a long stretch. And while I hadn't seen G-pur, I had seen a fair number of colonies by then, and most of the ones built since the late 1990s had relatively similar features.[122]

As a postscript to my 2015 visit, in 2020 I learned that B-ji, who had been clinging to his old life in the hills, which in many ways was clearly a good life for him, in the end, has also accepted a resettlement package. It's not clear if he himself will move to the plains, but he has taken the land that was offered, giving it to a relative to farm. This type of situation is not altogether uncommon; Bhils are not hapless victims without any agency in the resettlement process, as is often portrayed. Some have first accepted resettlement down in the plains, secured their rehabilitation packages, and then returned to the hills. Others, who are still awaiting relocation but feel stuck in the hills, build new buildings close to the brink of the water, hoping to make the list of families slated for resettlement.

At least one recent survey conducted in the region has had similarly nuanced findings—namely that 'those displaced were far better off than their former forest neighbours in ownership of a range of assets including TVs, cellphones, vehicles, access to schools and hospitals, and agricultural markets.... and that fears that resettlement will destroy the lives and lifestyles of tribals have been grossly exaggerated'. But material comfort is not everything. This same study found that, '54% of displaced folk wished to return to their old habitat, showing that nostalgia for ancestral land can matter

---

[122] Thakur in a personal communication (20 Apr 20) noted to me: 'G-pur is poor... because [a] it has many residents from outside of submergence zone who are not genuine PAFs and [b] there was a lot of corruption involved in purchase of land, etc. So, [c] NBA/PSS never got involved, while [d] the locals lacked a vocal leader like A-bhai or B-ji, as [e] the local leaders there didn't want any extra attention due to fear of being found out'.

more than ownership of assets and economic wellbeing'. Also, in forest areas, there were similar levels of yearning, where in at least one village, 52% of respondents wished to be 'resettled with the full compensation package'.[123] Yet, as usual, complex realities have led to polarized interpretations. Unfortunately, one of the authors of this survey quickly published a popular discussion of his findings in *The Times of India* under the absurd title, 'Why many tribals don't mind being ousted by dams'. Following this, he was rightly criticized for employing 'his data to draw sweeping but unwarranted generalisations'. Still, the actual survey findings, as opposed to the author's corollary claims that 'activists are denying tribals the right to development', do appear somewhat representative of the situation on the ground.[124] Rather than a single narrative of cultural endangerment and extinction, moving beyond the slogans, we find complex realities.

## A Brief Review

In the early through mid-nineteenth century, the British largely blamed other Indian powers for trying to exterminate the Bhils and believed that Bhils could only be 'saved' if they were 'civilized'. In this context, 'protection' clearly meant 'improvement' in the minds of colonial administrators. (This, in many ways, could be compared to the integrationist policies promoted in by Indian nationalists over a century later.) By the late nineteenth century, following the rise of Darwinism and social Darwinism, the Bhils came to be seen as a doomed race, losers in the struggle for survival. As awareness of environmental destruction spread, and as Bhil power in the hills had declined to the point of disappearing, they were no longer compared to predatory wild beasts, but rather to endangered species of wildlife, and they were gradually reinvented as a primitive forest tribe rather

---

[123] Swaminathan S. Anklesaria Aiyar and Neeraj Kaushal, 'Are Resettled Oustees from the Sardar Sarovar Dam Project Better Off Today Than Their Former Neighbors Who Were Not Ousted?' *NBER Working Paper Series*, 24423 (National Bureau of Economic Research, March 2018), 1. http://www.nber.org/papers/w24423

[124] See: S.A. Aiyar, 'Why Many Tribals Don't Mind Being Ousted by Dams', *The Times of India*, 10 Sep 2017. https://timesofindia.indiatimes.com/blogs/Swaminomics/why-many-tribals-dont-mind-being-ousted-by-dams/; Shripad Dharmadhikary and Nandini Oza, 'No, Swaminathan Aiyar, Adivasis Ousted by the Narmada Project Aren't Lovin' It. They Are Desperate', *Scroll.in*, 17 Sep 2017. https://scroll.in/article/850777/no-swaminathan-aiyar-adivasis-ousted-by-the-narmada-project-arent-lovin-it-they-are-desperate

than as predatory brigands. Paternalistic protection became the new norm. (Here parallels to indigenous rights activists today start coming in.) Those who did remember that the Bhils had been a substantial power just half a century previously excused this as an aberration that arose in a time of lawlessness following the collapse of the Maratha empire.

By the early twentieth century, isolationist policies began to dominate in colonial circles. The only way to save the Bhils was to remove the harmful influences of mainstream society and preserve them in their simple ways in their forest redoubts. (The romantic inclinations here were somewhat similar to that of certain NBA activists of the 1980s–1990s.) The Indian nationalist backlash to isolationist policies then worked to integrate the Bhils into mainstream India more than ever before, and by the 1980s, this project was nearly complete. Similarly, nationalist development policies responded to colonial underdevelopment by advocating the building of monumental architecture like big dams and began to revolutionize the countryside.

However, as discussed in this chapter, for a variety of reasons, the 1980s saw a revolution in the global politics of indigeneity and environmentalism, which again reshaped the way that the Bhils and their forests were conceived by the general Indian public, and by left-leaning activists in particular, thus leading to a resurgence in tribal endangerment discourse much akin to that of the early twentieth century. External activists in the Narmada Valley who imported global discourses of indigenous rights activism latched on to endangerment discourse as a way to save the Bhils despite the fact that these communities were (a) numerically massive, and so under no demographic threat of extinction, and (b) did not fit neatly into the box of the (other) 'ecologically noble Indian' which they had dreamed up for them, so too raising into question claims of ethnocide due to loss of forest-based ways of life. This certainly does not mean that the damming of the Narmada and the forcible displacement of hundreds of thousands of people were therefore 'right' or 'good'. Nor does it mean that environmental and social activists were wrong to oppose the dam and push for adequate resettlement. Rather, it is primarily an observation about continuous use and abuse of what I refer to in this book as tribal endangerment and extinction discourses, which date all the way back to the very outset of the colonial encounter in India.

# 6
# A National Park for the Gond & Baiga

The more I see of this district the more I come to the conclusion that the fundamental problem is the effective protection of the aboriginal... The Gond and the Baiga simply cannot cope with modern conditions: they are really incapable of looking after themselves and their own interests

E.S. Hyde, 1942[1]

In 1986, there was a signboard outside Kanha National Park, that read (Dhaknae ke vastyae—Sher, Cheetah, Bear and Gond aur Baiga Adivasi.) Object [sic] of interest include Lion, Chetha [sic], Bear and Gond & Baiga tribals

Pris Weeks and Shalina Mehta, 'Managing People and Landscapes', *Journal of Human Ecology*[2]

Baigas ... survive[d] under British pressures to 'reform or perish'. Though only some Baigas 'reformed', and though at times others faced near starvation, the Baiga and their culture did not 'perish'. Their growth in numbers at a minimum suggests survival and there is some indication of cultural survival and continuity

Philip McEldowney, 'The Threatened Tribal'[3]

---

[1] Cambridge Center for South Asian Studies Archive (CCSASA), Hyde Papers, Letter to W.V. Grigson from E.S. Hyde about allotment of land by aboriginal patels, 27 Jan 1942.
[2] Pris Weeks and Shalina Mehta, 'Managing People and Landscapes: IUCN's Protected Area Categories', *Journal of Human Ecology* 16, no. 4 (2004): 253–263.
[3] Philip McEldowney, 'Colonial Administration and Social Developments in Middle India: The Central Provinces, 1861–1921' (PhD Diss., University of Virginia, 1980), 479.

One of the more prominent sites of struggle over implementation of the 2006 Scheduled Tribes and Other Forest Dwellers (Recognition of Forest Rights) Act, or Forest Rights Act, has been Kanha National Park. Located on some 2000 square kilometres of expansive forests and meadows in the southeast corner of the state of Madhya Pradesh, since the Banjar Valley Reserve Forest was first formed here in 1879, Kanha has a long history as a protected area and a similarly lengthy record of conservation-induced displacement. In recent years, the story of the eviction of the Gonds and Baigas of Kanha National Park has become so well known that it has attracted the attention of a large cadre of global non-governmental organizations as well as domestic activists. Survival International's 'Parks Need People' Campaign, for instance, has been heavily involved in the area since the latest round of removals began in 2012. 'Tribal peoples like the Baiga are the best conservationists. But they face eviction from their ancestral homelands in the name of tiger conservation', proclaims a Survival International press release. 'The area is the ancestral home of the Baiga and Gond tribes, who face a desperate future without their forests', says the organization[4] (see Figure 6.1).

Such attempts to 'defend' and 'protect' the tribes of Kanha have led to a major amplification in comparisons between human and wildlife endangerment in the region.[5] Writing in *The Ecologist*, an activist with Survival put it this way: what is 'endangered' in Kanha is 'not just tigers', it is 'indigenous communities'. 'The Baiga's survival is endangered.... Conservation will never truly be a success until it recognizes the rights and needs of all parties involved. The tiger might be safe for now, but India's tribes need our help'.[6] In 2013, one of India's top papers, *The Hindu*, also tapped perfectly into the analogy of disappearing wildlife and forest-based ways of life, with Divya Trivedi's article headline: 'Like Tiger, Like Tribal'. 'The

---

[4] Survival International, 'Tribespeople Illegally Evicted from "Jungle Book" Tiger Reserve', 14 Jan 2015. http://www.survivalinternational.org/news/10631

[5] In the 'About Us' section of its webpage, Survival International describes itself this way: 'We are Survival, the global movement for tribal peoples' rights... We help them *defend* their lives, *protect* their lands and determine their own futures' (my emphasis in italics). https://www.survivalinternational.org/info

[6] Tom Linton, 'India's Indigenous Evictions—The Dark Side of the Jungle Book', *The Ecologist*, 6 Feb 2015. http://www.theecologist.org/News/news_analysis/2741085/indias_indigenous_evictions_the_dark_side_of_the_jungle_book.html

**Figure 6.1.** Endangered: 'The Baiga'.
Fair use. *Conservation Threatens India's Baiga Tribe*. Fusion Media Company. Screenshot from: https://youtu.be/NQbcW1B4cis

Baiga tribe in Kanha is dwindling fast, unnoticed by the heralders of development', Trivedi writes.

> After being removed from the Kanha National Park in Madhya Pradesh without any alternate means of livelihood, the Baiga tribals seem a lost and confused lot.... But it [Kanha] is most famous for its Royal Bengal tiger, an animal fast on the brink of extinction. Both the tiger and the Baiga are in need of urgent saving.[7]

This trope of Gond and Baiga endangerment and extinction comes up time and again in the popular press. Once more, we find it in a June 2016 piece appearing in the British tabloid *The Daily Mail*. 'A five-minute walk through patches of stately Sal forests on the outskirts of Kanha National Park in Central India leads to hamlets inhabited by the Baigas—one of the country's oldest tribal communities, which is now on the verge of extinction', writes the *Mail's* correspondent Rakesh Ranjan.[8] Similarly, in a

---

[7] Divya Trivedi, 'Like Tiger, like Tribal', *The Hindu*, 9 Feb 2013. www.thehindu.com/news/national/other-states/like-tiger-like-tribal/article4389793.ece

[8] Rakesh Ranjan, '"We Cannot Pollute Our Surroundings": Madhya Pradesh's Deprived Baiga Tribe is Learning to Survive Outside Forests After Being Evicted from Kanha National Park',

pair of articles appearing in the national newspaper *The Hindu*, S. Harpal Singh asks the eschatological question, 'Is Gond culture fading into oblivion?' and then reports that the 'Knowledge system of tribal people faces extinction'.[9]

Asking 'What happens when the needs of endangered tigers and endangered people collide?', Moushumi Basu again advocates for protecting both tigers and tribals:

> Tigers are classified as endangered Schedule I species under India's Wildlife Protection Act, which offers them a high degree of protection from human activities such as hunting and poaching. The Baiga, for their part, are categorized as Particularly Vulnerable Tribal Group by the Indian government, a designation that safeguards the community's traditional rights with respect to identity, habitat, sources of subsistence and culture in natural surroundings.... In short, the government has guaranteed both tigers and the Baiga protection to live in their native forest habitat.[10]

A noteworthy feature of this endangerment discourse is that it never actually defines what it is that is 'endangered' about the Baiga. Is it the Baiga as a population that is threatened with extinction? Ostensibly not: with an estimated population of some 400,000, as one demographic study puts it, 'The Baiga population has grown steadily since the first anthropological study of the tribe in the 1930s'.[11] Is it the Baiga language,

---

*Daily Mail*, 12 Jun 2016. http://www.dailymail.co.uk/indiahome/indianews/article-3636991/We-pollute-surroundings-Madhya-Pradesh-s-deprived-Baiga-tribe-learning-survive-outside-forest-evicted-Kanha-National-Park.html

[9] S. Harpal Singh, 'Is Gond Culture Fading into Oblivion?' *The Hindu*, 4 Nov 2010. http://www.thehindu.com/todays-paper/tp-national/tp-andhrapradesh/Is-Gond-culture-fading-into-Oblivion/article15675160.ece. S. Harpal Singh, Knowledge System of Tribal People Faces Extinction', *The Hindu*, 6 Apr 2015. http://www.thehindu.com/news/national/telangana/knowledge-system-of-tribal-people-faces-extinction/article7072372.ece

[10] Moushumi Basu, 'What Happens When the Needs of Endangered Tigers and Endangered People Collide?' *Ensia*, 2 Aug 2016. https://ensia.com/features/endangered-tigers-endangered-people-collide-central-india/

[11] For an estimate of 390,000 Baigas in 2011 see M. Gangwar and P. Bose, 'A Sociological Study of the Livelihoods of the Baigas in Baiga-Chak Belt of Dindori, India', *Peoples of the World Foundation* (2012). http://www.peoplesoftheworld.org/hosted/baigas/. For the demographic history of the Baigas see P.H. Reddy and B. Modell, 'The Baigas of Madhya Pradesh: A Demographic Study', *Journal of Biosocial Science* 1 (29 Jan 1997): 19–31. McEldowney summarizes the history of Baiga population growth: 'The Baiga population (in the three districts of

then, that is endangered? Again, no: one could perhaps argue that the Baiga language is 'extinct', though there is no real evidence of it ever having existed. Already in the 1860s, it was reported that the Baigas did not have their own language, and today they speak various local dialects of Hindi, Gondi, Chattisgarhi, etc., though these are sometimes called Baigani. Thus, linguistic endangerment and extinction are universally neglected in contemporary writings on the Baiga. Still, many people believe that the Baiga are 'endangered'. A 2014 internet poll appearing on the Times Group's internet outlet asked—'Baiga Tribe: Are they on the verge of extinction?' 50% of respondents voted 'Yes', 50% voted 'Can't Say', and nobody voted 'No'—an internet poll, of course, being obviously the best way to determine the endangered status of any tribal community.[12]

The refrain that the Baigas and Gonds, like the Bhils (discussed in the previous chapter), are endangered derives from the perception that they are forest-based communities being deprived of their forests.[13] The removal of people from their forests is seen as a form of necropolitics, *à la* Mbembe. Plunging indigenous peoples into 'death-worlds', whole populations are said to face what Fanon, in *Black Skins/White Masks*, called a 'zone of non- being'.[14] No longer connected with their traditional forest-based cultures, the view goes, 'vast populations are subjected to living conditions that confer upon them the status of the *living dead*'.[15]

Yet the usual tension between economic development and ecological preservation is a paradox that pervades endangerment discourse about these communities.[16] Consider the following recent text by Rajesh Gautam, titled *Baigas: The Hunter Gatherers of Central India*: 'The earlier

---

Balaghat, Mandla and Bilaspur) grew from about fifteen thousand in the 1860s to eighteen thousand in the 1890s, twenty-eight thousand in the 1930s, and forty-three thousand in the 1960s'. McEldowney, 'Colonial Administration', 479.

[12] Susash Sumanta Sarathi Sharma, 'Baiga Tribe: Are They on the Verge of Extinction?', *The Times of India*, 24 Oct 2014.

[13] This perspective thrives in Hindi language publications as well as. See, e.g. Vijay Chaurasiya, *Prakriti Putra Baiga* (Bhopal: Madhya Pradesh Hindi Granth Academy, 2004).

[14] 'Il y a une zone de non-être, une région extraordinairement stérile et aride, une rampe essentiellement dépouillée, d'où un authentique surgissement peut prendre naissance'. Frantz Fanon, *Peau Noire, Masques Blancs* (Paris: Éditions du Seuil, 1952), 26.

[15] Achille Mbembe, *Necropolitics*, trans. Steven Corcoran (Durham: Duke University Press, 2019), 92. Italics in original.

[16] Here, I draw on Derrida's fundamental insight that all texts are burdened with irresolvable internal contradictions and logical disjunctions, or aporias, and so are open to deconstruction.

form of agriculture is "shifting cultivation" which [is] now extinct among the Baigas', mourns the author.[17] Gautam tells us, 'But alas! … science and technology has failed to eradicate poverty and illiteracy. It has failed to save the population standing on the verge of extinction. And we, the civilized people, have failed in bringing our counterpart along with us'.[18] In the very same text, on the one hand, the argument runs that the Baiga's 'survival is at stake' because of their poverty and illiteracy. On the other, the belief is that the Baiga's 'pre-agricultural' way of life in the forest— or even the Baiga's 'primitivity' itself—is threatened with disappearing. Similarly, *The Times of India* celebrates the 'primitive and endangered' Baiga's 'exotic ethnic attire' as it simultaneously bemoans their 'poverty-haunted existence':

BAIHAR (Balaghat): India's most primitive and endangered tribe, Baigas, shook off their poverty-haunted existence to dress up in exotic ethnic attire to lift the spirit of sport and leave their stamp in the first-ever Olympics in Madhya Pradesh's tribal district of Balaghat, bordering Chhattisgarh. There were no modern-day athletics, but young tribal boys and girls from the Baiga heartland played to tradition with aplomb.[19]

Survival International carries this fetishization of Gond and Baiga primitivity a step even further, stereotypically presenting the Adivasis of Kanha as the Disney cartoon version of Kipling's Mowgli (see Figure 6.2). 'Tribespeople illegally evicted from "Jungle Book" tiger reserve', announces one Survival International headline. In its campaign poster, we are informed, 'Mowgli's been kicked out. His jungle is now a reserve. But tourists are welcome'. Such infantilizing antics can only serve as a distraction from real issues of trauma and precarity in these people's lives. Still, the main aim of this type of activism appears to be to project the Gond and Baiga as true children of nature and to preserve their forest-based ways of

---

[17] Rajesh K. Gautam, *Baigas: The Hunter Gatherers of Central India* (Delhi: Readworthy, 2011), vii, 7.
[18] Gautam, *Baigas*, 113.
[19] Amarjeet Singh, 'Baiga Olympics: Tribal Spirit, Tradition & Mahua', *The Times of India*, 5 Apr 2015. http://timesofindia.indiatimes.com/city/bhopal/Baiga-Olympics-Tribal-spirit-tradition-mahua/articleshow/46810933.cms

Figure 6.2. Mowgli's been kicked out. His jungle is now a tiger reserve. Fair use. Survival International. Source: https://www.survivalinternational.org/articles/india-evictions-jungle-book

life within the boundaries of Kanha National Park. This, I think, is worthwhile considering in historical context.

## Elwin's Park for the Gond & Baiga

The attempt to preserve Adivasi forest culture within the bounds of a national park is by no means new. In central India in 1939, anthropologist Verrier Elwin proposed a plan to establish 'a sort of National Park, in which not only the Baiga, but the thousands of simple Gond in their neighbourhood might take refuge'.[20] His intention was to counteract what he saw as 'an over-hasty and unregulated process of "uplift" and civilization' for central India's tribes. This park was to be established in a '"wild and largely inaccessible" part of the country, under the direct

[20] Verrier Elwin, *The Baiga* (London: J. Murray, 1939), 515.

control of a Tribes Commissioner... Inside this area, the administration was to allow the tribesmen to live their lives with the "utmost possible happiness and freedom".[21] According to Elwin: 'It was not a question of preserving Baiga culture—for the Baigas have very little culture: it was a question of keeping them alive, saving them from oppression and exploitation, giving them a simple form of development'.[22]

Elwin's proposition quickly came under heavy fire, however. The Hindu nationalist sociologist G.S. Ghurye, in particular, launched a sustained attack on Elwin, calling him an 'isolationist', an 'anthropological dictator', and accusing him of wanting to keep tribes in a 'zoo' or 'museum'.[23] Ghurye fervently believed that the so-called aborigines of India were actually 'backwards Hindus' who needed to be re-assimilated into the mainstream of the nation.[24] With specific reference to Elwin's national park proposal, Ghurye criticized:

> As we have seen, his scheme of a 'National Park' is intended to apply to that section of the so-called aborigines which has still kept itself vigorously tribal. In that 'park' there will be no schools, education being not considered good for the people of the 'park'. Outsiders will be licensed so that only amiable and amenable sorts of people get within the charmed circle. The people will practise shifting cultivation and will be governed by their own customs through their own elders. They will be encouraged to keep to their own ideas of aesthetics, etc. In short, there will be nothing that will present a contrast, either visual or mental, to the full-blooded tribal culture of the Baigas, the Murias, and others. Thus are they to be kept in 'innocence and happiness for a while till civilization is more worthy to instruct them and until a scientific age has learnt how to bring development and without causing despair'. For all practical purposes Dr. Elwin must be considered to be not only an isolationist but a no-changer as far as the uncontaminated

---

[21] Verrier Elwin, *Tribal World of Verrier Elwin: An Autobiography* (Oxford: Oxford University Press, 1989), 291–292.
[22] Elwin, *Tribal World*, 291–292.
[23] A.C. Sinha, 'Colonial Anthropology vs. Indological Sociology: Elwin and Ghurye on Tribal Policy in India' in *Between Ethnography and Fiction: Verrier Elwin and the Tribal Question in India*, eds T.B. Subba and Sujit Som (Delhi: Orient Blackswan, 2005), 71.
[24] K.S. Singh, 'G.S. Ghurye, Verrier Elwin, and Indian Tribes' in *The Legacy of G.S. Ghurye: A Centennial Festschrift*, ed. A.R. Momin (Bombay: Popular Prakashan, 1996), 39.

aborigines are concerned, in spite of his disclaiming himself to be an isolationist.[25]

To Ghurye, as well as many other nationalists at the time, the idea of a national park for the scheduled tribes was an anathema. Elwin summarized their position in his own words rather well:

> My views on the protection of the tribes caused a regular flutter, and for many years, indeed right up to the present time, I have been accused of wanting 'to keep them as they are', to hold up their development, to preserve them as museum specimens for the benefit of anthropologists. This is, and always has been, nonsense.[26]

Though Elwin never stopped defending his intention to protect the Gond and Baiga, following Ghurye's attack, he did eventually apologize for using the expression 'National Park', saying he 'should have realized the unfortunate connotations'.[27] He argued that, in all but name, his plan was not so far from the consensus opinion on national policy towards the tribes that emerged in independent India. 'In actual fact', he claimed in the 1950s, 'the Government of India has now appointed a Tribes Commissioner and established Tribal Welfare Departments in several States, as well as Scheduled and Tribal Areas, which in practice are not unlike what I suggested so long ago'.[28] Elwin's point here is not merely semantic. His park was to have been established in the Mandla District, precisely where Kanha National Park, one of the India's most successful tiger sanctuaries, is now located. Mandla District—referred to as the 'Ultima Thule of civilization, the dreaded home of the tiger, the Gond, and the devil' as late as 1912[29]— is also the site of one of the earliest colonial experiments in preserving and assimilating central India's tribal populations: the Baiga Chak (or

---

[25] G.S. Ghurye, *The Scheduled Tribes,* 3rd ed. (Bombay: Popular Press, 1963), 164.
[26] Elwin, *Tribal World,* 291-292.
[27] Verrier Elwin, 'Growth of a 'Philosophy', in *Anthropology in the Development Process,* ed. Hari Mohan Mathur (New Delhi: Vikas, 1977), 476. Also, Elwin, 'Beating a Dead Horse', *Seminar* 14 (Oct 1960).
[28] Elwin, *Tribal World,* 291-292.
[29] British Library, India Office Records (IOR) V/27/65/66, F.R.S. Rudman, *Mandla District Gazetteer,* vol. A, descriptive (Bombay: Times Press, 1912), 2.

'Baiga Reservation'), established in 1890, which will be discussed here at length.[30]

Taking Elwin's 1939 call for 'a sort of National Park' for the Gond and Baiga as a 'sort of' historical centrepoint, this chapter asks readers to consider the remarkable similarities between various colonial and contemporary attempts to demarcate protected areas for India's endangered 'tribal' populations. In this region of central India, there was not only the Baiga Chak, which still serves as an administrative entity to this day. There was also the colonial policy, dating back at least to 1874, of 'Scheduled Districts', 'Excluded and Partially Excluded Areas', and 'Backward Tracts', now renamed 'Scheduled Areas' for 'Scheduled Tribes', which will be explored here as well. Then there is the contemporary biocultural diversity conservation paradigm as expressed in the Scheduled Tribes (Recognition of Forest Rights) Act of 2006, which attempts to assert Adivasi land rights even within protected areas. What substantive differences are there between all these various modes of tribal conservation? Aren't they all, in some sense, aiming to create 'a sort of National Park' for the Gond and Baiga?

## The Gond Rajas of Garha Mandla

Before we can delve into answering these questions, it is important to understand that part of the irony in the idea of preserving Gond society's forest-based ways of life—especially within the bounds of a national park—is that it completely overlooks Gond history. As discussed in Chapter 2, the Gonds (like the Bhils) have been continuously constructed as endangered 'aboriginal children of the forest' ever since the colonial period. This, despite the fact that Raj Gond rulers had built architecturally significant palaces and forts centuries before the British ever arrived on the scene (see Figure 6.3). They also founded several cities (e.g. the founding of the city of Nagpur, for instance, is attributed to the Gond Raja Bakht Buland Shah of Devagad in the year 1702. Nagpur fell the Marathas in 1742).

---

[30] Archana Prasad, 'The Baiga: Survival Strategies and Local Economy in the Central Provinces', *Studies in History* 14, no. 2 (1998): 325–348.

**Figure 6.3.** Palace of the Gond Kings of Garha-Mandla at Ramnagar.
Public domain. Source: Russell, R.V. and Hira Lal, *The Tribes and Castes of the Central Provinces of India* (London: Macmillan, 1916), 47.

Chronologically speaking, it is important to understand that much of central India, which is today called Madhya Pradesh, was historically known as Gondwana, and that for hundreds of years, from at least the twelfth century, a series of Gond kingdoms had reigned over the area. One of the major kingdoms of Gondwana was Garha-Mandla, which controlled the area where Kanha National Park is now located. Famous figures in the history of Garha-Mandla include Jadurai or Yadavaraya, the founder of the dynasty,[31] and Rani Durgavati, who rose to become Gondwana's most celebrated queen. Durgavati occupied the resplendent Madan Mahal at present-day Jabalpur (see Chapter 2, Figure 2.1), and died a martyr's death while fighting the Mughal emperor Akbar's forces in battle in 1564.

As the Royal Anthropological Institute's description of a documentary film released in the 1980s put it: 'The once-powerful Raj or ruling Gonds have now been reduced to the status of a tribe that needs the protection of the Indian government for their survival'.[32] Understanding the history

---

[31] Eyre Chatterton, *Story of Gondwana* (London: Sir Isaac Pitman & sons, 1916), 30–31.
[32] Michael Yorke et al., 'Raj Gonds—Reflections in a Peacock Crown' (BBC Two, 24 Sep 1982).

of this decline means starting at least in the mid-1700s with power in the region transferring from the Raj Gonds to the Bhonsle Marathas—a process culminating in the utter destitution of most Gond communities by the early twentieth century. By the late 1700s, Raj Gond power had been all but supplanted by the Marathas. The anthropologist Stephen Fuchs, for example, describes: 'In 1781 the last Gond ruler of Mandla, Narhar Shah, was tortured to death by the Maratha general Moraji, and Mandla became a dependency of the Saugor Marathas. In 1799 Mandla fell to the Bhonsla king of Nagpur, till in 1818 the British took over and assumed the rule also over Mandla'.[33] It was in this period that many Gonds and other independent peoples of central India began their retreat into the forests and hills as a means of escape and resistance. As A.C. Lyall described in the 1867 *Gazetteer of the Central Provinces*, 'the wild original tribes... had begun to recede before the more skilful and superior settlers'. Lyall recorded that, 'In Bukht Boolund's time (A.D. 1700) the bulk of the population was undoubtedly Gond; but.... The Gonds are now as 1 to 18 of the strictly Hindoo population'.[34] After the British used the doctrine of lapse in 1853 to seize Nagpur from the heirless Maratha Bhonsle Maharaja Raghoji III, the British formed the Central Provinces in 1861 on top of what was once largely the territories of Raj Gond kingdoms, many of which had fallen under Maratha rule. In 1857, the last of the Raj Gond kingdoms fell to the British. The British executed the Gond Raja of Jabalpur by cannon for his part in the 1857 'mutiny', and the annexation was complete. Describing this situation, Helen Douglas Mackenzie, the wife of an Army officer, put it starkly in 1854: 'The result to the Gonds is nothing less than gradual extermination.... Should the present system be persisted in, the Gonds will be extinct in ten or fifteen years, and these lovely hills will become the abode of robbers, who may make us pay dearly for our apathy towards the sufferings of their harmless predecessors'. Thus, she argued, 'The only way to secure the Gonds from undue taxation and breaches of faith, is to... restore the Rajas to their hereditary rights'.[35]

---

[33] Stephen Fuchs, 'Folk Tales of the Gond and Baiga in Eastern Mandla', *Asian Folklore Studies* 24, no. 2 (1965): 53–116.
[34] M. Low, 'Nagpur', in *Gazetteer of the Central Provinces*, Part I, ed. Alfred Comyn Lyall (Nagpur: Chief Commissioner's Office Press, 1867), 266.
[35] Helen Douglas Mackenzie, *Life in the Mission, the Camp, and the Zenáná, or, Six years in India*, vol. 2 (London: Richard Bentley, 1854), 365.

Far from respecting the position of Gonds as former elites, however, most colonial texts were riddled with internal inconsistencies about how they understood these communities. Some colonial officials as well as Indian martial elites could not accept the idea that such formerly powerful kingdoms were established by 'aboriginal tribes', and so argued that Raj Gond dynasties were founded by 'kshatriyas' who married with local 'aborigines'. Official gazetteers and administrative texts often in one breath described the Gonds' accomplishments of the past and then in the next nonetheless rendered them at the bottom of the scales of humankind in their unilineal theories of sociocultural evolution.[36] Archaeology texts would similarly contradict one another. So, for example, the Archaeological Survey of India in the 1880s clearly documented a palace of the Gond Rajas of Garha Mandala, Moti Mahal at Ramnagar, amongst numerous other Gond remains (see Figure 6.3).[37] Yet Fergusson's *History of Indian and Eastern Architecture* from the same period completely denied the existence of such Gond antiquities, writing:

> Side by side with the intellectual Brahman caste, and the chivalrous Rajput, are found the wild Bhil and the naked Gond... living now as they have done for thousands of years.... these tribes are in too rude a state to have any architecture of their own in a sufficiently advanced state for our purposes.[38]

In 1868 a British Ethnological Committee—adopting all the usual metaphors of dehumanization, disappearance, extermination, as well as a total dismissal of Adivasi history—reported:

> The Central Provinces, from their geographical position, and still more from their natural features, form exactly the tract in which one would expect to find waifs and relics of aboriginal tribes. It is like a thick bit of cover in the middle of open country; when the plains all round have

---

[36] Charles Grant, ed., *The Gazetteer of the Central Provinces of India*, 2nd ed. (Bombay: Education Society's Press, 1870), xiv–xv.
[37] Alexander Cunningham, *Report of a Tour of the Central Provinces and Lower Gangetic Doab in 1881–82* (Calcutta: Government Printing, 1884), 46–55.
[38] James Fergusson, *History of Indian and Eastern Architecture*, vol. 3 (London: J. Murray, 1876), 3, 319.

been swept by hunters or cleared by colonists, you are sure to find in such a thicket all the wild animals that have not been exterminated. In the present instance the cover has never yet been properly beaten. Up to a very recent date that part of the Central Provinces which used to be called Gondwana was entirely unexplored, and it has no history prior to the time of the Maharattas.[39]

Since Gondwana had 'no history prior to the time of the Maharattas', of course such committees assumed it was the Gonds' essential primitivity that explained why the onslaught of each successive wave of invaders drove them to escape deeper into the forest. By 1867 it was said that the Gonds 'cannot compete' with Hindu agriculturalists, who were 'slowly, but surely, driving them out'.[40] Ignoring or dismissing the community's former status as rulers of the region, colonial sources typically reported that the Gonds were 'hunting tribes' in the past. In the words of one: 'The primary occupation of the Gonds in former times was hunting and fishing'.[41] Another wrote: 'These castes are really hunting tribes, for whom grain is a luxury and jungle roots and berries their ordinary diet, which they are said to supplement by eating field mice, lizards, and snails'.[42]

In what may very well have been a pastiche of colonial ethnology, in 1882, Shoshee Chunder Dutt published *The Wild Tribes of India* under the pseudonym Horatio Bickerstaff Rowney, where he mimicked the colonizer's appraisal of the Gonds. 'Some parts of the territory', he wrote, 'are well suited for European settlement, while the rest are fit only for the habitation of tigers or other wild animals; and it is here that the Gonds have existed for ages, and gradually degenerated'. Dutt in the voice of Rowney continues some pages later: 'Where the seclusion of life is very great, the chief occupation of the Gond still is to rove about his forests... with the wild beasts that go prowling about him'.[43]

---

[39] *Report of the Ethnological Committee on Papers Laid Before Them and Upon Examination of Specimens of Aboriginal Tribes Brought to the Jubbulpore Exhibition of 1866–67* (Nagpore: M. Lawler, 1868), 2.
[40] IOR V/27/314/440A, W.B. Thomson, *Report on the Land Revenue Settlement of the Seonee District, on the [sic] Central Provinces* (Bombay: Education Society's Press, 1867), 42.
[41] R.V. Russell and Hira Lal, *The Tribes and Castes of the Central Provinces of India*, vol. 3 (London: Macmillan, 1916), 141.
[42] A.H.L. Fraser, *Report on the Famine in Central Provinces in 1899–1900*, vol. 1 (Nagpur, 1901), 3.
[43] Shoshee Chunder Dutt [Pseud. Horatio Bickerstaff Rowney], *The Wild Tribes of India* (London: Thos. de la Rue, 1882), 1, 11.

In contrast to this type of colonial anthropology, in the mid-twentieth century, many nationalist scholars who were interested in the integration of Adivasis into the mainstream of Indian society, explained the disappearance of 'tribal' culture not in terms of 'degeneration' but rather in terms of 'upward' assimilation, Sanskritization, and Rajputization. As Surajit Sinha once put it in an article on 'State Formation and Rajput Myth in Tribal Central India', this type of evidence was often deployed to argue that, 'State-formation in the tribal belt of central India' was 'very largely a story of Rajputisation of the tribes'.[44] According to B.C. Mazumdar in *The Aborigines of the Highlands of Central India*, Gonds were 'of low culture' and resided in 'the deepest recesses of the wild forests'. 'In the scale of the civilized peoples they are even lower than the Bhils of the Nerbudda basin'.[45] And pointing to 'visible remnants of tribal society... only in marginal, undeveloped areas', D.D. Kosambi would argue that, 'The entire course of Indian history shows tribal elements being fused into a general society'. Kosambi was also critical of so-called tribal elements that fought against this tide, writing that, 'What has fossilized them is refusal' (to assimilate), as they 'cling desperately to primitive outward forms' (of tribal life).[46] Thus, viewing the 'conversion' of tribes into Rajputs as 'a general feature' of Indian history, the mainstream view has been that Raj Gonds aspired towards kshatriya status.

So, for example, there was the case of Queen Durgavati, who was mentioned at the outset of this section. Though there is some dispute as to her origins, most sources hold that Durgavati was born the daughter of a Chandela Rajput king (meaning that she was a kshatriya, not an 'Adivasi'). Her marriage to the Gond prince Dalpat Shah worked not only to cement an alliance between neighbouring kingdoms but also to elevate the status of this Raj Gond dynasty, serving to shift the perception away from one that saw all Gonds as a primitive tribe, but only through intermarriage, Rajputization, and upward assimilation. All of this, in any case, speaks quite strongly against the notion that, historically, all Gonds

---

[44] Surajit Sinha, 'State Formation and Rajput Myth in Tribal Central India', *Man in India* 42, no. 1 (1962): 36.
[45] B.C. Mazumdar, *The Aborigines of the Highlands of Central India* (Calcutta: University of Calcutta, 1927), 5.
[46] D.D. Kosambi, *An Introduction to the Study of Indian History* (Bombay: Popular Book Depot, 1956), 24–25.

were vanishing forest communities whose endangered ecological traditions are best protected in parks. And furthermore, it helps highlight the awkwardness of any position holding that only those people with the proper 'primitive' credentials are worthy of inhabiting protected areas such as parks.

## *Bewar* to Baiga Chak

As far as the Baigas are concerned—in contrast to the Raj Gonds—there is much evidence to suggest that these people had long lived as forest communities; thus, they have often been romanticized as one of India's quintessential endangered forest tribes. Traditionally, in addition to other forest-based livelihood activities, Baigas practiced *bewar*, a form of shifting cultivation, which Verrier Elwin called *swidden* agriculture.[47] Early British administrators in the Central Provinces, however, were unanimous in their view that *bewar* was a form of slash-and-burn cultivation immensely destructive to the timber resources from which they hoped to derive their revenue. Remarking that 'The Byga is the most terrible enemy to the forests we have anywhere in these hills', Captain James Forysth described what he felt was an 'inborn destructiveness of these jungle people to trees'.[48] And Captain Ward, who produced the first *Land Revenue Settlement of the Mundlah District* in 1869, felt that 'It is much to be regretted that these people have caused such devastation in the forests; and it is really difficult to believe that so few people could sweep the earth so clear of timber as they have done'.[49] (Here it might be noted that while

---

[47] Nehru Memorial Museum and Library (NMML), Verrier Elwin Papers (VEP), 'Papers Regarding Forests', file no. ATA/Pol/6, sn. 127, letter to AG, signed 31 May 1955. 'There is no word in English for a forest-clearing or jhum… bewar in MP… podu in Orissa… Swedish anth. KG Izikowitz [wrote]… "There is no ordinary word in ordinary English which covers this meaning, since the method is no longer used in England. In contrast to English, the Swedish language has a single word swedja e.g. a burnt clearing (noun) and to burn a clearing (verb) in ordinary use today, because the method has been continued up to modern times. In searching for an English word I have taken the helpful suggestion of Professor Eilert Ekwall, a dialect word, swidden." Personally [Elwin writes] "I like this word, and have used it in my latest book on the Soras, for it has a rural air"'.

[48] James Forsyth, *The Highlands of Central India: Notes on Their Forests and Wild Tribes, Natural History, and Sports* (London: Chapman and Hall, 1871), 304, 306.

[49] IOR V/27/314/413, H.C.E. Ward, *Report on the Land Revenue Settlement of the Mundlah District of the Central Provinces, 1868–69* (Bombay: Education Society's Press, 1870), 39.

the colonial prejudice against the Baigas and *bewar* appears to have been just that, a prejudice—the jury is still out on the environmental impact of this form of 'slash-and-burn' agriculture, and thus also Baiga status as 'ecologically noble'.)

The colonial administration in the first decades after founding the Central Provinces in 1861 was also convinced that in order to uplift and civilize the Baiga, they must be converted to plow-based sedentary agriculture. The Chief Commissioner hoped 'the wild tribes' would eventually 'settle down permanently' and 'adopt more civilized ways'.[50] But since the Baigas maintained a track record of resistance to sedentary agriculture, it was felt that 'the work of civilizing the Byga is much more difficult' than 'the civilizing' of other tribes.[51] At least in part, this resistance was because, as Elwin reported, the Baigas believed that their *bhagvan* (lord) barred them from using the plow, commanding: 'You must not tear the breasts of your Mother the Earth with the plough like the Gond and Hindu. You will cut down trees and burn them and sow your seed in the ashes. But you will never become rich, for if you did you would forsake the earth'.[52] Given this opposition to the plough, the preface of the Mandla settlement report was clear that, 'It has been not the least important problem ... to break these wild nomads of their wandering habits, and induce them to settle down within fixed areas. Hitherto they have roamed about the jungle very much at their pleasure, ruining the forest growth'.[53] John Morris, the Chief Commissioner of the Central Provinces, also believed that, 'So long as these people do nothing but grow kodo or koatkee on dhya patches for their own food... they can never improve, they can never rise in the human scale, but must continue to be wild men of the woods as they are now'.[54]

The question, then, is: if *bewar* was seen both as a tremendous scourge to forests and as an insurmountable obstacle to civilizing the Baiga, why

---

[50] IOR V/27/314/440A, J.H. Morris, Chief Commissioner of the Central Provinces in W.B. Thomson, *Settlement of the Seonee District*, 13 (*memorandum*); cited by Elwin, *The Baiga*, 112 and McEldowney, 'Colonial Administration', 444.

[51] Ward, *Mundlah*, 35.

[52] Elwin, *The Baiga*, 106–107. Some recent scholars have claimed that it was Elwin himself who invented the notion of Baiga religious objections to plow cultivation, since his goal was to 'save' the Baiga's tribal way of life. See Prasad, *Against Ecological Romanticism*.

[53] J.H. Morris, in Ward, *Mundlah*, 2.

[54] J.H. Morris cited in Elwin, *The Baiga*, 111.

did the colonial authorities always make concessions for its continuation? They did so in the form of an administrative unit they called the Baiga Chak or Baiga Reservation, a region of land where Baigas could (re)settle in and continue to practice their traditional form of cultivation, *bewar*. Baiga Chak was established after almost three successive decades where the administration had offered the shifting cultivators numerous incentives to adopt settled plough-driven agriculture, but at each step of the way, *bewar* was always allowed to endure. Calling the Baigas 'as wild as the forest they live in', Ward already in the late 1860s found it to be 'quite impracticable, as well as hard and impolitic' to force the Baigas to 'take to the plow'. He thus labelled 'the settlement with them' as 'simply the attempt to continue their destructive propensities within a ring fence'. Whereas 'formerly the areas claimed by these people amounted to over 30,000 acres' for *bewar*, now '7,794 acres of land have been allotted to these people in twelve villages'.[55] In May 1890, after numerous such concessions over the previous two decades, the area the administration set aside for *bewar*-cutting grew again to about 24,000 acres (about 37.5 square miles)—'Baigas were to move into the Chak as *bewar* would be strictly prohibited outside the area'.[56] According to Ward, the Baigas supposedly 'expressed themselves quite satisfied with the arrangement'.[57] However, we find direct evidence of Baiga complaints about the resettlement process of 1890 in the following translation of a statement made by one Dharmi Byga upon being ordered to move into the Chak:

> I am residing in Mauza Udhor, and am cutting bewar in this village for last 3 years. Sixty families of Bygas inhabit this village, and they all live upon dahia cultivation. We have now been ordered by government to leave this village and to remove to Dhurkata—a forest reserve that has been allotted by government for bewar cutting and colonization of Bygas. This reserve is situated at a distance of about 12 miles from our habitation. It has very little jungle as most of it was cut down by its old Byga settlers, and consequently it cannot support us and other Bygas of different villages. In our village too (viz. Udhor) there is now very

---

[55] Ward, *Mundlah*, 35, 36, 39.
[56] Philip F. McEldowney, 'Colonial Administration', 468.
[57] Ward, *Mundlah*, 39.

little forest. Part of it was cut down in last 3 years of our cultivation. We therefore pray that we may be able to allowed bewar cutting in the adjoining villages of Madiares and Kharidih so that we may be able to live with ease. We cannot take to plough as we have no agricultural stock or implements. We have no other course of livelihood but to stick to dahia cultivation. We do not wish to be removed from Udhor, but if Government intends to remove us from the village, we are willing to do so and to take up our abode in the adjoining village of Madiaras instead. But we do not want to go to Dhur Kata.[58]

All this provokes the question: was Baiga Chak a space where the Baiga could preserve and maintain their ecological and cultural traditions, or a space designed to facilitate their conversion to other ways of life and livelihoods? Verrier Elwin himself explicitly argued that: 'The Chak was not... as sometimes has been supposed, a sort of National Park where the Baiga would be allowed to carry on their ancient tribal life, but a Reformatory where the Baiga, under strict supervision and increasing official pressure, would be slowly "weaned" from their primitive habits'.[59] A forest department official writing in 1892 suggested the same: 'the true policy is to wean the Baigas from such cultivation by the grant of such privileges as will enable them to take to plough cultivation...'[60]

In contrast, Philip McEldowney insightfully recognizes how Baiga Chak was established on what he calls, 'a mixture of confusing, or even contradictory, ideas'.[61] In his 1980 PhD thesis chapter titled 'The Threatened Tribal', McEldowney describes the policy of colonial forestry in reference to the forest dwellers as one of 'new rules and procedures... which confiscated much of their land for forest conservation', and reflected 'a policy of transforming the[m] from forest to regular field cultivators'.[62] Yet the apparent logic of the Chak—to provide a refuge for *bewar*-cutting shifting cultivators, seemed to fly in the face of the anti-*bewar* sentiments so far discussed. Thus, some contemporary scholars

---

[58] Madhya Pradesh State Archives, Bhopal (MPSA), Rev. For. Comp., VIII, Forest Dept., no. 233, statement made by Dharmi Byga of Mauza Udhor, before Tehsildar of Ramgarh, dated 22 Apr 1891.
[59] Elwin, *The Baiga*, 118.
[60] MPSA, Rev. For. Comp. B26 f336–345, 1890–1892.
[61] McEldowney, 'Colonial Administration', 467.
[62] McEldowney, 'Colonial Administration', abstract.

and activists considering the *de facto* impact of Baiga Chak (rather than colonial anti-bewar discourse) have insisted that it was 'an area specially designated for the Baiga tribe to safeguard its livelihood and culture'.[63]

If Baiga Chak had not originally been formed as a space to preserve the Baiga's forest-based way of life, it quickly transformed into one. In 1885, Bloomfield's *Notes on the Baigas* reported concern that, although the Baigas themselves said their population was as numerous as ever, 'there can be little doubt that, like all wild tribes, they are gradually decreasing and disappearing'.[64] By the end of the 1890s, numerous colonial administrators seemed to begin to favour preserving the Baiga's way of life in Baiga Chak, especially with regard to *bewar*. In 1897 M.C. McCrie, the District Forest Officer in Mandla, 'reported that "the figures clearly show that bewar-cutting does not entail the permanent extinction of forest growth on the areas on which it is practised. Indeed it would probably do little harm or permanent damage."'[65] Similarly, Sir Bampfylde Fuller, writing in 1898, spoke of 'the past rather exaggerated ideas… of the injurious effects of bewar'.[66] Administrators also used the language of extinction to describe the loss of shifting cultivation. Sainthill Eardley-Wilmot, the Inspector General of Forests, for instance, suggested that the reason that the Karen of Burma had 'escaped the fate that overtakes most savage tribes in India, that of absorption with the mixed races of Hindustan', was because of 'allotting areas' for 'shifting cultivation', observing in 1910 that, 'in the Central Provinces the practice is fast dying out'.[67] The trend of pro-*bewar* sentiments continued through the first decades of the twentieth century with, in 1916, the Central Provinces passing a law allowing *bewar* in regulated areas even beyond the Chak.[68]

Not every administrator was of the same mind. Whereas some argued that 'Shifting cultivation… enables men to eke out an existence in the

---

[63] Ashish Kothari and Shiba Desor, 'Baigas' Battle: The Fight of the Baigas of Madhya Pradesh to Regain Their Traditional Rights is also a Fight to Restore the Diversity of Their Forests and to Protect National Wealth', *Frontline*, 1 May 2013. www.frontline.in/environment/conservation/baigas-battle/article4653458.ece

[64] A. Bloomfield, *Notes on the Baigas of the Central Provinces* (Balaghat: Self-Published, 1885), 1.

[65] Elwin, *The Baiga*, 126.

[66] Fuller cited in Elwin, *The Baiga*, 129.

[67] Sainthill Eardley-Wilmot and Mabel Eardley-Wilmot, *Forest Life and Sport in India* (London: E. Arnold, 1910), 280.

[68] McEldowney, 'Colonial Administration', 473.

tropics and at the same time preserves the stability of the soil', Rudman in his 1912 *Mandla District Gazetteer*, did not see Baiga Chak in a particularly positive light.[69] Writing of the negative impact of *bewar*, he stated:

> axes, traps, and arrows of the Baiga have cleared his once teeming jungles of every vestige of animal life, so that the advent of a hare within his limits is a red-letter day celebrated by the whole village turning out for a hunt. Elsewhere however the jungles teem with game, and a morning stalk through the Motinala, Phen, or Banjar Reserves is usually rewarded by the sight of scores of animals of half a dozen different varieties.[70]

Still, by the 1930s and 1940s, a considerable group of like-minded British anthropologists and administrators had come to agree that the Baigas and their way of life in the forest were under threat. Chief among them were J.H. Hutton, director of the 1931 census; Wilfrid Grigson, Deputy Commissioner of the Central Provinces and Berar, author of several works on 'the aboriginal problem'; and Verrier Elwin, the famed 'philanthropologist' who married a Gond woman. Grigson, who quietly agreed with Elwin's call for a Baiga national park, was also supportive of the rights of the Baiga to carry out *bewar*. 'I think it fairly obvious', wrote Grigson, 'that for Baiga additional bewar could be given in forest villages outside the chak as well as inside it, perhaps on the scale of one acre per man, with all or some of the conditions suggested at page 520 of Mr. Elwin's *The Baiga*'.[71] Notably, page 520 of Elwin's book elaborated on his national park idea for the Baiga.

By the early 1930s, the call for the Baigas' protection and preservation was popular in the colonial administration. Certainly not exclusively Verrier Elwin's position, many European scholar-administrators, and also some Indians, agreed. As T.C.S. Jayaratnam wrote in 1930, almost a decade before Elwin produced his 1939 magnum opus *The Baiga*, 'The complete extinction in the district of these rapidly disappearing tribes

---

[69] G.V. Jacks and R.O. Whyte, *The Rape of the Earth* (London: Faber and Faber, 1939), cited in IOR V/14725, W.V. Grigson, *Notes on the Aboriginal Problem in the Mandla District* (Nagpur: Government Printing, 1940), 23.
[70] IOR V/27/65/66, Rudman, *Mandla District Gazetteer*, 10.
[71] IOR V/14725, Grigson, *Notes on… Mandla*, 23.

can only be prevented by securing to them beora patches [beora was the local term for Bewar in Bilaspur] in such areas as are of no value as forests provided also, of course, that the cutting is controlled'.[72] And in 1931, M. Ikramullah, an Indian Civil Service Officer, complained that Baiga Chak was becoming too civilized:

> The Baiga Chak is a small block of Government Forest in Karanja range where a special reserve for Baigas has been created. Its area is 20,000 acres. Baigas used to practice Bewar cultivation whenever they were found but this was stopped by Government and they were settled in the 'Chak'. Here they are allowed to practise Bewar cultivation and live their own lives. I was rather disappointed when I visited the place because I found them wearing more clothes than I liked. In fact they are getting civilized. I missed the fine physique which has been described in Russell's book. They have started regular cultivation side by side with bewar. They are, however, still a very amiable set of people jolly and inquisitive. They would insist on having a ride in the car![73]

## Excluded Areas & Backward Tracts

As Verrier Elwin points out, the 'curious criticism' that anthropologists wanted to 'keep the tribesmen in zoos or museums' was first made 'in the Legislative Assembly in February 1936 in a debate on the Excluded Areas'. During this debate, 'a number of speakers attacked anthropologists as wishing to keep the primitive people of India "uncivilized" and "in a state of barbarism"'.[74] However, the controversial colonial logic of protected or 'excluded' areas for India's tribes dates back not just to the 1930s but at least to 1874, with the passage of the Scheduled Districts Act. This

---

[72] IOR V/27/314/392, T.C.S. Jayaratnam, *Report on the Revision of the Land Revenue Settlement of the Bilaspur Zamindaris in the Bilaspur District of the Central Provinces Effected during the Years 1928–1930* (Nagpur: Government Printing, 1931); cited in W.V. Grigson, *The Aboriginal Problem in the Central Provinces and Berar* (Nagpur: Government Printing, 1944), 264.

[73] W.H. Shoobert, *Census of India 1931, vol. XII: Central Provinces & Berar, Part I—Report* (Nagpur: Government Printing, 1933), appendix III, 404. Notes recorded by Mr. M. Ikramullah, I.C.S.

[74] Verrier Elwin, 'Do We Really Want to Keep Them in a Zoo?' *The Adivasis* (Delhi: Ministry of Information and Broadcasting, 1960 [1955?]), 8.

Act marked the establishment of a national policy that continues to this day in the form of India's constitutional categories of Scheduled Areas for Scheduled Tribes.[75] First named 'Scheduled Districts' in 1874, these areas (which included the Baiga Chak) were already called 'backward' at this time but were officially labelled as 'Backward Tracts' under the 1919 Government of India Act. By 1935, they were renamed again, this time as 'Excluded and Partially Excluded Areas'. Finally, in 1950, a Congress leadership that had previously claimed to reject the protectionist and isolationist logic of these zones, itself enshrined them into Schedule V and VI of the Constitution of India.

Conservatism and conservation went together in the colonial regime, and by the late nineteenth century, conserving both the social order and forests heavily preoccupied the administration. Both the Scheduled Districts Act of 1874 and the Indian Forest Act of 1878 can be seen as products of this dual conservative-conservationist impulse. Both, as Chandra puts it, 'effectively identified tracts for the conservation of forests and their tribal inhabitants'.[76] Colonial officials strongly believed they had to protect the forest from tribes, and then some also began to believe that they had to protect the tribes from losing the forest. This back-and-forth swing between attempts to preserve forests and tribes in central India eventually made up the crux of colonial policy towards both. As one colonial administrator in Bastar State wrote in 1940:

> On the one hand there have been ardent anthropologists with a strong affection for the inhabitants of this area. Their main preoccupation has been to prevent a violation of the peace and primeval contentment of the people of this area, even to the extent of retaining the area as a tribal reserve. On the other hand there have been the forestry experts, who have felt, as is clear from their writings, an equally sincere concern for the destruction of fine forests, with its results of erosion and the advent

---

[75] Sanjukta Das Gupta argues we can see this 'principle of administrative exception' for tribal areas date back to at least 1837 in India with the establishment of the Kolhan Government Estate for the Ho people of western Singhbhum (now in Jharkhand State). See: Sanjukta Das Gupta, 'A homeland for "tribal" subjects Revisiting British colonial experimentations in the Kolhan Government Estate', in *Subjects, Citizens and Law: Colonial and Independent India*, eds Gunnel Cederlöf and Sanjukta Das Gupta (Delhi: Routledge, 2016).

[76] Uday Chandra, 'Liberalism and Its Other: The Politics of Primitivism in Colonial and Postcolonial Indian Law', *Law & Society Review* 47, no. 1 (2013): 144.

of desert conditions. The views of both sides must command sympathy. If I may venture to express a personal opinion, I would say on the one hand that everything should be done to prevent any such degradation of the people of this area as has taken place among the Gonds in many districts of the Central Provinces. On the other hand, any one who has seen the appalling desolation which has resulted in the mountains of Waziristan (and probably many other place in India) as a result of ruthless destruction of forests, must equally agree that it is the duty of administration to do all that it can in the way of preservation.[77]

According to critics within the Indian National Congress of the 1930s and 1940s, the same logic of isolationism and protectionism for tribes that was central to Elwin's national park idea was also at the heart of the policy of the Backward Tracts and Excluded Areas. Though Elwin had attempted to claim that it was just the words 'National Park' that his opponents had objected to, in examining the history of Indian nationalist opposition to colonial tribal policy, we can see that there was something far more substantive at stake. The 1935 Government of India Act had implemented new constitutional reforms based on the recommendations of the much-despised Simon Commission, or Indian Statutory Commission, which did not include a single Indian member. In the face of protests of '*Simon Vapas Jao*' and 'Simon Go Home', the Simon Commission not only proposed separate communal electorates for Hindus and Muslims, and the separation of Burma from India, but also Excluded Areas for India's tribes. Each of these measures was felt to be an attack on the unity of the nation and nationalist movement, working by dividing and conquering. As G.S. Ghurye put it, such separate tribal areas, splitting the tribes from the mainstream, would contribute to the 'balkanization of Bharat [India]'.[78]

Numerous nationalist critics of every bent aligned themselves against the policy of excluded areas. Typical of the Congress Party view, L.P. Vidyarthi, for example, called this the 'policy of segregation

---

[77] CCSASA, Hyde Papers, Box I, #8: 3 'Office of the Administrator. Bastar State. Jagdalpur. No. C/339', dated camp Bijapur, 8 Apr 1940. A.N. Mitchell, Administrator, Bastar State to the Political Agent, Chhattisgarh States, Raipur, C.P.

[78] Carol Upadhya, 'The Hindu Nationalist Sociology of G.S. Ghurye', *Sociological Bulletin* 51, no. 1 (2002): 28–57.

in pre-independence period'.[79] A pamphlet of the Communist Party of India on 'the Tribal Problem' also argued that the 'British imperialists kept the tribal people and the areas they inhabit deliberately isolated from the rest of the Indian people', because they: 'did not wish them to become a part of the national movement. The areas inhabited by the tribal people were converted by the imperialists into excluded areas in an effort to keep them as exclusive preserves of the foreign administration and the Christian missionaries'.[80]

Colonial racial theory also saturated the state's exclusionary policies.[81] Referring to the tribes as 'backward races', the Simon Commission wrote that, 'The degree of exclusion of the various backward tracts... is not uniform, the differences being due to the varying estimates formed of the degree of backwardness of the inhabitants'. 'These backward races', it was said, were 'commonly supposed to be remnants of pre-Aryan autochthonous peoples into whose strongholds in the hills and forests the invader found it difficult and unprofitable to penetrate'.[82]

It was primarily colonial administrators who defended this policy of exclusion. W.V. Grigson, in his article on the 'The Aboriginal in the Future India', argued that the 1935 partially excluded areas did not go far enough: 'in the Central Provinces and Berar, for example, the partially excluded areas contain only 833,000 out of nearly three million aboriginals, and those who are outside these areas are often the worst exploited and most in need of protection'. According to Grigson:

> Congress and other critics without pausing to reflect on the real purpose and legal consequences of these provisions fiercely attacked the anthropologists accused of having inspired them, and the provisions themselves as intended to remove from ministerial control the rich

[79] Lalita Prasad Vidyarthi and Binay Kumar Rai, *The Tribal Culture of India* (Delhi: Concept Publishing Company, 1977), 413.
[80] Ardhendu Bhushan Bardhan, *The Tribal Problem in India*, Pamphlet no. 12 (New Delhi: Communist Party of India, 1973), 8.
[81] Much the same debate about the purpose of protected areas for tribal people was taking place amongst administrators in Australia at roughly the same moment, in this case, in the name of 'aboriginal reserves' rather than 'excluded areas' or 'national parks'. See Russell McGregor, 'The Aboriginal Reserves Debate of the Inter-War Years', Presented at the Society Conference 7 Aug 1993, 545.
[82] *Indian Statutory Commission*: Volume 1, part II, Ch. 7, p. 158 'Backward Tracts'. http://www.southasiaarchive.com/Content/sarf.140888/201594

natural resources of the areas partially excluded, as protecting peoples who needed no protection, and as based on distrust of Indian fairplay towards backward Indians.[83]

Grigson defended the 1935 Government of India Act, dismissing the nationalist position that the tribes should not be separated into a new minority, saying that they already constituted an old and beleaguered one. 'Driven as they have been by man or by circumstances into the hills and the backwoods and the malaria belt, these backward peoples are a real minority... still clinging to an ancient way of life.'[84]

More recently, postcolonial scholars following in the spirit of the Indian nationalist critique, have argued that the policy of excluded areas/ backward tracts/ scheduled areas had relegated their denizens to 'the waiting room of history', i.e. that these areas, founded on the liberal premise that the tribes were in need of 'protection', also simultaneously denied their readiness to participate in their own democratic governance.[85] Uday Chandra, in particular, has focused on the paradox of colonial 'liberalism' and 'primitivism' in India's Scheduled Areas. Asking, 'how can the ideal of universal liberal citizenship overcome paternalistic notions of protection', Chandra argues that 'liberal theorists and lawmakers have struggled to defend the rights and freedoms of political subjects whom they regard as "primitive," "backward," or in more politically-correct terms, "indigenous"'.[86] Exclusion in this context meant several things: that 'non-tribals' could not purchase land in these areas, and that efforts would be made to protect 'tribals' against predatory merchants and money lenders, but most importantly, it meant that, whereas in the rest of colonial India administrative power was being dissolved to Indians at the provincial level, these tribal areas would remain under direct rule of the colonial authorities. Thus, much as previously colonialism had justified itself by claiming that all of India was unqualified to govern itself and in need of a paternalistic British hand, now it was only those tribes perceived to be lowest on

---

[83] W.V. Grigson, 'The Aboriginal in the Future India', *Man* 46 (Jan–Feb 1946): 16–17.

[84] W.V. Grigson 'Foreword', in *Tribal Hyderabad: Four Reports,* ed. Christoph von Fürer-Haimendorf (Hyderabad: Government of H.E.H. the Nizam Revenue Department, 1945), v–vii.

[85] Dipesh Chakrabarty, *Provincializing Europe: Postcolonial Thought and Historical Difference* (Delhi: Oxford University Press, 2001).

[86] Chandra, 'Liberalism and Its Other', 135.

the scale of civilization who were still branded as incapable of defending their own economic and political interests. This is largely the same logic that critics feared was being applied in the case of Elwin's call for 'a sort of national park' for the Gond and Baiga.

## 'Particularly Vulnerable Tribal Groups' Gain 'Habitat Rights'

Much as the government of India has revised colonial nomenclature with reference to the places where Adivasis live, now referring to them as 'scheduled areas' rather than 'backward tracts', the government has also made some modicum of effort to re-label the communities themselves in less stigmatizing terms. Formerly identified as 'Primitive Tribal Groups' by the Indian government, in the 2006 Forest Rights Act these communities were renamed 'Particularly Vulnerable Tribal Groups'. Should this evolution in nomenclature be seen as yet another example of 'The Return of the Native', as Adam Kuper might suggest?[87]

In 2012, an amendment to the Forest Rights Act defined the concept of 'Habitat Rights' for Particularly Vulnerable Tribal Groups. Since then, several environmental and social activist publications have celebrated the fact that the Baigas were the first community in India to be awarded these rights. Billed as a landmark win for the tribal forest rights movement, the environmentalist magazine *Down To Earth* describes 'Habitat rights' as going 'beyond the individual and community rights conferred under the Act. They aim to protect not just land rights and livelihoods of the people living in forests, but encompass their whole culture and way of life'.[88] The Hindi language press has similarly celebrated this phenomenon.[89]

Yet in this context, the term 'habitat' reeks of animal analogy. By most definitions, a 'habitat' is an ecological or environmental area of a non-human animal, plant or other species; according to the Forest Rights Act

---

[87] Adam Kuper argues that, 'In the rhetoric of the indigenous peoples movement the terms "native" and "indigenous" are often euphemisms for what used to be termed "primitive"'. 'The Return of the Native', *Current Anthropology* 44, no. 3 (Jun 2003): 389–402.

[88] Anupam Chakravartty, 'Baiga Get Home', *Down to Earth*, 15 Feb 2016.

[89] 'Baiga Janjati ko Mila Habitat Adhikar', *Navbharat Times*, 29 Dec 2015. https://navbharattimes.indiatimes.com/other/good-governance/madhya-pradesh/habitat-rights-for-baiga-tribes/articleshow/50370504.cms

' "Habitat" includes the area... in reserved forests and protected forests of primitive tribal groups and pre-agricultural communities and other forest dwelling Scheduled Tribes'.[90] Considering the long history of racist animalizing metaphors for tribal peoples around the world, it is somewhat surprising that activists and administrators would promote this language without considering its dehumanizing implications.

The communities affected by this law are also confused about the language of 'habitat rights' for different reasons as well. The Hindi term chosen as the translation for 'habitat' by the Indian government is *aawas*, but a literal translation of word *aawas* actually means 'home'. Thus, as one NGO enthusiastically in support of habitat rights explains, 'this has created confusion and due to misinterpretation, many states have equated the term "habitat" to mean providing housing facilities as under Indira Awas Yojana and other such housing scheme'.[91] In my own field experience with Baiga communities living in or around Kanha National Park and Baiga Chak in 2006 and 2016, few if any had ever heard of the Forest Rights Act, let alone their supposed victory for habitat rights. Most people I spoke with, on hearing the expression '*aawas adhikar*', reasonably assumed the legislation was about 'housing rights'.

Important to appreciate here is that the area where the Baigas have been granted 'habitat rights' is precisely in Baiga Chak. 'We have recognised Baiga Chak as the tribe's habitat', said Chavi Bharadwaj, the district collector of Dindori in Madhya Pradesh, in an interview with *The Economic Times*. But then added: 'Even we are not sure what a Baiga habitat is. But like a tiger's habitat, we consider it as all the areas the tribe routinely wanders into, including distant forest shrines'.[92] Thus, the same area where in 1890 the colonial authorities began their experiment with conserving the Baiga, or more specifically the traditional Baiga land use method of *bewar*, is again centre stage in the historic effort to save India's tribes.[93]

Here, again, I think it is necessary to reflect on the concept of protected areas for indigenous peoples, and to consider how closely habitat rights

---

[90] FRA 2006, Section 2 (h).
[91] Subrat Kumar Nayak, 'Habitat Rights Under FRA', *Vasundhara* (Aug 2016): 6.
[92] Dinesh Narayanan, 'Forest Rights Act: How Rules Fail in the Jungle', *Economic Times*, 1 Oct 2015. http://blogs.economictimes.indiatimes.com/it-doesnt-add-up/forest-rights-act-how-rules-fail-in-the-jungle/
[93] Chakravartty, 'Baigas Get Home', reports that in about a year since notification started, in Nov 2015, 'the right has been granted over 9,300 hectares (ha) to about 900 families in seven villages' in the Samnapur block of Dindori.

resemble not only the original intention of Baiga Chak but also Elwin's initiative of a national park for the Baiga. Referring specifically to Dindori District, the area where habitat rights have now been granted, in 1941, Edward Hyde, a colonial deputy commissioner in the region, argued: 'I consider that the greater part of this district ought to become an aboriginal preserve. It is, as Mr. Rudman said of the Gond 30 years ago in the Mandla Gazetter, "their last strong-hold against Hindu aggression"'. Without such a 'preserve', Hyde feared:

> the more I see of conditions in primitive areas, the more convinced I am that our policy, or lack of it, is wrong and unsuitable and is leading towards the extermination of the primitive tribes as such… They are losing not only their peculiar but their better features and are being degenerated into a series of low caste Hindus, losing their primitive virtues and acquiring evil customs.[94]

## Tribal Hunting & Cultural Conservation

What the new biocultural diversity conservation paradigm proposes, and the 2006 Scheduled Tribes and Other Forest Dwellers (Recognition of Forest Rights) Act promises, is the protection of traditional ecological lifestyles and livelihoods. Neither, though, would allow for either hunting or *bewar* agriculture within India's national parks. Yet in the mid-twentieth century, the disappearance of hunting (along with the disappearance of *bewar*) was one of the main sites where administrator-anthropologists saw endangered ecological traditions and applied pressure for protection. Elwin firmly believed that, 'What the Baiga needs above all else is the restoration of the freedom of the forest' and argued that 'the Game Act has pressed heavily upon the Baiga and has served still further to devitalize the tribal life'. To quote Elwin,

> It is a shame and a disgrace that a tribe that has lived for millennia by hunting should now have to witness the spectacle of any townsman who

---

[94] CCSASA, Hyde Papers, Letter to W.V. Grigson from ESH about aboriginal reserves, 14 Jan 1941, Box VII, file C.

can afford a licence coming into his country and slaughtering its animals for pleasure, while they who depend on their bows and arrows for food should have to hide them in their huts.[95]

The Baigas had long been seen by the colonial authorities as 'the wildest of these tribes, inhabiting the most inaccessible hills and the remotest forests' of the Central Provinces, and they were said to 'subsist on what they can secure with their bows and arrows, in the use of which they are very skilled, and on the forest produce, or whatever they can get in exchange for it, and the small crops, which they raise on the hill sides, of kodo, kootkee, rehuar'.[96] Banned from hunting and cultivating in the forest, a section titled 'The Disappearance of the Ritual Hunt' would become a cornerstone of Elwin's famous most pamphlet on the tribal problem, *Loss of Nerve*.

Grigson, in his 1940 *Notes on the Aboriginal Problem in the Mandla District*, mentions several instances where those in power abused the game laws, including one case where, 'six or seven Baigas in 1937 [were excessively fined] for killing a *sambhar* [deer] which they said had entered their fields. The case was reported by a notorious Hindu "leader" who, according to the Baigas, only reported them because they refused to give him the meat'.[97] In 1939, Grigson, Elwin, and others succeeded in having the Game Act partly reversed and Baigas were again permitted to hunt with their traditional bows and arrows in Mandla, but as Grigson wrote: 'Some Baiga still believe that it was an offence to kill a pig. I think however that the ignorance of the Act cuts both ways; some are so ignorant that they have never taken any notice of its provisions'.[98] Later, in his 1944 *Notes on the Aboriginal Problem in the Central Provinces*, Grigson put it this way: 'The tribal hunt possibly is not yet a dead institution in some parts of the province... if it does survive, then it should not be interfered with'.[99]

[95] Elwin, *The Baiga*, 516–517.
[96] IOR V/27/314/440A, Thomson, *Settlement of the Seonee District*, 39.
[97] IOR V/14725, Grigson, *Notes on... Mandla*, 19.
[98] Ibid., 26.
[99] Grigson, *Aboriginal Problem in the Central Provinces*, 346.

In the 1950s, Stephen Fuchs also worried about some of the changes that conservation laws brought about in forest societies:

> The Gond and Bhumia... [i]n former times ... were free to hunt in the forests and to complement their otherwise mainly vegetarian diet with the meat of all kinds of wild animals. But the present game laws of the Government restrict hunting severely and they have either to apply for a hunting licence, which is not easy for them to procure, or to get meat in some other way. Some of course resort to poaching, but they risk severe punishment if they are caught.[100]

All this is to say that just as individuals in early to mid-twentieth century India were beginning to think about wildlife conservation, many anthropologists had already long been thinking about the conservation of hunting and hunting cultures. Wildlife and hunting were inextricably linked in the colonial imagination. If wildlife were to disappear, the loss of hunting would be tragic. Some even believed that if hunting were to go extinct, that there would not be any point of wildlife existing (see Chapter 3).

In the pre-independence period, what we would today call 'wildlife conservation' was still more controversial than tribal conservation, and efforts were equally being made at protecting hunting interests. As one sceptical administrator asked in the 1930s after Kanha was first declared a game sanctuary, 'What exactly are these sanctuaries for?' At the time, the administrator argued, 'There is not the slightest fear of the fauna of the Central Provinces disappearing at any time in the foreseeable future'. Complaining that, 'the sanctuary at Kanha is attracting outside tigers with the result that the barasingha [*Rucervus duvaucelii*], the only really scarce species, are now getting reduced', and that 'the large herds of chital [*Axis axis*] which get out of the sanctuary are doing immense damage', he proposed 'that all [game] sanctuaries in this province be abolished and that... shooting in such areas be reintroduced'.[101] Soon after Kanha's

---

[100] Stephen Fuchs, *The Gond and Bhumia of Eastern Mandla* (Bombay: Asia Publishing, 1960), 69.
[101] Francis Wyle and Mr. Maitland quoted in W.V. Grigson, *The Aboriginal Problem in the Balaghat District: A Preliminary Report* (Nagpur: Government Printing, 1941), 46 and Grigson, *Aboriginal Problem in the Central Provinces*, 347.

initial notification as a game sanctuary in 1935, shooting blocks were reopened to keep down both deer and tiger populations.

## Displacement from Kanha National Park

From the moment of Kanha's inception as a reserve forest in 1879, a year after the passage of the Indian Forest Act, powerful external forces have been at work in Gondwana and Baiga *desh*, or Baiga country, to remove the Gonds and Baigas from their forests. Brander's working plan for the Banjar Reserve records some of the first removals of the 1870s:

> Kanha, &c. In these places the Baigas had apparently made more or less permanent settlements, but owing to the severe famine of 1874 they were abandoned and have not been re-occupied. The subsequent creation of the reserve in 1879 has since excluded them. The present generation of Baigas have not as yet settled down to cultivation. They still largely depend on the reserve for their subsistence, into which they make excursions for several days at a time, collecting fruits, hunting and fishing.[102]

Brander writes: 'There are two forest villages situated inside the Reserve… It is highly undesirable that more villages should be created inside the Reserve'. He then goes on to assert that 'the Reserve is free from all rights', meaning the rights of its Baiga and Gond inhabitants.[103] Today, Kisli, one of the two forest villages named in Brander's report, is no longer a living village for local people, but rather a headquarters for park administration, for lavish tourist resorts, and for jeep safari expeditions into the park. When I first visited there in 2006, I could immediately see that local people living in and around Kisli who were not working in the tourism industry were deeply resentful of the intrusion, with many expressing wariness of the rapid expansion of the tourist sector there. By the third time I visited Kisli in 2016, the village was almost

---

[102] A.A. Dunbar Brander, *Working Plan for the Forests of the Banjar Valley Reserve, Mandla Forest Division, Northern Circle, CP, for the Period 1904–1935* (Allahabad: Pioneer Press, 1906), 2.
[103] Brander, *Working Plan*, 3.

unrecognizable with the number of new luxury hotels that had been built in the interceding decade.

This process arguably began in 1973–1974 when Kanha was declared a Tiger Reserve (TR). Lasgorceix and Kothari document what happened around this time:

> 24 villages (around 650 families) were displaced outside the boundaries of the TR. These villages were reportedly relocated voluntarily. Some villagers resisted at the beginning of the process, but after a better understanding of the relocation package, this resistance dwindled… It was most likely the first relocation from a PA [Protected Area] after independence. As reported by H.S. Panwar, the then director of the TR, this relocation was made in a participatory and transparency way [sic]; youth and elders of the villages participated in decision-making and in the implementation of the relocation package. The park officials apparently had only an advisory role. More recent research, however, suggests that there was a significant 'discontent and disillusionment following the displacement of the locals leading to an ambiance of latent conflict', which also showed up in numerous acts of illegal use of resources from within the park.[104]

Anthropologist Shalina Mehta also reports how at least one of the first villages displaced from Kanha in the 1970s was 'relocated out of the park onto to land that was not owned by either the Forest or Revenue Departments':

> Consequently neither of these government entities felt responsible for the villagers, arguing that the village was outside of their administrative zone. The people inhabiting these villages did not have access to safe drinking water or other amenities. Nor did they have means to level the rough lands that were allotted to them. They were neither allowed to collect fodder nor minor forest produce from land that was once their home.[105]

---

[104] Antoine Lasgorceix and Ashish Kothari, 'Displacement and Relocation of Protected Areas: A Synthesis and Analysis of Case Studies', *Economic & Political Weekly* 44, no. 49 (5 Dec 2009): 40.
[105] Weeks and Mehta, 'Managing People and Landscapes', 253–263.

In my experience of collecting Adivasi oral histories of conservation-induced displacement in central India, a certain amount of 'discontent and disillusionment' certainly exists within Baiga and Gond communities who were removed from Kanha. In 2006, and again in 2011 and 2016, I visited numerous villages displaced from the core of the Kanha, resided in several of these villages, and conducted video interviews with current and former park residents, primarily in local dialects of Hindi. Most recently, in 2016, I resided in two villages in Kanha's buffer zone that had been recently shifted out of the core area of the park. Along with interviewing residents of these and neighbouring villages, I also interviewed several elderly gentlemen from another village who had been shifted from the centre of the core area to just within the boundary of the core area, and who feared their village might be removed again, as the forest department was currently in talks with their village about just such a move. I also interviewed several families that had been shifted out of the park, and now lived individually in scattered homes not located in resettlement colonies.

Free Prior Informed Consent (FPIC) is today considered the gold standard for both conservation and development-induced displacement and resettlement. Most evictees I interviewed around Kanha did report giving free, prior, consent to move, but this consent did not seem to be particularly well informed. While some people in some villages reported that men and unmarried women over 18 received 10 Lakh Rupees to move (approximately $16,000 in 2016), as well as five acres of land, others reported only receiving money and no land, and in several instances, they reported not receiving anything at all. Some villages were resettled together, but other villages were split apart. In one case, a single village was split in half and resettled in two different locations. In another case, individuals from the same village each chose to resettle wherever they could find the best land to purchase, allegedly because the government did not provide them with land. Furthermore, in two of the villages where I worked, the majority of interviewees reported being deeply unhappy about the move and their new situation for a variety of reasons. For example, they felt that the old village community had been disrupted. Other major complaints ranged from lack of employment in the new setting, to lack of access to forest resources, to lack of water for crops. Several people reported that what they initially thought was a tremendous sum of money, 10 Lakh Rupees per adult, soon ran out, others that now they regretted moving because only after moving did they realize what they had lost.

Paradoxically, considering all of the media and activist hype surrounding the eviction of the Gonds and Baigas from Kanha, one of my more concerning findings was that evictees reported a near-universal lack of outside support during the resettlement process. The people I interviewed, both in the park and in resettlement, have universally made (or are currently making) the decision to leave without any outside, third party, consultation. Negotiations are solely between themselves and park officials. All villagers reported that no outside NGOs or lawyers were involved in their decision to leave the protected area, either helping them to remain, or negotiating the terms of their resettlement packages.

People resettled outside of the park expressed a wide range of emotions about the move. Some larger families with multiple sons and unmarried daughters, aged 18 and over, seem to have been able to build large, rather impressive, houses for themselves by combining resettlement packages (see Figure 6.4). Many in this category reported that they felt satisfied with the resettlement package, especially if they were previously poor and/or landless in their former villages. Clearly, the issue of resettlement was a divisive one within communities; everybody seemed to have a different opinion or feeling about it. Generally, from my experiences, poorer families with less to lose were more eager to leave the park than families that were well off in their current

**Figure 6.4.** A home resettled outside of Kanha National Park.
Photo by author.

situation, and the younger generation was more amenable to life in resettlement than the older generation. Furthermore, it was primarily outside activists who subscribe to and perpetuate the narrative that 'tribals', their culture, and their way of life in the forest, are all in danger of vanishing as a result of conservation-induced displacement in Kanha. Average villagers rarely, if ever, spoke of their transition out of the park in terms of grand narratives of cultural and ecological loss, being more concerned with the logistics, economics, and other complex practicalities of resettlement.

## Among Believers

On my third fieldwork trip to Kanha National Park and Baiga Chak since 2006, during my sabbatical year in the autumn of 2016, I knew I wanted to see the area from the perspective of the activists who worked there, particularly those who espoused Adivasi endangerment discourse. When planning this trip, I was generously put in contact with some of these activist networks by the well-known environmentalist Ashish Kothari, founder of Kalpavriksh.

Ashish Kothari and I had met briefly after he had delivered a keynote address at a 'Local Futures' conference on 'the Economics of Happiness' in the beautiful *Teatro Verdi* in Florence, Italy (a city where I was then located as a visiting guest lecturer). Kothari's talk on 'Radical Ecological Democracy / EcoSwaraj' was packed with powerful rhetorical points, stating, for instance, that 'the development process today, especially the globalized development process, is a process of violence against nature, against communities, against culture, against each one of us'. Yet while maintaining that this situation was a 'crisis', he never resorted to claims of cultural extinction for India's Adivasis, instead regaling his audience with uplifting stories of 'indigenous villages in central India' who were 'reclaiming their livelihoods and the political and economic spaces', stopping big dams, reviving traditional agricultural diversity, becoming self-sufficient, and building sustainable communities.[106]

---

[106] For the full speech, see: Ashish Kothari, 'Radical Ecological Democracy/EcoSwaraj', Presentation at Economics of Happiness gathering, 2 Oct 2016. https://youtu.be/SG0uarfxmv4

**Figure 6.5.** Save the Real Avatar Tribe.
Fair use. Survival International. Source: https://www.survivalinternational.org/news/9478

Sitting on the steps outside the theatre with Kothari after his talk, I complimented him on his work and outlined my critique of sensationalist endangerment discourse by groups such as Survival International that depicted indigenous communities around Kanha as Disney cartoon versions of Kipling characters and portrayed groups such as the Dongria Kondh as the threatened Na'vi, animated science fiction characters from James Cameron's *Avatar* (see Figure 6.5).[107] While it appeared Kothari appreciated my perspective, he also pointed to the important work that was happening on the ground, countering that Adivasi communities such as the Dongria Kondh were not just being used by outside activists and were themselves leading the struggle against Vedanta's destruction of their lands. Kothari then put me in touch with Meenal Tatpati, who was working for Ekta Parashad, one of India's leading social movements

---

[107] A quick sidebar: I once visited Zhangjiajie National Park in Hunan, China. Its phenomenal karst mountain-scape is said to be the inspiration James Cameron's 2009 movie *Avatar*. And on top of some of the most popular mountains in the centre of the park, which you can reach by riding what's been billed as the tallest outdoor glass elevator in the world, and with walkways as crowded as the Shanghai subway, tourists were posing for photos alongside life-size statues of the *Na'vi*. Meanwhile, speaking to some locals who still worked inside the park, they described how at least one mountaintop village had been evicted to make room for a McDonalds.

working on forest rights. It was thanks to Meenal that I was able to connect with activists working on the ground in Kanha.

So, when I travelled to Madhya Pradesh later that month, this was how I came to be teamed up with the indigenous rights activist, J- Yadav. I first met J- at a *dhaba* (or roadside restaurant) in the plains just below the Pachmarhi Biosphere Reserve, another one of my fieldwork sites. We sat sipping chai and eating samosas, and I immediately recognized that J- would be the perfect person to explore Mandla, Balaghat, and Dindori districts with. Not only did J- already have an extensive network of connections in the region, he also had a firmly held conviction that Gond and Baiga Adivasi cultures and traditions were threatened with extinction. Before I ever met J-, I knew a bit about his perspective, because I had seen him appear in a TV documentary about Kanha National Park, where he was quoted as saying of Gonds and Baigas: 'Their culture, their society—everything is going to be destroyed. These tribes are about to disappear'. Now, speaking with J- in person, he told me about how he had previously worked with Survival International, how he believed that 'Adivasis are happiest in forests', and how displacement equals death for these communities.

From the *dhaba* where we had our first meeting, we then hiked several kilometres to a nearby *basti*, one of the roughest resettlement colonies of people displaced from the Pachmarhi Biosphere Reserve. This small hamlet, which I had visited on several occasions over the years, and which I have previously published an account of in an edited volume on *Memory, Identity, and the Colonial Encounter in India*, was one of the first to be evicted from Pachmarhi, and was one of the poorest resettlement colonies in the area.[108] The elderly residents there recounted how in the early days of the park in the 1980s, the *forest-wale* or forest officers had driven them out of their original forest village by setting fire to it. While over the previous several days, my friend K- Rajak and I had visited half a dozen much more recently built colonies around Pachmarhi, where the large majority of residents reported feeling happy with, or at least neutral towards, their new situation in resettlement, this horror story of an arson

---

[108] Ezra Rashkow, 'Dispossessing Memory: Adivasi Oral Histories from the Margins of Pachmarhi Biosphere Reserve, Central India', in *Memory, Identity and the Colonial Encounter in India: Essays in Honor of Peter Robb*, eds Ezra Rashkow, Sanjukta Ghosh, and Upal Chakrabarty (New York: Routledge, 2017), 151–175.

event which happened roughly forty years ago, of course, confirmed J-'s view of the destructive violence of conservation-induced displacement.

K- Rajak, in contrast to J- Yadav, was not an activist. He was a local from Pachmarhi who I had first met years ago in the forest surrounding the town while he was out hiking with his dogs Balu and Judy, just as one of them had killed a baby *jangli suar* or wild pig. The second time we happened to run into each other in the same forest, we also happened to come across some of his friends who were carrying pots full of *mahua* liquor to sell (illegally) in town. We all had a good drink together and our friendship was cemented. K- was working as a *dhobi* or laundryman at the time, washing clothing for hotels guests in the nearby forest streams. But after we became friends, he gladly put a pause to this unpleasant work in order to accompany me as I travelled to surrounding forest villages to conduct oral history interviews. He was an invaluable help in my work in Pachmarhi, as he not only knew all the local trails and villages but also helped ease the conversations between my American-accented standard Hindi and the local dialects spoken in the area. Now, after we finished another round of fieldwork in Pachmarhi together, J-, K-, and I proceeded to travel together to Kanha. On the long bus and train rides together, we had ample opportunity to have a conversation about Adivasi politics. And over the next few weeks of such conversations about activism, K- Rajak would become influenced by J- Yadav, and also began express concerns about the problems of Adivasi endangerment and extinction.

One of our first stops on the outskirts of Kanha was a celebration of Birsa Munda's birthday or *Birsa Jayanti* in Baihar town. Birsa Munda was a late nineteenth-century Adivasi freedom fighter in India's independence movement, and this was a celebration of his 141st birthday. It was a rally under a large tent, by my estimates attended by well over 1,000 people. We arrived in town just in time to see the leadership of the Birsa Munda Brigade, Adivasi Mulniwasi Adhikar Parishad (Indigenous Rights Council), Self-Respect Movement, Gond Mahasabha (Gond Assembly), and the Adivasi Bachao Andolan (Save the Adivasis Movement), and others, march into the tent (see Figure 6.6). They were accompanied by flagbearers who waved the multicoloured banner of the Gondwana movement, while the crowd chanted slogans such as '*Birsa Munda Amar Rahe*' (Long live Birsa Munda), '*Jo zamin sarkari hai, wo zamin hamara hai*'

**Figure 6.6.** Leadership of the Birsa Munda Brigade, Adivasi Mulniwasi Adhikar Parishad (Indigenous Rights Council), Self-Respect Movement, Gond Mahasabha (Gond Assembly), and the Adivasi Bachao Andolan (Save the Adivasis Movement), and others, march into the tent.
Photo by author.

(government land belongs to us) and '*Jai Adivasi*' (Victory to Adivasis) (see Figure 6.7).

Along with entertainment which included traditional Baiga dancers in full regalia, about a dozen Adivasi leaders and other local VIPs were seated in three or four rows on stage. They took turns delivering speeches as the crowd either sat on the ground in front of the stage or stood listening from the rear. I could see immediately that this was a carefully choreographed spectacle. And like many other such rallies that happen on a regular basis in central India, it was part of a broad-based movement for Adivasi empowerment and equality. Major demands included land and forest rights, an end to conservation and development-induced displacement, as well as more ambitious goals such as a 'Tribal Religion' category

**Figure 6.7.** Birsa Munda Jayanti celebration and rally.
Photo by author.

in the census (a highly divisive proposition by BJP standards), and a demand for a separate Gondwana state.

I spent the first half-hour or so standing respectfully on the sidelines, taking it all in. But then, much to my embarrassment, I was dragged on stage in front of the huge crowd attending the rally, and offered a VIP seat, for no apparent reasons besides my skin colour and a good dose of traditional hospitality. As this happened, I could not help recall the words of the Adivasi poet Waharu Sonavane:

> We didn't go to the stage
> nor were we called.
> With a wave of the hand
> we were shown our place.
> There we sat
> and were congratulated,
> and 'they', standing on the stage

>    kept on telling us of our sorrows.
>    Our sorrows remained ours,
>    they never became theirs.[109]

After several other speakers, eventually Satish Pendam, leader of the Birsa Brigade and Adivasi Bachao Andolan ('Save the Adivasis Movement'), rose to the podium. Pendam was a popular leader, in his early 40s, who years ago gave up a government job in order to lead the fight for Adivasi rights. And, like many organic intellectuals, he was used to speaking at multiple registers for different audiences. Here, in front of his people, he delivered a rousing speech in Hindi, calling for Adivasi unity, asserting land and water rights, demanding an end to evictions from Kanha National Park, and acknowledging on the ground complexities. In a recent interview in *The Times of India,* however, speaking to an English language national audience, he adopted more generic forms of endangerment discourse, arguing 'that the government is out to destroy tribals of this country', and that the mainstream is destroying traditional forest-based ways of life:

> Tribals have for centuries survived off the land but that is being snatched from them and given to corporates at throwaway prices. The unique culture has been suppressed and not allowed to flourish, thus alienating them with their roots. And the constitutional right that they have to live in their unique way, to survive is all being taken away.... These people have been uprooted from their centuries old ecosystem and thrown into the urban cesspool, a lifestyle which they have no idea about. It's like going to Mars for them.

Pendam also aptly critiqued the unfortunate tendency in mainstream discourse to dehumanize Adivasis, however:

> Don't put us in front of spectators as a show piece. That's not the kind of promotion tribals want. Understand one thing, we (tribals) are the

---

[109] Waharu Sonavane, 'Stage', in *Godhad*, trans. Bharat Patankar, Gail Omvedt, and Suhas Paranjape (Pune: Sugava Prakashan, 1987), 35. For a discussion of this poem (and problem) in the Narmada context, see: Gail Omvedt, 'An Open Letter to Arundhati Roy', *Roundtable India*, 12 Jul 2011. https://roundtableindia.co.in/index.php?option=com_content&view=article&id=2671:an-open-letter-to-arundhati-roy

real owners of this land. We were here before anyone else. Today we are called 'van-vaasi' (forest dwellers) as if we are some kind of hybrid animal species roaming in the jungles.[110]

After the rally, J-, K-, and I were hosted at the district collector's house, where we had an interesting exchange about Adivasi leadership. J- specifically argued that poor, illiterate Adivasis needed educated leadership from outside. 'They cannot help themselves, they need to be helped', he said. 'They don't have leaders, and they need to be led'. Meanwhile, K- recalled conversations we had had with villagers who complained that Adivasi leaders just 'eat money' (*paisa khate*), and so he argued that 'they are just thieves' (*voh sirf chor hai*), for example, collecting 5,000 Rupees for an ST certificate (used to claim Scheduled Tribe status for purposes of government accommodations). J- then conceded that traditional leaders, Gond Rajas and Thakurs, were 'only for themselves' and 'do not help the people of the jungle', but that activists, like the ones we had just heard speak, truly had the people's interests at heart and were 'not corrupt'.[111]

For the next ten days or so, our plan was to tour the periphery of Kanha, visiting villages that had been resettled outside of the national park, before heading into Baiga Chak in neighbouring Dindori district. J- had some previous experience leading foreign activists and journalists on tours of villages around Kanha—these were typically passionate young advocates of protecting tribespeople from endangerment and extinction, usually without any Indian language skills—and I believe he expected my case to be no different. His goal was always to present the loss of the forests as an existential threat to these communities, and largely he succeeded. Asking Adivasi interviewees leading questions like 'is Adivasi culture disappearing along with forests' and 'can Adivasi culture survive without forests' often led to predictably bleak replies: '*Hamare sanskriti khatam ho jayega*' and '*sab khatam hai*'—'our culture will be finished',

---

[110] Abhishek Choudhari, 'Government Destroying Tribals, Attacking Their Basic Rights', *The Times of India*, 24 Nov 2019. https://timesofindia.indiatimes.com/city/nagpur/govt-destroying-tribals-attacking-their-basic-rights/articleshow/72200790.cms

[111] This reminded me, to some extent, of a comment by E.S. Hyde already in the 1940s that, 'there is a controversy between the Gond leaders themselves: some urge that all Gonds should be called themselves [sic] as Hindu whereas others urge equally strong that they should return their religion as tribal'. CCSASA, Hyde Papers, Box VIII, File D, E.S. Hyde to R.K. Ramadhyani, superintendent of census operations, C.P. & W.V. Grigson, Pachmarhi, 19 May 1941.

'everything is finished'. But when I occasionally moved away from my 'embedded' tour, and eschewed such leading questions, the situation appeared more complex.

Residents, as usual, reported a range of responses to removal from the park. Some even reported that they had proactively approached the forest department themselves to request resettlement, before anyone from the government had ever sought to remove their village. Many family members who combined their resettlement packages now lived in large, well-appointed houses they had built with the money. And although there were clearly many economic complaints (especially aggravated because this was autumn of 2016 and right in the middle of demonetization), tractors were scattered around the villages, as were motorcycles, and many homes contained televisions and other indicators of a certain degree of material prosperity. In many instances, villagers also reported that they preferred their current situation to the life they had previously had inside the park. One middle-aged gentleman, for instance, recounted how tigers used to kill several head of cattle from his old village inside the park each month, and spoke of how glad he was that now there were no problems like that.[112] Another said that it was good that slash and burn *bewar* cultivation was ending, since there was not enough forest left. This should not be taken as a simple preference for development over culture, however. Some respondents explicitly rejected the notion that their culture was vanishing in resettlement, saying that Adivasi culture and tradition, *sanskriti aur parampara*, remained strong.

Later, in Baiga Chak, we saw many examples of thriving Adivasi culture as well as more explicit activist efforts at cultural conservation. In the first home where we resided, for example, the owner proudly took us to a nearby hillside to show us his *bewar* crops. Here he was growing at least a dozen varieties of traditional millets such as *kodon* and *kutki*, as were many other families (see Figure 6.8). He did this, he said, in order to save these traditional crops from extinction, and later that day, he showed us how he was featured in a calendar and other publications dedicated to saving biodiversity and agrodiversity. In the evenings, as we sat around

---

[112] Incidentally, on the same day that we heard this account of human-wildlife conflict, we also read reports in the local newspaper that a tiger had killed a 17-year-old girl in Pachmarhi, quite near to the roadside *dhaba* and resettlement colony where we had originally met J- Yadav.

**Figure 6.8.** A Baiga farmer displaying traditional *bewar* millets.
Photo by author.

the fire, a neighbour would often come to visit. She was a dance instructor who had written a Hindi language book about traditional Baiga music or *lokgit,* and spent her days teaching dance to the local youth. And yet she also feared that these dances were disappearing. She said that 'people were forgetting everything—tradition, culture, songs, dances, everything'. Both of these neighbours were heavily involved in keeping Baiga tradition and culture alive. And as tends to be the case, the same people who most actively celebrate and promote a culture are the same people who also express the deepest concern and sadness for cultural loss.

In Baiga Chak, there was much pride in and celebration of cultural heritage, yet there were also many examples of dire poverty. It happened to be on Thanksgiving Day 2016 that we stayed in one of the poorest, most dilapidated one-room huts I'd ever spent the night in. The hut's owner generously invited us in, provided my friends with what was probably his only blanket, and shared the food from his own *bewar* fields with us. Late that evening, under a waning moon and bright stars, the owner called me away from the hut for 'hauling wood' (*lakri lene ke liye*) but it was really to drink *mahua* liquor down where they were brewing it at a nearby stream. Unfortunately, at that point, our host, his wife, and some of their friends proceeded to get extremely drunk. Alcoholism was a major problem in many Adivasi villages where I had stayed over the years. And so, the next morning as we said our goodbyes, while I would normally have given a thank you gift directly to our host, I quietly gave a handful of rupee notes to his daughter instead, telling her not to let her father spend it on alcohol.

Our next stop was to visit another Gond activist friend of J-'s. His well-appointed home, made from solid concrete construction, and filled with Gondwana and Bara Dev (Gond political and religious) paraphernalia, stood in stark contrast to the poverty where we had stayed the night before. The most interesting conversation of that day revolved around Naxalism. One of the residents of this household in eastern Madhya Pradesh had recently returned from the Bastar region of Chhattisgarh, and he was full of cautious praise for the Naxalites. According to him, Naxals and Andolan activists were fighting for the same thing—*jal, jangal, aur zamin* (water, forest, and land rights)—only their methods to achieve them were very different. He described how the Naxalites collected 200 rupees per month from villagers as tax and recruited children at the age of 10. Every second child was required to join, he said. They would then be 'fully educated' to grade twelve. He agreed that common people were caught between the Naxals and the state, and also admitted there was a tension between the desire to build roads and protect forests. But normal Adivasi politicians do nothing, he claimed, and he wondered if Naxals were in power, would they be any different.

Our final stop on our several-week-long tour (before heading to Amarkantak, the origin point of the Narmada River, and also a UNESCO biosphere reserve) was a traditional village in Baiga Chak where J- knew some more activist colleagues involved in the preservation of *bewar* agriculture. This was a hillside village set several kilometres away from the nearest road and surrounded by many kilometres of teak (*sagwan*) plantations on several sides. We hiked nearly twelve hours to get there, arriving in the village well after dark, wondering along the way if we should overnight at another village in between. Thankfully we did not, because after having the next day to settle in and do some interviews, the following night was Baiga Dussehra, one of the most spectacular village festivals I had ever attended. This was a harvest festival bringing together boys and girls who were eligible for marriage, with the boys and girls of each village taking turns visiting the neighbouring villages. Baiga teenagers and adults, all wearing their traditional dress and elaborate flower head ornaments (*kalgi*), with women displaying their heaviest silver jewellery

**Figure 6.9.** Baiga Dussehra: Gathering around the fire after midnight.
Photo by author.

and *godna* tattoos, began singing around the fire only at midnight. The festival lasted throughout the night (see Figure 6.9). As the sun began to rise and warm us after the crisp cold night, men and women danced and sang separately in circles, with men taking turns playing the *dhol* drum. As I sat watching these beautiful festivities continue throughout the day, I couldn't help but be reminded of my anthropologist colleague Vikram Thakur's words the previous year at a wedding celebration in a resettlement colony in Nandurbar for people ousted from the Narmada Valley: 'See, here are your endangered tribals'.

## People Parks in Comparative Perspective

In many regards, the call for a national park for the Baiga and Gond, which Elwin eventually retracted, reflects the broader arch of the debate over the shape of protected areas around the world. Elwin's concern for saving the Baiga from tribal extinction and Ghurye's reaction that this would prevent assimilation and national progress both resonate with wider debates that have taken place repeatedly over the fate of indigenous peoples and their lands. For example, at roughly the same moment that anthropologists, colonial administrators, and nationalists in India were debating the policy of 'excluded areas' for tribes, and Elwin's 'national park' idea, Australians were also debating the merits of protected areas or 'Aboriginal reserves'. As Russell McGregor writes:

> On one side were those who argued that reserves should preserve a remnant of the Aboriginal race and culture in its pristine state by completely cutting off their inhabitants from all outside contacts. On the other side were those who maintained that, while reserves should shelter Aborigines from the corrupting edge of European civilisation, their paramount purpose was to instruct their inmates in Western ways of life and thought. It may be easy to interpret both options as symptomatic of a white Australian disdain for Aborigines: the former seeking to marginalise them by shutting them away in closed communities; the latter seeking merely to destroy Aboriginal culture. Yet a closer examination of the reserves debate in its contemporary intellectual context may reveal more complex motivations...[113]

Elwin's plan for a national park for the Baigas and Gonds may not have been actualized in his lifetime, but by 1956 India did establish a 'tribal reserve' very much along the lines of what he had envisioned—not in central India, but in the Andaman Islands in the Bay of Bengal. Perhaps the clearest case in independent India of a protected area for tribal peoples or 'aborigines', paralleling Elwin's idea of a tribal national park, the Jarawa Tribal Reserve was founded shortly after the passage of the Andaman and Nicobar Islands (Protection of Aboriginal Tribes) Regulation of 1956. Since this chapter considers overlapping discourses of biological and cultural diversity conservation in India, as well as the role of protected areas in conserving tribal populations, the Jawara Tribal Reserve makes for a fascinating alternative example of a case where a bounded geographical

---

[113] McGregor, 'The Aboriginal Reserves Debate', 545, focuses on three main protagonists in this debate: Fredric Wood Jones and Donald Thomson, who stood for closed reserves, and A.P. Elkin who wanted the opposite.

territory was set aside in Indian law for the isolation and protection of a tribal community.

In contrast to the Baigas and the Gonds of central India, various tribes of Andaman Islanders have been far more threatened with biological extinction, and thus an 'endangered' status also applies more plainly here. As Thomas Headland put it in an open letter to the Indian government in 1999: 'Reports say that the Jarawa have declined greatly in this century, from 500 in 1901 to 250 today. There is therefore an immediate call for concern for these indigenous people. If the Indian government does not take steps to protect them now, they will surely be another tragic example of a Negrito population going extinct'.[114] Indeed, it is widely accepted that several Andaman tribes have become extinct since the turn of the twentieth century.

However, even in the cases of Andaman populations that are documented as extinct, the precise boundaries of each 'population' are far from settled; confusion and misinformation seem to proliferate in both activist and official accounts. For example, several articles mention that only two Andaman populations have gone extinct since the beginning of the twentieth century: a group called the Jangil said to have gone extinct in 1907, and the Aka Bo whose last member, Bo Senior, died in 2010.[115] Yet other sources paint a far more complicated picture. While some sources put the date of the Jangil's extinction at 1907, others say 1931.[116] This confusion seems to arise because the 1931 census stated that 'there was a fourth clan of Jarawas of which nothing has been seen since 1907'.[117] This census report, in turn, points to a far deeper set of problems: that of defining tribal populations, the debates between

---

[114] Thomas N. Headland, 'An Open Letter to the Government of India Concerning the Human Rights Situation of the Jarawa Tribal Minority in the Andaman Islands', 13 Jul 1999. http://www-01.sil.org/~headlandt/jarawa.htm

[115] Stefan Kirschner, 'Don't Let the Jarawa Become Another Onge', *Indigenous Policy Journal* 23, no. 1 (2012). www.indigenouspolicy.org/index.php/ipj/article/view/43/102

[116] George van Driem, *Languages of the Himalayas: An Ethnolinguistic Handbook of the Greater Himalayan Region: Containing an Introduction to the Symbiotic Theory of Language* (Leiden: Brill, 2001), 215 writes that 'the Aka-Bea of South Andaman and Rutland Island were extinct by 1931'. Anvita Abbi, 'The situation in India and adjacent areas' in *The Languages and Linguistics of South Asia: A Comprehensive Guide*, eds Hans Henrich Hock and Elena Bashir (Berlin: Walter de Gruyter GmbH, 2016), 636 lists the Jangil language as becoming extinct in 1925.

[117] C.C. Bonington, *Census of India, 1931, Vol. II: The Andaman and Nicobar Islands* (Calcutta: Central Publication Branch, 1932), 8.

lumpers and splitters that occur in any system of taxonomy, and specifically the confusion between the Jangil and the Jarawa. While many historical sources say that the Jangil were a group of Jarawa, and refer to this community as the Rutland Jarawa of Rutland Island, most contemporary authors define them as a distinct and now 'extinct' tribal group. To further complicate this picture, as George Weber observes, there was a general 'interchangeability of the terms "Jarawa" and "Onge" during the 19th century and into the 1930s'. Thus, according to Weber, the 1931 census reference to 'four "Jarawa" tribes does not refer to what we today call Jarawas. It meant all members of the Onge-Jarawa group: the Onge, the Sentineli, the Jarawa proper as well as the Jangil'.[118] In contrast, by most contemporary definitions, the Onge are those people who now 'inhabit the southernmost island of Little Andaman and number about 100 members'.[119] Thus, exactly how many Andaman tribal groups are extinct is a subject of debate.[120] Does this mean that each of these groups listed should be considered a distinct tribe that is extinct, or conversely, could it be argued that they are in some sense all are surviving populations since they have merged into a single group now referred to as the Great Andamanese?

This focus on tribal endangerment and extinction in the Andaman Islands leads to other problems as well: particularly the problem of saving endangered tribes in tribal reserves, which is at the heart of this chapter. As Satadru Sen writes in the conclusion to his history of the concept of

---

[118] George H.J. Weber, *Lonely Islands: The Andamanese* (Liestal, Switzerland: The Andaman Association, 1998). https://web.archive.org/web/20130520161055/http://www.andaman.org/BOOK/chapter8/text8.htm#jangil

[119] According to the organization *Cultural Survival*, 'In 1976 the Andaman administration set put on [sic] a deliberate scheme to "resettle" the Onge to an area... known as Dugong Creek, providing them with mainstream amenities and coconut plantations. This "resettlement" has set in motion the biological social, and cultural death of the On[g]e'. D. Venkatesan, 'Ecocide or Genocide? The Onge in the Andaman Islands', *Cultural Survival Quarterly* 14, no. 4 (Dec 1990): 49–51. www.culturalsurvival.org/ourpublications/csq/article/ecocide-or-genocide-the-onge-andaman-islands

[120] Pranab Ganguly, 'The Negrito of Little Andaman Island a Primitive People Facing Extinction', *Indian Museum Bulletin* 10, no. 1 (1975): 7–27, writes: 'The aborigines of the Andaman Islands fall into two separate divisions-the Great Andamanese Division and the Jarawa-Sentinelese-Onge Division. The ten tribes of Great Andaman which once constituted the Great Andamanese Division, viz., the Bea, Balawa, Bojigyab, Juwai, Kol, Kede, Yere, Tabo, Kora and Chariar, are already extinct. Only [a] hybrid group of 24 individuals remains (as per the Census of India 1971) which is also on the verge of extinction'. Other sources list the extinct divisions of the Great Andamanese as follows: Bale, Bea, Juwoi, Kede, Kol, Kora, and Pucikwar, with the Bo, Jeru, and Cari still extant.

A NATIONAL PARK FOR THE GOND & BAIGA    311

savagery in the Andaman Islands: 'Today, the nearly-extinct status of the Andamanese is a matter of national regret and regret management. From a liberal anti-imperialist perspective, the colonial intervention appears "ethnocidal" or "genocidal", and post-1947 interventions disagreeably quasi-colonial'. Sen refers to what has happened to the Jarawa as a 'secret theater and an unfinished project, consisting of tribal reserves', and points to the paradoxical nature of policies geared towards saving this endangered tribe.[121]

Similarly, Vishvajit Pandya, another author working on the history and anthropology of the Andamans, points out the paradoxical nature of the contemporary official policy towards the Andaman islanders that has not advanced past the mid-twentieth century debates over isolation vs. integration. The official policy towards the Jarawa today is still 'protection, preservation, and conservation' as well as 'providing provisions', and according to Pandya there is an 'inherent contradiction' between schemes of 'providing for' and 'preserving' the islanders.[122]

Over the years, the size of the Jarawa Tribal Reserve shrank significantly. Jarawa territory was reduced from 6408 sq. km in 1858 to 1689 sq. km in 1957, and then was reduced again in 1984, to 856.72 sq. km,

---

[121] Satadru Sen, *Savagery and Colonialism in the Indian Ocean: Power, Pleasure and the Andaman Islanders* (New York: Routledge, 2010), 211. Sen further comments: 'So the Anthropological Survey attempts to restrict contact between the dying insider (who is an outsider in the nation) and the living outsider (who is the insider in the nation)... Elwin ran into trouble when he suggested that "national parks" be created in India for aborigines as spaces where they would remain "sovereign". The irony of seeking sovereignty from the nation in the national park probably did not elude Elwin, but such was the ideological bind... The aborigine in the nation-state is thus doomed both in the jungle and in the park, particularly if aboriginality is differentiated from peasant-hood... Within the ideology of aboriginality, it is worse to nationalize a 'tribal' than to nationalize a non-tribal peasant, because it is assumed that whereas the peasant is merely being awakened to a dormant identity, the aborigine is being destroyed... A "national" policy that seeks to preserve and sustain aboriginality requires the accommodation and recuperation of "colonial" practices; the dilemma is woven into the fabric of the liberal nation-state'.

[122] Vishvajit Pandya, *In the Forest: Visual and Material Worlds of Andamanese History (1858–2006)* (Lanham, MD: University Press of America, 2009), 11, 227. As Pandya puts it: 'The possibility of preserving tribal society in a "human zoo" continues to be debated with those who want to bring tribes into mainstream India... so those on the Islands who believe the Jarawa should continue to be treated as a people with their own territory are at odds with those who feel they should be brought out and made to join the "democratic and progressive mainstream"... The most likely future may well be a repetition of the past, and the Jarawa will eventually lose their territory, like the Ongee and the Great Andamanese who have been resettled in areas assigned by the authorities... The assumed binary between "mainstreaming" and "museumizing" is false, for periodic intrusions and attempts to establish settlements in the forest have meant that that outside world has impinged on Jarawa society for many decades'.

an approximately 50% reduction compared to 1957.[123] And in recent decades, one major incursion into the reserve has come in the form of the Andaman Trunk Road. Following allegations of 'human safaris', India's Supreme Court ordered the road closed in 2002, but only briefly. A decade later, in 2012, still dealing with the problem of 'human safaris' the Supreme Court again tried to act by banning 'commercial and tourist activity inside a 5km buffer zone' around the Jarawa's reserve, but this attempt to rein in impact on the Jarawa also seems to have failed to produce much result.[124] As in the cases of Verrier Elwin's call for a National Park for the Gond and Baiga of central India, as in the case of the Baiga Chak, and as in the case of Excluded and Scheduled Areas, the main goal in the formation of the Jarawa Tribal Reservation was to protect the local population from deleterious external pressures. Again, the question that must be explored in further research is how to untangle, compare, and contrast, these various forms of protected areas, especially in light of new movements towards biocultural diversity conservation.

Most histories of indigenous peoples in national parks have largely focused on the dispossession of resident populations in the making of uninhabited wilderness areas. Only since around 2014 has the similarly problematic history of the idea of preserving human communities today referred to as 'indigenous' in parks and other protected areas been studied in much depth.[125] Yet in the very first-ever call for a national park, as well as in frequent proposals for national parks throughout the nineteenth, twentieth, and now the twenty-first century, protected areas have been envisioned as places of conservation not only of endangered species but also of human groups perceived to be vanishing or endangered.

As discussed in Chapter 1, since the very inception of the national park concept, the idea that protected areas should be spaces for indigenous peoples has competed with the dominant paradigm of indigenous removal and the idea that wilderness should be uninhabited. From antebellum calls in the United States to preserve 'Indian wilderness' to today's

---

[123] Swapan Kumar Biswas, 'Vulnerability among Primitive Tribal Groups in Andaman', *International Journal of Academic Research* 4, no. 3 (March 2017): 38.
[124] Gethin Chamberlain, 'Human Safaris May Be Banned, but Still Tourists Flock to Andaman Islands', *The Guardian*, 1 Sep 2012.
[125] For a global overview of the history of preserving indigenous peoples in parks, see: Ezra Rashkow, 'Idealizing Inhabited Wilderness: A Revision to the History of Indigenous Peoples in National Parks', *History Compass* 12, no. 10 (2014): 818–832.

international campaigns for biocultural diversity conservation, the underlying point that indigenous peoples should be allowed to maintain forest-based ways of life in protected areas such as national parks has been constant through all of the variations on this theme.

By the 1970s, the United Nations Educational and Scientific Organization (UNESCO) would emerge as one of the dominant global institutions to promote the goal of conservation of indigenous cultures within protected areas through its world network of Biosphere Reserves. This was in large part thanks to Raymond Dasmann, a prominent figure in UNESCO and a founder of the Man and Biosphere Programme, which administers these reserves. Inspired by the likes of Paul Sarasin's *Weltnaturschutz* of the 1910s and the 'anthropological reserves' proposed by the International Union for the Protection of Nature (IUPN) in the 1940s, Dasmann was also a member of Survival International, then still called the Primitive People's Fund.[126] And following the centennial celebrations of the world's first national park (Yellowstone, established in 1872) where Dasmann praised George Catlin's 1830s vision of 'A nation's Park, containing man and beast, in all the wild and freshness of their nature's beauty!', he wrote, 'I believe that this is a good time to re-examine the entire concept of national parks and all equivalent protected areas'. He was upset that, as he put it, 'animals were given the first national park. The Indians had a different appointment with destiny'. Somewhat patronizingly calling indigenous peoples 'ecosystem people', Dasmann argued that 'Ecosystem people have always lived in the equivalent of a national park. It is the kind of country that ecosystem people have always protected'.[127] Yet Dasmann did at least add one progressive element to this agenda. Arguing that moves to protect these communities 'should be determined by the "peripheral peoples" themselves. They alone have the right to determine their own future', his was one of the earlier expressions of the principal of self-determination that can today be found within most calls for preserving people in protected areas.[128] Since that

---

[126] Raf De Bont, '"Primitives" and Protected Areas: International Conservation and the "Naturalization" of Indigenous People, ca. 1910–1975', *Journal of the History of Ideas* 76, no. 2 (2015): 232.
[127] Raymond F. Dasmann, 'National Parks, Nature Conservation, and Future Primitive', *The Ecologist* 6, no. 5 (1977): 164–167.
[128] Raymond F. Dasmann, *The Conservation Alternative* (New York: Wiley, 1975).

time, conservation legislation around the world has emphasized a shift towards integrating local peoples' rights and interests into the maintenance of protected areas, though this has rarely succeeded.

This mode of thinking about conservation started gaining acceptance in the 1980s and 1990s when the indigenous peoples' rights movement merged with the politics of environmentalism on the global stage.[129] In this milieu, a large camp of academics, activists, policymakers, and conservationists have sided with what they understand to be the interests of indigenous communities. This new conservation paradigm emphasizes the rights of resident communities to continue to exist in national parks and other protected areas.[130] Unfortunately, however, as has been documented in numerous case studies, the wildlife conservation establishment in India has rarely ever embraced the idea of respecting Adivasi land and forest rights within the boundaries of these protected areas.[131] And in this regard, at least, the biosphere reserve designation has largely proven to be a meaningless bureaucratic label.[132] Considering the fact that biocultural diversity conservation is meant to be built into the foundations of the biosphere reserve concept, and yet it is usually failing in these reserves, it is hard to imagine other forms of protected areas such as national parks faring much better.

Again, one problem with this new people-centred model in protected areas management is also that it does not critically engage with the history of the idea it unwittingly repeats. Human endangerment discourse, along with fears of various forms of extinction, saturates much of the activist rhetoric when it comes to places like Kanha National Park and tribes like the Gonds and Baigas. As I have argued throughout this book, the problem here is not only that human societies that are demographically healthy are being projected as vanishing and in danger of becoming

---

[129] See Beth A. Conklin, 'Environmentalism, Global Community, and the New Indigenism', in *Inclusion and Exclusion in the Global Arena*, ed. Max Kirsch (New York: Routledge, 2006), 162–163.

[130] Marcus Colchester, 'Conservation Policy and Indigenous Peoples', *Cultural Survival Quarterly* 28, no. 1 Special Issue: 'Indigenous Lands or National Park?' (Spring 2004): 17–22.

[131] Rashkow, 'Dispossessing Memory'.

[132] Kaera L. Coetzer, Edward T.F. Witkowski, and Barend F.N. Erasmus, 'Reviewing Biosphere Reserves Globally: Effective Conservation Action or Bureaucratic Label?', *Biological Reviews* 89, no. 1 (2014): 1–23. Michael L. Lewis, *Inventing Global Ecology: Tracking the Biodiversity Ideal in India, 1947–1997* (Athens: Ohio University Press, 2004) makes a similar critique of the Biosphere Reserve network in India.

extinct, and therefore perceived as in need of protection from above. More to the point, it is that indigenous peoples are envisioned as endangered like wildlife, that these two forms of endangerment are seen as related, and ergo that endangered species and societies need to be granted similar forms of protected areas. This is deeply problematic for communities that have historically suffered the impact of racist, dehumanizing analogies, to say the least. While the experience of removing people from protected areas has often been tragic, and indeed is the much bigger problem for the people of Kanha, the history of advocating for people to remain in national parks, especially as central features of those parks, has also been fraught.

While, historically, this agenda has sometimes been based on romanticist visions of ecologically noble savages, or on paternalistic notions of saving vanishing tribes, today's biocultural diversity conservation agenda has evolved to become a rights-based discourse based on self-determination, which does represent a significant improvement over older versions of this phenomenon. But there are still problems with rhetoric that slips back into old habits, rhetoric that only pays lip service to ideas of rights and self-determination, and rhetoric that remains stuck as rhetoric and never transforms into action. The 2006 Scheduled Tribes and Other Traditional Forest Dwellers (Recognition of Forest Rights) Act, thus, for example, specifically frames itself not in terms of top-down protection, but rather in terms of fighting against historical injustices faced by forest-dwelling communities. Though still relying on contentious notions of tribal harmony with nature ('conservation is embedded in the ethos of tribal life'), the 2006 Forest Rights Act nonetheless appears to make significant progress in the struggle for Adivasi land rights. As discussed in the preface to this book, however: with the Indian Supreme Court ruling of February 2019, which ordered the eviction of millions of forest dwellers, this idealistic vision of preserving nature-bound tribal life seems to be again endangered for Kanha's Adivasis.

# Bibliography

## A. Fieldwork Recordings

Fieldwork interviews between 2005 and 2019 were primarily video recorded, totaling some 600 gigabytes of data and well over 100 hours of footage. A small number of interviewers (approximately 30) were audio recorded only. Recordings have been supplemented by field-notes.

## B. Archives

American Museum of Natural History, New York (AMNH)
    Faunthorpe-Vernay Expedition Archive, 1921— 1929
British Library, Asian and African Studies, London (Previously called the 'Oriental and India Office Library' (OIOC))
    Mss Eur D1156—Papers of David Symington, Indian Civil Service, Bombay
    Mss Eur D950—Papers of Verrier Elwin, anthropologist
    Mss Eur E267—Papers of Sir Malcolm Cotter Cariston Seton (1872–1940)
    Mss Eur F236—Papers of W G Archer, Indian Civil Service, Bihar (1931–1947)
    Mss Eur J624-26—Letter books of Sir Richard Jenkins (1785–1853)
British Library, India Office Records, London (IOR)
    F/4: Records of the Board of Commissioners for the Affairs of India, Board's Collections
    H/*: Home (Miscellaneous)
    L/E: Economic Department Records, Departmental Papers: Annual Files
    L/PJ: Public & Judicial Department Files
    V/*: Official Publications
Cambridge Center for South Asian Studies, Cambridge (CCSAS)
    E.S. Hyde Papers
Central Provinces Secretariat Record Room, Nagpur
    Berar Forest Department
Madhya Pradesh State Archives, Bhopal (MPSA)
    Central Provinces Forest Department
    Central Provinces Revenue and Agriculture Department
    Holkar State Series
National Archives of India, New Delhi (NAI)
    Central India Agency
    Foreign (Political)
    Home (Public)
    Forest Department
    Mewar Residency Office

Revenue and Agriculture Department
Vernacular Press Reports
Nehru Memorial Museum and Library, Delhi (NMML)
Verrier Elwin Papers (VEP)
Rajasthan State Archive, Bikaner (RSA)
Udaipur Jangalat Series
Udaipur Administration Reports
*Rewa State Administration Report, 1913–1914*
Maharaja Sadul Singh, *His Highnesses' General Shooting Diary*, vol. 2. Bikaner: Government Press, 1941
Royal Anthropological Society Library, British Museum, London
Collections of the Museum of Mankind
School of Oriental and African Studies (SOAS) Special Collections
PP MS 19 Christoph von Fürer-Haimendorf Collection
Pamphlet Collections
Tring Natural History Museum
A.O. Hume Manuscripts

## C. Published Sources

Abbi, Anvita. 'The Situation in India and Adjacent Areas'. In *The Languages and Linguistics of South Asia: A Comprehensive Guide*, edited by Hans Henrich Hock and Elena Bashir, 631–706. Berlin: Walter de Gruyter GmbH, 2016.

Abbi, B.L. and S. Saberwal, eds. *Urgent Research in Social Anthropology: Proceedings of a Conference*. Simla: Indian Institute of Advanced Studies, 1969.

Aborigines Protection Society. *The Second Annual Report of the Aborigines Protection Society, Presented at the Meeting in Exeter Hall, May 21st, 1839*. London, 1839.

Abu-Lughod, Lila. 'Do Muslim Women Really Need Saving? Anthropological Reflections on Cultural Relativism and Its Others'. *American Anthropologist* 104, no. 3 (2002): 789.

Adams, Archibald. *The Western Rajputana States: A Medico-Topographic and General Account of Marwar Sirohi and Jaisalmir*. London: Junior Army & Navy Stores, 1899.

Adams, William M. *Against Extinction: The Story of Conservation*. London: Earthscan, 2004.

Ahmad, Z.A. *Excluded Areas Under the New Constitution*. Congress Political and Economic Studies 4. Allahabad: Ashraf, 1937.

Aiyappan, A. 'Urgent Anthropology for Southern India'. In *Urgent Research in Social Anthropology: Proceedings of a Conference*, edited by B.L. Abbi and S. Saberwal, 34–40. Simla: Indian Institute of Advanced Studies, 1969.

Aiyar, Swaminathan S. Anklesaria. 'Why Many Tribals Don't Mind Being Ousted by Dams'. *Times of India*, 10 Sep 2017. https://timesofindia.indiatimes.com/blogs/Swaminomics/why-many-tribals-dont-mind-being-ousted-by-dams/

Aiyar, Swaminathan S. Anklesaria and Neeraj Kaushal. 'Are Resettled Oustees from the Sardar Sarovar Dam Project Better Off Today than Their Former Neighbors Who Were Not Ousted?' *NBER Working Paper Series*, 24423 (National Bureau of Economic Research, Mar 2018), 1. http://www.nber.org/papers/w24423

Akeley, Mary L. Jobe. *Carl Akeley's Africa*. New York: Dodd Mead, 1929.

Akeley, Mary L. Jobe. 'Summary of Talk Given for Society for the Preservation of the Fauna of the Empire by Mary L. Jobe Akeley, 10 December 1928'. *Journal of the Society for the Preservation of the Fauna of the Empire* 9 (1929): 15–21.

All-India Conference for the Preservation of Wild Life, 'Proceedings of the All-India Conference for the Preservation of Wild Life', 28–30 Jan 1935. Delhi: Government Press, 1936.

Allen, Jim et al. *The Last Tasmanian Extinction: A Search by Dr. Rhys Jones to Discover and Comprehend the Life and Death of the Tasmanian Aborigines*. California: CRM Films, 1998), video recording (61 min).

Altherr, Thomas L. and John F. Reiger. 'Academic Historians and Hunting: A Call for More and Better Scholarship'. *Environmental History Review* 19, no. 3 (1995): 39–56.

Ambedkar, B. 'Annihilation of Caste with a Reply to Mahatma Gandhi' (1936). *Writings and Speeches*, vol. 1. Bombay-Education Department: Government of Maharashtra, 1944.

Amte, Baba. 'Narmada Project: The Case Against and an Alternative Perspective'. *Economic & Political Weekly* (1990): 811–818.

*An Universal History, from the Earliest Account of Time*, vol. 18. London: T. Osborne, 1748.

Anand, D. *Hindu Nationalism in India and the Politics of Fear*. New York: Palgrave, 2011.

Ann Grodzins Gold and Bhoju Ram Gujar. *In the Time of Trees and Sorrows: Nature, Power, and Memory in Rajasthan*. Durham N.C.: Duke University Press, 2002.

Anon. 'From *The Oriental*, "Field Sports in India"'. *Littell's Living Age* 119, fifth series, 4 (Oct–Dec 1873): 63.

Anon. 'On the Practicability of Civilising Aboriginal Populations'. *Monthly Chronicle* 4 (Jul–Dec 1839): 309.

Anon. 'The Month'. *Oriental Sporting Magazine* 5 (May 1872): 238.

Anon. 'Two Great Shikaris'. *Blackwood's Edinburgh Magazine* 157, no. 956 (Jun 1895): 949–961.

Aristotle. *Politics*. Translated by Benjamin Jowett. Stillwell, KS: Digireads.com, 2005.

Arnold, David. 'Disease, Resistance and India's Ecological Frontier, 1770–1947'. In *Issues in Modern Indian History: For Sumit Sarkar*, edited by Biwamoy Pati, 1—22. Mumbai: Popular Prakashan, 2000.

Arouet, Francois Marie [Voltaire]. *Essais sur les Moeurs et L'esprit des Nations*, vol. 6. Neuchâtel, 1773.

Bacow, Lawrence S. 'Steering Committee on Human Remains in Harvard Museum Collections', *Harvard Office of the President*, 27 Jan 2021. https://www.harvard.edu/president/news/2021/steering-committee-on-human-remains-in-harvard-museum-collections/

Baden-Powell, B.H. *Report of the Proceedings of the Forest Conference, 1873–74: Held at Allahabad, 15–19 January 1874*. Calcutta: Office of the Superintendent of Government Printing, 1874.

Baden-Powell, Robert Stephenson Smyth. *Memories of India; Recollections of Soldiering, and Sport*. Philadelphia: D. McKay, 1915.

Baden-Powell, Robert Stephenson Smyth. *Sport in War*. London: William Heinemann, 1900.

Baer, Adela. 'Maintaining Biocultural Diversity'. *Conservation Biology* 3, no. 1 (Mar 1989): 97–98.
Bailey, Frederick George. *Tribe, Caste, and Nation: A Study of Political Activity and Political Change in Highland Orissa*. Manchester: Manchester University Press, 1960.
Baillie, W.W. *Days and Nights of Shikar*. London: J. Lane, 1921.
Baker, Edward B. *Sport in Bengal: And How, When, and Where to Seek It*. London: Ledger, Smith, 1887.
Bal, Hartosh Singh. *Waters Close over Us: A Journey Along the Narmada*. Delhi: Harper Collins, 2013.
Ballhatchet, K. *Social Policy and Social Change in Western India, 1817–1830*. London: Oxford University Press, 1957.
Bambach, Richard K. 'Phanerozoic Biodiversity Mass Extinctions'. *Annual Review of Earth and Planetary Sciences* 34 (2006): 127–155.
Banerjee, Rahul. 'Reasserting Ecological Ethics: Bhils Struggles in Alirajpur'. *Economic & Political Weekly* 32, no. 3 (Jan 18, 1997): 87–91.
Banerjee, Rahul. 'The Bhils: A People Under Threat'. *Humanscape* 8, no. 8 (Sep 2001) 21–24.
Banerjee, Rahul. 'The Forests of Shisewadi: Facing Displacement', *Anaarkali—The Saga of Bhil Adivasi Indigenous People*, 5 May 2013. http://anar-kali.blogspot.com/2013/05/mumbais-water-needs-versus-livelihoods.html
Barclay, Edgar. *Big Game Shooting Records*. London: Witherby, 1932.
Bardhan, A.B. *The Tribal Problem in India*. Delhi: Communist Party Publication, 1973.
Bardhan, Ardhendu Bhushan. *The Tribal Problem in India*, Pamphlet no. 12. New Delhi: Communist Party of India, 1973.
Barker, Joanne. 'The Human Genome Diversity Project: "Peoples", "Populations" and the Cultural Politics of Identification'. *Cultural Studies* 18, no. 4 (2004): 574–575.
Barnard, Alan. 'Kalahari Revisionism, Vienna and the "Indigenous Peoples" Debate'. *Social Anthropology* 14, no. 1 (2006): 1–16.
Barnett, Antony. 'In Africa the Hoodia Cactus Keeps Men Alive. Now Its Secret Is "Stolen" to Make Us Thin'. *Observer*, 21 Jun 2001. http://www.guardian.co.uk/world/2001/jun/17/internationaleducationnews.businessofresearch
Barrow, Mark. *Natures Ghosts*. Chicago: University of Chicago Press, 2009.
Barta, Tony. 'Mr Darwin's Shooters: On Natural Selection and the Naturalizing of Genocide'. *Patterns of Prejudice* 39, no. 2 (2005): 117–126.
Bashkow, Ira. 'On History for the Present: Revisiting George Stocking's Influential Rejection of "Presentism"'. *American Anthropologist* 121, no. 3 (2019): 709–720.
Basu, Amrita. *Two Faces of Protest: Contrasting Modes of Women's Activism in India*. Berkeley: University of California Press, 1994.
Bates, Crispin. 'Congress and the Tribals'. In *The Indian National Congress and the Political Economy of India*, edited by Mike Shepperdson and Colin Simmons, 231–252. Aldershot: Avebury, 1988.
Bates, Crispin. 'Lost Innocents and the Loss of Innocence: Interpreting Adivasi Movements in South Asia'. In *Indigenous Peoples of Asia*, edited by R.H. Barnes, A. Gray, and B. Kingsbury, 103–119. Ann Arbor: Association of Asian Studies, 1995.
Bauman, Zygmunt. *Modernity and the Holocaust*. Cambridge: Polity Press, 1989.
Baumann, Peter and Helmut Uhlig. *Rettet die Naturvölker: Kein Platz für "wilde" Menschen*. Berlin: Safari-Verlag, 1980.

Baviskar, Amita. *In the Belly of the River: Tribal Conflicts over Development in the Narmada Valley.* Delhi: Oxford University Press, 1995.
Baviskar, Amita. 'The Politics of Being "Indigenous" '. In *Indigeneity in India*, edited by Bengt Karlsson and Tanka Subba, 33–50. London: Kegan Paul, 2006.
Bechtel, Stefan. *Mr. Hornaday's War: How a Peculiar Victorian Zookeeper Waged a Lonely Crusade for Wildlife That Changed the World.* Boston: Beacon Press, 2012.
Beggiora, Stefano. 'The End of Time in Adivasi Traditions or the Time of the End for Adivasi Traditions?.' *Anglistica AION* 19, no. 1 (2015): 163–174.
Benjamin, N. and B.B. Mohanty. 'Imperial Solution of a Colonial Problem: Bhils of Khandesh up to c. 1850', *Modern Asian Studies* 41, no. 2 (2007): 343–367.
Berkhof, Ferdinand. 'Survival International Is Paternalistic'. *Sunday Standard* (Botswana), 27 Jan 2011. https://www.sundaystandard.info/ocsurvival-international-is-paternalisticoco/
Best, J.W. *Forest Life in India.* London: John Murray, 1935.
Best, J.W. *Shikar Notes for Novices.* Allahabad: The Pioneer Press, 1920.
Béteille, André. 'The Concept of Tribe with Special Reference to India'. *European Journal of Sociology/Archives Européennes de Sociologie* 27, no. 2 (1986): 297–318.
Béteille, André. 'The Idea of Indigenous People'. *Current Anthropology* 39, no. 2 (1998): 187–192.
Beverley, Eric Lewis. 'Frontier as Resource: Law, Crime, and Sovereignty on the Margins of Empire'. *Comparative Studies in Society and History* 55, no. 2 (2013): 241–272.
Bhukya, Bhangya. 'The Subordination of the Sovereigns: Colonialism and the Gond Rajas in Central India, 1818–1948'. *Modern Asian Studies* 47, no. 1 (2013): 288–317.
Bird-David, Nurit. 'Beyond "The Hunting and Gathering Mode of Subsistence": Culture-Sensitive Observations on the Nayaka and Other Modern Hunter-Gatherers'. *Man* 27, no. 1 (Mar 1992): 19–44.
BirdLife International. '*Perdicula manipurensis* (amended version of 2016 assessment)'. *The IUCN Red List of Threatened Species 2017.* https://dx.doi.org/10.2305/IUCN.UK.2017-1.RLTS.T22679012A112384972.en
Biswas, Swapan Kumar. 'Vulnerability Among Primitive Tribal Groups in Andaman'. *International Journal of Academic Research* 4, no. 3 (Mar 2017): 36–49.
Black, Jason Edward. 'Native Authenticity, Rhetorical Circulation, and Neocolonial Decay: The Case of Chief Seattle's Controversial Speech'. *Rhetoric & Public Affairs* 15, no. 4 (2012): 635–645.
Blanchard, Pascal et al., eds. *Human Zoos: Science and Spectacle in the Age of Colonial Empires.* Liverpool: Liverpool University Press, 2008.
Bloomfield, A. *Notes on the Baigas of the Central Provinces.* Balaghat: Self-Published, 1885.
Boas, Franz. 'Some Principles of Museum Administration'. *Science* 25 (1907): 920–933.
Bodley, John H. 'Alternatives to Ethnocide: Human Zoos, Living Museums, and Real People'. In *Western Expansion and Indigenous Peoples: The Heritage of Las Casas*, edited by Elias Sevilla-Casas, 31–51. The Hague: Mouton, 1977. https://sites.google.com/site/bodleyanthropology/books/victims-of-progress-2
Bodley, John H. *Victims of Progress*, 6th ed. London: Rowan & Littlefield, 2015.
Bonington, C.C. *Census of India, 1931: The Andaman and Nicobar Islands*, vol. 2. Calcutta: Central Publication Branch, 1932.

Bonwick, James. *The Last of the Tasmanians; Or, the Black War of Van Diemen's Land.* London: Sampson Low, 1870.
Bose, N.K. 'The Hindu Method of Tribal Absorption'. *Science and Culture* 7, no. 2 (1941): 188–194.
Botkin, Daniel B. *No Man's Garden: Thoreau and a New Vision for Civilization and Nature.* Washington, DC: Island Press, 2001.
Braddon, Edward. *Thirty Years of Shikar.* Edinburgh: William Blackwood, 1895.
Brander, A.A. Dunbar. *Working Plan for the Forests of the Banjar Valley Reserve, Mandla Forest Division, Northern Circle, CP, for the Period 1904–1935.* Allahabad: Pioneer Press, 1906.
Brandis, Dietrich. *Memorandum on the Forest Legislation Proposed for British India, Other Than the Presidencies of Madras and Bombay.* Simla: Government Press, 1875.
Brannen, Peter. 'Earth Is Not in the Midst of a Sixth Mass Extinction'. *Atlantic,* 13 Jun 2017. https://www.theatlantic.com/science/archive/2017/06/the-ends-of-the-world/529545/
Brantlinger, Patrick. *Dark Vanishings: Discourse on the Extinction of Primitive Races, 1800–1930.* Ithaca: Cornell University Press, 2003.
Brewster, David. *Edinburgh Encyclopaedia.* London: John Murray, 1830.
Briggs, John. 'Two Lectures on the Aboriginal Race of India, as Distinguished from the Sanskritic or Hindu Race'. *Journal of the Royal Asiatic Society of Great Britain and Ireland* 13 (1852): 275–309.
British Association for the Advancement of Science. *Report of the Eleventh Meeting of the British Association for the Advancement of Science: Held at Plymouth in 1841.* London: John Murray, 1842.
Brockington, Dan. *Fortress Conservation: The Preservation of the Mkomazi Game Reserve, Tanzania.* Bloomington: Indiana University Press, 2002.
Brosius, J. Peter and Sarah L. Hitchner. 'Cultural Diversity and Conservation'. *International Social Science Journal* 61, no. 199 (2010): 141–168.
Brosius, J. Peter. 'Endangered Forest, Endangered People: Environmentalist Representations of Indigenous Knowledge'. *Human Ecology* 25, no. 1 (Mar 1997): 47–69.
Brower, Barbara and Barbara Rose Johnston, eds. *Disappearing Peoples? Indigenous Minorities in South and Central Asia.* Walnut Creek, CA: Left Coast Press, 2007.
Brown, James Moray. *Shikar Sketches, with Notes on Indian Field-Sports.* London: Hurst & Blackett, 1887.
Brown, Robert. *Races of Mankind,* vol. 3. London: Cassell, Petter, & Galpin, 1873.
Brown, Robert. *The Peoples of the World: Being a Popular Description of the Characteristics, Condition, and Customs of the Human Family,* vol. 4. London: Cassell, 1892.
Browning, Frank. 'The Human Zoo: Invention of the Savage'. *Huffington Post,* 3 Feb 2012.
Buch, M.N. 'Is Verrier Elwin Still Relevant? A Study of the Bhils of Jhabua'. Centre for Governance and Political Studies, Vivekananda International Foundation. 17 Oct 2012. https://www.vifindia.org/article/2012/october/17/is-verrier-elwin-still-relevant-a-study-of-the-bhils-of-jhabua
Buchanan, Francis. *A Journey from Madras through the Countries of Mysore, Canara, and Malabar...,* 3 vols. London: Cadell [etc.], 1807.

Buell, Lawrence. *Writing for an Endangered World*. Cambridge, MA: Harvard University Press, 2009.

Burman, B.K. Roy. 'Basic Concepts of Tribal Welfare and Tribal Integration'. *Journal of Social Research* 3, no. 2 (1960): 17–18.

Burton, E.F. *An Indian Olio*. London: Spencer Blackett, 1888.

Burton, R.W. *The Preservation of Wild Life in India*. Bangalore: Bangalore Press, 1953.

Burton, R.W. 'Wild Life Preservation in India'. *Journal of the Bombay Natural History Society* 47, no. 4 (1948): 101.

Butt, Khan Saheb Jamshed. *Shikar*. Bombay: Rusi Khambatta, 1963.

Cameron, G. Poulett. *The Romance of Military Life*. London: Houlston and Wright, 1858.

Carrin, Marine. 'Engaging Scholarship in Understanding Endangered Societies with Special Reference to India'. In *Marginalised and Endangered Worldviews: Comparative Studies on Contemporary Eurasia, India and South America*, edited by Lidia Guzy and James Kapaló, 9–29. Münster: LIT Verlag, 2017.

Carter, Michael J. *Peasants and Poachers: A Study in Rural Disorder in Norfolk*. Suffolk: Boydell Press, 1980.

Cartmill, Matt. *A View to a Death in the Morning: Hunting and Nature Through History*. London: Harvard University Press, 1993.

Casas, Bartolomé de las. *Brevísima Relación de la Destrucción de las Indias*. Seuilla: En casa de Sebastian Trugillo, 1552.

Casas, Bartolomé de las. *Witness: Writing of Bartolomé de las Casas*. Edited and translated by George Sanderlin. Maryknoll: Orbis books, 1993.

Catlin, George. *Letters and Notes on the Manners, Customs, and Condition of the North American Indians*. London: Self-published, 1842.

Catton, Theodore. *Inhabited Wilderness: Indians, Eskimos, and National Parks in Alaska*. Albuquerque: University of New Mexico Press, 1997.

Ceballos, Gerardo, Ehrlich, Anne H., and Ehrlich, Paul R. *The Annihilation of Nature: Human Extinction of Birds and Mammals*. Baltimore: John Hopkins University Press, 2015.

Chakrabarty, Dipesh. *Provincializing Europe: Postcolonial Thought and Historical Difference*. Delhi: Oxford University Press, 2001.

Chakravartty, Anupam. 'Baiga Get Home'. *Down to Earth*, 15 Feb 2016. https://www.downtoearth.org.in/news/governance/baigas-get-home-52666

Chamberlain, Gethin. 'Human Safaris May Be Banned, but Still Tourists Flock to Andaman Islands'. *Guardian*, 1 Sep 2012.

Chandra, Uday. 'Liberalism and Its Other: The Politics of Primitivism in Colonial and Postcolonial Indian Law'. *Law & Society Review* 47, no. 1 (2013): 135–168.

Charsley, Katharine. '"Children of the Forest" or "Backwards Communities"? The Ideology of Tribal Development'. *Edinburgh Papers in South Asian Studies* 7 (1997): 1–17.

Chattapadhyay, K.P. 'The Tribal Problem and Its Solution'. *Eastern Anthropologist* 3, no. 1 (Sep 1949): 3–21.

Chatterji, Angana. 'Commentary: Anthropology and Cultural Survival'. *Anthropology News* 45, no. 3 (Mar 2004): 7–8.

Chatterton, Eyre. *Story of Gondwana*. London: Sir Isaac Pitman & Sons, 1916.

Chattopadhyay, Sohini. 'Exclusive: Inside a Hindutva Hostel: How RSS Is Rewiring the Tribal Mind'. *Catch News*, 19 Dec 2015. http://www.sacw.net/index.php?page=imprimir_articulo&id_article=12762

Chaurasiya, Vijay. *Prakriti Putra Baiga*. Bhopal: Madhya Pradesh Hindi Granth Academy, 2004.

Chopra, Suneet. 'Revolt and Religion: Petty Bourgeois Romanticism'. *Social Scientist* 16, no. 2 (Feb 1988): 60–67.

Choudhari, Abhishek. 'Government Destroying Tribals, Attacking Their Basic Rights'. *Times of India*, 24 Nov 2019. https://timesofindia.indiatimes.com/city/nagpur/govt-destroying-tribals-attacking-their-basic-rights/articleshow/72200790.cms

Churchill, Ward. 'An American Holocaust? The Structure of Denial'. *Socialism and Democracy* 17, no. 1 (2003): 28.

Cobbett, William. *Cobbett's Weekly Register*. London: J.M. Cobbett, 1822.

Coetzer, Kaera L., Edward T.F. Witkowski, and Barend F.N. Erasmus. 'Reviewing Biosphere Reserves Globally: Effective Conservation Action or Bureaucratic Label?' *Biological Reviews* 89, no. 1 (2014): 1–23.

Colchester, Marcus. 'Conservation Policy and Indigenous Peoples'. *Cultural Survival Quarterly* 28, no. 1 Special Issue: 'Indigenous Lands or National Park?' (Spring 2004): 17–22.

Coldstream, J.C. 'Shikar Rules of Shimla Hill States and Shimla District'. Shimla, 1924.

Cole, Simon A. 'Do Androids Pulverize Tiger Bones to Use as Aphrodisiacs?' *Social Text* 42 (Spring 1995): 173–193.

Conklin, Beth A. 'Environmentalism, Global Community, and the New Indigenism'. In *Inclusion and Exclusion in the Global Arena*, edited by Max Kirsch, 162–188. New York: Routledge, 2006.

Cooch Behar, Maharajah of. *Thirty Seven Years of Big Game Shooting*. Bombay: Times Press, 1908.

Corry, Stephen. 'Interview 1: Stephen Corry, Survival International, 4 December 2007'. In *The Politics of Indigeneity: Dialogues and Reflections on Indigenous Activism*, edited by Venkateswar and E. Hughes, 193–206. New York: Zed Books, 2011.

Corry, Stephen. *Tribal Peoples for Tomorrow's World*. Alcester: Freeman Press, 2011.

Cotton, James Sutherland and William Stevenson Meyer. *Imperial Gazetteer of India*. Oxford: Clarendon Press, 1908.

Cowles, Henry. 'A Victorian Extinction: Alfred Newton and the Evolution of Animal Protection'. *British Journal for the History of Science* 46, no. 4 (Dec 2013): 695–714.

Crosby, Percy Leo. *Patriotism: A Dialogue*. New York: Percy Crosby, 1932.

Cumming, W.G. *Wild Men and Wild Beasts: Scenes in Camp and Jungle*. London: Hamilton Adams, 1871.

Cunningham, Alexander. *Report of a Tour of the Central Provinces and Lower Gangetic Doab in 1881-82*. Calcutta: Government Printing, 1884.

Czech, Kenneth P. *An Annotated Bibliography of Asian Big Game Hunting Books, 1780 to 1980*. St. Cloud, MN: Land's Edge Press, 2003.

Daley, Ben and Peter Griggs. '"Loved to Death": Coral Collecting in the Great Barrier Reef, Australia, 1770–1970'. *Environment and History* 14, no. 1 (2008): 89–119.

Dalrymple, William. *The Age of Kali: Travels and Encounters in India*. London: HarperCollins, 1998.

Damodaran, Vinita. 'Book Review: Environment and Ethnicity in India 1200-1991, by Sumit Guha. Cambridge: Cambridge University Press, 1999'. *Journal of Political Ecology* 7, no. 1 (2000): 12–17.
Damodaran, Vinita. 'Colonial Constructions of Tribe in India'. *Indian Historical Review* 30, no. 1 (Jan 2006): 44–76.
Darwin, Charles. *Journal and Remarks, 1832–1836* [AKA *Voyage of the Beagle*], vol. 1. London: Colburn, 1839.
Darwin, Charles. *The Descent of Man, and Selection in Relation to Sex*. London: Murray, 1871.
Darwin, Charles. *The Descent of Man, and Selection in Relation to Sex*. London: Penguin Classics, 2004.
Das, Durga, ed. *Sardar Patel's Correspondence 1945–50, vol. 7 Integrating Indian States, Police Action in Hyderabad*. Ahmedabad: Navajivan, 1973.
Das, Tarak C. 'Cultural Anthropology in the Service of the Individual and the Nation: Presidential Address Delivered in the Section of Anthropology'. In *Proceedings of the Twenty-Eighth Indian Science Congress*, 1–29. Benares, 1941.
Das, Tarak C. 'Nature and Extent of Social Change in Tribal Society of Eastern India'. *Sociological Bulletin* 11, no. 1–2 (1962): 221–238.
Dasmann, Raymond F. 'Future Primitive: Ecosystem People versus Biosphere People'. *CoEvolution Quarterly* 11 (1976): 26–31.
Dasmann, Raymond F. 'National Parks, Nature Conservation, and Future Primitive'. *Ecologist* 6, no. 5 (1977): 164–167.
Dasmann, Raymond F. *The Conservation Alternative*. New York: Wiley, 1975.
Dasmann, Raymond F. 'The Importance of Cultural and Biological Diversity'. In *Biodiversity: Culture, Conservation, and Ecodevelopment*, edited by M.L. Oldfield and J.B. Alcorn, 7–15. Boulder, CO: Westview, 1991.
Dattatri, Shekar. 'How a Social Justice Tool Became a Means to Grab Land in India's Forests'. *Hindustan Times*, 2 Jul 2019. https://www.hindustantimes.com/analysis/how-a-social-justice-tool-became-a-means-to-grab-land-in-india-s-forests/story-TPm9hWnFzRJavD1bKN2grM.html
Dave, Parag. 'Concrete Used in Narmada Dam Can Build a Road Around Equator'. *Rediff News*, 29 Sep 2006. https://www.rediff.com/news/2006/sep/29dam.htm
Davidson, Lawrence. *Cultural Genocide*. New Brunswick: Rutgers University Press, 2012.
Davies, David M. *The Last of the Tasmanians*. Sydney: Shakespeare Head Press, 1973.
Dawkins, Richard. *The Selfish Gene*. Oxford: Oxford University Press, 1976.
De, Debasree. *A History of Adivasi Women in Post-Independence Eastern India: The Margins of the Marginals*. Delhi: Sage, 2018.
De Bont, Raf. '"Primitives" and Protected Areas: International Conservation and the "Naturalization" of Indigenous People, ca. 1910–1975'. *Journal of the History of Ideas* 76, no. 2 (2015): 215–236.
Dean, Dennis R. *James Hutton and the History of Geology*. Ithaca: Cornell University Press, 1992.
Deepak, Mahesh Kumar. 'Communal Politics and the Role of Various Political Ideologies in Bihar: 1940–45'. *Scholarly Research Journal for Interdisciplinary Studies* 4, no. 30 (Mar 2017): 5018–5022. http://www.srjis.com/pages/pdfFiles/1497252864Mahesh%20Kumar%20Deepak.pdf

Derrida, Jacques. *De la Grammatology*. Paris: Éditions de Minuit, 1967.
Deshpande, Arvind M. *John Briggs in Maharashtra: A Study in District Administration under Early British Rule*. Delhi: Mittal, 1987.
Devi, Savitri. *A Warning to the Hindus*. Calcutta: Brahmachari Bijoy Krishna, Hindu Mission, 1939.
Dharmadhikary, Shripad and Nandini Oza, 'No, Swaminathan Aiyar, Adivasis Ousted by the Narmada Project Aren't Lovin' It. They Are Desperate'. *Scroll*, 17 Sep 2017. https://scroll.in/article/850777/no-swaminathan-aiyar-adivasis-ousted-by-the-narmada-project-arent-lovin-it-they-are-desperate
Dhillon, Amrit. 'Millions of Forest-Dwelling Indigenous People in India to be Evicted'. *Guardian*, 22 Feb 2019. https://www.theguardian.com/world/2019/feb/22/millions-of-forest-dwelling-indigenous-people-in-india-to-be-evicted
Diamond, Jared M. *Collapse: How Societies Choose to Fail or Survive*. London: Allen Lane, 2005.
Dickens, Charles. 'The Noble Savage'. *Household Words* VII (11 Jun 1853): 337–339.
Dikötter, Frank. *The Discourse of Race in Modern China*. London: Hurst, 1992.
Dippie, Brian W. *The Vanishing American: White Attitudes and U.S. Indian Policy*. Lawrence, KS: University Press of Kansas, 1991.
Divyabhanusinh. 'Junagadh State and Its Lions: Conservation in Princely India, 1879–1947'. *Conservation and Society* 4, no. 4 (2006): 522–540.
Divyabhanusinh. *The End of a Trail: The Cheetah in India*, 2nd ed. Delhi: Oxford University Press, 2002.
Divyabhanusinh. *The Story of Asia's Lions*. Mumbai: Marg Publications, 2005.
Dovers, Stephen R. 'On the Contribution of Environmental History to Current Debate and Policy'. *Environment and History* 6 (2000): 131–50.
Driem, George van. *Languages of the Himalayas: An Ethnolinguistic Handbook of the Greater Himalayan Region: Containing an Introduction to the Symbiotic Theory of Language*. Leiden: Brill, 2001.
Dube, S.C. 'Five Research Proposals'. In *Urgent Research in Social Anthropology: Proceedings of a Conference*, edited by B.L. Abbi and S. Saberwal, 61–69. Simla: Indian Institute of Advanced Study, 1969.
Dube, S.C. 'The Kamars and Some Problems of Tribal Adjustment'. *Eastern Anthropologist* 2, no. 4 (Jun 1949): 192–200.
Dube, S.C. ed. *Tribal Heritage of India*, vol. 1. Delhi: Vikas, 1977.
Dunbar Brander, A.A. *Wild Animals in Central India*. London: Edward Arnold, 1923.
Dunbar, Samuel. *The Presence of God with His People*. Boston: S. Kneeland, 1760.
Durbach, Nadja. 'London, Capital of Exotic Exhibits from 1830 to 1860'. In *Human Zoos: Science and Spectacle in the Age of Colonial Empires*, edited by Pascal Blanchard, et al., 81–88. Liverpool University Press, 2008.
Dutt, Shoshee Chunder [Pseud. Horatio Bickerstaff Rowney]. *The Wild Tribes of India*. London: Thos. De la Rue, 1882.
Dwivedi, Ranjit. 'Displacement, Risks and Resistance: Local Perceptions and Actions in the Sardar Sarovar'. *Development and Change* 30, no. 1 (1999): 43–78.
Eardley-Wilmot, Sainthill and Mabel Eardley-Wilmot, *Forest Life and Sport in India*. London: E. Arnold, 1910.
Edye, J.S. *Sport in India and Somali Land*. London: Gale & Polden, 1895.

Ellis, Clyde. 'Paradise Lost: Dismantling the Trope of Nature's Children'. *Ethnohistory* 49, no. 3 (2002): 717–719.
Ellis, George E. *The Red Man and the White Man in North America*. Boston: Little, Brown, 1882.
Ellison, Bernard C. *H R H The Prince of Wales's Sport In India*. London: William Heinemann, 1925.
Elwin, Verrier. 'Beating a Dead Horse'. *Seminar* 14 (Oct 1960): 35–38.
Elwin, Verrier. 'Do We Really Want to Keep Them in a Zoo?' In *The Adivasis*, 8–20. Delhi: Ministry of Information & Broadcasting, 1960 [1955].
Elwin, Verrier. 'Growth of a 'Philosophy''. In *Anthropology in the Development Process*, edited by Hari Mohan Mathur, 468–84. New Delhi: Vikas, 1977.
Elwin, Verrier. *The Baiga*. London: J. Murray, 1939.
Elwin, Verrier. *Tribal World of Verrier Elwin: An Autobiography*. Oxford: Oxford University Press, 1989.
'Endangered Elms', *New York Times*, 9 Sep 1933.
Erskine, K.D. *Rajputana Gazetteer: Imperial Gazetteer of India*, vol. 18. Calcutta: Government Printing, 1908.
Erskine, K.D. *The Mewar Residency*, 2 vols. Ajmer: Scottish Mission Industries, 1908.
Evans, D. *History of Nature Conservation in Britain*. London: Routledge, 1992.
'Existence of Jews held Endangered', *New York Times*, 24 Dec 1945.
Fabian, Johannes. *Time and the Other: How Anthropology Makes Its Object*. New York: Columbia University Press, 1983.
Fanon, Frantz. *Peau Noire, Masques Blancs*. Paris: Éditions du Seuil, 1952.
Fanon, Frantz. *Les Damnés de la Terre*. Paris: F. Maspero, 1961.
Farhadinia, M.S. et al. 'Status of Asiatic Cheetah in Iran: A Country-scale Assessment'. *Tehran, Iran: Iranian Cheetah Society*, 2014. https://ptes.org/wp-content/uploads/2015/01/Iran-cheetah-population-final-report-fall-2014.pdf
Farnham, Timothy J. *Saving Nature's Legacy: Origins of the Idea of Biological Diversity*. New Haven: Yale University Press, 2007.
Farrier, David. *Anthropocene Poetics: Deep Time, Sacrifice Zones, and Extinction*. Minneapolis: University of Minnesota Press, 2019.
Fattori, Marco. 'The Bhils and the Rajput Kingdoms of Southern Rajasthan'. In *Narratives from the Margins: Aspects of Adivasi History in India*, edited by Sanjukta Das Gupta and Raj Sekhar Basu, 127–152. Delhi: Primus Books, 2012.
Felix [pseud]. *Recollections of a Bison & Tiger Hunter*. London: J.M. Dent, 1906.
Fergusson, James. *History of Indian and Eastern Architecture*. London: J. Murray, 1876.
Fernando Vidal and Nélia Dias, 'The Endangerment Sensibility'. In *Endangerment, Biodiversity and Culture*, edited by Fernando Vidal and Nélia Dias, 1–38. New York: Routledge, 2016.
Ferris, Elizabeth G. *The Politics of Protection: The Limits of Humanitarian Action*. Washington: Brookings Institution Press, 2011.
Findly, Ellison B. 'Jahangir's Vow of Non-Violence'. *Journal of the American Oriental Society* 107, no. 2 (Apr–Jun 1987): 245–256.
Finzsch, Norbert. '"[ … ] Extirpate or Remove that Vermine": Genocide, Biological Warfare, and Settler Imperialism in the Eighteenth and Early Nineteenth Century'. *Journal of Genocide Research* 10, no. 2 (2008): 215–232.

Fiskesjö, Magnus. 'The Animal Other: China's Barbarians and Their Renaming in the Twentieth Century'. *Social Text* 29, no. 4 (Winter 2012): 57–79.
Fitter, R.S.R. and P. Scott, *The Penitent Butchers: The Fauna Preservation Society 1903–1978*. London: Collins, 1978.
Forsyth, James. *The Highlands of Central India: Notes on Their Forests and Wild Tribes, Natural History, and Sports*. London: Chapman and Hall, 1871.
Fox, Richard. '"Professional Primitives": Hunters and Gatherers of Nuclear South Asia'. *Man in India* 49 (1969): 139–160.
Franklin, Benjamin. *Mémoires de la Vie Privée de Benjamin Franklin*. Paris: Buisson, 1791.
Fraser, A.H.L. *Report on the Famine in Central Provinces in 1899–1900*. Nagpur, 1901.
Freitag, Jason. *Serving Empire, Serving Nation: James Tod and the Rajputs of Rajasthan*. Leiden: Brill, 2009.
Frere, H. Bartle. 'On the Laws Affecting the Relations Between Civilized and Savage Life, as Bearing on the Dealings of Colonists with Aborigines'. *Journal of the Anthropological Institute of Great Britain and Ireland* 11 (1882): 313–354.
Froude, James Anthony. *Oceana: Or, England and Her Colonies*. New York: C. Scribner's Sons, 1886.
Fuchs, Stephen. *The Gond and Bhumia of Eastern Mandla*. Bombay: Asia Publishing, 1960.
Fuchs, Stephen. 'Folk Tales of the Gond and Baiga in Eastern Mandla'. *Asian Folklore Studies* 24, no. 2 (1965): 53–116.
Fürer-Haimendorf, Christoph von. 'Fundamental Research in Indian Anthropology'. In *Urgent Research in Social Anthropology: Proceedings of a Conference*, edited by B.L. Abbi and S. Saberwal, 77–82. Simla: Indian Institute of Advanced Study, 1969.
Fürer-Haimendorf, Christoph von. 'The Tribal Problem in All-India Perspective'. In *Tribes of India: Struggle for Survival*, edited by Christoph von Fürer-Haimendorf, 313–322. Berkeley: University of California Press, 1982.
Fürer-Haimendorf, Christoph von. *Tribal Populations and Cultures of the Indian Subcontinent*. Leiden: Brill, 1985.
Gadgil, Madhav and Kailash C. Malhotra, 'Adaptive Significance of the Indian Caste System: An Ecological Perspective'. *Annals of Human Biology* 10, no. 5 (1983): 465–477.
Gadgil, Madhav and Ramachandra Guha. *Ecology and Equity*. London: Routledge, 1995.
Gadgil, Madhav and Ramachandra Guha. *This Fissured Land: An Ecological History of India*. Berkeley: University of California Press, 1993.
Gadgil, Madhav. 'Diversity: Cultural and Biological'. *Trends in Evolution and Ecology* 2, no. 12 (1987): 369–373.
Gaillard, Gerald. *The Routledge Dictionary of Anthropologists*. London: Routledge, 2004.
Gandhi, Mohandas K. *Constructive Programme: Its Meaning and Place*. Ahmedabad: Navajivan, 1941.
Gandhi, Mohandas K. 'Discussion on Fellowship'. *Young India*, 19 Jan 1928. In *The Collected Works of Mahatma Gandhi*, vol. 41 (2 Dec 1927–1 May 1928). https://www.gandhiashramsevagram.org/gandhi-literature/mahatma-gandhi-collected-works-volume-41.pdf

Gandhi, Mohandas K. *The Collected Works of Mahatma Gandhi*, vol. 7 (15 Jun 1907–12 Dec 1907). http://www.gandhiserve.org/cwmg/VOL007.PDF
Gandhi, Mohandas K. *The Collected Works of Mahatma Gandhi*, vol. 76 (31 May 1939–15 Oct 1939). http://www.gandhiserve.org/cwmg/VOL076.PDF
Ganguly, Pranab. 'The Negrito of Little Andaman Island a Primitive People Facing Extinction'. *Indian Museum Bulletin* 10, no. 1 (1975): 7–27.
Gangwar, M. and P. Bose, 'A Sociological Study of the Livelihoods of the Baigas in Baiga-Chak Belt of Dindori, India'. *The Peoples of the World Foundation* (2012). http://www.peoplesoftheworld.org/hosted/baigas/
Gardner, Nora. *Rifle and Spear with the Rajpoots: Being the Narrative of a Winter's Travel and Sport in Northern India*. London: Chatto & Windus, 1895.
Gautam, Rajesh K. *Baigas: The Hunter Gatherers of Central India*. Delhi: Readworthy, 2011.
Gautier, Francois. 'The Hindu Future of the World'. *Times of India Blog*, 27 Jan 2017. https://timesofindia.indiatimes.com/blogs/francois-gautiers-blog-for-toi/the-hindu-future-of-the-world
Gerard, Montague Gilbert. *Leaves from the Diaries of a Soldier and Sportsman During Twenty Years' Service in India, Afghanistan, Egypt, and Other Countries, 1865–1885*. London: John Murray, 1903.
Gerland, Georg. *Über Das Aussterben Der Naturvölker*. Leipzig: Verlag Friedrich Fleischer, 1868.
Ghurye, G.S. *The Scheduled Tribes*, 3rd ed. Bombay: Popular Press, 1963.
Gidwani, Vinay. 'The Unbearable Modernity of Development? Canal Irrigation and Development Planning in Western India'. *Planning and Progress* 58 (2002): 1–80.
Glasfurd, A.I.R. *Rifle and Romance in the Indian Jungle*. London: J. Lane, 1905.
Glavin, Terry. *The Sixth Extinction: Journeys Among the Lost and Left Behind*. New York: Macmillan, 2007.
Godbole, Madhav. 'Is India a Secular Nation?' *Economic & Political Weekly* 51, no. 15 (9 Apr 2016). https://www.epw.in/journal/2016/15/web-exclusives/india-secular-nation.html
Godden, Jon and Rumer. *Shiva's Pigeons: An Experience of India*. New York: Knopf, 1972.
Goldsmid, Frederic John. *James Outram: A Biography*. London: Smith, Elder, 1880.
Golwalkar, M.S. *Bunch of Thoughts*. Bangalore: Vikrama Prakashan, 1966.
Golwalkar, M.S. *We, or, Our Nationhood Defined*. Nagpur: Bharat Publications, 1939.
Gospel Tract Society, *Endangered Species: Our Children*. Independence, MO: Gospel Tract Society, nd [1970?].
Gouldsbury, Charles Elphinstone. *Tiger Slayer by Order: Digby Davies, Late Bombay Police*. London: Chapman & Hall, 1915.
Government of India. *Census of India*. Home/PCA/A-11, 'Individual Scheduled Tribe Primary Census Abstract Data and its Appendix'. Office of the Registrar General & Census Commissioner, India, 2011. http://www.censusindia.gov.in/2011census/PCA/ST.html
Government of India. *Constituent Assembly Debates (Proceedings), 9 Dec 1946 to 24 Jan 1950*. Delhi: Lok Sabha Secretariat, 1966. http://164.100.47.194/Loksabhahindi/cadebatefiles/cadebates.html
Government of India. *Constitution of India*, Articles 341 and 342.

Government of India. *Scheduled Tribes and Other Traditional Forest Dwellers (Recognition of Forest Rights) Act, 2006* (FRA).
Gqola, Pumla Dineo. 'A Question of Semantics? On *Not* Calling People "Endangered"'. In *Perspectives on Endangerment*, edited by Graham Huggan and Stephan Klasen, 51–60. Hildesheim: Georg Olms Verlag, 2005.
Grant, Charles, ed. *The Gazetteer of the Central Provinces of India*, 2nd ed. Bombay: Education Society's Press, 1870.
Griffiths, Jay. *Wild: An Elemental Journey*. London: Hamish Hamilton, 2007.
Grigson, W.V. 'The Aboriginal in the Future India'. *Man in India* 46 (Jan–Feb 1946): 16–17.
Grigson, W.V. 'Foreword'. In *Tribal Hyderabad: Four Reports*, edited by Christoph von Fürer-Haimendorf, v–vii. Hyderabad: Government of H.E.H. the Nizam Revenue Department, 1945.
Grigson, W.V. *Notes on the Aboriginal Problem in the Mandla District*. Nagpur: Government Printing, 1940.
Grigson, W.V. *The Aboriginal Problem in the Central Provinces and Berar*. Nagpur: Government Printing, 1944.
Grigson, W.V. *The Aboriginal Problem in the Balaghat District: A Preliminary Report*. Nagpur: Government Printing, 1941.
Grove, Richard. 'Environmental History'. In *New Perspectives on Historical Writing*, edited by Peter Burke, 261. Pennsylvania: Penn State Press, 2001.
Grove, Richard. *Green Imperialism: Colonial Expansion, Tropical Island Edens, and the Origins of Environmentalism, 1600-1860*. Cambridge: Cambridge University Press, 1995.
Grove, Richard. 'The Origins of Environmentalism'. *Nature* 345 (May 1990): 11–14.
Gruber, Jacob W. 'Ethnographic Salvage and the Shaping of Anthropology'. *American Anthropologist*, New Series 72, no. 6 (Dec 1970): 1289–1299.
Guha, Ramachandra. 'An Early Environmental Debate: The Making of the 1878 Forest Act'. *Indian Economic & Social History Review* 27, no. 1 (1990): 65–84.
Guha, Ramachandra. 'Between Anthropology and Literature: The Ethnographies of Verrier Elwin'. *Journal of the Royal Anthropological Institute* 4, no. 2 (Jun. 1998): 325–343.
Guha, Ramachandra. 'Ecology for the People'. *Telegraph of Calcutta*, 14 Nov 2005.
Guha, Ramachandra. 'Lost in the Woods'. *Hindustan Times*, 23 Oct 2008. https://www.hindustantimes.com/india/lost-in-the-woods/story-gbX8spVkWcqrgjhzuLDHnO.html
Guha, Ramachandra. 'Savaging the Civilised: Verrier Elwin and the Tribal Question in Late Colonial India'. *Economic & Political Weekly* 31, no. 35/37 (Sep 1996): 2375–2389.
Guha, Ramachandra. *Savaging the Civilized: Verrier Elwin, His Tribals, and India*. Chicago: University of Chicago Press, 1999.
Guha, Sumit. *Environment and Ethnicity in India, 1200-1991*. Cambridge: Cambridge University Press, 1999.
Guha, Sumit. 'Forest Polities and Agrarian Empires: The Khandesh Bhils, c. 1700-1850'. *Indian Economic & Social History Review* 33, no. 2 (1996): 133–153.

Guitar, Lynne. 'Criollos: The Birth of a Dynamic New Indo-Afro-European People and Culture on Hispaniola'. *KACIKE, Journal of Caribbean Amerindian History and Anthropology* 1 (2000): 1–17.

Guitar, Lynne. 'Documenting the Myth of Taíno Extinction'. *KACIKE, Journal of Caribbean Amerindian History and Anthropology*, Special Issue (Dec 2002). https://ia800309.us.archive.org/5/items/KacikeJournal/GuitarEnglish.pdf

Gupta, Sanjukta Das. 'A Homeland for "Tribal" Subjects Revisiting British Colonial Experimentations in the Kolhan Government Estate'. In *Subjects, Citizens and Law: Colonial and Independent India*, edited by Gunnel Cederlöf and Sanjukta Das Gupta, 112–131. Delhi: Routledge, 2016.

Guzy, Lidia and James Kapaló, eds. *Marginalised and Endangered Worldviews: Comparative Studies on Contemporary Eurasia, India and South America*. Münster: LIT Verlag, 2017.

Hakim, Roxanne. 'Vasava Identity in Transition: Some Theoretical Issues'. *Economic & Political Weekly* 31, no. 24 (Jun 15, 1996): 1492–1499.

Hamilton, Walter. *The East-India Gazetteer*, vol. 1, 2nd ed. London: Parbury, 1828.

Hanbury-Tenison, Robin. *Report of a Visit to the Indians of Brazil on Behalf of the Primitive Peoples Fund/Survival International, January–March, 1971*. London: Survival International, 1971.

Hand, Eric. 'Sixth Extinction, Rivaling That of the Dinosaurs, Should Join the Big Five, Scientists Say'. *Science Magazine*, 16 Apr 2015. http://www.sciencemag.org/news/2015/04/sixth-extinction-rivaling-dinosaurs-should-join-big-five-scientists-say

Haraway, Donna, Noboru Ishikawa, Scott F. Gilbert, Kenneth Olwig, Anna L. Tsing, and Nils Bubandt. 'Anthropologists Are Talking–About the Anthropocene'. *Ethnos* 81, no. 3 (2016): 535–564.

Haraway, Donna. 'Anthropocene, Capitalocene, Plantationocene, Chthulucene: Making Kin'. *Environmental Humanities* 6, no. 1 (2015): 159–165.

Haraway, Donna. 'Teddy Bear Patriarchy: Taxidermy in the Garden of Eden, New York City, 1908–1936'. *Social Text* 11 (Winter, 1984–1985): 20–64.

Hardiman, David. *Gandhi in His Time and Ours: The Global Legacy of His Ideas*. New York: Columbia University Press, 2003.

Hardiman, David. *The Coming of the Devi: Adivasi Assertion in Western India*. Delhi: Oxford University Press, 1995.

Hardinge, Charles. *The Historical Record of the Imperial Visit to India 1911*. London: Murray, 1914.

Harmon, D. and L. Maffi. 'Are Linguistic and Biological Diversity Linked?' *Conservation Biology in Practice* 3, no. 1 (2002): 26–27.

Headland, Janet and Thomas N. Headland. 'Westernization, Deculturation, or Extinction Among Agta Negritos? The Philippine Population Explosion and Its Effect on a Rainforest Hunting and Gathering Society'. In *Hunters and Gatherers in the Modern Context*, vol. 1, edited by Linda J. Ellanna, 272–284. Fairbanks: University of Alaska, 1994.

Heise, Ursula K. *Imagining Extinction: The Cultural Meanings of Endangered Species*. Chicago: University of Chicago Press, 2016.

Heise, Ursula K. 'Lost Dogs, Last Birds, and Listed Species: Cultures of Extinction'. *Configurations* 18, no. 1–2 (2010): 60.

Hendley, T.H. 'An Account of the Maiwár Bhíls'. *Journal of the Asiatic Society of Bengal* 44, no. 4 (1875): 347–388.
Henen, Brian. 'Do Scientific Collecting and Conservation Conflict?' *Herpetological Conservation and Biology* 11, no. 1 (2016): 13–18.
Hewett, John Prescott. *Jungle Trails in Northern India: Reminiscences of Hunting in India*. London: Methuen, 1938.
Hicks, F.C. *Forty Years Among the Wild Animals of India from Mysore to the Himalayas*. Allahabad: The Pioneer Press, 1910.
Hinton, Alexander Laban. 'The Dark Side of Modernity: Towards an Anthropology of Genocide'. In *Annihilating Difference: The Anthropology of Genocide*, edited by Alexander Laban Hinton, 1–40. Berkeley: University of California, 2002.
Hippler, Arthur E. 'Comment on "Development in the Non-Western World"'. *American Anthropologist* 81 (1979): 348–349.
Hitchcock, Robert K. 'International Human Rights, the Environment, and Indigenous Peoples'. *Colorado Journal of International Environmental Law and Policy* (special issue: *Endangered Peoples: Indigenous Rights and the Environment*) 5, no. 1 (1994): 1–22.
Hohenwart-Gerlachstein, Anna. 'The International Committee on Urgent Anthropological and Ethnological Research'. *Current Anthropology* 10, no. 4 (Oct 1969): 376–377.
Holden, William N. and R. Daniel Jacobson. 'Ecclesial Opposition to Nonferrous Metals Mining in Guatemala and the Philippines: Neoliberalism Encounters the Church of the Poor'. In *Engineering Earth: The Impacts of Mega engineering Projects*, edited by Stanley D. Brunn, 383–411. Heidelberg: Springer, 2011.
Holly Jr., Donald H. 'The Beothuk on the Eve of their Extinction'. *Arctic Anthropology* 37, no. 1 (2000): 79–95.
Hopkins, Harry. *The Long Affray: The Poaching Wars, 1760–1914*. London: Papermac, 1986.
Hornaday, William Temple. *Our Vanishing Wild Life: Its Extermination and Preservation* (New York: C. Scribner's sons, 1913).
Hornaday, William Temple. 'The Passing of the Buffalo'. *Cosmopolitan* 4 (1887): 85–98, 231–243.
Hornaday, William Temple. *The Destruction of Our Birds and Mammals: A Report on the Results of an Inquiry*. New York: New York Zoological Society, 1901.
Hornaday, William Temple. *The Extermination of the American Bison*. Washington: Government Printing Office, 1889.
Hornaday, William Temple. *Two Years in the Jungle: The Experiences of a Hunter and Naturalist in India, Ceylon, the Malay Peninsula and Borneo*. London: Kegan Paul, 1885.
Hufford, Marry. 'Introduction: Rethinking the Cultural Mission'. In *Conserving Culture: A New Discourse on Heritage*, edited by Marry Hufford, 1–11. University of Illinois Press, 1994.
Huggan, Graham and Stephan Klasen, eds. *Perspectives on Endangerment*. Hildesheim: Georg Olms Verlag, 2005.
Hughes, Julie E. 'Royal Tigers and Ruling Princes: Wilderness and Wildlife Management in the Indian Princely States'. *Modern Asian Studies* 49, no. 4 (2015): 1210–1240.
Hull, Pincelli. 'Life in the Aftermath of Mass Extinctions'. *Current Biology* 25, no. 19 (2015): R943.

Hume, Allan Octavian. 'Perdicula manipurensis, sp. Nov.' *Stray Feathers* 9 (1880): 467–471.
IANS. 'PM Modi to Inaugurate World's Second Biggest Dam on September 17'. *Indian Express*, 14 Sep 2017.
Indian Board for Wild Life. *Project Tiger: A Planning Proposal for Preservation of Tiger (Panthera tigris tigris Linn.) in India*. New Delhi: Government of India, Ministry of Agriculture, 1972.
'India Tiger Census Shows Rapid Population Growth'. BBC, 29 Jul 2019. https://www.bbc.com/news/world-asia-india-49148174
*Indian Forest Act, 1878, as Modified up to the 1st December, 1903*. Calcutta: Superintendent Government Printing, 1903.
Ingen, E. van and van Ingen, 'Interesting Shikar Trophies: Hunting Cheetah *Acinonyx jubatus* (Schreber)'. *Journal of the Bombay Natural History Society* 47, no. 4 (1948): 718–720.
Irwin, Paul G. *Losing Paradise: The Growing Threat to Our Animals, Our Environment, and Ourselves*. New York: Square One Publishers, 1999.
Islam, Shuja ul and Zohra Islam. *Hunting Dangerous Game with the Maharajas in the Indian Sub-Continent*. New Delhi: Himalayan Books, 2004.
Jacks, G.V. and R.O. Whyte, *The Rape of the Earth*. London: Faher and Faher, 1939.
Jacoby, Karl. '"The Broad Platform of Extermination": Nature and Violence in the Nineteenth Century North American Borderlands'. *Journal of Genocide Research* 10, no. 2 (Jun 2008): 249–267.
Jadhava, Khasherao Bhagvantrao. *Opinion on the Revision Settlement Report of Mahuva Taluka*. Baroda: Government Press, 1914.
Jaffrelot, Christophe. *The Hindu Nationalist Movement and Indian Politics: 1925 to the 1990*. London: C Hurst, 1996.
Jain, Lakshmi Chand. *Dam Vs Drinking Water: Exploring the Narmada Judgement*. Delhi: Parisar, 2001.
Jakoby, Karl. '"The Broad Platform of Extermination": Nature and Violence in the Nineteenth Century North American Borderlands'. *Journal of Genocide Research* 10, no. 2 (Jun 2008): 249–267.
Jal, Murzban. 'Historical Materialism and a Relook at the "Tribal Question" in India'. *Mainstream Weekly* 55, no. 1 (24 Dec 2016). https://www.mainstreamweekly.net/article6908.html
James, William. *The Meaning of Truth, a Sequel To 'Pragmatism'*. New York: Longmans, 1909.
Jaulin, Robert. *La Paix blanche: introduction à l'ethnocide*. Paris: Éditions du Seuil, 1970.
Jayaratnam, T.C.S. *Report on the Revision of the Land Revenue Settlement of the Bilaspur Zamindaris in the Bilaspur District of the Central Provinces Effected during the Years 1928–1930*. Nagpur: Government Printing, 1931.
Jepson, Paul and Robert Whittaker. 'Histories of Protected Areas: Internationalisation of Conservationist Values and Their Adoption in the Netherlands Indies (Indonesia)'. *Environment and History* 8 (2002): 129–172.
Jepson, Stanley, ed. *Big Game Encounters: Critical Moments in the Lives of Well-Known Shikaris*. London: Witherby, 1936.

Johar, Roshni. 'Stepping into a World of Charm'. *Tribune* (India), 27 Nov 1999. https://www.tribuneindia.com/1999/99dec04/saturday/head7.htm

Johari, Aarefa. 'In Gujarat's Adivasi Belt, BJP has to Contend with Bhilistan Separatists, Boycotts and "Big People"'. *Scroll*, 6 Nov 2017. https://scroll.in/article/856382/in-gujarats-adivasi-belt-bjp-has-to-contend-with-bhilistan-separatists-boycotts-and-big-people

Johnson, W.T. *Twelve Years of a Soldier's Life*. London: A.D. Innes, 1897.

Kala, D.C. *Jim Corbett of Kumaon*. Delhi: Ravi Dayal, 1979.

Kalof, Linda and Amy Fitzgerald. 'Reading the Trophy: Exploring the Display of Dead Animals in Hunting Magazines'. *Visual Studies* 18, no. 2 (2003): 112–122.

Karve, I. 'The Tribals of Maharashtra'. In *Urgent Research in Social Anthropology: Proceedings of a Conference*, edited by B.L. Abbi and S. Saberwal, 94–100. Simla: Indian Institute of Advanced Studies, 1969.

Kela, Shashank. *A Rogue and Peasant Slave: Adivasi Resistance, 1800–2000*. Delhi: Navayana, 2012.

Kelly, Robert L. and Mary M. Prasciunas. 'Did the Ancestors of Native Americans Cause Animal Extinctions in Late-Pleistocene North America? And Does It Matter If They Did?' In *Native Americans and the Environment: Perspectives on the Ecological Indian*, edited by Michael Harkin and David Lewis, 96. Lincoln: University of Nebraska Press, 2007.

Khan, Mohd Momin. *The Malayan Tiger*. Kuala Lumpur: Institut Terjemahan & Buku Malaysia, 2014.

Khanna, Monit. 'With Less Than 3,000 Alive, Indian Wolf Is Most Endangered Wolf Species: Study'. *India Times*, 4 Sep 2021. https://www.indiatimes.com/technology/science-and-future/indian-wolf-endangered-species-study-548691.html

Khatri, Dipal. 'Aboriginal Culture Village Shows Tribal Lifestyles'. *China Post*, 19 Apr 2007.

Kipling, John Lockwood. *Beast and Man in India*. London: MacMillan, 1891.

Kipling, Rudyard. 'The Tomb of His Ancestors'. *McClure's Magazine* 10, no. 2 (Dec 1897): 99–120.

Kirschner, Stefan 'Don't Let the Jarawa Become Another Onge'. *Indigenous Policy Journal* 23, no. 1 (2012). www.indigenouspolicy.org/index.php/ipj/article/view/43/102

Kirsh, Stuart. 'Lost Worlds: Environmental Disaster, "Culture Loss," and the Law'. *Current Anthropology* 42, no. 2 (Apr 2001): 167–198.

*Kohelet/Ecclesiastes* KJV, 3:19–20.

Kolbert, Elizabeth. *The Sixth Extinction: An Unnatural History*. New York: Henry Holt, 2014.

Kosambi, D.D. *An Introduction to the Study of Indian History*. Bombay: Popular Book Depot, 1956.

Kothari, Ashish and Shiba Desor, 'Baigas' Battle: The Fight of the Baigas of Madhya Pradesh to Regain Their Traditional Rights is also a Fight to Restore the Diversity of Their Forests and to Protect National Wealth'. *Frontline*, 1 May 2013. www.frontline.in/environment/conservation/baigas-battle/article4653458.ece

Krupat, Arnold. 'Chief Seattle's Speech Revisited'. *American Indian Quarterly* 35, no. 2 (2011): 192–214.

Kuhn, Thomas. *The Structure of Scientific Revolutions*. Chicago: University of Chicago Press, 1962.

Kuper, Adam. 'The Return of the Native'. *Current Anthropology* 44, no. 3 (Jun 2003): 389–402.

Kupfer, Matthew and Thomas de Waal. 'Crying Genocide: Use and Abuse of Political Rhetoric in Russia and Ukraine'. *Carnegie Endowment for International Peace*, 28 Jul 2014. https://carnegieendowment.org/2014/07/28/crying-genocide-use-and-abuse-of-political-rhetoric-in-russia-and-ukraine-pub-56265

Ladle, Richard J. and Paul Jepson. 'Origins, Uses, and Transformation of Extinction Rhetoric'. *Environment and Society: Advances in Research* 1 (2010): 102–103.

Lal, Parmanand. 'The Tribal Man in India: A Study in the Ecology of the Primitive Communities'. In *Ecology and Biogeography in India*, edited by M.S. Mani, 281–329. The Hague: W. Junk, 1974.

Langa, Mahesh. 'Gujarat's Pride Grows as It Now Hosts 674 Gir lions'. *The Hindu*, 11 Jun 2020. https://www.thehindu.com/sci-tech/energy-and-environment/gujarats-pride-grows-as-it-now-hosts-674-gir-lions/article31799404.ece

Lasgorceix, Antoine and Ashish Kothari. 'Displacement and Relocation of Protected Areas: A Synthesis and Analysis of Case Studies'. *Economic & Political Weekly* 44, no. 49 (5 Dec 2009): 37–47.

Laughlin, Charles and Ivan A. Brady, eds, *Extinction and Survival in Human Populations*. New York: Columbia University Press, 1978.

Lawrence, D.H. *Lady Chatterley's Lover*. Firenze: Tipografia Giuntina, 1928.

Lawrence, Marilyn. 'Loving Them to Death: The Anorexic and Her Objects'. *International Journal of Psychoanalysis* 82, no. 1 (2001): 43–55.

Leakey, Richard and Roger Levin. *The Sixth Extinction*. New York: Double Day, 1995.

Lee, Richard and Irene Devore. 'Problems in the Study of Hunters and Gatherers'. In *Man the Hunter: The First Intensive Survey of a Single, Crucial Stage of Human Development—Man's Once Universal Hunting Way of Life*, edited by Richard Lee and Irene Devore, 3–12. Chicago: Aldine, 1968.

Lee, Richard B. 'Indigenism and Its Discontents'. In *Inclusion and Exclusion in the Global Arena*, edited by Max Kirsch, 141–172. New York: Routledge, 2006.

Lemkin, Raphael, *Axis Rule in Occupied Europe*. Washington, DC: Carnegie Endowment for International Peace, 1944.

Lenin, Vladimir Ilyich. 'Report On The Work Of The All-Russia Central Executive Committee And The Council Of People's Commissars Delivered At The First Session Of The All-Russia Central Executive Committee, Seventh Convocation' (2 Feb 1920). In *Lenin's Collected Works*. Translated by George Hanna, 4th English ed., vol. 30, 315–336. Moscow: Progress Publishers, 1965. https://www.marxists.org/archive/lenin/works/1920/feb/02.htm

Lenin, Vladimir Ilyich. 'The Heritage We Renounce'. In *Lenin's Collected Works*, vol. 2, 491–534. Moscow: Progress Publishers, 1972. http://www.marxists.org/archive/lenin/works/1897/dec/31c.htm

Leopold, Aldo. *A Sand County Almanac and Sketches Here and There*. New York: Oxford, 1949.

Leopold, Aldo. 'The Game Situation in the Southwest'. *Bulletin of the American Game Protective Association* 9, no. 2 (1920): 3–5.

Lévi-Strauss, Claude. 'Anthropology: Its Achievements and Future'. *Current Anthropology* 7, no. 2 (Apr 1966): 124–127.
Lévi-Strauss, Claude. *Tristes Tropiques*. Paris: Plon, 1955.
Lewis, Michael L. *Inventing Global Ecology: Tracking the Biodiversity Ideal in India, 1947–1997*. Athens: Ohio University Press, 2004.
Li, Tania Murray. 'Indigeneity, Capitalism, and the Management of Dispossession'. *Current Anthropology* 51, no. 3 (2010): 385–414.
Linton, Tom. 'India's Indigenous Evictions—The Dark Side of the Jungle Book'. *Ecologist*, 6 Feb 2015. http://www.theecologist.org/News/news_analysis/2741085/indias_indigenous_evictions_the_dark_side_of_the_jungle_book.html
Lizarralde, M. 'Biodiversity and Loss of Indigenous Languages and Knowledge in South America'. In *On Biocultural Diversity: Linking Language, Knowledge, and the Environment*, edited by Luisa Maffi, 265–281. Washington, DC: Smithsonian Institution Press, 2001.
Lodge, Thomas, trans. *The Famous and Memorable Works of Josephus: A Man of Much Honor and Learning Among the Jews*. London: F.L., 1655.
Lokur, B.N. et al., *The Report of the Advisory Committee on the Revision of the Lists of Scheduled Castes and Scheduled Tribes*. New Delhi: Department of Social Security, Government of India 1965.
Lopez, K.L. 'Returning to Fields'. *American Indian Culture and Research Journal* 16 (1992): 165–174.
Lu, Xing. *Rhetoric of the Chinese Cultural Revolution: The Impact on Chinese Thought, Culture, and Communication*. Columbia: University of South Carolina Press, 2004.
Lutkehaus, Nancy. *Margaret Mead: The Making of an American Icon*. Princeton: Princeton University Press, 2008.
Lyall, Alfred Comyn, ed. *Gazetteer of the Central Provinces*. Nagpur: Chief Commissioner's Office Press, 1867.
M.R. 'The Erosion of Secular India', *The Economist*, 4 Feb 2020. https://www.economist.com/the-economist-explains/2020/02/04/the-erosion-of-secular-india
Macdonald Jr., Theodore. 'Introduction: 25 Years of the Indigenous Movement in the Americas and Australia'. *Cultural Survival Quarterly*, Jun 1997. https://www.culturalsurvival.org/publications/cultural-survival-quarterly/introduction-25-years-indigenous-movement-americas-and
MacDonald, Robert H. *Language of Empire: Myths and Metaphors of Popular Imperialism, 1880–1918*. Manchester: Manchester University Press, 1994.
Mace, G.M. and A. Balmford. 'Patterns and Processes in Contemporary Mammalian Extinction'. In *Priorities for the Conservation of Mammalian Diversity: Has the Panda Had Its Day?*, edited by A. Entwistle and N. Dunstone, 28–52. Cambridge: Cambridge University Press, 2000.
Mackenzie, Helen Douglas. *Life in the Mission, the Camp, and the Zenáná, or, Six years in India*. London: Richard Bentley, 1854.
MacKenzie, John M. *Empire of Nature: Hunting, Conservation, and British Imperialism*. Manchester: Manchester University Press, 1988.
Maconochie, Evan et al. *Papers Relating to the Original Survey Settlement of 148 Government Villages of the Nandurbar Taluka (Including Navapur Petha), Shirpur and Shahada of the Khandesh Collectorate*. Bombay: Government Central Press, 1904.
Maconochie, Evan. *Life in the Indian Civil Service*. London: Chapman and Hall, 1926.

Madhusudan, M.D. and K. Ullas Karanth. 'Hunting for an Answer: Is Local Hunting Compatible with Large Mammal Conservation in India?' In *Hunting for Sustainability in Tropical Forests*, edited by John Robinson and Elizabeth Bennett, 339–355. New York: Columbia University Press, 2000.
Maffi, Luisa. 'Biocultural Diversity and Sustainability'. In *The SAGE Handbook of Environment and Society*, edited by Jules Pretty et al., 267–278. Los Angeles: SAGE, 2008.
Maffi, Luisa. *Biocultural Diversity Conservation*. London: Earthscan, 2012.
Maffi, Luisa. 'Linguistic, Cultural, and Biological Diversity'. *Annual Review of Anthropology* 34 (2005): 599–617.
Maffi, Luisa. Ed. *On Biocultural Diversity: Linking Language, Knowledge, and the Environment*. Washington, DC: Smithsonian Institution Press, 2001.
Maharatna, Arup. 'How Can "Beautiful" Be "Backward"? Tribes of India in a Long-term Demographic Perspective'. *Economic & Political Weekly* 46, no. 4 (Jan 2011): 42–52.
Mainwaring, Henry Germain. *A Soldier's Shikar Trips*. London: Grant Richards, 1920.
Majumdar, D.N. *The Fortunes of Primitive Tribes*. Lucknow: Universal Publishers, 1944.
Majumdar, D.N. 'Tribal Rehabilitation in India'. *International Social Science Bulletin: Documents on South Asia* 3, no. 4 (Winter 1951): 769–1010.
Malcolm, John. *Report on the Province of Malwa, and Adjoining Districts*. Calcutta: Government Gazette Press, 1822.
Mandala, Vijaya Ramadas. *Shooting a Tiger: Big Game Hunting and Conservation in Colonial India*. New Delhi: Oxford University Press, 2019.
Mankekar, D.R. *Accession to Extinction: The Story of the Indian Princes*. Delhi: Vikas, 1974.
Manson, Richard. 'Little White Lies of Endangerment: The Scary World of Supremacists and Separatists in the United States'. In *Perspectives on Endangerment*, edited by Graham Huggan and Stephan Klasen, 87–96. Hildesheim: Georg Olms Verlag, 2005.
Marks, Jonathan. 'The Human Genome Diversity Project: Impact on Indigenous Communities'. In *Encyclopedia of the Human Genome*, 1–4. MacMillan, 2003.
Martin, Anthony J. *Introduction to the Study of Dinosaurs*. London: Blackwell Publishing, 2005.
Martin, P.S. 'Catastrophic Extinctions and Late Pleistocene Blitzkrieg: Two Radiocarbon Tests'. In *Extinctions*, edited by M.H. Nitecki, 153–189. Chicago: University of Chicago Press, 1984.
Martinez, Dennis. 'Protected Areas, Indigenous Peoples, and The Western Idea of Nature'. *Ecological Restoration* 21, no. 4 (2003): 247–250.
Marx, Karl. *Das Kapital*, vol. 1. Moscow: Progress Publishers, 2010.
Mathew 20:16.
Maybury-Lewis, David 'Genocide of Indigenous Peoples'. In *Annihilating Difference: The Anthropology of Genocide*, edited by Alexander Laban Hinton, 43–53. Berkeley: University of California Press, 2002.
Mazower, Jonathan. 'Modi's Escalating War Against India's Forests and Tribal People'. *CounterPunch*, 31 May 2019. https://www.counterpunch.org/2019/05/31/modis-escalating-war-against-indias-forests-and-tribal-people/

Mazumdar, B.C. *The Aborigines of the Highlands of Central India*. Calcutta: University of Calcutta, 1927.
Mbembe, Achille. *Necropolitics*. Translated by Steven Corcoran. Durham: Duke University Press, 2019.
McBrien, Justin. 'This Is Not the Sixth Extinction. It's the First Extermination Event'. *Truthout*, 14 Sep 2019. https://truthout.org/articles/this-is-not-the-sixth-extinction-its-the-first-extermination-event/
McCracken, Eileen. *The Irish Woods since Tudor Times: Distribution and Exploitation*. Newton Abbot: David & Charles, 1971.
McLaughlin, Tim. 'Review of Jimmy Nelson, Before They Pass Away'. *Image on Paper*, 2 Jan 2014. http://imageonpaper.com/2014/01/02/before-they-pass-away/
Mead, Margaret and Ken Heyman. *World Enough: Rethinking the Future*. Boston: Little Brown, 1975.
Mehta, B.H. *Gonds of the Central Indian Highlands*, 2 vols. Delhi: Concept, 1984.
Mehta, B.H. 'The Problem of the Aborigines'. In *Thakkar Bapa Eightieth Birthday Commemoration Volume*, edited by T.N. Jagadisan and Shyamlal, 236–240. Madras: Diocesan Press, 1949.
Mehta, Prakash Chandra. *Changing Face of the Bhils*. Udaipur: Shiva, 1998.
Menezes, Mary. *British Policy Towards the Amerindians in British Guiana, 1803–1873*. Oxford: Clarendon Press, 1977.
Menon, Vivek. *Under Siege: Poaching and Protection of Greater One-Horned Rhinoceroses in India*. Cambridge: Traffic International, 1996.
Middleton, Townsend. 'Scheduling Tribes: A View from Inside India's Ethnographic State'. *Focaal* no. 65 (2013): 13–22.
Mina, Jagdish Chandra. *Bhil Janjati ka Sanskritik evam Arthik Jivan*. Udaipur: Himanshu, 2003.
Mishra, Suresh. *Madhya Pradesh ke Gond Rajya*. Bhopal: Madhya Pradesh Hindi Granth Academy, 2000.
Moore, J.L. et al. 'The Distribution of Cultural and Biological Diversity in Africa'. *Proceedings of the Royal Society of London* 269 (2002): 1645–1653.
Morris, P.A. *Van Ingen & Van Ingen: Artists in Taxidermy*. Ascot: MPM, 2006.
Morse, Bradford and Thomas Berger. *Sardar Sarovar: Report of the Independent Review*. Ottawa: Resource Futures International, 1992.
Mouffe, Chantal. 'Civil Society, Democratic Values and Human Rights'. In *Globality, Democracy and Civil Society*, edited by Terrell Carver and Jens Bartelson, 101. New York: Routledge, 2011.
Mühlhäusler, P. 'The Interdependence of Linguistic and Biological Diversity'. In *The Politics of Multiculturalism in the Asia/Pacific*, edited by D. Myers, 154–161. Darwin: North Territory University Press, 1995.
Munshi, Surendra. 'Tribal Absorption and Sanskritisation in Hindu Society'. *Contributions to Indian Sociology* 13, no. 2 (1979): 293–316.
Naik, Thakorlal Bharabhai. *The Bhils: A Study*. Delhi: Bharatiya Adimjati Sevak Sangh, 1956.
Narain, Sunita et al. *The Report of the Tiger Task Force: Joining the Dots*. Delhi: Union Ministry of Environment and Forests, 2005. http://projecttiger.nic.in/TTF2005/pdf/full_report.pdf

Narayanan, Dinesh. 'Forest Rights Act: How Rules Fail in the Jungle'. *Economic Times*, 1 Oct 2015. http://blogs.economictimes.indiatimes.com/it-doesnt-add-up/forest-rights-act-how-rules-fail-in-the-jungle/
Nash, Roderick Frazier. *Wilderness and the American Mind*. New Haven: Yale University Press, 1967.
*Navbharat Times*. 'Baiga Janjati ko Mila Habitat Adhikar'. 29 Dec 2015. https://navbharattimes.indiatimes.com/other/good-governance/madhya-pradesh/habitat-rights-for-baiga-tribes/articleshow/50370504.cms
Nayak, Subrat Kumar. 'Habitat Rights Under FRA'. *Vasundhara Newsletter* (Aug 2015): 6. https://www.academia.edu/15358454/Habitat_Rights_under_Forest_Rights_Act_Newsletter
Nehru, Jawaharlal. 'Foreword' in Verrier Elwin, *A Philosophy for NEFA*. Elaborated in: *Report of the Committee on Special Multipurpose Tribal Blocks*. New Delhi: Government of India, Ministry of Home Affairs, 1960.
Nehru, Jawaharlal. 'The Tribal Folk: Speech at the Opening Session of the Scheduled Tribes and Scheduled Areas Conference', New Delhi, 7 Jun 1952, *Speeches*, vol. 2, 576–583. Delhi: Government of India Publications Division, 1954.
Nehru, Jawaharlal. 'Tribal Panchsheel'. In *Report of the Third Tribal Welfare Conference Held at Jagdalpur, Bastar District (Madhya Pradesh), 13–15 March 1955*, Bharatiya Adimjati Sevak Sangh, 13–15.
Nelson, Jimmy. *Before They Pass Away*. Kempen, Germany: TeNeues, 2013.
Neumann, Roderick P. *Imposing Wilderness: Struggles Over Livelihood and Nature Preservation in Africa*. Berkeley: University of California Press, 1998.
Newkirk, Pamela. *Spectacle: The Astonishing Life of Ota Benga*. New York: Amistad, 2015.
Nietschmann, B. 'The Interdependence of Biological and Cultural Diversity'. In *Center for World Indigenous Studies Occasional Papers*, no. 21, 1–8. Olympia, WA: Center for World Indigenous Studies, 1992.
Nietzsche, Friedrich. *Morgenröthe: Gedanken über die moralischen Vorurteile*, 2nd ed. Leipzig: Verlag von E.W. Fritzsch, 1887.
Nietzsche, Friedrich. 'On the Uses and Disadvantages of History for Life'. In *Untimely Meditations*. Translated by R.J. Hollingdale, 57–123. Cambridge: Cambridge University Press, 1983.
Nilsen, Alf Gunvald. *Adivasis and the State: Subalternity and Citizenship in India's Bhil Heartland*. Cambridge: Cambridge University Press, 2018.
Nisbet, Robert. 'Idea of Progress: A Bibliographical Essay'. *Literature of Liberty: A Review of Contemporary Liberal Thought* 2, no. 1 (Jan 1979): 13–15.
Niyogi, M. Bhawani Shankar, et al. *Report of the Christian Missionary Activities Enquiry Committee, Madhya Pradesh 1956*. Nagpur: Government Printing, 1957.
Norton, David A. et al. 'Over-Collecting: An Overlooked Factor in the Decline of Plant Taxa'. *Taxon* 43 no. 2 (May 1994): 181–185.
*OED Online*. 'endangered, adj.' Oxford: Oxford University Press, 2017. http://www.oed.com/view/Entry/61876?redirectedFrom=endangered
Omvedt, Gail. 'An Open Letter to Arundhati Roy'. *Roundtable India*, 12 Jul 2011. https://roundtableindia.co.in/index.php?option=com_content&view=article&id=2671:an-open-letter-to-arundhati-roy&catid=118:thought&Itemid=131

Osborn, Henry F. and Harold E. Anthony. 'Can We Save the Mammals?' *Natural History: The Journal of the American Museum of Natural History* 22, no. 5 (Sep–Oct 1922): 388–405.

Osborn, Henry F. and Harold E. Anthony. 'Vanishing Wild Life of Southern Asia'. *Natural History: The Journal of the American Museum of Natural History* 22, no. 5 (Sep–Oct 1922): 402–403.

Ostler, Rosemarie. 'Disappearing Languages'. *Futurist* 33, no. 7 (1999): 16–22.

Oviedo, G., L. Maffi, and P.B. Larsen. *Indigenous and Traditional Peoples of the World and Ecoregion Conservation: An Integrated Approach to Conserving the World's Biological and Cultural Diversity*. Gland, Switzerland: WWF International, 2000.

Pachpore, Virag. 'The Legend Called Balasaheb Deshpande'. *Organizer*, 23 Dec 2013. http://organiser.org/Encyc/2013/12/23/The-legend-called-Balasaheb-Deshpande.aspx

Padel, Felix and Samarendra Das. 'Cultural Genocide: The Real Impact of Development-Induced Displacement'. In *India Social Development Report 2008: Development and Displacement*, edited by Hari Mohan Mathur, 103–115. Oxford: Oxford University Press, 2008).

Padel, Felix. 'How Best to Ensure Adivasis' Land, Forest and Mineral Rights?' *Institute of Development Studies Bulletin* 43, no. S1 (Jul 2012): 49–57.

Pandian, Anand. 'Predatory Care: The Imperial Hunt in Mughal and British India'. *Journal of Historical Sociology* 14 (2001): 79–107.

Pandya, Vishvajit. *In the Forest: Visual and Material Worlds of Andamanese History (1858–2006)*. Lanham, MD: University Press of America, 2009.

*Papers Relative to the Meywar Bheel Corps under the Command of Major William Hunter*. London: Acton Griffith, 1856.

Parkman, Francis. *The Oregon Trail: Sketches of Prairie and Rocky-Mountain Life*. New York: G.P. Putnam, 1849.

Parmar, Pooja. 'Undoing Historical Wrongs: Law and Indigeneity in India'. *Osgoode Hall Law Journal* 49, no. 3 (Summer 2012): 512–513.

Patel, Ashok. *Bhil Janjivan aur Sanskriti*. Bhopal: Madhya Pradesh Hindi Granth Academy, 1998.

Pearson, G.F. 'The Degeneration of Tigers'. *Indian Forester* 35 (1909): 273.

Pels, Peter. 'From Texts to Bodies: Brian Houghton Hodgson and the Emergence of Ethnology in India'. In *Anthropology and Colonialism in Asia: Comparative and Historical Colonialism*, edited by Jan van Bremen and Akitoshi Shimiz, 65–92. New York: Routledge, 2013.

Pels, Peter. 'The Rise and Fall of the Indian Aborigines'. In *Colonial Subjects: Essays on the Practical History of Anthropology*, edited by Peter Pels and Oscar Salemink, 82–116. Ann Arbor: University of Michigan Press, 1999.

Pester, John. *War and Sport in India 1802–1806, an Officer's Diary*. London: Heath, Cranton & Ouseley, 1913.

Peters, Hans Peter. 'Gap Between Science and Media Revisited: Scientists as Public Communicators'. *Proceedings of the National Academy of Science USA* 110, Suppl. 3 (2013): 14102–14109.

Petras, James. 'NGOs: In the Service of Imperialism'. *Journal of Contemporary Asia* 29, no. 4 (1999): 429–440.

Philip, Kavita. *Civilizing Natures: Race, Resources, and Modernity in Colonial South India*. New Delhi: Orient Longman, 2003.
Phillips, Tom. 'No, Redheads Are Not in Danger of Going Extinct'. *BuzzFeed*, 9 Jul 2014. https://www.buzzfeed.com/tomphillips/gingergeddon-is-cancelled
Pinney, Roy. *Vanishing Tribes*. London: Arthur Baker, 1968.
Pinney, Roy. *Vanishing Wildlife*. New York: Dodd, Mead, 1963.
Pocock, R.I. *Fauna of British India: Including Ceylon and Burma*, vol. 1. London: Taylor & Francis, 1939.
Pohl, Greg R. 'Why We Kill Bugs—The Case for Collecting Insects'. *Ontario Lepidoptera* 7 (2008): 7-15.
Pollock, Steve. *Atlas of Endangered Peoples*. New York: Facts on File, 1995.
Possey, Darrell A. 'Biological and Cultural Diversity: The Inextricable, Linked by Languages and Politics'. In *On Biocultural Diversity: Linking Language, Knowledge, and the Environment*, edited by Luisa Maffi, 379-396. Washington, DC: Smithsonian Institution Press, 2001.
Powell, Miles A. *Vanishing America: Species Extinction, Racial Peril, and the Origins of Conservation*. Cambridge: Harvard University Press, 2016.
Pranvendra, Sangeeta. 'Bhil Tribals Forge Political Unity, Give BJP, Congress Jitters in Several States; Community Alleges Neglect from Govt'. *Firstpost*, 4 May 2019. https://www.firstpost.com/politics/bhil-tribals-forge-political-unity-give-bjp-congress-jitters-in-several-states-community-alleges-neglect-from-govt-6572111.html
Prasad, Archana. *Against Ecological Romanticism: Verrier Elwin and the Making of an Anti-Modern Tribal Identity*. Delhi: Three Essays Collective, 2003.
Prasad, Archana. 'The Baiga: Survival Strategies and Local Economy in the Central Provinces'. *Studies in History* 14, no. 2 (1998): 325-348.
Pretty, Jules. *The Edge of Extinction: Travels with Enduring People in Vanishing Lands*. Ithaca, NY: Cornell University Press, 2014.
Price, Samantha A. and John L. Gittleman. 'Hunting to Extinction: Biology and Regional Economy Influence Extinction Risk and the Impact of Hunting in Artiodactyls'. *Proceedings of the Royal Society B* 274 (2007): 1845-1851.
Prichard, James C. 'On the Extinction of Human Races'. *Monthly Chronicle* (1839): 497.
Qureshi, Sadiah. *Peoples on Parade: Exhibitions, Empire, and Anthropology in Nineteenth-Century Britain*. Chicago: University of Chicago Press, 2011.
Rampino, Michael R. and Shu-Zhong Shen. 'The End-Guadalupian (259.8 Ma) Biodiversity Crisis: The Sixth Major Mass Extinction?' *Historical Biology* 33, no. 5 (2021): 716-722.
Rangarajan, Mahesh. *Fencing the Forest: Conservation and Ecological Change in India's Central Provinces, 1860-1914*. Delhi: Oxford University Press, 1996.
Rangarajan, Mahesh. *India's Wildlife History: An Introduction*. Delhi: Permanent Black, 2001.
Rangarajan, Mahesh. 'The Raj and the Natural World: The War Against "Dangerous Beasts" in Colonial India'. *Studies in History* 14, no. 2 (Jul-Dec 1998): 265-299.
Ranjan, Rakesh. '"We Cannot Pollute Our Surroundings": Madhya Pradesh's Deprived Baiga Tribe Is Learning to Survive Outside Forests After Being Evicted from Kanha National Park'. *Daily Mail*, 12 Jun 2016. http://www.dailymail.co.uk/indiahome/indianews/article-3636991/We-pollute-surroundings-Madhya-

Pradesh-s-deprived-Baiga-tribe-learning-survive-outside-forest-evicted-Kanha-National-Park.html

Rashkow, Ezra. 'Dispossessing Memory: Adivasi Oral Histories from the Margins of Pachmarhi Biosphere Reserve, Central India'. In *Memory, Identity and the Colonial Encounter in India: Essays in Honor of Peter Robb*, edited by Ezra Rashkow, Sanjukta Ghosh, and Upal Chakrabarty, 151–175. New York: Routledge, 2017.

Rashkow, Ezra. 'Idealizing Inhabited Wilderness: A Revision to the History of Indigenous Peoples in National Parks'. *History Compass* 12, no. 10 (2014): 818–832.

Rashkow, Ezra. 'Making Subaltern Shikaris: Histories of the Hunted in Colonial Central India'. *South Asian History and Culture* 5, no. 3 (2014): 292–313.

Rashkow, Ezra. 'Wilding the Domestic: Camp Servants and Glamping in British India'. *Indian Economic & Social History Review* 58, no. 3 (2021): 361–391.

Reddy, P.H. and B. Modell. 'The Baigas of Madhya Pradesh: A Demographic Study'. *Journal of Biosocial Science* 1 (29 Jan 1997): 19–31.

Redford, Kent H. 'The Ecologically Noble Savage'. *Orion Nature Quarterly* 9, no. 3 (1990): 25–29.

Reid, Walter V. and Kenton R. Miller. *Keeping Options Alive: The Scientific Basis for the Conservation of Biodiversity*. Washington, DC: World Resources Institute, 1989.

Reining, Priscilla. 'Urgent Research Projects'. *Current Anthropology* 8, no. 4 (Oct 1967): 362–416.

Remsen, J.V. 'The Importance of Continued Collecting of Bird Specimens to Ornithology and Bird Conservation'. *Bird Conservation International* 5, no. 2–3 (1995): 146–180.

*Report of the Commission for Scheduled Tribes and Scheduled Castes*. Delhi: Government of India, 1990.

*Report of the Ethnological Committee on Papers Laid Before Them and Upon Examination of Specimens of Aboriginal Tribes Brought to the Jubbulpore Exhibition of 1866-67*. Nagpore: M. Lawler, 1868.

*Report of the Parliamentary Select Committee on Aboriginal Tribes*. London: W. Ball, A. Chambers, Hatchard & Son, 1837.

Reynolds, Henry. *Fate of a Free People*. Camberwell: Penguin, 2004.

Rice, William. *Tiger-Shooting in India: Being an Account of Hunting Experiences on Foot in Rajpootana, During the Hot Seasons, from 1850 to 1854*. London: Smith, Elder, 1857.

Richards, Robert J. and Lorraine Daston, eds. *Kuhn's Structure of Scientific Revolutions at Fifty: Reflections on a Science Classic*. Chicago: University of Chicago Press, 2016.

Richardson, John. *A Dictionary, Persian, Arabic, and English*, vol. 1. Oxford: Clarendon Press, 1777.

Risley, H.H. 'The Study of Ethnology in India'. *Journal of the Anthropological Institute of Great Britain and Ireland* 20 (1891): 235–263.

Ritchie, James. *The Influence of Man on Animal Life in Scotland: A Study in Faunal Evolution*. Cambridge: Cambridge University Press, 1920.

Rittel, Horst and Webber, Melvin. 'Dilemmas in a General Theory of Planning'. *Policy Sciences* 4 (1973): 155–169.

Ritvo, Harriet. *The Animal Estate: The English and Other Creatures in the Victorian Age*. Cambridge, MA: Harvard University Press, 1987.

Roberts, Leslie. 'A Genetic Survey of Vanishing Peoples'. *Science* 252 (1991): 1614–1617.

Robertson, William and Dugald Stewart. *The Works of William Robertson, D.D.*, vol. 10. London: Cadell and Davies, 1817.
Rogers, Brudenell. 'The Destruction of Human Life and Property in India by Noxious Wild Animals'. London: W. Wilfred Head, 1873.
Rosaldo, Renato. 'Imperialist Nostalgia'. *Representations* 26 (Spring 1989): 107–122.
Rose, Deborah Bird. *Wild Dog Dreaming: Love and Extinction*. Charlottesville: University of Virginia Press, 2011.
Rothman, Hal. 'Review of Green Imperialism: Colonial Expansion, Tropical Island Edens and the Origins of Environmentalism, 1600–1860, by R. H. Grove'. *Environmental History* 1, no. 1 (1996): 112–113.
Rousseau, Jean-Jacques. *Discourse on the Origin of Inequality*. Translated by Donald A Cress. Cambridge: Hackett, 1992.
Roy, Arundhati. 'The Greater Common Good'. *Outlook India*, 24 May 1999.
Roy, Sarat Chandra. 'The Aborigines of Chota Nagpur. Their Proper Status in the Reformed Constitution of India'. *Man in India* 26, no. 2 (1946): 120–136.
Roy, Sarat Chandra. *The Birhors: A Little-known Jungle Tribe of Chota Nagpur*. Ranchi: Mission Press, 1925.
Roy, Sarat Chandra. 'The Effect on the Aborigines of Chotanagpur of Their Contact with Western Civilization'. *Journal of the Bihar and Orissa Research Society* 17, no. 4 (1931): 358–394.
Rudman, F.R.S. *Mandla District Gazetteer*, vol. A. Bombay: Times Press, 1912.
Runte, Alfred. *National Parks: The American Experience*. Lincoln: University of Nebraska Press, 1979.
Ruse, Michael. *The Darwinian Revolution: Science Read in Tooth and Claw*. Chicago: University of Chicago Press, 1979.
Rushdie, Salman. 'The Firebird's Nest'. *New Yorker*, 23 Jun 1997.
Russell, R.V. *Central Provinces Gazetteer: Imperial Gazetteer of India*, vol. 10. Calcutta: Government Printing, 1908.
Russell, R.V. and Hira Lal. *The Tribes and Castes of the Central Provinces of India*. London: Macmillan, 1916.
Schaller, George. *The Deer and the Tiger*. Chicago: University Press, 1972.
Saha, Suranjit Kumar. 'Historical Premises of India's Tribal Problem'. *Journal of Contemporary Asia* 16, no. 3 (Jan 1, 1986): 274–319.
Said, Edward W. *Beginnings: Intention and Method*. New York: Basic Books, 1975.
Said, Edward W. *Orientalism*. New York: Pantheon Books, 1978.
Salt, Henry S., ed. *Killing for Sports*. London: G. Bell, 1915.
Sanderson, G.P. *Thirteen Years among the Wild Beasts of India: Their Haunts and Habits*. London: Wm. H. Allen, 1878.
Sankhala, Kailash. *Tiger! The Story of the Indian Tiger*. Delhi: Rupa, 1978.
Sanyal, S. 'Primitive Tribes of Bihar: Strategy for Development'. *Man in India* 68, no. 4 (1988): 356–368.
Sarasin, Paul. *Über die Aufgaben des Weltnaturschutzes: Denkschrift gelesen an der Delegiertenversammlung zur Weltnaturschutzkommission in Bern am 18. November 1913*. Basel: Helbing & Lichtenhahn, 1914.
Saraswati, Dayananda. *Gokarunanidhi: Ocean of Mercy for the Cow*. Lahore: Virajanand Press, 1889.

Saussure, Ferdinand de, *Saussure's First Course of Lectures on General Linguistics, 1907: From the Notebooks of Albert Riedlinger/Premier cours de linguistique general, 1907: d'après les cahiers d'Albert Riedlinger*. Oxford: Pergamon, 1996.
Schaller, George. *The Deer and the Tiger*. Chicago: University Press, 1972.
Schleiter, Markus. 'Enduring Endangerments: Constructing the Birhor "Tribe", Development Officers and Anthropologists from Early Twentieth-Century Colonial India to the Present'. In *Perspectives on Endangerment*, edited by Graham Huggan and Stephan Klasen, 73–84. Hildesheim: Georg Olms Verlag, 2005.
Scott, James C. *Seeing Like a State: How Certain Schemes to Improve the Human Condition Have Failed*. New Haven: Yale University Press, 1998.
Sen, Satadru. *Savagery and Colonialism in the Indian Ocean: Power, Pleasure and the Andaman Islanders*. New York: Routledge, 2010.
Sepkoski, David. *Catastrophic Thinking: Extinction and the Value of Diversity from Darwin to the Anthropocene*. Chicago: University of Chicago Press, 2020.
Sepkoski, David. 'Extinction, Diversity, and Endangerment'. In *Endangerment, Biodiversity and Culture*, edited by Fernando Vidal and Nélia Dias, 62–86. New York: Routledge, 2016.
Seton-Karr, Henry. 'The Preservation of Big Game'. *Journal of the Society for the Preservation of the Wild Fauna of Empire* 4 (1908): 26.
Sharma, Asavari Raj. 'The "Other" in the Forest Rights Act Has Been Ignored for Years'. *Wire*, 1 Jul 2018. https://thewire.in/rights/the-other-in-the-forest-rights-act-has-been-ignored-for-years
Sharma, Susash Sumanta Sarathi. 'Baiga Tribe: Are They on the Verge of Extinction?' *Times of India*, 24 Oct 2014. http://ww.itimes.com/poll/baiga-tribe-are-they-on-the-verge-of-extinction/result
Shorey, C.J. 'Shikar Tales'. *Journal of the Bengal Natural History Society* 20, no. 3 (Jan 1946): 87.
Shoobert, W.H. *Census of India 1931: Central Provinces & Berar, Part I—Report*, vol. 12. Nagpur: Government Printing, 1933.
Sikaligar, Punamchand. *Van evam Adivasi Samajik Jivan*. Udaipur: Shiva, 1994.
Sikand, Yoginder. 'Simple Ways of Life'. *Deccan Herald*, 23 Dec 2012. https://www.deccanherald.com/content/300193/simple-ways-life.html
Silver Hackle [pseud]. *Indian Jungle Lore and the Rifle. Being Notes on Shikar and Wild Animal Life*. Calcutta: Thacker, 1929.
Simcox, Arthur Henry A. *A Memoir of the Khandesh Bhil Corps, 1825–1891: Compiled from Original Records*. Bombay: Thacker, 1912.
Simon, John Allsebrook. *Report of the Indian Statutory Commission*, 3 vols. London: His Majesty's Stationery Office, 1930.
Simson, Frank B. *Letters on Sport in Eastern Bengal*. London: R.H. Porter, 1886.
Singh, Amarjeet. 'Baiga Olympics: Tribal Spirit, Tradition & Mahua'. *Times of India*, 5 Apr 2015. http://timesofindia.indiatimes.com/city/bhopal/Baiga-Olympics-Tribal-spirit-tradition-mahua/articleshow/46810933.cms
Singh, K.S. 'G.S. Ghurye, Verrier Elwin, and Indian Tribes'. In *The Legacy of G.S. Ghurye: A Centennial Festschrift*, edited by A.R. Momin, 39–46. Bombay: Popular Prakashan, 1996.
Singh, Kesri. *Hints on Tiger Shooting*. Bombay: Jaico Publishing House, 1969.

Singh, S. Harpal. 'Is Gond Culture Fading into Oblivion?' *The Hindu*, 4 Nov 2010. http://www.thehindu.com/todays-paper/tp-national/tp-andhrapradesh/Is-Gond-culture-fading-into-oblivion/article15675160.ece

Singh, S. Harpal. 'Knowledge System of Tribal People Faces Extinction'. *The Hindu*, 6 Apr 2015. http://www.thehindu.com/news/national/telangana/knowledge-system-of-tribal-people-faces-extinction/article7072372.ece

Sinha-Kerkhoff, Kathinka. 'Voices of Difference: Partition Memory and Memories of Muslims in Jharkhand, India'. *Critical Asian Studies* 36, no. 1 (2004): 113–142.

Sinha, A.C. 'Colonial Anthropology vs. Indological Sociology: Elwin and Ghurye on Tribal Policy in India'. In *Between Ethnography and Fiction: Verrier Elwin and the Tribal Question in India,* edited by T.B. Subba and Sujit Som, 71–85. Delhi: Orient BlackSwan, 2005.

Sinha, Kirtyanand. *Shikar in Hills and Jungles*. Calcutta: Newman, 1934.

Sinha, Subir, Shubhra Gururani, and Brian Greenberg. 'The "New Traditionalist" Discourse of Indian Environmentalism'. *Journal of Peasant Studies* 24, no. 3 (1997): 65–99.

Sinha, Surajit. 'State Formation and Rajput Myth in Tribal Central India'. *Man in India* 42, no. 1 (1962): 36.

Sinha, Surajit. 'Tribe-Caste and Tribe-Peasant Continua in Central India'. *Man in India* 45, no. 1 (1965): 57–83.

Skaria, Ajay. *Hybrid Histories: Forests, Frontiers, and Wildness in Western India*. Delhi: Oxford University Press, 1999.

Skaria, Ajay. 'Shades of Wildness: Tribe, Caste, and Gender in Western India'. *Journal of Asian Studies* 56, no. 3 (1997): 726–745.

Skaria, Ajay. 'Writing, Orality and Power in the Dangs, Western India, 1800s–1920s'. In *Subaltern Studies* 9, edited by Dipesh Chakrabarty and Shahid Amin, 13–58. Oxford: Oxford University Press, 1996.

Sleeman, W.H. *Rambles and Recollections of an Indian Official*, vol. 1. London: Archibald Constable, 1893 [1844].

Smith, Brian. 'Eaters, Food, and Hierarchy in Ancient India: A Dietary Guide to a Revolution of Values'. *Journal of the American Academy of Religion* 58, no. 2 (1990): 177–205.

'Smithsonian-Wenner-Gren Conference'. *Current Anthropology* 8, no. 4 (Oct 1967): 355–361.

Smythies, Evelyn Arthur. *Big Game Shooting in Nepal*. Calcutta: Thacker, Spink, 1942.

Sonavane, Waharu. 'Stage'. In *Godhad*. Translated by Bharat Patankar, Gail Omvedt, and Suhas Paranjape, 35. Pune: Sugava Prakashan, 1987.

Sonntag, Selma K. 'Self-Government, Indigeneity and Cultural Authenticity: A Comparative Study of India and the United States'. In *Indigeneity in India*, edited by B.T. Karlsson and T.B. Subba, 190–191. London: Kegan Paul, 2006.

Sontag, Susan. 'Notes on "Camp"'. In *Against Interpretation and Other Essays*, 275–292. New York: Farrar, Straus & Giroux, 1966.

Sousa, Ashley Riley. '"They Will be Hunted Down Like Wild Beasts and Destroyed!": A Comparative Study of Genocide in California and Tasmania'. *Journal of Genocide Research* 6, no. 2 (Jun 2004): 193—209.

Sparks, Jared, ed. *The Writings of George Washington: Being His Correspondence, Addresses, Messages and Other Papers, Official and Private, Selected and Published from the Original Manuscripts*, vol. 8. Boston: Ferdinand Andrews, 1839.

Spence, Mark David. *Dispossessing the Wilderness: Indian Removal, National Parks, and the Preservationist Ideal*. New York: Oxford University Press, 1999.

Spencer, Herbert. *Social Statics*. London: John Chapman, 1851.

Spiro, Jonathan. *Defending the Master Race: Conservation, Eugenics, and the Legacy of Madison Grant*. Burlington: University of Vermont Press, 2009.

Srinivas, M.N. 'A Note on Sanskritization and Westernization'. *Far Eastern Quarterly* 15, no. 4 (Aug 1956): 481–496.

Srinivas, M. N. *Social Change in Modern India*. Bombay: Allied Publishers, 1966.

Srivastava, Vinay Kumar and Sukant K. Chaudhury. 'Anthropological Studies of Indian Tribes'. In *Sociology and Social Anthropology in India*, edited by Yogesh Atal, 50–119. Delhi: Pearson Education India, 2009.

Staffner, Hans. *Baba Amte: A Vision of New India*. Delhi: Popular Prakashan, 2000.

Stanyan, Abraham, *An Account of Switzerland: Written in the Year 1714*. London: Jacob Tonson, 1714.

Stewart, Arthur Easdale. *Tiger and Other Game: The Practical Experiences of a Soldier Shikari in India*. London: Longmans, 1927.

Stocking, George. 'On the Limits of 'Presentism' and 'Historicism' in the Historiography of the Behavioral Sciences'. *Journal of the History of the Behavioral Sciences* 1, no. 3 (1965): 211–218.

Stracey, P.D. *Wild Life in India: Its Conservation and Control*. New Delhi: Department of Agriculture, 1963.

Subba, T.B. and Sujit Som, eds. *Between Ethnography and Fiction: Verrier Elwin and the Tribal Question in India*. Delhi: Orient Longman, 2005.

Suckling, K. Anim. 'A House on Fire: Linking the Biological and Linguistic Diversity Crises'. *Animal Law Review* 6 (2000): 93–202.

Sutherland, John. *Original Matter Contained in Lieut.-Colonel Sutherland's Memoir on the Kaffers, Hottentot, and Bosjemans of Southern Africa*. Cape Town: Pike & Philip, 1847.

Sutherland, William J. 'Parallel Extinction Risk and Global Distribution of Languages and Species'. *Nature* 423 (15 May 2003): 276–279.

Sysling, Fenneke. '"Protecting the Primitive Natives": Indigenous People as Endangered Species in the Early Nature Protection Movement, 1900–1940'. *Environment and History* 21, no. 3 (2015): 381–399.

Talbot, Lee Merriam. *A Look at Threatened Species: A Report on Some Animals of the Middle East and Southern Asia Which Are Threatened with Extermination*. London: Fauna Preservation Society, 1960.

Thakkar, A.V. 'The Problem of the Aborigines'. Poona: R.R. Kale Memorial Lecture, Gokhale Institute of Politics and Economics, Sep 1941.

Thakur, Vikramaditya. 'Learning and Leading: Resistance, Subaltern Leadership and the Making of Two Bhil Community Leaders from the Narmada Valley, Western India'. *South Asia Multidisciplinary Academic Journal* 21 (2019): 1–19. http://journals.openedition.org/samaj/5661

Thapar, Valmik. *Battling for Survival: India's Wilderness Over Two Centuries*. New Delhi: Oxford University Press, 2003.

Thapar, Valmik. *Saving Wild Tigers, 1900–2000: The Essential Writings*. New Delhi: Permanent Black, 2001.
Thapar, Valmik. *Tiger: Portrait of a Predator*. London: Collins, 1986.
*The Indian's Friend*. 'The Indian Association' 16, no. 2 (Oct 1903), 2.
*The Modern Part of an Universal History*, vol. 4. London: S. Richardson, etc., 1759.
*The Parliamentary Register: Or, History of the Proceedings and Debates of the House of Commons*, vol. 37. London: J. Debrett, 1794.
*The Portfolio: A Collection of State Papers*. London: F. Shoberl, 1836.
*The Times*. 'Dr. A.R. Wallace on Darwinism'. 23 Jan 1909.
*The Times*. 'Fauna of the Empire'. 28 Dec 1939.
Thompson, E.P. *Whigs and Hunters: The Origin of the Black Act*. London: Allen Lane, 1975.
Thompson, Liz and Simon Coate. *Fighting for Survival: The Bhils of Rajasthan*. Melbourne: Reed Education, 1997.
Thomson, W.B. *Report on the Land Revenue Settlement of the Seonee District, on the [sic] Central Provinces*. Bombay: Education Society's Press, 1867.
Thoreau, Henry David. *The Maine Woods*. Cambridge: Harvard, 1884.
Thornton, Russell. *American Indian Holocaust and Survival: A Population History Since 1492*. University of Oklahoma Press, 1987.
Tivari, Shiv Kumar. *Madhya Pradesh ki Janjati Sanskriti*. Bhopal: Madhya Pradesh Hindi Granth Academy, 2005.
Tod, James. *Annals and Antiquities of Rajasthan: or the Central and Western Rajput States of India*, 3 vols. 2nd ed. Madras: Higginbotham, 1873.
Todd, Zoe. 'Indigenizing the Anthropocene'. *Art in the Anthropocene: Encounters Among Aesthetics, Politics, Environments and Epistemologies*, edited by Etienne Turpin and Heather Davis, 241–254. Open Humanities Press, 2015.
Totten, Samuel, William S. Parsons, and Robert K. Hitchcock, 'Confronting Genocide and Ethnocide of Indigenous Peoples an Interdisciplinary Approach to Definition, Intervention, Prevention, and Advocacy'. In *Annihilating Difference: The Anthropology of Genocide*, edited by Alexander Laban Hinton, 54–93. Berkeley: University of California, 2002.
Totten, Samuel. ' "Genocide", Frivolous Use of the Term'. *Encyclopedia of Genocide*, edited by Israel W. Charny et al., 35–36. Santa Barbara: ABC-CLIO, 1999.
Trautmann, Thomas R. *Aryans and British India*. Berkeley: University of California Press, 1997.
Travers, Robert. *The Tasmanians; The Story of a Doomed Race*. Melbourne: Cassell Australia, 1968.
Trevelyan, G.M. *English Social History*. London: Longmans, Green, 1942.
Trivedi, Divya. 'Like Tiger, like Tribal', *The Hindu*, 9 Feb 2013. www.thehindu.com/news/national/other-states/like-tiger-like-tribal/article4389793.ece
Trotter, Lionel James. *The History of the British Empire in India: From the Appointment of Lord Hardinge to the Political Extinction of the East-India Company, 1844 to 1862*. London: W.H. Allen, 1866.
Turnbull, Clive. *Black War: The Extermination of the Tasmanian Aborigines*. Melbourne: Cheshire-Lansdowne, 1948.
Upadhya, Carol. 'The Hindu Nationalist Sociology of GS Ghurye'. *Sociological Bulletin* 51, no. 1 (2002): 27–56.

Vanita, Ruth. 'Gandhi's Tiger: Multilingual Elites, the Battle for Minds, and English Romantic Literature in Colonial India'. *Postcolonial Studies* 5, no. 1 (2002): 95–110.

Velho, Nandini Krithi K. Karanth, and William F. Laurance. 'Hunting: A Serious and Understudied Threat in India, a Globally Significant Conservation Region'. *Biological Conservation* 148 (2012): 210–215.

Venkatesan, D. 'Ecocide or Genocide? The Onge in the Andaman Islands'. *Cultural Survival Quarterly* 14, no. 4 (Dec 1990): 49–51. www.culturalsurvival.org/ourpublications/csq/article/ecocide-or-genocide-the-onge-andaman-islands

Verghese, Boobli G. 'A Poetic License'. *Outlook India*, 5 Jul 1999. https://www.outlookindia.com/magazine/story/a-poetic-licence/207723

Verghese, Boobli G. 'Sardar Sarovar Project Revalidated by Supreme Court'. *International Journal of Water Resources Development* 17, no. 1 (2001): 79–88.

Vidyarthi, Lalita Prasad and Binay Kumar Rai, *The Tribal Culture of India*. Delhi: Concept, 1976.

Vidyarthi, Lalita Prasad. 'Conference on Urgent Social Research in India'. *Current Anthropology* 10, no. 4 (Oct 1969): 377–379.

Viren, Sarah. 'The Native Scholar Who Wasn't'. *New York Times*, 25 May 2021. https://www.nytimes.com/2021/05/25/magazine/cherokee-native-american-andrea-smith.html

W. 'Tigers'. *Journal of the National Indian Association in Aid of Social Progress in India*, no. 14 (Oct 1873): 442.

Wakefield, W. *Our Life and Travels in India*. London: Sampson Low, 1878.

Walker, Henry. *Saturday Afternoon Rambles Round London: Rural and Geological* (London: Hodder and Stoughton, 1871.

Walker, Ruth. 'Is the Paragraph an Endangered Species?' *Christian Science Monitor*, 11 Jun 2015. https://www.csmonitor.com/The-Culture/Verbal-Energy/2015/0611/Is-the-paragraph-an-endangered-species

Warren, Louis S. *Buffalo Bill's America*. New York: Knopf Doubleday, 2007.

Weber, George H.J. *Lonely Islands: The Andamanese*. Liestal, Switzerland: The Andaman Association, 1998.

Weber, Thomas. 'Gandhi, Deep Ecology, Peace Research and Buddhist Economics'. *Journal of Peace Research* 36, no. 3 (May 1999): 349–361.

Weeks, Pris and Shalina Mehta. 'Managing People and Landscapes: IUCN's Protected Area Categories'. *Journal of Human Ecology* 16, no. 4 (2004): 253–263.

Weiss, Gerald. 'The Tragedy of Ethnocide: A Reply to Hippler'. *American Anthropologist* 83, no. 4 (Dec 1981): 899–900.

Weslager, Clinton Alfred. *The Delaware Indians: A History*. New Brunswick: Rutgers University Press, 1989.

Western Bhil Agency. *Annual Reports on the Working of the Western Bhil Agency*. Bombay: Government Central Press, 1875–1905.

White, Hayden. *Tropics of Discourse: Essays in Cultural Criticism*. Baltimore: Johns Hopkins University Press, 1978.

Whitehead, Judith. 'Submerged and Submerging Voices: Hegemony and the Decline of the Narmada Bachao Andolan in Gujarat, 1998–2001'. *Critical Asian Studies* 39, no. 3 (2007): 339–421.

Whitehead, Judith. 'The Bhils'. In *Disappearing Peoples? Indigenous Groups and Ethnic Minorities in South and Central Asia*, edited by Barbara Brower and Barbara Rose Johnston, 73–90. Walnut Creek, CA: Left Coast Press, 2007.

Wilkinson, T.S. 'Isolation, Assimilation and Integration in Historical Perspective'. *Bulletin of the Tribal Research Institute, Chhindwara*, M.P. 2, no. 1 (Jun 1962): 19–28.

Willcocks, James. *The Romance of Soldiering and Sport*. London: Cassell, 1925.

Williams Jr, Robert A. 'Encounters on the Frontiers of International Human Rights Law: Redefining the Terms of Indigenous Peoples' Survival in the World'. *Duke Law Journal* 1990, no. 4 (Sep 1990): 660–665.

Wilson, Edward O., ed. *Biodiversity*. Washington, DC: National Academy Press, 1988.

Wilson, Edward O. *The Diversity of Life*. Cambridge, MA: Belknap Press, 1992.

Wöbse, Anna-Katharina. 'Paul Sarasins "anthropologischer Naturschutz": Zur "Größe" Mensch im frühen internationalen Naturschutz: Ein Werkstattbericht'. In *Naturschutz und Demokratie!?*, edited by Gert Gröning and Joachim Wolschke-Bulmahn, 207–214. München: Martin Meidenbauer, 2006.

Wöbse, Anna-Katharina. '"The World After All was One": The International Environmental Network of UNESCO and IUPN, 1945–1950'. *Contemporary European History* 20, no. 3 (2011): 331–348.

Wolf, Cary. 'Foreword'. In *Extinction Studies: Stories of Time, Death, and Generations*, edited by Deborah Bird Rose, Thom van Dooren, and Matthew Chrulew, vii–xvi. New York: Columbia University Press, 2017.

Woodyatt, Nigel. *My Sporting Memories: Forty Years with Note-book & Gun*. London: Herbert Jenkins, 1923.

World Commission on Dams. *Dams and Development: A New Framework for Decision-Making: The Report of the World Commission on Dams*. London: Earthscan, 2000.

Wright, Glen W. 'NGOs and Western Hegemony: Causes for Concern and Ideas for Change'. *Development in Practice* 22, no. 1 (2012): 123–134.

Xaxa, Virginius. 'Tribes as Indigenous People of India'. *Economic & Political Weekly* 34, no. 51 (18–24 Dec 1999): 3589–3595.

Young, Robert. *Postcolonialism: An Historical Introduction*. Oxford: Blackwell, 2001.

Yule, Henry, and Arthur Coke Burnell. *Hobson-Jobson: Being a Glossary of Anglo-Indian Colloquial Words and Phrases and of Kindred Terms Etymological, Historical, Geographical and Discursive*. London: John Murray, 1886.

Zachariah, Benjamin. 'A Voluntary Gleichschaltung? Indian Perspectives Towards a Non-Eurocentric Understanding of Fascism'. *Journal of Transcultural Studies* 5, no. 2 (2014): 63–100.

Zachariah, Benjamin. 'At the Fuzzy Edges of Fascism: Framing the Volk in India'. *South Asia: Journal of South Asian Studies* 38, no. 4 (2015): 639–655.

Zinkin, Maurice. 'From Revolt to Love'. In *Sahibs who Loved India*, edited by Khushwant Singh, 124–134. Delhi: Penguin, 2008.

## D. Conferences & Unpublished Papers

Anon. 'Community Conservation in South Asia: An Annotated Bibliography' http://www.umich.edu/~infosrn/CICB/CICB_SA1.doc

Davis, Wade. 'Dreams from Endangered Cultures', TED Talks, 2003. https://www.ted.com/talks/wade_davis_on_endangered_cultures/

Kari-Oca Declaration. 'The Indigenous Peoples' Earth Charter'. In *World Conference of Indigenous Peoples on Territory, Environment and Development*, 25–30. 1992, Kari-Oca.

Kothari, Ashish. 'Radical Ecological Democracy / EcoSwaraj'. Economics of Happiness Gathering, Florence, Italy, 2 Oct 2016. https://youtu.be/SG0uarfxmv4

Kumar, V.M. Ravi. 'Multiple Voices: Evolution of Colonial Forest Policies in Madras Presidency, an Enquiry into Ideas and Legal Discourses, 1800–1882'. Conference on Livelihoods, Environment, and History at Calcutta University, Mar 2005.

McGregor, Russell. 'The Aboriginal Reserves Debate of the Inter-War Years', *Journal of the Royal Historical Society of Queensland* 15, no. 11 (1995): 545–552..

Pretty, Jules et al. 'How Do Biodiversity and Culture Intersect?' Plenary Paper for Conference on 'Sustaining Cultural and Biological Diversity in a Rapidly Changing World: Lessons for Global Policy'. American Museum of Natural History, New York, 2–5 Apr 2008. https://www.amnh.org/research/center-for-biodiversity-conservation/convening-and-connecting/2008-biocultural-diversity

Thakur, Vikramaditya. 'Merchants of Mobilization: Representing Anti-dam and Resettlement Claims in Western India'. *Agrarian Crisis Conference*, Cornell University, 5–6 Apr 2013.

Woof, Jonathan. 'Indigeneity and Development in Botswana: The Case of the San in the Central Kalahari Game Reserve'. *IDGS—Research Papers*. University of Ottawa, 2014. https://ruor.uottawa.ca/handle/10393/32350

# E. Dissertations

Chattopadhyay, Sutapa. 'Involuntary Migration and the Mechanisms of Rehabilitation: The Discourses of Development in Sardar Sarovar, India'. PhD diss., Kent State University, 2006.

Dongol, Yogesh. 'Cultural Politics of Community-Based Conservation in the Buffer Zone of Chitwan National Park, Nepal'. PhD diss., Florida International University, 2018.

Martini, Elspeth. 'The Tides of Morality: Anglo-American Colonial Authority and Indigenous Removal, 1820–1848'. PhD diss., University of Michigan, 2013.

McDuie-Ra, Duncan. 'Civil Society and Human Security in Meghalaya: Identity, Power and Inequalities'. PhD diss., University of New South and Wales, 2007.

McEldowney, Philip. 'Colonial Administration and Social Developments in Middle India: The Central Provinces, 1861–1921'. PhD diss., University of Virginia, 1980.

Sills, Mark Allan. 'Ethnocide and Interaction Between States and Indigenous Nations: A Conceptual Investigation of Three Cases in Mexico'. PhD diss., University of Denver, 1992.

Thakur, Vikramaditya. 'Unsettling Modernity: Resistance and Forced Resettlement Due to a Dam in Western India'. PhD diss., Yale University, 2014.

## F. Non-Government & Web Documents

Agrawal, Arun et al., 'An Open Letter to the Lead Authors of "Protecting 30% of the Planet for Nature: Costs, Benefits and Implications"', 12 Jan 2021. https://openlettertowaldronetal.wordpress.com/

American Museum of Natural History, 'Northwest Coast Hall'. https://www.amnh.org/exhibitions/permanent/northwest-coast

Basu, Moushumi. 'What Happens When the Needs of Endangered Tigers and Endangered People Collide?' *Ensia*, 2 Aug 2016. https://ensia.com/features/endangered-tigers-endangered-people-collide-central-india/

Bosshard, Peter. 'New Independent Review Documents Failure of Narmada River Dam'. *World Rivers Review: Special Focus on River Restoration*. Oakland, CA: International Rivers, 15 Dec 2008. http://web.archive.org/web/20140910090656/https://www.internationalrivers.org/resources/new-independent-review-documents-failure-of-narmada-river-dam-1806

Corbett National Park, 'About Edward James Jim Corbett'. http://www.corbett-national-park.co.in/About-Edward-James-Jim-Corbett.html

Headland, Thomas N. 'An Open Letter to the Government of India Concerning the Human Rights Situation of the Jarawa Tribal Minority in the Andaman Islands', 13 Jul 1999. http://www-01.sil.org/~headlandt/jarawa.htm

International Union for Conservation of Nature [IUCN] Red List of Threatened Species. <www.iucnredlist.org>.

International Work Group for Indigenous Affairs [IWGIA], 'India'. https://www.iwgia.org/en/india.html

Kawasaki, Ken and Visakha Kawasaki, eds. 'Jataka Tales of the Buddha: Part III'. Kandy, Sri Lanka: Buddhist Publication Society, 1998. http://www.accesstoinsight.org/lib/authors/kawasaki/bl142.html

Monish [pseud.], 'Kenneth Anderson (1910–1974)', 27 Apr 2010. https://www.africahunting.com/threads/kenneth-anderson.2771/

Munda, Ram Dayal, 'Adi-Dharam'. https://www.goodreads.com/quotes/8540290-to-separate-the-adivasi-from-his-land-is-to-stop

Narmada Bachao Andolan, 'Narmada Satyagraha 2002—A Call to the Conscience of the Nation', 15 Jun 2002. https://www.wussu.com/roads/r02/r0206281.htm

Povos Indígenas no Brasil, 'Xingu: O Parque'. https://pib.socioambiental.org/pt/povo/xingu/1539

Rettet die Naturvölker, http://www.naturvoelker.de

Right Livelihood Award, 'Acceptance Speech—Medha Patkar and Baba Amte/Narmada Bachao Andolan', 31 Dec 1991. https://youtu.be/he0oXpq5gS4 https://rightlivelihood.org/speech/acceptance-speech-medha-patkar-and-baba-amte-narmada-bachao-andolan/

Survival International, 'About Us'. https://www.survivalinternational.org/info

Survival International, 'Progress Can Kill: How Imposed Development Destroys the Health of Tribal Peoples', 2007. http://assets.survivalinternational.org/static/lib/downloads/source/progresscankill/full_report.pdf

Survival International. '"Disaster" as Indian Supreme Court Orders Eviction of "8 million" Tribespeople', 21 Feb 2019. https://www.survivalinternational.org/news/12083

Survival International. 'Survival International Launches Campaign to Stop "30x30"—"The Biggest Land Grab in History"', 22 Apr 2021. https://www.survivalinternational.org/news/12570

Survival International. 'Tribespeople Illegally Evicted from "Jungle Book" Tiger Reserve', 14 Jan 2015. http://www.survivalinternational.org/news/10763

The Environmental Planning & Coordination Organisation (EPCO), 'Projects: Domestic Projects: Biosphere Reserves'. http://www.epco.in/epco_projects_domestic_biosphere.php

The Formosan Aboriginal Culture Village, 'About Us>Our Roots'. www.nine.com.tw/webe/html/introduction/index.aspx

United Nations Development Programme (UNDP), 'Consultation on Indigenous Peoples' Knowledge and Intellectual Property Rights', Suva Fiji, Apr 1995.

United Nations Environmental Programme (UNEP), *Global Environmental Outlook: Environment for Development*. Nairobi: UNEP, 2007.

United Nations Educational, Scientific and Cultural Organization (UNESCO), 'World Network of Biosphere Reserves (WNBR)'. http://www.unesco.org/new/en/natural-sciences/environment/ecological-sciences/biosphere-reserves/world-network-wnbr/

United Nations Educational, Scientific and Cultural Organization (UNESCO), 'Main Characteristics of Biosphere Reserves'. http://www.unesco.org/new/en/natural-sciences/environment/ecological-sciences/biosphere-reserves/main-characteristics/

United Nations Educational, Scientific and Cultural Organization (UNESCO), 'Biological and Cultural Diversity'. http://www.unesco.org/new/en/natural-sciences/environment/ecological-sciences/biodiversity-and-climate-change/science-and-research-for-management-and-policy/biological-and-cultural-diversity/

United Nations High Commissioner for Human Rights (UNHCHR), 'Convention on the Prevention and Punishment of the Crime of Genocide', *Adopted by Resolution 260 (III) A of the United Nations General Assembly on 9 December 1948.*

United Nations High Commissioner for Human Rights (UNHCHR). 'India Must Prevent the Eviction of Millions of Forest Dwellers, Say UN Experts', 4 Jul 2019. https://www.ohchr.org/EN/NewsEvents/Pages/DisplayNews.aspx?NewsID=24786

Vanavasi Kalyan Ashram Delhi, 'Welcome to the Vanavasi Kalyan Ashram Delhi', http://vanvasikalyanashramdelhi.org/index.php/2-uncategorised/16-welcome-to-vanvasi-kalyan-ashram-delhi

Vanavasi Kalyan Ashram, 'About Us'. http://vanvasi.org/about-us/

Wildlife First, 'About Us'. http://www.wildlifefirst.info/about.html

## G. Video

Armstrong, Franny, dir. *Drowned Out*. Spanner Films, 2002. https://spannerfilms.net/films/drownedout

British Film Institute. *Queen Elizabeth Visits Nepal in Time for a Massive Tiger Hunt.* Newsreel Highlights of 1961 (UE61019).

Coville, Pru, et al. *India's Maoist Revolt* [transcript]. SBS Dateline, 2013. https://www.journeyman.tv/film_documents/4103/transcript/

Grzimek, Bernhard and Michael Grzimek, dir. *Kein Platz für wilde Tiere.* West Germany: Okapia, 1956.

Macfarlane, A. 'Interview with Professor Christoph von Fürer-Haimendorf' [Video file], 2003. http://www.dspace.cam.ac.uk/handle/1810/28

Oza, Nandini. *Oral Histories of the Narmada Struggle.* https://oralhistorynarmada.in/

Yorke, Michael, et al., 'Raj Gonds—Reflections in a Peacock Crown', 1982. http://www.therai.org.uk/film/volume-ii-contents/raj-gonds-reflections-in-a-peacock-crown/

# Index

*For the benefit of digital users, indexed terms that span two pages (e.g., 52–53) may, on occasion, appear on only one of those pages.*

Tables and figures are indicated by *t* and *f* following the page number

30x30 Campaign for Nature, xi–xii

Aborigines Protection Society, 28–30, 43, 86
activists, xi–xii, xvi, 16–17, 68, 69, 167, 259–60, 296–307
   Adivasi, 76, 101–2, 228–29, 249–59, 303–5
   anthropologist, 52–53, 81
   biocultural diversity, 8–9, 17–18, 69, 262–63
   brochures, 11–12
   celebrity, 218–19
   critique of, 63, 216–17
   discourse of, 11
   elite, 66, 214, 218–19, 248
   environmental, 216–17, 228–29, 287
   external, 101, 217–19, 229, 246–48, 259–60, 262, 295–307
   forest rights, xiv–xv, 287–88
   Gandhian, 208
   human endangerment discourse of, 314–15
   indigenous peoples as, 37–38
   internet, 101–2
   left and right wing, 81–82, 182–83, 260
   local, 249–59
   middle-class, xvii, 71, 246–48
   misinformation, 309–10
   performing for, 246–47, 249–50
   as polemical, xvii–xviii
   pro-tribal, xvi, 210, 244–45, 279–80, 314
   public positions of, xxii
   second-generation, 101–2
   social, xiv–xv, 287
   study of, xx–xxi, 299
   tourist, 248
   tribal fetishization in, 266–67
   western, 62–63
   See also *Ekta Parashad*; Kalpavriksh; NBA; NGOs; Survival International
Adivasi, xii, 15–16, 70–103, 166–204, 205–60, 261–315
   Adivasi Bachao Andolan, 299–300, 300f, 302
   Adivasi Mahasabha, 76, 194–95
   as *anusuchit janjati* (scheduled tribes), 78
   as *asuras* or *rakshasas* (demons), 77
   as *bhumijan* (people of the soil), 76
   as colonial construct, 76
   as conquered by Aryans, 77–78
   as divisive, 76–77
   as ecological Indians, 92–95, 246–47 (*see also* 'as living in harmony with nature')
   as endangered, 17–18, 75, 81–82, 98–99, 102, 206–19, 245–46, 262–67, 296–307
   as euphemism, 76–77
   as forest dwellers, xiv, 15–16, 74–75, 79–80, 81–83, 203–4
   as forest rights advocates, xiv–xv
   as *Girijan* (mountain folk), 76, 78, 80
   as in need of protection, xvi
   as indigenous peoples of India, xii, 84–92
   as *Janglijati* (jungle castes), 78

Adivasi (cont.)
- as living in harmony with nature, xiv–xv, 15–16, 81–83, 175
- as original peoples of India, 76–77, 84–92
- as political category, 102–3
- as *Raniparaj* (wild people), 76
- as rulers of kingdoms, 74–75, 79–80, 98–99, 270–76
- as term used by others, 76
- as tourist attractions, 261
- as vanishing, 15–16, 95–100
- as *Vanvasi* (forest dwellers), 78, 80–81, 84
- as victims of ethnocide, 81
- as victims of progress, 181
- as warriors, 193–94, 224, 226–27
- assimilation of, 177–85, 275
- biological extinction of, 72–73
- Bollywood depictions, 254
- comparisons to endangered species, 71–72, 81–82
- comparisons to other indigenous communities, 71–72
- conforming to stereotypes, 247
- cotton farming, 253
- dehumanization of, 181
- emic vs etic perspectives, 71
- endangered lifestyles and livelihoods of, 72
- etymology of, 76
- Gandhi's attitude towards, 177–79
- hunting, 111, 148–49
- identity of, 75
- 'improvement' of, 181
- leaders, 248, 249–59
- naming of, 73–84
- preserving racial purity of, 180
- protected areas for, 267–70, 287–89 (*see also* activists; Scheduled Tribes; Tribe)
- self-identification as, 76, 76n.14
- solidarity with, 71–72
- stereotypes, 15–16, 266–67
- western perspectives on, 14

Adivasistan, 169–70, 194–96
Africa, 28–29, 36, 42–43, 50–52, 54–55, 84–85, 89, 90, 93, 108, 205, 237
*Against Ecological Romanticism* (Prasad), 94
agrarianization, 100
agricultural expansion, 112, 115, 202, 210
Akeley, Carl and Mary Jobe, 50–53
Akkalkuwa, 254–55
Akrani Mahal, 243
alarm/alarmism, xi–xii, xv, 4–6, 13–14, 26–27, 42–43, 102, 185–86
Alaska National Interest Lands Conservation Act, 53
alienation (Marxist, *entfremdung* and *entäußerung*), 192–93
Ambedkar, Bhimrao, 177–79
American Museum of Natural History, 50–51, 56–57, 66, 118–22
Amte, Murlidhar (Baba Amte), 208–9
analogy, 11–12, 14–15, 25–26, 87–88, 199, 262–63, 287–88
Andaman and Nicobar Islands (Protection of Aboriginal Tribes) Regulation of 1956, 308–9
Andaman Islands, 308–12
animal protection (vs conservation), 20n.5
animists, 76, 182
*Annihilation of Caste, The* (Ambedkar), 178–79
Anthropocene, 5–6
anthropocentrism, 20–21, 61
*anthropologischer naturschutz*, 49, 52–53, 63–64
anti-dam movement. *See* dams; Narmada Bachao Andolan; Sardar Sarovar Dam
anxiety
- colonial, 115, 171
- of endangerment, 1–2
- racist, 142–43, 180–81
- scientific, 56
- upper-caste, 178–79
- Victorian, 20–21

apartheid, 253
apocalypse, 102
- apocalyptic predictions of extinction, 8

INDEX 357

apocalyptic rhetoric, 6–7
apocalypse, religious, 102
arson, 298–99
Aryan Invasion Theory, 77–78, 85–86, 88–89
Aryan race. See *Aryan Invasion Theory*
Asiatic Cheetah (*Acinonyx jubatus venaticus*), 115, 116, 128n.68
Asiatic Lion (*Panthera leo persica*), 113–115, 120, 128n.67
assimilation, 16–17, 88–89, 177–85, 217–18, 221, 239–40, 244–46, 268–70, 275–76, 307–8
  into Aryan community, 77–78
  cultural, 68
  fighting against, 99–100
  into Hinduism, 79
  tribal, 172–75
  vs. isolation and integration, 16–17, 167–70
*Atlas of Endangered Peoples* (Pollock), 208–9
*Ausrottung* and *Aussterbung* (extermination and extinction), 41–42, 50n.89
Australia, 31, 121
  aboriginal reserves in, 307–8
  aborigines, 85–86, 91–93, 240
  Protector of Aborigines in, 30
authenticity, 48
  of Indian wildness, 48
  outsiders' criteria of, 65, 95–97
  preserving, 26–27
  protecting in parks, 45
  tribal or Adivasi, 96–97, 99–102, 246–47
*Avatar* (Cameron), 297–98

backward Hindus, 16–17, 167–68, 180, 206
backward races, 285
Backward Tracts, 270, 282–87
backward tribes, 75–76, 99, 193–94
backwardness, 79, 99, 189–93, 285
Baiga, 17–18, 84–85, 148, 261–315
  Baiga Chak (Baiga Reservation), 269–70, 276–83, 288–89, 303–6, 311–12

Baiga Dussehra, 306–7, 307*f*
*Bewar* agriculture, 276–82, 288, 289, 304–7
  godna tattoos, 306–7
Balaghat, xx, 266, 298
barasingha (*Rucervus duvaucelii*), 115n.34, 156*t*, 291–92
barbarians/barbarism, 3–4n.10, 25–26, 28–29, 38, 77, 89, 91–92, 144–45, 166–67, 171, 192–93, 229–30, 232, 282–83
Bastar, 283, 306
Bates, Crispin, 76, 84, 184–85
Baviskar, Amita, 247, 247n.113
bears, 47–48, 81, 107n.7, 132–33
  bear-baiting, 20n.5
  Indian Sloth Bear (*Melursus ursinus*), 116n.35, 128–30, 140, 160*t*
*Before They Pass Away* (Nelson), 26–27, 28*f*
Béteille, André, 93
Bheel. See Bhil
Bhil, xvi, 14–17, 72–76, 205–60
  as Adivasi, 76
  as *anusuchit janjati* (scheduled tribes), 78
  as backward, 75–76
  as criminal, 238
  as endangered, 73
  as forest tribes, 74–76
  as hunter-gatherers, 219–26
  as *jatis* (castes), 76n.14
  as Kshatriya or Rajput, 74–75, 79–80, 226–27
  as regionally dominant, 73
  as rulers, 74–75, 226–29
  as threatened with extermination, 229–40
  as *vanvasi* (forest dwellers), 78–81, 84
  as wild, 75–76
Bhilala, 76n.14, 207–8n.7, 247n.113
demographics, 72
in danger of extinction, 72
in need of protection, 229–40
leaders, 218–19
Muslim, 235n.81

Bhil (cont.)
  nomenclature, 73–84
  Padvi, 76n.14, 250, 254–58
  Pawra, 76n.14
  Tadvi, 76n.14, 207–8
  Vasava/Vasave, 76n.14, 207–8, 249, 250–54
Bhil Corps, 241–42
  Khandesh, 230–31, 236–238
  Mewar, 227–28
Bhilistan, 228–29
  See also Adivasistan; Gondwana Movement
Bhil Pradesh. See Bhilistan
Bhonsle Marathas, 271–72
  See also Maratha Empire
*Bhumijan* (people of the soil), 76
big game, 105–6, 108–9, 110–11, 115, 119–20, 147–48, 148n.136, 149, 154*t*
Bihar, 173, 194–95, 254n.119
Bikaner, 146–48
biocultural diversity, xii–xiii, xviii, 7–12, 14–16, 45, 61–68, 69, 100–3, 217, 270, 289, 311–15
biodiversity, xi–xii, xv, 5n.15, 10, 12–13, 62–63, 65–66, 100, 304–5
biopiracy, 36
biosphere people, 42n.70
Biosphere Reserves, 66–67, 313–14
biosphere, the, 8
Birhor, 173–74
Birsa Munda, 299–300, 301*f*
Birsa Munda Brigade, 299–303, 301*f*
bland/blanding, 59, 59n.118
Bodley, John, 29, 59–60, 84–85. See also *Victims of Progress*
Bombay
  Army, 90
  city, 246–47, 252–53
  Government of, 171–72, 230–31
  Governor of, 89–90, 230–31
  Presidency, 243
  State, 256
Bo Senior (last of the Aka Bo), 309–10
Brahmin/Brahminical/Brahminism, 177, 183–84, 210–11, 221, 224, 230–31, 233–34, 248, 273

Brantlinger, Patrick, 28–29, 84–85, 149–50. See also *Dark Vanishings*
Brazil, 52–53
Briggs, John, 86–89, 235–37
British Empire. See empire
buffalo, 70–71, 115n.34, 117–20, 155*t*
Buffalo Bill Cody, 53–54
Burma, 280, 284
Bushmen, 36, 54–55, 89–90, 205, 237
  See also San
Buxton, Edward N. and Thomas, 43

California, 34–35, 40
carnivores, 16, 38, 104–65, 234–35
Casas, Bartolomé de las, 22–25, 30
caste, 70, 78–80, 178–79, 183–84, 197–98, 226, 244–45, 249, 273, 289
  absorption of tribes into caste system, 183–84
  caste-tribe continuum, 79
  relationship between caste and tribe, 79, 90–91, 274
  Scheduled Castes, 191, 203–4
  upper caste, 221
Catlin, George, 45–47, 313–14
*Census of India,* 72, 75–76, 91, 176, 281, 309–10
  Tribal religion category in, 300–1
Central Provinces, 113, 116, 119–20, 130–31n.77, 136, 139, 156*t*, 235n.81, 271–85, 290–92
Chicken Little, 214–16
  See also 'The Sound the Hare Heard'
Chief Seattle's speech, 61–62
China, 38, 192–93
Chital (*Axis axis*), 148, 155*t*, 291–92
Chota Nagpur, 173, 193
Christianization, 75–76
Christian missionaries, 63, 175–76, 182–83, 191, 195–96, 284–85
  negative impact on tribes, 175–76
Christians/Christianity, 31–32, 102, 180
civilization
  advance of, 106
  Aryan, 77–78, 85–86, 88–89

backwardness on the scale of civilization, 190
becoming too civilized, 281–82
British superiority, 85–86
capacity for becoming civilized, 233, 234, 236
civilizational hierarchies, 179
civilized off the face of the earth, 47–48
civilized people, 39–42, 47, 86, 150
civilizing discourse, 176–77
civilizing influences, 41, 51, 177, 230–31,
civilizing mission, 69, 171, 194, 242–43,
civilizing process, 89
civilizing the Baiga, 277–78
civilizing the Bhils, 241–42
civilizing the savage, 89, 105–6, 169–70, 194
civilizing tribes, 178–81, 186, 233
comparisons between tribes, 235, 275, 277
considering oneself civilized, 186
contrasting civilized vs tribal life, 185–86
enemy of, 107n.7
as an evil that destroys ancient customs, 233n.76
as extermination, 41
failures of, 265–66
forces of de-civilization, 59
future, 46
Hindu, 80, 85–86
as imperialist ideology, 169–70
as incapable of bringing development without despair, 268–69
incorporating tribes into Hindu, 183–84
as encroaching, 77–78, 224
Indian, 88–89
living outside of, 226–27
measuring distance from, 230–31
necessity to wipe out primitivity to advance, 25–26
new to, 240–41
origins of, 56–57
progress of, 41, 233n.76
as salvation, 259–60
scale of, 85–86, 88–89, 238, 275, 286–87
semi-civilized, 239–40
transition from primitiveness to, 188
Ultima Thule of, 269–70
uncivilized, 282–83
unregulated process of, 267–68
vanishing archaic, 70, 199
western, 41–42, 52–53
co-endangerment, 8, 62
Columbus, Christopher, 11, 21
Congo, Belgian, 50–53, 142–43
conservation-induced displacement, xvi, 249–50, 252–53, 261–315
Constitution of India, 75–76, 99–100, 172, 189–91, 282–84, 302
conversion, 182–83, 279
criminal tribes, 178–79, 193–94, 238
cultural ecology, 15–16, 74–75, 96–97
cultural imperialism, 9, 14–15, 54–55, 169–70, 184, 247
Cultural Survival (NGO), 11, 201
culture
  absorption of, 183–84, 188, 190–91, 249
  Adivasi, 15–17, 71, 74–75, 81, 84, 101–2
  as changing, 59–60, 197–98, 213
  conservation of, 9, 30–31, 43, 45, 65, 69, 289–92, 304–5, 308–9, 311–15
  contact between, 172–73
  as data, 199–200
  death of, 58–59, 213–14, 261, 302
  decline of, 96–97, 100, 176–77, 275, 295–96
  destruction of, 57–59, 298
  disappearing, 37, 56, 92, 146, 175–76, 196–97, 212, 302
  diversity of (*see* biocultural diversity)
  domination of, 102–3, 213–14, 302
  endangered, 9–10, 15–16, 36–37, 37n.56, 60, 81–82, 96–97, 169–70, 202–3, 204, 212, 217, 234–35, 249–50, 256

culture (*cont.*)
  eradicating, 16–17, 167–68
  essentialist idea of, 62–63
  evolution of, 25–26
  extermination of, 58–59, 81
  extinction of, 36–37, 60, 199–200, 213–14, 239–40, 249–50, 263–64
  forced modification of, 59–60
  forest, xiv–xv, 149–50, 203–4, 211–12, 239–40, 265, 267–68, 279, 287
  fossil, 226
  genocide of, 58–60, 81, 208–10, 213
  heritage, 73, 174–75, 305–6
  Hindu, 179
  of indigenous people, 11, 53–54, 56–57, 64, 211–12, 223, 246–47, 249, 253, 254, 298, 304, 308
  isolation of, 189
  *laissez-faire*, 184
  material, 81
  mourning the loss of, 58–59
  old, 192–93
  preserving, 53–54, 97–98, 174–75, 180, 188, 198, 199–200
  protecting, 16–17, 167–70, 174–75, 190–91, 200
  saving, 197–98, 228–29
  as species, 226
  survival of, 146, 212, 261, 302
  threats to, 7–9, 17
  traditional, 99–100, 174, 208
  tribal, xvi, 99, 102, 166–70, 173–76, 179, 185, 187, 188, 190–93, 200, 202–3, 208, 229, 267–68, 275, 295–96
  vanishing, 3–4, 30–31, 67, 99–100, 197–98, 201, 212
  vs nature, 82
Curtis, Edward, 26–27, 27*f*
Cuvier, Georges, 19–20, 24–25

dams, xvi, 17, 83*f*, 102n.75, 187–88. *See also* Sardar Sarovar Dam
dance, 53–54, 186, 221, 247, 253, 254, 300–1, 304–7
dark age. *See* Kali Yug

*Dark Vanishings* (Brantlinger), 28–31, 84–85
Darwin, Charles, 3–4, 19–21, 31–33, 238, 259–60
Das, T.C. 175–76
Dasmann, Raymond, 63–64, 313–14
Davis, Wade, 7–8, 58–59
decolonization, 150n.139
decolonizing discourse, 69
dehumanization, 9, 14–15, 17–18, 21n.7, 37–38, 42–43, 87–88, 181, 192–93, 231–32, 234–35, 239–40, 273, 287–88, 302, 314–15
demographics, 72, 102–3, 200, 260, 264–65
Derrida, J. x, 265n.16
Deshpande, Ramakant Keshav (Balasaheb Deshpande), 182–83
detribalization, 75–76, 174–75
development, 16–17, 40–41, 59, 66–67, 75, 80, 102–3, 168–70, 174–75, 182–83, 186–92, 200, 202–4, 210–11, 214, 217–18, 218n.36, 221–22, 244–45, 247n.113, 258–60, 262–63, 265–66, 268–69, 296, 304
development-induced displacement, xvi, 205–19, 249–59
Dickens, Charles, 95–96
dinosaurs, 5n.15, 19–20
disappearing, x, 8, 15–16, 19–21, 23n.13, 25–34, 37, 40–41, 56, 59, 65, 67–69, 72, 73, 84–85, 91–92, 95–98, 105, 112, 116, 118, 121, 132–33, 145, 146, 173–76, 184–85, 196, 210, 212, 239–40, 259–60, 262–63, 265–66, 273, 275, 280–82, 289–92, 298, 303–5
*Disappearing Peoples?* (Brower and Johnston), 221–22
discourse, xii, 16, 71, 183–84
  activist, 11
  biocultural, 9, 82, 107n.7, 111–12, 210, 308–9, 315
  colonial vs. contemporary, 75–76, 82–83, 105–6, 133, 176–77, 229–40, 279–80
  cultural conservation, 9, 245–46
  dehumanizing, 181, 302

dominant, 98, 204
endangerment and extinction, xviii, 1–4, 9–16, 19–69, 72, 84–85, 102, 196, 207–9, 214–17, 219–20, 229–40, 250, 256, 260, 264–66, 296–98, 302, 314–15
   global mismatch with local situations, 71–72, 217, 249–50, 260
   Nazi, 180–81
   primitivist, 96–97
   protectionist, 106
   revisionist, 82
   romanticist, 94, 246–47
displacement. *See* conservation-induced displacement; development-induced displacement
diversity. *See* biocultural diversity; biodiversity
Divyabhanusinh, 114
*Do Muslim Women Really Need Saving?* (Abu-Lughod), 63
Domestication, 40–41, 46, 51, 105–6, 125–27, 180, 235, 236
Dongria Kondh, 297–98
Dube, S.C. 73, 188, 200–1
Duddubha Jataka: The Sound the Hare Heard, 70–71
dying
   customs, 280
   races, 26, 56, 238–40
   tribes, 92, 173–74, 311n.121
   world, 196
*Dying Speeches of Several Indians,* 24–25

ecocide, 57–61, 82–83, 207–8, 210
ecofetishism, 65
*Ecological Indian, the* (Krech), 15–16, 64–65, 92–101
ecological nobility, 92–97, 101, 248, 260, 276–77, 315
ecological refugees, 42n.70
Ecosystem People, 42n.70, 313–14
education (Adivasi) xv, 101–2, 166–67, 172, 182–83, 186–87, 191, 193, 221, 243–45, 248, 252–59, 268–69, 303, 306

*Ekta Parashad,* 297–98
Elphinstone, Mountstuart, 86–87, 230–32, 235, 236
Elwin, Verrier, 17–18, 52–53, 76, 169, 172, 176, 185–87, 198–99, 267–70, 276–77, 279, 281–90, 307–9, 311–12
empire, 23, 38, 75, 108, 139–40, 224–27, 231–32
   age of, 3–4, 24–25, 39, 69
   British, 2–3, 3n.6, 30, 114, 130, 133, 136, 139–40
   Maratha, 17, 228–29, 231–32, 259–60
   Mughal, 253, 271
   Spanish, 22–23
end times, end of the world, 6–7, 102
   *See also* apocalypse
England, 25n.21, 39, 40, 47–48, 86–88, 127–28, 132–35, 140, 276n.47
English (language) xvii, 2–4, 3–4n.10, 25n.21, 41–42, 59–60, 75–76, 78, 85–86, 88–89, 100–1, 169–70, 179, 248, 253–54, 276n.47, 302
environmental history, xviii, 90–91, 100, 222
environmentalism, 3–4, 23–25, 64, 94, 96, 133, 142–43, 245–46, 260, 314
environmentalists, xi–xii, 6, 12–13, 23, 41–43, 62, 84, 93, 94, 96, 101, 142–45, 204, 207–8, 210–11, 217n.35, 245–46, 248, 287, 296
erasure, 26–27, 75–76, 143, 148–49, 242–43
eschatological thinking, 102
essentialism, 101
   *See also* strategic essentialism
ethnocide, 29, 57–61, 81–83, 170, 201–4, 207–10, 213, 214–17, 260, 310–11
ethnographic state, the, 99–100
ethnography, 71, 173
Ethnological Society of London, 86–87
ethnology, 85–87, 91, 274
ethnosphere, 8
eugenics, 44, 50–51, 56–57

eviction, xi, xin.2, 249–50, 262, 267f, 295, 302, 315
  See also conservation; development-induced displacement
Excluded Areas, 167, 171, 172, 191, 243–44, 270, 282–87, 307–8
  See also Backward Tracts; national parks; protected areas; Scheduled Areas; Scheduled Districts
exhibitions (tribal), 54–57
  See also museums
existential crisis, 8, 100–1
existential denial, 34n.48
existential threat, 303–4
exploitation, 36n.54, 102–3, 109–10, 136, 167, 175, 185, 188–92, 197, 202–3, 240–41, 242–44, 267–68, 285
extinction, xi–xiii, xvii–xviii, 2–16, 17–69, 70–73, 75, 84–85, 89–90, 95–100, 101–6, 110–28, 130–33, 137–38, 140–50, 167, 171–75, 177, 180–81, 196–202, 207–10, 213–20, 222, 228–29, 237–41, 249–50, 258–60, 263–66, 280–82, 291, 296–99, 303–5, 307–11, 314–15
extinct languages, 24–25
extinct species
  dodo, 20–21
  mammoth, 19–20, 37n.56
  mastodon, 19–20, 24–25
  passenger pigeon, 37n.56, 118
  sabre-tooth tiger, 5–6, 37n.56
  Stellar's sea cow, 20–21
  whooping crane, 37n.56

'fake' tribes, 34n.48
Fanon, Franz, 150n.139, 265
forest, xi–xviii, 14–16, 25–26, 41, 47–48, 51, 54–55, 70–84, 83f, 89, 90–91, 100–4, 108–10, 115, 120–21, 130–31, 133–39, 146, 148, 150, 151t, 168–70, 172–75, 184–87, 204, 208, 210–12, 217, 219–29, 239–40, 244–45, 248, 253, 254, 258–60, 262–64, 265, 271–99, 303–6

Forest Department, 136, 142, 256–57, 279, 294, 298–99, 304
Forest Peoples Programme, 213
Formosan Aboriginal Culture Village, 53–54
Forsyth, James, 90–91, 108–9, 162t
fortress conservation, xiii, xiiin.6
fortresses, 74–75, 232–33
fossils, 19–20
  cultural, 226
  hunter-gatherers as, 226
  tribes as, 275
fragility, 8, 60
Franklin, Benjamin, 25–26
Frere, Henry Bartle, 89–90
funeral dirges, xviiin.20, 69
Fürer-Haimendorf, Christoph von, 70, 167, 198–99, 221–23, 286

game, 47–48, 105, 109–10, 113, 119, 125–27, 138, 139–41, 142, 147–49, 281
  See also big game; hunting; wildlife
game laws/protection, 44, 109–11, 120–21, 131–38, 135f, 289–291
game reserves, 48–49, 116, 291–92
Gandhi, Mohandas, 76, 144–45, 177–79
Gandhians, 191, 208, 245–47
Garden of Eden, 56–57, 94–95
Garha-Mandla, 74f, 270–76, 271f
*Gattungswesen / Gattungsleben* (species-being / species-life), 192–93
gaur (Indian bison, *Bos gaurus*), 119–20
genocide, 11–12, 22n.9, 32, 57–61, 70, 81, 201–2, 207–10, 213–17, 249
German (language), 41–42, 43f
Germany, 1n.1, 26–27, 28f, 41–42, 43f, 180
Ghurye, G.S. 76–77, 80, 169, 177, 183–84, 268–70, 284, 307–8
*girijan* (mountain folk), 76, 78, 80, 180
Glacier Park Indians, 53–54
Golwalkar, M.S. 179–80, 182–83

Gond, xvi, 14, 15–18, 72–81, 74*f*, 83*f*, 84–86, 89, 90, 98–101, 110, 198, 203–4, 261–315
   Raj Gond, 74–75, 77n.18, 98–99, 270–76
   Gondwana, 74–75, 77n.18, 270–76, 292
   Gondwana movement, 299–301, 301*f*, 306
   Gond Mahasabha, 301*f*
Grant, Madison, 44
Great Andamanese, 309–10
*Green Imperialism* (Grove), 133
Grove, Richard, 23–25, 133
Grzimek, Bernhard, 41n.69, 43*f*
Guha, Ramachandra, 169, 178, 179, 222
Guha, Sumit, 81–82, 224
Gujarat, 128n.67, 210–11, 228–29, 249, 251–52

harmony with nature, xv, 62, 73, 94–95, 101–2, 219–20, 229–30, 315
Headland, Thomas and Janet, 58–59, 309
heritage, 53n.101, 65–67, 71, 73, 76–77, 90, 99–100, 101–2, 174–75, 189, 305–6
Hindi, 78, 86, 219–20, 228–29, 243–44, 253–54, 264–65, 287, 288, 294, 299, 302, 304–5
*Hindu, The,* 262–64
Hinduism, 79, 92, 146–47, 174–75, 176, 179, 182, 197–98
Hinduization, 79, 92, 182–84, 244–45
Hindus, 1–2, 16–17, 80, 86–88, 172, 175–85, 188, 202–3, 221, 248, 249, 274, 277, 284, 288–90, 303n.111
   as indigenous peoples of India, 76–77, 85–86
   *See also* backward Hindus
Hindustan, 116, 193–94, 280
*Hindutva* (Hindu nationalism), 1–2, 80, 179–85, 221, 268
hippies, 199–200, 245–46
Hispaniola, 21–23
Hobbes, Thomas, 94–95
Hodgson, Brian, 87–89
Holocaust, 11–12, 35–36, 57–58, 180–83, 214
Hornaday, William T. 41, 70, 117–18, 142–43, 143n.122
horror, 4–5, 122, 136–37, 148, 234, 298–99
Human Genome Biodiversity Project, 67–68
human populations, xiii–xiv, xvi, 3–4n.10, 9, 12–13, 15–18, 22–24n.15, 29, 32–33, 42–43, 55–56, 68, 72–75, 81–82, 86–88, 91, 104–6, 111–12, 131–32, 171, 175–79, 189–90, 192–93, 198–99, 202–3, 209–11, 223, 224, 226, 232, 239–40, 242–43, 256–57, 264–66, 269–72, 280, 308–12
   human race, 34
   mono- & poly-genesis, 34n.47
   problems defining, 33–38, 73
   possibility of extinction of, 36–37, 68
   (*see also* demographics)
human remains, 55–57
human safaris, 311–12
human zoos, 54–57, 62, 311n.122
humanitarians, 42–43, 175, 177, 189
hunter-gatherers, 5–6, 47–48, 72, 219–26, 228–31, 245–46, 265–66, 274
   extinction of, 222–23, 226, 228–29
hunting, 15–16, 20n.5, 25–26, 38–44, 104–65, 205, 264, 273–74, 281, 289–92
   hunting humans, 38–44, 62, 72, 106–9, 205, 227–28, 232–33, 238, 239–40, 242–44
   See also *shikar* (hunting)
Hutton, James, 19–21
Hutton, J.H. 176, 281
Hyde, E.S. 166, 261, 288–89
hyperbole, xvii, 6, 22n.9, 60–61, 70, 102–3, 119–20, 214–17, 258–59, 280

identity politics, 66, 101

imperialism, 38, 108, 116, 149–50, 166–67, 171, 188, 189, 191, 284–85, 310–11
  *See also* cultural imperialism; *Green Imperialism*; NGO imperialism
Indian Civil Service (ICS), 243–44, 281–82
Indian Forest Act of 1878, 90–91
Indian wilderness, 45, 47, 312–13
Indigenous People's Earth Charter of 1992, 64–65
indigenous peoples, xi–xv, 3–4, 8–9, 11–18, 21–25, 30–31, 33–38, 41–103, 110–11, 138, 146, 148–50, 166–315
  *See also* Adivasi
indigenous rights, xi, 11, 168–69, 201–4, 314
Indonesia, 50, 93
industrial economy, xvi, 36, 93, 94, 146, 186–88, 190–91, 230–31, 292–93
integration (of Adivasis), 16–17, 66–67, 81–82, 97–98, 166–204, 217–18, 226–27, 243–46, 259–60, 275, 311, 313–14
intellectual history, 9–10, 14, 16–17, 24–25, 44n.74, 61, 71, 94–95
Ishi, 34–35
isolation, xvi, 16–17, 73, 79, 81–82, 93, 97–99, 133, 166–204, 217, 219–24, 226, 229–31, 239–41, 242–46, 247n.113, 260, 267–70, 282–87, 308–9, 311
IUCN (International Union for the Conservation of Nature, formerly the IUPN), 64, 66, 128nn.66, 313

Jackson, Andrew, 30
James, William, xvii–xviii
Jangil, 309–10
*Janjati* (folk caste), 78, 287n.89
Jarawa, 308–12
Jarawa Tribal Reservation, 308–12
*jati* (caste), 76n.14, 78
Jaulin, Robert, 59–60
Jefferson, Thomas, 19–20, 25–26

Jews, 2–3, 37, 57–58, 180–81
Jharkhand, 13n.39, 98–99, 193–96, 283n.75
Jinnah, M.A. 194–95
Jones, William, 86
jungle, 78, 106, 109, 116, 148–49, 180, 226–27, 232–33, 235, 236, 256, 266–67, 267f, 274, 276–79, 281, 302–3, 311n.121

Kali Yuga, 102
Kalpavriksh, 296
Kanha National Park, xxii, 17–18, 83f, 148, 261–315
Karen, 280
*Kein Platz für wilde Tiere* (Grzimek), 41–42, 43f
Khandesh, 86–87, 229–34, 236–42, 250–51
Kipling, Rudyard, 266–67, 267f
Korwa, 173
Kothari, Ashish, 296–98
Krech, Shepard, 93
Kruger National Park, 51–52
kshatriyas, 207–8n.7, 226–27, 273, 275–76
*Kulturvölker,* 41–42
Kuper, Adam, 69, 76–77

land grab, xi–xii, xiv
last of their kind, 34–36, 121, 271–72
Lemkin, Raphäel, 57–58
Leopold, Aldo, 142–44
Lepchas, 92
Lévi-Strauss, Claud, 196–97
lions. *See* Asiatic Lions
Lokur Comission, 99
Lorentz National Park, 50

Madhya Bharat, 256
Madhya Pradesh, xxii, 14, 17–18, 228–29, 262, 263, 266, 271, 288, 298, 306
Maffi, Luisa, 9–10
Maharashtra, xxii, 14, 219f, 228–29, 243, 250–52, 251f, 254–55
mainstream, 16–17, 80, 85–86, 97–98, 167–70, 176–85, 202–3, 206, 213,

217–18, 226, 236, 244–45, 249, 260, 268, 275, 284, 302, 310n.119, 311n.122
Majumdar, D.N. 172–75
Malthus, Thomas, 32–33, 32n.39
Malwa, 230–31, 233
mammoths. *See* extinct species
Man and Biosphere Programme, 63–64, 66–67, 313–14
Mandla District, 264–65n.11, 269–70, 277, 280–81, 288–90, 298
Maori, 40–41
Maratha Empire. *See* Empire
marginalization, xi–xii, 8–9, 36–38, 76–77, 98, 180, 226, 239–40, 275, 308
Marx, Karl, 42–43, 192–93, 192n.67
Marxism/Marxists, 192–93
massacre, 60–61, 107n.7, 125–27, 206, 241–42
Mead, Margaret, 8, 58–59
media, 206–7, 216–17, 217n.35, 246–48, 295
  *See also* social media
Mehta, B.H. 167, 189, 203–4, 204n.96
memory, 46, 56–57, 212, 298–99
metanarratives, 75, 249–50
metaphor, 9, 38, 42–43, 181, 228, 238, 247, 273, 287–88
middle class, 9, 38, 42–43, 181, 228, 238, 247, 273, 287–88
  tribal, 98–99
missionaries. *See* Christian missionaries
modernization, 177
Montesinos, Antonio de, 21, 24–25
monuments, 46, 47, 50, 56–57, 108–9, 260
mourning, 30–31, 58–59, 59n.118, 110–11, 143, 222, 228–29, 251–52, 265–66
Mowgli, 266–67, 267f
Mughal Empire. *See* empire
Müller, Max, 87–89
Munda, 173, 176, 193, 198, 213–14, 299–300
murder, 57–58, 95–96, 209–10, 241–42

museums, 16–17, 46, 50–51, 54–57, 66, 117–21, 167–68, 186–87, 268, 269, 282–83, 311n.122
Muslim League, 178, 194–96

Nandurbar, 240–41, 250–52, 251f, 254n.120, 306–7
*Narmada Bachao Andolan* (Save the Narmada Movement) (NBA), 17, 168–69, 204, 205–60
Narmada River, 17, 139, 161t, 205–60
narrative
  of biocultural diversity loss, 15–16, 84–85, 100–1, 295–96
  colonial, 69, 89
  complex vs. simple, 6–7, 11–12, 64, 249–50, 258–59, 295–96
  crisis, 6
  of decline, 223
  popular, 81–82, 221, 224–25
  standard, 100, 248
  *See also* metanarrative
national parks, xi–xiii, xvi, 17–18, 44–55, 62, 66–67, 83f, 261–315
Native Americans, 30, 48–49, 90, 93
  Cherokee, 34
  Extinction or extermination of, 91–92
  Lenni Lenape or Delaware, 34
  Powhatan, 34
  as Red Indians or Red Skins, 29, 40–41, 93, 240
  Yahi, 34–35
  *See also* Ishi; Shawahdunit; Trail of Tears; Vanishing American
*Naturvölker* (nature folk), 41–42, 43f, 50n.89
Nazis, 37, 180–82
necropolitics, 265
Nehru, Jawaharlal, 185–96
Nelson, Jimmy, 26–27, 28f
Nepal, 88, 116, 127, 154t
NGO-imperialism, 63
noble savage, 94–96, 214–16
Non-Government Organizations (NGOs), 8–9, 65, 96–98, 245–46, 248, 254, 288, 295
nostalgia, 40, 252–53, 258–59

Onge, 309-10
oppression, 21, 57-58, 65, 66, 97-98, 149-50, 241-42, 267-68
oral history, xvi, 17, 194-95, 201, 216n.33, 244, 249-59, 294, 296-307
Oraon, 96-97, 173, 183
orientalism, 96-97, 176-77, 219-20, 244
Ota Benga, 54-55
*Our Vanishing Wild Life* (Hornaday), 142-43

Pachmarhi Biosphere Reserve, 298-99
pacification, 75-76, 86-87, 229-30, 233
Padel, Felix, 81, 209-10, 213-14
Pakistan, 169-70, 193-96
palaces, 74-75, 74f, 146-48, 270, 271f, 273
Palawa community. *See* Tasmanians
*panchsheel* (tribal development plan), 187
paper genocide, 22n.9
paradigm shift, 16, 105, 133
*Parc National Albert*, 50-52
*Parque Indígena* (indigenous park), 53
passenger pigeon. *See* extinct species
paternalism, 9, 17, 65, 90-91, 97-99, 101
Patkar, Medha, 208-9, 212, 215f, 219f, 251-52
peripheral peoples, 313-14
plastic shamans, 36n.54
playing Indian, 36n.54
polygyny, 256-57, 256n.121
population. *See* human populations
precarity, 22n.9, 102-3, 249-50, 266-67
predators, 44, 104-8, 128-31, 139, 141, 144-45, 259-60
  *See also* carnivores
predatory people, 17, 87-88, 106-9, 134-35, 144-45, 229-31, 234-35, 237, 242-43, 259-60, 286-87
preservation, xii-xiii, 2n.5, 9, 13-14, 16-18, 26-27, 30-31, 33n.42, 45-50, 51-57, 65, 67, 71, 92, 97-100, 104-6, 109-11, 114, 115, 117, 122, 130-43, 166-70, 172, 174-75, 178-79, 180, 184, 188, 189, 191, 196-200, 232-33, 240-45, 248, 260, 265-70, 279-85, 288-89, 306-8, 311, 311-15
Prichard, James Cowles, 31-32
primitive, 25-26, 28-29, 32-33, 45, 46, 49, 50-52, 56, 69, 73, 75-80, 88, 90-99, 166-74, 178-79, 182, 187-94, 196, 198, 200, 223, 226, 228-30, 237, 239-40, 259-60, 265-67, 274-76, 279, 282-83, 287-89
Primitive Peoples Fund. *See* Survival International
primitivism, 96-98, 199-200, 217, 228-29, 239-40, 244, 286-87
progress, 8, 25-26, 41, 59-60, 68, 69, 143, 168-70, 187-88, 192-93, 202-3, 218, 230-31, 233n.76, 244-45, 307-8, 313-15
protected areas, xi-xviii, 17-18, 44-54, 66-67
'protecting' people, xii, 1-2, 12-13, 16-18, 20-25, 28-30, 37, 40-54, 62-65, 69, 71, 86-87, 90-91, 96-101, 106, 144-45, 166-75, 184, 185
Protector of Aborigines/Indians, 22-30
pygmies, 50-53, 142-43

Quakers, 30, 43

Racism, 9, 12-15, 44, 51-52, 54-58, 68, 76-77, 91, 142-44, 179, 180-81, 236, 285, 287-88, 314-15
Raj Gond. *See* Gond
Rajasthan / Rajputana, 14, 113-14, 146, 148-49, 219-21, 228-29
Rajput, 74-75, 226-27, 231-33, 237, 253, 273, 275-76
Rajputization, 79, 275-76
Rangarajan, Mahesh, 108-9, 128-30, 132-33
*Raniparaj*. *See* Adivasi
rehabilitation, 174, 216-19, 222, 249, 258
remoteness, 119-20, 166, 230-33, 244, 290
*Report of the Christian Missionary Activities Enquiry Committee* (Niyogi), 195-96

Reserve Forests, 90–91, 120–21, 136, 262, 287–88, 292
resettlement, xv–xvi, 17, 206, 213, 216–19, 246–47, 249–60, 277–78, 294–96, 295f, 303–4
resettlement colonies, xvi, 17, 246–47, 249, 250–55, 251f, 257–58, 298–99, 306–7
*Rettet die Naturvölker: Kein Platz für "wilde" Menschen* (Baumann and Uhlig), 41–42, 43f
Rewa, 146–47
rewards for exterminating wild animals, 104–5, 115, 125, 128–33, 139, 140–42, 158t
rhetoric, xii, 5–30, 37, 38, 42–43, 63, 68–69, 101–3, 171–72, 202–3, 207–8, 212, 214–17, 231–32, 234–35, 249, 296, 314–15
rhinoceros, 70–71, 114n.29, 115–16, 116n.36, 156t
Right Livelihood Award, 208–9, 251
Risley, H.H. 91–92
romanticism, 26–27, 43, 45, 46, 47, 51, 53, 62–63, 93, 94–95, 97–98, 101, 176–77, 185–88, 199–200, 214–20, 233n.76, 246–47, 260, 276–77, 315
ecological, 64, 96, 246–47
See also *Against Ecological Romanticism*; ecological Indians; ecologically noble savage; primitivism
Roosevelt, Theodore, 48–49
Rousseau, Jean-Jacques, 94–95
Roy, Arundhati, 70, 214–16, 215f, 246–47
Roy, S.C. 172–74

salvage anthropology, 32, 56, 68, 196–97, 201
San, 36
See also Bushmen
Sanskritization, 275
Santal, 72, 73, 198
Sarasin, Paul, 49–50, 52–53, 63–64
Sardar Sarovar Dam, 17, 83f, 206–19, 244–59, 260

Satpura Mountains, 241–42, 247n.113, 256–57
savages, 25–26, 41, 48–49, 70, 88–90, 94–96, 106–8, 109, 171, 175, 178–79, 230–33, 235, 237, 242
See also civilizing the savage; ecologically noble savage; noble savage
Scheduled Areas, 189–90, 270, 282–83, 286–87, 311–12
Scheduled Districts Act of 1874, 90–91, 270, 283
Scheduled Tribes, 90–91, 99, 179, 189–91, 203–4, 206–7, 243–44
See also Adivasi; *anusuchit janjati*
Scheduled Tribes and Other Forest Dwellers (Recognition of Forest Rights) Act of 2006 (FRA), xiii, 79–80, 262, 287–89, 315
segregation, 189, 242–44, 284–85
sensationalism, xii, 216–17, 297–98
sensibility, 1, 13–14, 22–23
Serengeti National Park, 51–52
Shahada, 254
Shawahdunit, 34–35
shifting agriculture, 188, 211–12, 265–66, 268–69, 276–82
See also *bewar*; slash-and-burn
*shikar*, 104–65, 227–28
Singh, Jaipal, 193–95
Sixth Extinction, 4–7
slash-and-burn, 221–24, 276–82
slavery, 3–4n.10, 42–43, 88–89, 134–35
Smithsonian Museum, 117–18
snakes, 128–32, 140
Social Darwinism, 50–51, 238–39, 259–60
social media, 101–2, 228–29
social movements, 168–69, 245–49
Society for Preservation of Wild Fauna of Empire, 43, 51–52, 110–11, 122
South Africa, 36, 51–52, 54–56, 67, 89, 91–92, 113–14, 117–24, 167–68, 186–87, 237, 269
specimens, 45–47
Spencer, Herbert, 32–33, 32n.40

sportsmen, 19, 44, 106, 110–11, 113, 115, 116, 118–20, 133–45
Srinivas, M. N. 79n.27, 183–84
state formation, 224–25, 248, 275
state of nature, 94–95
statelessness, 79
stereotypes, 15–16, 51–52, 64–65, 73, 84, 95–98, 102–3, 247
strategic essentialism, 84
struggle for existence, 32–33, 239
struggle for survival, 149–50, 223, 238–39, 259–60
subaltern *shikaris* (hunters), 137–40, 148–49
subjugation, 69, 77–78, 132–33, 150, 238, 239–40, 244–45
suffering, 3–4n.10, 17, 23, 139, 173, 175, 208, 216–17
Supreme Court of India, xi–xii, xiii, 214–18, 311–12, 315
survival, 71, 73, 84, 132–33, 145, 146, 149–50, 167, 188, 201–4, 210–12, 219–20, 223, 238–39, 243–44, 259–61, 265–66
Survival International, xi–xii, xiv–, 11, 16–17, 52–53, 97–98, 201, 262–63, 266–67, 267*f*, 271–72, 297–98, 297*f*, 313–14
sustainability, xv, 66–67, 111, 239–40, 296
Symington, David, 171–72, 205, 243–44

Taino, 22
Taiwan, 53–54*f*
Tasmanians, 30, 35–36, 39
taxidermy, 41, 50–51, 56, 104, 117–18, 122, 151*t*
Terralingua, 66
Thapar, Valmik, xiii–xiv
Thoreau, Henry David, 47–49
Tienhoven, P.G. van, 50–51
tiger (*Panthera tigris*) CP, 16–18, 81–83, 83*f*, 104–65, 204, 210, 234–36, 242–44, 262–70, 274, 288, 291–93, 304
Tod, James, 86, 232–33, 233n.76
tradition, 15–16, 62–63, 101–2, 203–4, 208, 247, 250–51, 253, 266
  disappearing, 212
  ecological, 36, 66–67, 72, 96–97, 101, 110–11, 133–34, 138, 146, 149, 176, 203–4, 211–12, 217, 222, 265, 275–79, 288
  lifestyle, 45, 58–59, 73, 99–102, 187, 192–93, 249
  new traditionalism, 94
  preserving, 249, 264
Trail of Tears, 30
transition, tribes in, 81–82, 174, 188, 200, 213, 223, 295–96
Truganini, last of the Tasmanians, 30, 34–35

United Nations Educational, Scientific and Cultural Organization (UNESCO), 63–67, 174, 306–7, 313–14
United Nations Environmental Programme (UNEP), 65–66
Universal Declaration on Cultural Diversity, 65–66
urgency, 10, 31, 42–43, 49–50, 68, 70, 118–19, 121, 185, 196–201, 203–4, 263
urgent anthropology, 196–201

vanishing
  Indian, the, 37–38, 68, 95–100, 101
  peoples, 3–4, 9–13, 12*f*, 15–16, 21, 26–37, 40–41, 44–45, 54–56, 67–68, 70, 72–73n.8, 77–78, 84–85, 90–91, 94–100, 117–18, 197–201, 212, 237, 275–76, 295–96, 304, 312, 314–15
  wildlife, 12*f*, 44–45, 56, 118–19, 121
  *Vanishing American, The* (Dippie), 25–26, 30–31, 118
  *Vanishing of the Great Race, The* (Grant), 44
  *Vanishing Race, The* (Curtis), 26–27, 27*f*
*vanvasi. See* Adivasi; Bhil; Gond
Vanvasi Kalyan Ashram, 80, 183
Vedanta, 297–98
Verghese, B.G. 214–17
vermin eradication, 16, 17, 38–39, 44, 105–8, 113, 128–33, 144,

145, 152t, 233n.77, 234–35, 238, 254n.119
victims, 58–59, 67–68, 76, 84–85, 107n.7, 172, 217, 221, 258
*Victims of Progress* (Bodley), 84–85, 187–88, 191–92
Villas-Bôas brothers, 52–53
Vindhyas, 247n.113, 256–57
*Volkskultur*, 181
Voltaire, 22

Waiting room of history, 90–91, 286–87
Wallace, A.R. 32–33n.42
war, 21, 67–68, 89, 94–95, 214
   Anglo-Maratha, 228–30, 235
   comparisons to hunting, 108–9, 117–18, 134
   crimes, 61
   on dangerous beasts, 16, 106–8, 128–30, 132–33
   of extermination, 40, 95–96, 117–18, 140, 231–32
   Indo-Pak, 195–96
   Vietnam, 61
   World War I era, 242–43
   World War II, 63–64, 194–95, 198–99
Washington, George, 25–26
*Weltnaturschutz* (world nature conservation), 49–50, 63–64, 313–14
Wenner-Gren Foundation, 196–97
white
   race as endangered, 37–38, 44
   racism, 39–40, 51–55, 106, 109, 145, 197, 265, 308
   saviour complex, 43, 62–63
   supremacists, 37–38
Whitehead, Judith, 221–22, 246–47
wild
   animals, 14–16, 19, 40–43f, 45–46, 48–49, 90, 95–96, 180, 233, 235, 236, 239–42, 273–74, 291
   beasts, 25–26, 38, 39–41, 69, 82–83, 232, 234–35, 238, 259–60, 274, 313–14
   children, 240–41, 243–44
   Indians, 34–35, 48

   life, 16, 51, 72, 78, 104–65, 174–75, 207–8, 234–35, 236
   men, 38–40, 69, 82–83, 234–35, 241–42, 277, 313–14
   peoples, 41–43f, 45–46, 51, 76, 82, 86, 90, 172, 205, 227, 230–32, 235, 239–42, 273, 275, 277–78
   places, 17–18, 45–49, 235, 236, 267–68, 277–78
   races, 19, 40–41, 236–37
   tribes, 14–16, 72, 75–76, 170, 232–33, 236, 239–41, 271–72, 277, 280
*Wild Tribes of India, The* (Rowney / Dutt), 274
wild west shows, 53–54
wilderness, 15–18, 34–35, 44–52, 72, 110, 143, 312–13
   *See also* Indian wilderness
wildlife, xi–xiv, xvi–xvii, 9, 12–13, 12f, 14–16, 17–18, 33, 39, 43–46, 51–52, 56, 71–72, 81, 97–98, 100–1, 104–65, 199, 208, 210, 220, 235, 259–60, 262–64, 291–92, 314–15
Wildlife First, xiv
wildness, 16, 45–49, 79, 109–10, 190–91, 242–43
wolf (*Canis lupus*), 25–26, 104, 128–30, 132–33, 143
World Bank, 206, 244
World Commission on Dams, 206–7, 213
World Wildlife Fund, xi–xii

Xaxa, Virginius, 96–97
Xingu National Park, 52–53

Yellowstone National Park, 51–52, 313–14

*zamin* (land), 299–300, 306
*zamindars* (landlords), 79–80
*Zivilisationsmenschen* (civilization people), 41–42
zoologists, 70, 88, 199
zoos, 16–17, 167–68, 268, 282–83
   Alipore Zoo, 55–56
   Bronx Zoo, 44, 54–55, 142–43
   *See also* human zoos

Ingram Content Group UK Ltd.
Milton Keynes UK
UKHW021814230423
420652UK00004B/145